The Progressive Era

THE PROGRESSIVE ERA

*Primary Documents on Events
from 1890 to 1914*

Elizabeth V. Burt

Debating Historical Issues in the Media of the Time
David A. Copeland, Series Editor

GREENWOOD PRESS
Westport, Connecticut • London

Library of Congress Cataloging-in-Publication Data

Burt, Elizabeth V., 1943–
    The Progressive era : primary documents on events from 1890 to 1914 / Elizabeth V.
Burt.
        p. cm.—(Debating historical issues in the media of the time ; ISSN 1542–8079)
    Includes bibliographical references and index.
    ISBN 0–313–32097–7 (alk. paper)
    1. United States—History—1865–1921—Sources. 2. Progressivism
(United States politics)—Sources. 3. American newspapers. I. Title. II. Series.
E661.B98   2004
973.8–dc22   2003027518

British Library Cataloguing in Publication Data is available.

Library of Congress Catalog Card Number: 2003027518
ISBN: 0–313–32097–7
ISSN: 1542–8079

First published in 2004

Greenwood Press, 88 Post Road West, Westport, CT 06881
An imprint of Greenwood Publishing Group, Inc.
www.greenwood.com

Printed in the United States of America

The paper used in this book complies with the
Permanent Paper Standard issued by the National
Information Standards Organization (Z39.48–1984).

10 9 8 7 6 5 4 3 2 1

To my family, whose interest and support have sustained and encouraged me in all my endeavors, and to my grandparents, who lived through the events described in this book.

Contents

Contents

Acknowledgments

R esearch for this project was partially funded by a summer stipend from the National Endowment for the Humanities and several re-search grants from the University of Hartford. Research assistance was provided by the Wisconsin State Historical Society, Madison, Wisconsin; the Simsbury Public Library, Simsbury, Connecticut; and Suzanna Cecchin.

Series Foreword

As the eighteenth century was giving way to the nineteenth, the *Columbian Centinel* of Boston, quoting a wise judge in its January 1, 1799 issue, said, "Give to any set men the command of the press, and you give them the command of the country, for you give them the command of public opinion, which commands everything." One month later, Thomas Jefferson wrote to James Madison with a similar insight. "We are sensible," Jefferson said of the efforts it would take to put their party—the Republicans—in power, "The engine is the press."

Both writers were correct in their assessment of the role the press would play in American life in the years ahead. The press was already helping to shape the opinions and direction of America. It had been doing so for decades, but its influence would erupt following the Revolutionary War and continue into the 1920s and farther. From less than forty newspapers in 1783—each with circulations of around 500—the number of papers greatly increased in the United States. By 1860, newspaper circulation exceeded 1 million, and in 1898, Joseph Pulitzer's *World* alone had a daily circulation of 1.3 million. By the beginning of World War I, about 16,600 daily and weekly newspapers were published, and circulation figures passed 22.5 million copies per day, with no slowdown in circulation in sight. Magazines grew even more impressively. From around five at the end of the Revolution, journalism historian Frank Luther Mott counted 600 in 1860 and a phenomenal 3,300 by 1885. Some circulations surpassed 1 million, and the number of magazines continued to grow into the twentieth century.

The amazing growth of the press happened because the printed page of periodicals assumed a critical role in the United States. Newspapers and magazines became the place where Americans discussed and debated the issues that affected them. Newspapers, editors, and citizens took sides, and they used the press as the conduit for discussion. The *Debating Historical Issues in the Media of the Time* series offers a glimpse into how the press was used by Americans to shape and influence the major events and issues facing the nation during different periods of its development. Each volume is based on the documents, that is, the writings that appeared in the press of the time. Each volume presents articles, essays, and editorials that support opposing interests on the events and issues; and each provides readers with background and explanation of the events, issues, and, if possible, the people who wrote the articles that have been selected. Each volume also includes a chronology of events and a selected bibliography. Books in the *Debating Historical Issues in the Media of the Time* series cover the following periods: the Revolution and the young republic, the Federalist era, the antebellum period, the Civil War, Reconstruction, the Progressive Era, and World War I.

This volume focuses upon the issues that affected America as it moved from the nineteenth to the twentieth century. The Progressive Era witnessed the growth of investigative journalism—often referred to as Muckraking. It was also the zenith of newspaper circulation in America with some papers in New York exceeding 1 million in daily circulation. As immigrants landed in the United States in record numbers and modern business demanded more workers than ever, Americans turned to the press to stay abreast of their quickly changing world. There, the issues surrounding the development of business versus labor, the rights of women, and increasing American involvement in world politics played out in events that would shape America's direction throughout the twentieth century.

Chronology of Events

1890   The nation's 11th census notes an increase in the foreign-born
population, an increase of the proportion of the population
living in cities, and a widening gap between the rich and the
poor
United Mine Workers formed
Farmers organize to form People's Party
Federal Territory of Oklahoma established in Indian Territory
Death of Sitting Bull
Battle of Wounded Knee, South Dakota
National Woman Suffrage Association (NWSA) and American
Woman Suffrage Association (AWSA) unite to form National
American Woman Suffrage Association (NAWSA)

1891   Congress creates the Office of Superintendent of Immigration
President Harrison opens additional 900,000 acres of Oklahoma
Indian Territory to white settlers

1892   Ellis Island opened to process immigrants
The Geary Act extends the Chinese Exclusion Act for 10 years
Cholera epidemic in port cities increases fear of immigrants
Lynching reaches an all-time high in southern states
Homestead Strike begins July, ends December
Queen Liliukalani of Hawaii deposed
President Grover Cleveland (Dem.) reelected

1893   Stock market crash, financial panic
Colorado votes for woman suffrage

1894 American businessmen under Judge Sanford B. Dole proclaim a
            Hawaiian constitution
        Coxey's Army of jobless men marches on Washington, D.C.
        Anti-Saloon League formed
        The frontier is declared closed by historian Frederick Jackson
            Turner at convention of the American Historical Association
1896 William McKinley (Rep.) elected president
        Alaskan gold rush begins
        Utah becomes the 45th state
        Utah and Idaho vote for woman suffrage
        Supreme Court rules in *Plessy v. Ferguson* that it is constitutional
            for public places to have separate accommodations for
            Negroes if those accommodations are equal
1897 Utah elects the nation's first woman state senator, M. H. Cannon
1898 U.S.S. *Maine* explodes in Havana harbor
        United States defeats Spain in the Spanish-American War;
            American soldiers use the newly developed Gattling gun,
            which uses an electric motor to feed cartridges and shoots
            3,000 rounds per minute
        United States annexes Hawaiian Islands
        United States annexes Philippine Islands, Guam, and Puerto Rico
1899 Philippine Republic is formed and rebels against the United States
        Anti-Imperialist League formed in the United States
        Samoan Islands divided among the United States, Britain, and
            Germany
        Carrie Nation starts saloon-smashing in Kiowa, Kansas
1900 President William McKinley (Rep.) reelected
        Turn of the century brings predictions of progress
1901 President McKinley assassinated; succeeded by Vice President
            Theodore Roosevelt
        Financial panic, stock market collapses
        Socialist Party founded
1902 Death of suffragist Elizabeth Cady Stanton
1903 United States recognizes Republic of Panama, assists revolution
            against Colombia, wins concession to build Panama Canal
1904 Construction of Panama Canal begins
        Steerage fare on trans-Atlantic liners is slashed to $10 in
            competition for immigrant passengers
        Socialist Party candidate Eugene Debs wins significant number
            of votes in presidential election

President Theodore Roosevelt (Rep.) is elected for second term
1905 Radical Industrial Workers of the World (IWW) is founded
1906 Death of suffragist Susan B. Anthony
Oklahoma becomes the 46th state; Indian Territory and
Oklahoma Territory merged
1908 William Howard Taft (Rep.) elected president
1909 Alabama defeats bill for prohibition
Lumber strike in Montana led by IWW
Press gets the wireless; first message transmitted from New York
to Chicago
1910 Congress amends Immigration Act of 1907 to bar paupers,
criminals, anarchists, and diseased persons
Twelfth census reveals new information on immigration; 8.7
percent of U.S. population had arrived since 1900.
Victor Berger of Wisconsin is first Socialist elected to
Congress
Ohio local elections outlaw liquor in 58 of state's 88 counties
National Association for the Advancement of Colored People
(NAACP) is organized in Chicago
Congress passes law requiring all U.S. passenger ships to carry
radio equipment
Washington votes for woman suffrage; first suffrage parade is
held in New York
1911 Triangle shirtwaist factory fire kills 146 workers
Journalist Will Irwin publishes series "The American
Newspaper" in *Collier's Magazine*
Texas defeats statewide prohibition; Ohio defeats state
constitutional prohibition amendment; Maine retains
prohibition
Congressman Richard Hobson introduces prohibition
amendment to House of Representatives
California votes for woman suffrage
1912 The *Titanic* sinks on maiden voyage
Nation's first minimum-wage law passed in Massachusetts
Democrat Woodrow Wilson is elected president
Arizona, Kansas, and Oregon vote for woman suffrage; suffrage
defeated in Ohio, Michigan, and Wisconsin
Radio Act of 1912 requires license for radio operators, to be
granted by Department of Commerce and Labor
Nine states are dry

1913 States ratify Sixteenth Amendment to allow federal income tax

States ratify Seventeenth Amendment, which calls for direct election of senators

Congress passes Webb-Kenyon Act, which forbids shipping of liquors into prohibition states

Woman Suffrage parade held in Washington, D.C. is mobbed by rowdies

1914 Striking miners and their families killed in the Ludlow Massacre, Ludlow, Colorado

Fourteen states are dry

Nevada adopts woman suffrage

Panama Canal is opened for commercial traffic

U.S. troops depose Mexican president Victoriano Huerta; support Huerta's rival, Constitutionalist General Obregon

Assassination of Archduke Ferdinand; German invasion of Belgium; England declares war on Germany after invasion of Belgium; President Wilson pledges neutrality in European war

Introduction: The Progressive Era and Newspapers

The Progressive Era and Progressive Reformers

Few historians agree on what the Progressive Era was, who the progressives were, and whether reforms of the period actually were progressive. What they do agree on, however, is that during the period roughly between 1890 and 1917, a positive and optimistic spirit infused segments of the American intellectual, political, and social reform communities and spread throughout the general culture and society.[1] Most also agree that the Progressive Era was a period of social, political, and economic reform that had far-reaching influence on the history of the United States for the greater part of the twentieth century.

This was a period during which the United States experienced unprecedented growth and development—in its population, its cities and towns, settlement of the West, commerce and industry, transportation, and technology. While such growth generally brought a better standard of living to the nation, it often occurred as a result of the exploitation of immigrants, the poor, and racial and ethnic minorities. Along with the positive and optimistic spirit of the age came moments of doubt and anxiety. Financial panics, labor unrest, regulatory efforts to limit immigration, and attempts to reform business and industries punctuated the years of the Progressive Era and illustrated the contradictory and sometimes conservative nature of the period.

There are also contradictions in the characteristics used to define the progressives. Most agree they were reformers rather than revolutionaries who hoped to mend, not destroy, the country's existing social and political structure. The progressives were united in a general viewpoint that

1

embraced many or all of a number of beliefs that facilitated change, including optimism, leadership by an enlightened elite, environmentalism, romantic individualism, and cultural nationalism. More importantly, however, they were united by a specific belief in their own power to transform the world, which was a marked change from the passive belief in automatic progress expressed earlier in the nineteenth century.

This activism, however, was expressed in different fashions, with progressives sometimes taking opposing positions on a given issue. While some, for example, supported increased popular political participation through liberalized suffrage, the referendum, and the recall, others called for the increased professionalization of government by the creation of a class of professional managers, a process that would actually *decrease* popular participation.[2] While some supported prohibition in the belief that it would improve moral behavior and living conditions among the poor and working class, others saw the restriction of the manufacture, sale, and consumption of alcohol as a restriction of individual rights. Labor reformers sought to improve working conditions in mines, factories, and transportation, but opposed any reforms that would open jobs to African Americans.

It is also difficult to predict who might have become a progressive based on individuals' demographic characteristics or motivations. Many historians have found that progressives were generally of a common social type composed mainly of those who were native-born, white, Anglo-Saxon, Protestant, middle-class, and well educated. These characteristics, however, also accurately identify conservative and reactionary activists of the period. Thus individuals of the same class and background often found themselves on opposite sides of some of the issues of the period.

But while it may be difficult to predict who might be found among the progressives, historians as well as contemporaries were able to identify some individuals as most definitely in the progressive camp. These individuals, who consistently supported a wide range of progressive reforms, included political leaders like Presidents Theodore Roosevelt and Woodrow Wilson and Wisconsin Senator Robert L. La Follette, social reform leaders like Jane Addams and Florence Kelley, and intellectuals like Charlotte Perkins Gilman and Walter Lippmann. A number of journalists could also be identified as progressives, especially those who wrote exposés on big business and corrupt government such as San Francisco editor Fremont Older, New York publisher Joseph Pulitzer, and muckrakers Ida Tarbell and Lincoln Steffens. Progressives also included reform journalists like Ida B. Wells-Barnett, who campaigned against lynching, and Jacob Riis, whose photographs revealed the deplorable conditions of life in city tenements.

Issues of the Progressive Era

Many of the issues of the Progressive Era were closely related to the country's growth and development, which brought wealth and well-being to some but poverty, insecurity, and loss to others. During this period, the country moved from one that was largely rural and agricultural to one that was increasingly urban and industrial. In 1890 about one-third of the nation's population was urban; that increased to more than 50 percent by 1920. Many of those flocking to the cities were immigrants, with the result that in 1900, 40 percent of New York's inhabitants were foreign-born. Many of these immigrants were poor, unskilled, and illiterate peasants from southern and eastern Europe, while those immigrating to the West Coast included Japanese and Chinese, as well.[3] Unfortunately, these immigrants came to America when the supply of unskilled labor far outweighed the demand for it, and many were unable to find work. The growth of the urban population outpaced the development of a social infrastructure; social problems such as vagrancy, poverty, disease, and crime became associated with the people who crowded into city slums and tenements. Many of the nation's more established citizens responded by calling for restrictions on immigration. In 1882 this resulted in the nation's first immigration law restricting a particular nationality—the Chinese. Others, such as journalist Jacob Riis, instead tried to expose the miserable living conditions in the slums to bring about housing reform and social assistance.

While cities grew in size, the concept of the American West changed. The "last frontier," Oklahoma Indian Territory, was opened for settlement in the land rush of 1889, and in 1893 historian Frederick Jackson Turner declared that the frontier was closed in a famous speech before the American Historical Association. Native Americans made a few last vain attempts to retain their lands and their rights, but were gradually overcome by superior forces, shortage of game, and harsh conditions. Apache Chief Geronimo was forced to surrender to the U.S. Army after 15 years of rebellion in 1886, and Sioux Chief Sitting Bull was killed shortly before the Massacre at Wounded Knee in 1890. Surviving Native Americans were eventually restricted to reservations, where every aspect of life was controlled and regulated by the federal government.

When westward expansion of the United States reached its natural boundary of the Pacific Ocean, some Americans began to eye territories off American shores. Both the Monroe Doctrine (which in 1823 declared that the Western Hemisphere should no longer be a target for European colonization) and the policy of Manifest Destiny (which reified the nation's determination to occupy the North American continent from the Atlantic to the Pacific) were reinterpreted in such a way as to encourage a new policy of imperialism and expansionism. The first step toward imperialism was taken in the Hawaiian Islands, some 2,000 miles off the coast of California. In 1893 a coup led by American businessmen deposed the native Hawaiian ruler and established a provisional government that was quickly replaced by an American-dominated republic. By 1898 the islands' sovereignty had been transferred to the United States. In the Caribbean, the United States became embroiled in a short war with Spain in 1898 in support of Cuban rebels. The United States's victory in the Spanish-American War led to its annexation of Puerto Rico and the Philippines. Over the next 17 years, the United States's territorial ambitions led to brief military actions in the Samoan Islands, Panama, Nicaragua, Haiti, Santo Domingo, and Mexico. Proponents of expansionism gave a number of reasons to justify these acts, including the protection of American business interests, the liberation of the native people from tyrannical or corrupt governments, and the improvement of local living conditions for the native people. Some Americans, however, opposed expansionism. They formed organizations such as the Anti-Imperialist League, established in 1899, and protested expansionism on both moral and practical grounds. First, they maintained that America was corrupting its own democratic institutions by colonizing other peoples. Second, they argued that by assuming control of these lands the nation was taking on significant economic and military responsibilities.

Commerce and industry also grew during this period, and much of that growth was linked to new developments in technology. Cities began to light their streets and buildings with electricity, making 24-hour workdays possible. Elevated railways in cities made it easier for workers to travel to and from work, which in turn encouraged the growth of suburbs, and, ironically, extended the length of the workday for suburban commuters. The telephone and wireless made instant communication possible, which speeded up the commercial cycle. Automobiles began to replace foot and horse transportation, and the need for oil, gasoline, new roads, and bridges created giant industries and public projects that would come to dominate the American economy in the next 50 years. Steamships became larger and faster, bringing more immigrants to America at cheaper fares and making intercontinental travel a recreational option feasible for the upper middle class, as well as the wealthy, for the first time. The scientific and technological revolution was sometimes a two-edged sword. While inventions could improve daily life and assist the nation's growth and development, they also posed certain dangers. Faster ships could collide with icebergs. Automobiles caused traffic fatalities and demanded the costly construction of roads. Electricity could light up the night and drive machines, but it could also electrocute.

By the beginning of the Progressive Era, the nation's economy was dominated by an industrial elite that controlled the majority of the nation's resources and capital, and this was only tightened during the period. In 1890 more than half the nation's wealth was owned by just 1 percent of the population; in 1900 90 percent of the nation's wealth was owned by just 10 percent of the population. As commerce and industry grew, so did the gulf between the haves and the have-nots. While millionaires such as John D. Rockefeller and Andrew Carnegie measured their annual income in the hundreds of millions, workers in 1915 earned just $687 yearly in real wages.[4] Many others—blacks, Native Americans, and recent immigrants—lived in abject poverty. Workers attempted to increase wages and improve working conditions through the organization of unions, strikes, and walkouts. The organization of unions, however, was almost always opposed by factory and mine owners. When workers protested, owners often brought in outside muscle such as the Pinkertons, the National Guard, or the U.S. Army to protect their interests. The conflicts that resulted, such as the Homestead Strike in 1892 and the Colorado mine wars in 1914, nearly always ended in the arrest of union leaders and the defeat of the strikers.

Even as some tried to organize unions to improve working and economic conditions, others focused on a more conventionally legitimate solution by establishing political parties such as the People's Party (or Populists) in 1890 and the Socialist Party in 1901. The Populists gained significant support in the Midwest and farming communities during the 1890s, and the Socialists succeeded in winning office in a number of municipal governments. Neither, though, ever gained a significant presence in the nation's established two-party system. They did succeed, however, in bringing issues to national attention through party conventions, presidential debates, and the actions of their leaders. The Socialist Party, for example, nominated its leader, Eugene Debs, for president five times. The last time he was nominated, in 1920, he won nearly 1 million votes while serving a jail sentence for his support, during World War I, of pacifism, the radical International Workers of the World, and the Russian Revolution.

Even those who were well established in the political system saw the need for political reform during the Progressive Era. On the municipal level, some reformers proposed removing party interests and ward politics from the political process by making elections nonpartisan. Some advocated structural changes, such as replacing mayors and aldermen elected by districts with professional managers and administrators chosen in citywide elections. At the state level, reforms tended to give voters a greater voice in the electoral process. The initiative and referendum allowed voters to express their opinions directly through a vote on specific issues. The recall allowed them to remove unsatisfactory or corrupt elected public officials. The threat of intimidation at the polls was removed through the adoption of the secret ballot, known as the "Australian ballot," first introduced in 1888 and used in all the states by 1910. Direct primaries, which allowed party members rather than just party leaders to select candidates for office, were introduced in 1903 and adopted by most states by the end of the period. On the national level, reform focused on increasing voter representation. The Reapportionment Act of 1882 increased the number of delegates in the House of Representatives to be more reflective of the nation's growing population, and in 1913, the Seventeenth Amendment to the Constitution allowed citizens to vote directly for U.S. senators.

Ironically, however, popular political participation did not actually increase during the Progressive Era. Voter participation in elections after the turn of the century actually *decreased* as the influence of the parties in individual lives decreased, and voters lost interest or motivation in the election process. In addition, some segments of the population—African Americans, Native Americans, and women—were actually *restricted* from the voting process for most of the period. African Americans had won their citizenship and the right to vote under the Fifteenth Amendment, but after the Reconstruction Era, poll taxes, literacy tests, and intimidation were used, particularly in the South, to prevent them from registering and voting. Women did not win the right to vote until the ratification of the Nineteenth Amendment in 1920. The Progressive Era, in fact, was one of energetic organization and campaigning for woman suffragists who only eventually overcame entrenched opposition from political, religious, and social conservatives as well as some industries, notably the alcohol and beer industries.[5]

For African Americans, this was a period of diminishing opportunity during which they faced racism and discrimination in both the North and the South. In 1890 more than 60 percent of blacks in the rural South lived in poverty as sharecroppers and tenant farmers. Those who fled economic hardship to settle in northern cities found themselves in competition with immigrant labor for the poorest paying manual jobs. "Jim Crow" laws segregated public and private buildings, schools, and transportation, and in some southern cities residential segregation was put into law. These laws were legitimized in 1896 by the Supreme Court, when it ruled that public accommodations could be segregated as long as they were "separate but equal."[6] Blacks who stepped out of line were intimidated, brutalized, and murdered; more than two thousand black men and youths were lynched between 1890 and 1920, mostly in the South. Some white reformers, such as settlement-house leader Lillian Wald and author Mark Twain, spoke out against racial injustice, but most of those who tried to improve the lives of African Americans were blacks who did so at great risk to themselves. These reformers included educator Booker T. Washington, who founded the

Tuskegee Institute for Negroes in 1881, journalist Ida B. Wells-Barnett, who led a crusade against lynching from 1892 until her death in 1931, and W. E. B. Du Bois, who in 1910 founded the *Crisis,* the magazine supported by the National Association for the Advancement of Colored People. It must be said that little happened during the Progressive Era to improve the lot of African Americans, but Wells-Barnett's crusade against lynching as well as the eruption of race riots in a number of cities during the period led social and political leaders to recognize that a "race problem" existed and begin to seek remedies.

Newspapers during the Progressive Era

The American newspaper industry expanded exponentially between 1880 and 1917. In that period, the number of English-language daily newspapers grew steadily from 850 in 1880 to 1,967 in 1900 and to 2,200 in 1910. (An additional 400 dailies of other types, including foreign-language and socialist newspapers were also published in that year.) National circulation also increased, aided by faster printing presses, growing advertising revenue, and better transportation. Daily circulation totals grew from 3.1 million in 1880 to 15.1 million in 1900 and to 22.4 million in 1910. In addition to daily newspapers, there was a thriving business in weeklies, biweeklies, and semiweekly newspapers. The number of weeklies increased from 12,000 in 1900 to about 14,000 in 1910. While the majority of these were published in English, there was also a boom in foreign-language publications, which reached their peak in 1917 at 1,325 papers. Nearly half of these were published in German; the majority of the rest were published in Polish, Russian, Italian, and Yiddish. These newspapers played an important role in allowing a voice to recent immigrants, many of whom did not read or speak English.[7]

This period saw the emergence of giant metropolitan dailies, city newspapers such as the *New York World* and the *New York Journal,* which during the Spanish-American War occasionally reached daily circulations of more than one million. In an effort to appeal to all segments of the population, these newspapers continued an earlier trend of differentiating between different types of news. They appealed to a range of readers by developing specialty pages and sections devoted to sports, finance, women, entertainment, and society. In an effort to capitalize on the increased leisure time available to the growing middle class and even the working class, daily newspapers began to publish a Sunday edition. In 1890 about 250 dailies had Sunday editions; this number doubled by the turn of the century.

"The Press," *Fourth Estate*, 5 March 1896, cover. *This drawing by Charles Frederik Brisley won first place in a competition launched by the trade publication the* Fourth Estate *for the best illustration representing journalism. The figure wears the badge "Forever," which, according to the* Fourth Estate, *represented many of the ideals of modern journalism: "Forever is the right word. It stands for the truth that is eternal. It might also be considered to tell of the continuous labor that is characteristic of the journalist. Undoubtedly it speaks of the life that shall last forever with the freedom of speech in the land of liberty…. There is nothing common-place in this illustration of the familiar line, 'The pen is mightier than the sword.'"*

The Progressive Era also saw the explosion of special-interest newspapers, from those addressing foreign-language or ethnic audiences to those expressing specific political or social views. These publications, often referred to as the "alternative press," represented groups as widely different as the Socialist Party, the woman suffrage and antisuffrage movements, the prohibition movement, African Americans, German Americans, and the Methodist, Congregational, and Roman Catholic Churches. Some of these, like the National American Woman Suffrage Association's *Woman's Journal* and the Anti-Saloon League's *American Issue,* were established for the specific purpose of promoting the group's reform and ceased publication once that reform was accomplished. Others, like the NAACP's *Crisis* and the Catholic Church's *Boston Pilot,* continued publication into the twenty-first century.

The growth of newspapers was greatly fueled by a simultaneous growth in the advertising industry. By 1890 advertising was the chief means of promotion of national brand-name products. Department stores bought entire newspaper pages to promote sales or specific items. Advertising agencies, first established in the late 1860s, now began to do more than buy and resell bulk newspaper space. They began to design and write ads for customers, as well. During the 1880s advertising slowly began to replace sales and subscriptions as the chief source of newspaper revenue, so that by 1914, 66 percent of newspapers' revenues came from advertising.[8] Some newspaper critics began to fear the influence of advertising on journalism, and in 1911 journalist Will Irwin conducted an investigation of major newspapers across the country to discover how often they curbed their reporting to mollify advertisers and political allies. One proposed solution, which had little success, was to create an adless newspaper. Others designed codes of ethics they hoped would erect a wall between the advertising and news functions of newspapers.

Developments in technology also aided the growth of the newspaper industry. Advances in printing, which had been constant since the early nineteenth century, brought the invention and adoption of steam-powered rotary presses that in 1890 could print 72,000 eight-page papers—the average size of many dailies at that time—in an hour.[9] Another innovation in printing was the invention of color presses, which allowed newspapers to print color supplements and color comics, a strategy initially used to attract poor and immigrant readers. The *New York World* was one of the first newspapers to do this in 1893. Its use of yellow on the dress of the main character (the Yellow Kid) in the comic strip *Hogan's Alley* led to the derogatory term "yellow journalism" to refer to cheap or sensational journalism. Other technological developments introduced during the 1890s included the use of half-tone photographs, which allowed for realistic and sometimes lurid depictions of events, and the linotype, which allowed an operator to set lines of type at a keyboard similar to a typewriter. One linotype operator could do the work of five men, and this sped up the process of setting pages significantly.

Major advances in communication technology revolutionized the way reporters collected information and wrote stories. AT&T began to build telephone lines from New York to other cities and states in 1885. As telephone service became available, newspapers were quick to adapt the way they collected news. By 1898 a leading trade publication declared the telephone to be "absolutely essential to the newspaper."[10] Reporters covering breaking news on deadline could now phone their stories into the newsroom where "a deskman" would transcribe their story and prepare it for printing. The wireless was another technology that allowed for instant communication across vast spaces. In 1903 a regular news service opened between New York and London, and in 1909 newspapers started using the wireless on a regular basis.

For those who still relied on footwork, however, advances in transportation also made their jobs easier and more efficient. Elevated railways and underground streetcar services in cities like New York and Boston eased street congestion and made it easier and quicker for reporters to get from one part of the city to another. Automobiles were another invention that eventually made getting from one place to another easier and faster, especially for reporters working in rural areas or traveling from town to town. Motorcars were first introduced in the 1890s, and by 1908 Henry Ford had produced his Model T, billed as "a motorcar for the multitudes." The development of gasoline-powered trucks also affected the delivery of newspapers so that they could be distributed throughout cities and rural areas to more readers more quickly.

These technological developments also played a role in newspapers in that inventions and breakthroughs were often treated as stories and were frequently referred to with awe as miracles, magical, and awe-inspiring. Science and technology were often news-makers and became the frequent subject of editorial comment. Automobiles, which became ubiquitous by the mid-1920s, were initially seen as an oddity, then a fad, then a noisy, smoke-belching danger to all who used the road. Airplanes were later viewed in much the same way. Steamships, which by 1892 could carry more than two thousand passengers and cross the Atlantic in five and one-half days, seemed to pose at least two dangers.[11] First, because the larger passenger liners made cheaper fares possible for steerage passengers, more and poorer immigrants could now flood the country.[12] Second, because captains often raced to set a record for their steamship line, ships on the North Atlantic route faced an increased danger of running into icebergs. The sinking of the "unsinkable" *Titanic* in 1912 provided newspapers with a sensational chance to ponder the dangers of overreliance on technology while at the same time praising the miracle of the wireless that allowed the sinking ship to call for help and transmit information about the disaster to newspapers on the mainland.

Another development of the period, the consolidation of business interests in chains and monopolies, also affected the newspaper industry. Successful publishers began to acquire multiple newspapers, expanding their influence and power from the regional to the national level. One of the earliest of these, E. W. Scripps, established a chain of afternoon dailies in middle-sized cities through the Midwest. This became the Scripps-McRae League of Newspapers in 1889 and included 18 papers in states from Ohio to Colorado by 1893. One of the most notorious of chain owners was Californian William Randolph Hearst, who started out in 1887 as the editor of his father's *San Francisco Examiner.* In 1895 Hearst purchased the *New York Journal* and by 1920 he owned 11 newspapers, at least one magazine, and a press association, the International News Service. While chains made owners wealthy and even encouraged the establishment of new newspapers in some regions, more often they acted to put less powerful newspaper owners out of business. One such publisher, Frank Munsey, was infamous for buying newspapers in cities where he already owned a newspaper and then either combining them or shutting down his latest acquisition.

Competition in many cities was fierce because most had so many newspapers. Chicago and Boston, for example, each had eight dailies in 1900, while New York had nine. This competition led to circulation wars, whose aim was to gain more readers and advertisers. One method of gaining more readers was to lower prices from the average two or three cents of the period to just a penny. This might lure readers away from a competitor in the short run, but the competitor often responded by lowering its cost as well, and prices usually returned to normal within the year.

Newspapers in competition with each other also launched crusades or investigations to attract readers. Though publishers' true motivation might be to increase readership and promote themselves as champions of the people, these crusades often had the added benefit of actually bringing about positive change. In 1897, for example, Hearst's *New York Evening Journal* launched a crusade in support of striking miners in Pennsylvania. The *Journal* published more than 40 articles, editorials, and cartoons in support of the strike and demanding the punishment of local police who had fired on the miners, killing 20. Although the police were acquitted, Hearst did arouse sympathy for the plight of the miners, which might have contributed to later improvements in their working conditions. In another crusade, the *New York World* in 1905 launched an investigation of fraud in the powerful

Equitable Life Assurance Society that led to strict regulatory legislation of the insurance industry. Other crusades focused on political corruption. In San Francisco, Fremont Older's *San Francisco Chronicle* campaigned for civic reform, specifically targeting city machine politics and the corrupt party bosses.[13]

Though often well-investigated and documented, many crusades were based on flimsy evidence and promoted through lurid headlines, overimaginative illustrations, and sensational claims. Competition among newspapers sometimes led to poorly considered campaigns that backfired against specific publishers or the newspaper industry in general. In 1898, for example, Pulitzer's *New York World* and Hearst's *New York Journal* exploited the situation in Cuba and the explosion of the battleship the U.S.S. *Maine* to promote war with Spain. After the Spanish-American War was over and the bodies were counted, critics blamed the newspapers for jingoism and war-mongering. In another instance, Hearst's *New York Journal* ran a bitter campaign against President William McKinley's successful bid for reelection in 1900. When McKinley was assassinated in 1901 by an anarchist reportedly carrying a copy of the *Journal* in his pocket, many held Hearst responsible.

Examples like these led critics to attack any newspapers that used these promotional tactics—reduced prices, stunts, crusades, imaginative headlines, illustrations, cartoons, and color—as sensational or yellow journals. The news industry responded accordingly. In 1911, for example, Pulitzer's *New York World* established an internal Bureau of Accuracy to check facts and publish corrections of inaccurate stories. Press associations, established during the second half of the 1800s mostly by men working in the news industry, began to take up the issue of yellow journalism and seek ways to improve the industry. Bowing to critics and public pressure, newspapers began to publish corrections of inaccurate information and address readers' complaints on their editorial pages.

Newspapers reached their heyday during the Progressive Era, reaching peak circulations and enjoying a level of competition not seen since in the newspaper industry. They investigated, reported, and interpreted events as well as the important issues of the period. They played an important role in how Americans viewed the world. Immigrants turned to newspapers as a way of learning about this new land. The middle class looked to newspapers for a reinforcement of lifestyles and values they cherished and clung to in a changing world. Business leaders used newspapers to promote their speculations and business interests, carry advertisements for their products, and promote a spirit of consumerism across the land. Political leaders carried out their campaigns in newspapers and sought their endorsement. These groups and individuals also found themselves the subject of newspaper stories, sometimes to their detriment. Stories about the "immigration flood" that linked immigration to increases in crime provided fuel for the movement that sought to regulate or restrict immigration. Middle-class conservatives felt threatened by stories reporting advances made by the woman's movement and hardened their resistance to such change. Members of the industrial and commercial elite often found themselves at the wrong end of the pen in stories investigating the exploitation of workers, fraud, and corporate corruption. Likewise, public officials found themselves under increased scrutiny in the press.

Newspapers of the era also served as critics of the status quo and promoted many of the important political and economic reforms of the period. Paradoxically, many mainstream newspapers tended to be conservative in the face of social reform and lagged far behind the more radical reform papers such as those of the woman suffrage and labor movements. Regardless of their position on specific issues, however, newspapers of the Progressive Era were active in the national discussion of controversial issues. They brought these issues to the public's attention, promoted debate by publishing the positions of opposing sides, acted as both moderators and participants in many of these debates, and generally served as facilitators of public discussion.

PUBLICITY WILL KILL HIM

"Publicity Will Kill Him," *American Issue,* 17 July 1915, p. 9. *Newspapers of the Progressive Era believed in the power of the press to sway public opinion. In this cartoon in the Anti-Saloon League's* American Issue, *the press in the guise of St. George slays the dragon, "Demon Rum," with the sword of truth. This image plays on the words of the adage, "The pen is mightier than the sword."*

This book presents some of the debates on many of the issues of importance during the Progressive Era. Each chapter focuses on a specific event or issue, from the census of 1890 to the labor war in Ludlow, Colorado, in 1914. Each chapter examines the event or issue through the words of newspaper stories, editorials, and, occasionally, advertisements and political cartoons, and attempts to tease out the many perspectives involved in each issue. Many times, it is too simplistic to attempt to separate material into the arguments of two sides as being for or against something. In these cases, a variety of examples are provided in an attempt to reflect the diversity of perspectives on some very complicated issues.

Since so many newspapers were published during this period, it was impossible to represent their entire range here. Material is drawn from more than two dozen newspapers published during the period. Many of those selected were located in major cities like New York, Chicago, and San Francisco because those newspapers were particularly influential. An attempt was also made to provide some geographic and regional diversity, and newspapers used in this study ranged from Boston to San Francisco and Milwaukee to New Orleans. The material quoted in these chapters is written just as it was in the original publication. Capitalization is used here as it was in the original, and an attempt has been made to reproduce the formatting of multiple-deck headlines. The name of the writer is not provided in most cases, since bylines were rarely used during this period. Occasional words or phrases are inserted in brackets wherever a brief explanation is necessary.

The selection of events and issues for such a book is subjective to a certain degree, and examples of their coverage in newspapers is limited by the availability and accessibility of newspapers published during the period being examined. The chapters, which are organized chronologically, are generally anchored to a specific event but may broaden to discuss the issue as it developed over time. Twenty events or issues of concern of the Progressive Era are featured in this work, though some issues, such as immigration and labor, play a role in a number of chapters devoted to a more specific topic. Each chapter concludes with a list of questions for discussion.

NOTES

1. Paul Boyer, "The Progressive Era," in *The Enduring Vision* (Lexington, Mass.: D. C. Heath, 1990), p. 760.

2. John C. Burnham, "Essay," in *Progressivism*, ed. John D. Buenker, John C. Burnham, and Robert M. Crunden (Cambridge, Mass: Schenkman Publishing Co., 1980), pp. 9, 34.

3. Boyer, pp. 752–53.

4. Boyer, p. 757. Real wages are defined in terms of actual purchasing power after allowing for inflation.

5. Eleanor Flexner, *Century of Struggle: The Woman's Rights Movement in the United States*, rev. ed. (Cambridge: Belknap Press of Harvard University Press, 1975), pp. 256–338.

6. The U.S. Supreme Court reached this decision in *Plessy v. Ferguson*, a case in which a black man had argued his constitutional rights were being infringed when the East Louisiana Railroad refused to seat him in a coach reserved for whites only. By the time of the Court's ruling, "separate car laws," referred to as the "Jim Crow car" laws, had been passed by a number of southern states that required the railroads to provide separate cars for white and black passengers. The ruling was quickly used to justify the segregation of all public facilities, including schools, hotels, and restaurants.

7. A combination of economic, social, and political factors led to the steady decline of the number of newspapers after 1914. Circulation, however, continued to increase, though not nearly as rapidly as in the years given here.

8. Jean Folkerts and Dwight L. Teeter, Jr., *Voices of a Nation*, 3rd ed. (Boston: Allyn and Bacon, 1998), p. 316.

9. "Boston Herald's Big Presses," *Fourth Estate*, 14 May 1896, p. 4.

10. "The Telephone Monopoly," *Fourth Estate*, 10 March 1898, p. 2.

11. Advertisements, *Boston Traveller*, 28 July 1892; 4 and 17 December 1892, p. 10.

12. Warren Line advertisement, *Donahoe's Magazine*, 24 January 1891, p. 8.

13. Michael Emory and Edwin Emory, *The Press and America*, 7th ed. (Englewood Cliffs, N.J.: Prentice Hall, 1992), pp. 214–21.

CHAPTER I

The Census of 1890 Measures American Life and Defines Some of Its Problems

"When once I asked the agent of a notorious Fourth Ward alley how many people might be living in it, I was told: One hundred and forty families, one hundred Irish, thirty-eight Italian, and two that spoke the German tongue," wrote news reporter Jacob Riis in 1890. "The answer was characteristic of the cosmopolitan character of lower New York, very nearly so of the whole of it, wherever it runs to alleys and courts. One may find for the asking an Italian, a German, a French, African, Spanish, Bohemian, Russian, Scandinavian, Jewish, and Chinese colony. Even the Arab, who peddles 'holy earth' from the Battery as a direct importation from Jerusalem, has his exclusive preserves at the lower end of Washington Street."[1]

Riis, who was a police reporter first for the *New York Tribune* and then for the *New York Sun,* had made a name for himself during the 1870s and 1880s with his stories and photographs documenting life in the New York slums. An immigrant himself who had lived in abject poverty during his first three years in the United States, he was determined to bring the plight of the city's poorest inhabitants to the attention of middle-class reformers and politicians who had the power to effect change. In addition to his writing, he began to agitate for sanitary improvements, tenement control by the city, and assistance for widows and orphans. In 1887 he was appointed to the city's Tenement House Commission and between 1888 and 1890 worked on his book, *How the Other Half Lives*. Here he described the conditions of the working and immigrant classes in the city's tenements. His stories and photographs put faces on the people counted in the census of 1890 and put flesh and bone on the seemingly endless rows of statistics gathered by the census takers. Here is how he described a family of Jewish immigrants, who lived and worked in their Ludlow Street apartment, after following a man "groaning under a heavy burden of unsewn garments" into a tenement.

The Sweaters of Jewtown

Up two flights of dark stairs, three, four, with new smells of cabbage, of onions, of frying fish, on every landing whirring sewing machines behind closed doors betraying what goes on within, to the door that opens to admit the bundle and the man. A sweater this, in a small way. Five men and a woman, two young girls, not fifteen, and a boy who says unasked that he is fifteen, and lies in saying it, are at the machines sewing knickerbockers, "knee-pants" in the Ludlow Street dialect. The floor is littered ankle-deep with half-sewn garments. In the alcove, on a couch of many dozens of "pants" ready for the finisher, a bare-legged baby with pinched face is asleep. A fence of piled-up clothing keeps him from rolling off on the floor. The faces, hands, and arms to the elbows of everyone in the room are black with the color of the cloth on which they are working....

They are "learners," all of them, says the woman, who proves to be the wife of the boss, and have "come over" only a few weeks ago.... The workers work for a week's wages...from two to five dollars. The children—there are four of them—are not old enough to work. The oldest is only six.... There are ten machines in the room; six are hired at two dollars a month. For the two shabby smoke-begrimed rooms, one somewhat larger than the ordinary, they pay twenty dollars a month. She does not complain, "though times are not what they were, and it costs a good deal to live." Eight dollars a week for the family of six and two boarders. How do they do it? She laughs, as she goes over the bill of fare, at the silly question: bread, fifteen cents a day. Of milk two quarts a day at four cents a quart, one pound of meat for dinner at twelve cents, butter one pound a week at "eight cents a quarter pound." Coffee, potatoes and pickles complete the list. At the least calculation, probably, this sweater's family hoards thirty dollars a month, and in a few years will own a tenement somewhere and profit by the example set by their landlord in rent-collecting. It is the way the savings of Jewtown are universally invested, and with the natural talent of its people for commercial speculation the investment is enormously profitable.[2]

The conditions in which this particular family lived and worked were most likely described in numbers somewhere in the long lists of statistics produced by the census of 1890. This census, perhaps more than any before it, marked significant changes in American life. The total population had increased about 30 percent in the past decade, which was due more to the steady flood of immigrants and an improved life expectancy than to an increased birthrate. More Americans were living in cities than ever before, and cities in both the North and South had increased alarmingly in size. The census also revealed that the number of the foreign-born or those of foreign parentage had increased everywhere, particularly in northeastern and midwestern cities and in midwestern states. Those of native parentage in Wisconsin and Minnesota, for example, were outnumbered by those of foreign birth or parentage by three to one.[3] Modest growth was also reported in the black, Chinese, and Japanese populations, which caused concern for some who wished to keep the race "pure."[4] Indications of an apparent shift away from the dominant white Anglo-Saxon citizenry toward a more diverse population caused unease in some quarters and fueled the movement for increased immigration restrictions.

The collection of census data was begun June 1 and was completed by late summer of 1890. Preliminary reports of some findings were released as early as August 1890, while more comprehensive bulletins were released gradually over the next three years. The census highlighted many significant issues that were to dominate the years of the Progressive Era. The economic plight of blacks, Native Americans, and immigrants were there to be interpreted, as were the limited opportunities open to women through education and employment. Evidence of the miserable living conditions in the cities' teeming tenement districts and in rural shantytowns could be found in the housing statistics. The rate of unemployment and worker exploitation could be found in employment and income statistics. Reformers hoping to improve life, especially for the poor and powerless, could focus on these statistics and trends to promote their programs. Thus, as figures were released, various political, intellectual, and reform leaders used them to promote legislation and improvement. Others worried that these figures could be manipulated to promote political agendas.

Newspapers, for their part, used census figures to highlight particular trends, to warn against politicians' manipulation of the figures, or to argue for certain reforms. Because the findings of the census were to have political repercussions in the reapportionment of the U.S. House of Representatives and the allocation of resources, newspapers were particularly attentive to its accuracy, and criticism quickly became partisan. Democratic papers were particularly concerned over (Republican) President Benjamin Harrison's appointment of Robert B. Porter as superintendent of the census, who they believed would use the census to advance the Republican Party. In a period that was enchanted by statistics, critics quickly focused on the numbers. The 11th census was more ambitious, sweeping, and expensive than any of the 10 decennial population counts that had preceded it. Its census takers attempted to reach every habitable place in the country, but were avoided by immigrants and blacks, who feared being counted by government representatives. Likewise it surely missed many of the families living in rural areas off the beaten track. Its findings were used by the government to apportion legislative representation and distribute federal funds, but those same findings were debated by cities and regions that believed they had been undercounted or misrepresented. It resulted in accusations of fraud and misappropriation of funds, political maneuvering, and manipulation. For the press of the 1890s, the census provided provocative copy for nearly five years.

The following readings are organized in three sections. In the first section, the articles and editorials are critical of the census itself, either because of charges that the numbers were being manipulated for political reasons or due to reports that census takers were committing fraud. The readings in the second section relate to the growth in immigration, with the first editorial reflecting typical fears aroused by the specter of "alien invasion" and the second charging nativist politicians with intentionally misinterpreting immigration statistics to suit their own purposes. In the final section, the two readings reflect opposite responses to population growth in specific parts of the country. The first article quoted here welcomes growth in the South, while the second enumerates the many troubles resulting from unregulated growth in northern cities.

CRITICISMS OF POLITICAL MANIPULATION OF STATISTICS AND FRAUD

The first complaints against Porter began to surface as the preliminary counts were released in August. As has happened with nearly every census taken before and since, critics charged that the census takers had miscounted the population through both inefficiency and dishonesty. New York City, for example, claimed that the census had undercounted its population by some 100,000, or nearly 7 percent, which would reduce by one its Democratic representation in Congress. The mayor called for a recount, but his request was denied by the secretary of the interior, who oversaw the census.[5] The New York Times, *which wrote several editorials calling for a recount, concluded that the undercount was part of a political scheme to keep Republicans in the majority in Congress. In the following article the* Times *accuses Porter of deliberately manipulating the count for political reasons.*

New York Times, 10 November 1890

PORTER'S LITTLE SCHEME: A PLAN TO PERPETUATE REPUBLICAN CONTROL WHICH FELL THROUGH

WASHINGTON, Nov. 9—Superintendent of the Census Porter seems to have decided, as long ago as when Quay was trying to postpone action on the Force Bill in the Senate, that the population of the United States would not exceed 63,000,000.

It has just leaked out that when the anti–Force bill Republican Senators were dickering with the Democrats to shelve the Force bill and limit debate on the Tariff bill, Porter called upon Quay and a few other Republican Senators and Representatives and informed them that if the population of the country should turn out to be not more than sixty-three million it would be the easiest thing in the world to prepare a reapportionment scheme which would ensure Republican control of the Government for an indefinite number of years. The Census Superintendent had figured the thing down to a fine point, and was prepared to give the basis of representation upon which the reapportionment should be made to accomplish its purpose, provided that the census returns did not go above the sixty-three millions.

Porter urged the immediate preparation of the bill, and earnestly advised that it be taken up immediately after the Tariff bill and put through before the adjournment of the session. It happened, however, that one of the leading Democratic Senators got a hint of what Porter was at, and the result was the refusal of the Democrats to make the Force and Tariff bill bargain unless the Republicans pledged themselves to try no further legislation after finishing the Tariff bill, and Porter's little scheme had to be postponed.

This was long before the census returns had been counted in Porter's bureau. When the figures did come out, ten days ago, they gave the United States a population of 62,480,540.

Other newspapers criticized reports that created a rosy picture of the country's economic status. The New Orleans Times-Democrat, *for example, blasted the census for comparing apples to oranges in its report of economic growth between 1860 and 1890. The census report of 1890 had taken both the taxed and nontaxed wealth of the country and divided it by the number of inhabitants to come up with a per capita figure, while for the earlier census years, it had considered only the taxed wealth. This resulted in an inflated report of the per capita growth in wealth over the 30 years, the* Times-Democrat *pointed out. In the following editorial, the* Times-Democrat *attributes such an error to either Porter's ignorance or his willful misrepresentation of the facts.*

New Orleans Times-Democrat, 25 September 1891

MORE CENSUS BLUNDERING

Of the various sets of statistics issued by the census office there is no set perhaps on which the average American more congratulated himself than that in which the total and the individual wealth of the country in the year 1890 was set forth side by side with the total and individual wealth of the country at previous dates. The figures which Mr. Porter collected for the eleventh census made him draw the deduction that "the absolute wealth of the United States may be estimated at $62,620,000,000, or nearly $1000 per capita, as against $514 per capita in 1860, $780 per capita in 1870, and $870 in 1880." In other words, the gain in wealth of the country per capita in the thirty years 1860–1890, has been, according to the census superintendent, $486....

It is plain to the least intelligent person that, to arrive at a trustworthy comparison of the per capita wealth at two different dates, the same basis of comparison must be used. In other words, the taxed wealth alone, or both the taxed and untaxed wealth, must be taken into account of at both dates; no correct estimate could be obtained by taking merely the taxed wealth of one date and both the taxed and untaxed wealth at the other date.

This, however is the extraordinary error into which ignorantly or willfully Mr. Porter has fallen; and of course his calculations of per capita wealth in 1890 as compared with the same in 1860, are entirely vitiated and rendered worthless.

The taxed and untaxed wealth of the country being taken from the 1860 tables and being divided by the population in that year, the per capita wealth of the country is found to be in 1860, not the $514 which Mr. Porter fixed it at, but $993—within $7 of being as much as it was in 1890....

These modified results, which still show a substantial gain of wealth all round in the course of thirty years, will not of course be as gratifying to the national vanity as the "buckram" results arrived at by Mr. Porter, but they will have the recommendation over Mr. Porter's figures, which most people will value highly, that they are correct, whereas Mr. Porter's are grossly incorrect.

Porter's census easily continues to hold the record for being far and away the most unreliable and worthless compilation of statistics that has ever been foisted on the American people.

As the Census Bureau continued to release bulletins focusing on particular analyses of the numbers, stories of individual cases of fraud and forgery surfaced that brought the whole process under scrutiny. Thus, when one census taker in Philadelphia was arrested for fraud in 1892, his case got widespread attention.[6] Here, the New Orleans Times-Democrat *once again attacks the validity of the census, this time with wry humor.*

New Orleans Times-Democrat, 9 May 1892

THAT AWFUL CENSUS

The Times-Democrat has taken frequent occasions of pointing out the extraordinary vagariousness of the statistics compiled under various heads by Census Superintendent Porter's enumerators and employes [*sic*], and of deducing hence the unreliableness of some of the reports. But an incident happened in Philadelphia a few days ago that is calculated to bring out in clearer relief than ever this unreliable character of the eleventh census.

A census examiner of the name of Henry Huston sixty years of age, who some time ago was removed from the control of the industrial census in Philadelphia, was arrested that day on charges of fraud against the United States government and of forgery and perjury, growing out of a fraudulent performance of his census duties. The following two instances will tell sufficiently how Mr. Huston obtained his statistics, by aid of the directory instead of by the use of his legs and tongue:

In the first instance, according to the account, Mr. Huston returned the name of a young man as a carpenter and builder doing a business of $410,000 a year. The signature and address of the man were on the sheet, to which Huston appended his own sign manual, after swearing to the accuracy, so far as he knew, of the contents. The alleged carpenter and builder turned out, on investigation, to be a foreman in a dyeing establishment, and pronounced the signature purporting to be his to be a forgery.

In the second instance, the occupation of the enumerated person was given also as a carpenter and builder, and his business was rated at the goodly sum of $800,000. On investigation, it was found that the person entered on the sheet had been dead for years, and his widow declared that his business had not been of a carpenter and builder, but of a college professor!

It is comforting, of course, to know that the imaginative census man was held in $2000 bail to answer for making an exuberant imagination supply delusive fancies instead of getting prosaic judgment to provide hard facts; but any amount of punishment inflicted on the offender for his gross work of falsification will unfortunately neither impart accuracy and reliability to the census returns, nor confidence in these returns to the public for whose use they were compiled.

The author of a statistical work once added a fifty-page list of errata in the second edition, and a kind-hearted critic suggested to him that perhaps in the third edition he might see his way to put the whole work in the list of errata. Porter will not have to wait that long; the public will mentally put the entire census in the list of errata at the end of the first issue.

GROWTH IN IMMIGRATION

Another feature of the census to attract considerable attention was its identification of population trends. One set of statistics that caused considerable alarm in some quarters was that of the number of aliens living in the country and their increase in proportion to the number of native-born. The native-born population had grown from 43,475,840 in 1880 to 53,372,703 in 1890, an increase of 22.47 percent. The foreign-born population in the same period had increased from 6,679,943 to 9,249,547, or 38.47 percent. Some who promoted immigration restriction used these figures to support their warnings of the dangers posed by the poor, illiterate, and criminal classes they believed were flooding the country from abroad. The Boston Traveller, *which opposed immigration in general and Irish immigration in particular, was one of those to respond in alarm to the immigration figures provided by the census.*

Boston Traveller, 19 December 1892

THE IMMIGRATION RATE

If the immigration increases during the twenty years, from 1890 to 1910, as it did from 1870 to 1890, the alien arrivals will number over 30,000,000 and the government will be practically in the hands of and controlled by the alien-born citizens. If no restriction is put upon the immigration before the baby boy now born attains his majority the population of the United States will exceed 150,000,000 and the native-born citizen will have no more to say in the government of this country than the natives of Ireland now have in the government of Ireland. The man who was first in war, in peace, and in the hearts of his countrymen, was also first to warn his people of the dangers of immigration.

The Boston Pilot, *a Catholic newspaper that was particularly attentive to the interests of Irish Americans, instead saw the danger in the misinterpretation or misuse of immigration statistics. It feared that certain politicians, such as Massachusetts Senator Henry Cabot Lodge, would use these statistics to bolster their arguments for the restriction of immigration. Here is one of the many editorials it published in which it ridicules the use nativist politicians such as Lodge made of the statistics.*

Boston Pilot, 2 September 1893

LODGE MISINTERPRETS IMMIGRATION STATISTICS

If the Government of the United States were truly paternal, it would deprive Mr. Henry C. Lodge of the census reports. Whenever his eye beholds one, a divine madness seizes him, not to be appeased until he has drawn some dismal and wholly erroneous opinions from its innocent statistics and published them to a peaceful country, destroying all its comfort. His latest affliction is that whereas 62 percent of the population and 48 percent of the criminals are of native parentage, 38 percent of the population and 52 percent of the criminals are foreign, which he thinks is a reason for changes in immigrant legislation. Would it soothe the perturbed mind of Mr. Lodge to read his figures in this way? There are twelve Americans to every thirteen foreigners in the prisons. Of the entire native population, .0013 are in the prisons, reformatories of various sorts, and almshouses; of the foreign-born and natives of foreign parentage, .0028. That is to say, with every advantage of from a quarter millennial to thirty years in this country, America's virtue is .0015 greater than the foreign article. To put it in the way most in accord with Mr. Lodge's dolorous pitch, there are two of the foreign element not honest and self-supporting to every one American thief and pauper. It would be little to the credit of the Republic if the proportions were smaller. Does not an American citizen mean to be at least twice as good as any European, Asiatic, blameless Ethiopian, or dweller in the isles of the sea?

POPULATION GROWTH PROVOKES OPTIMISM AND FEARS

The census revealed many aspects of American life and these were interpreted broadly for the general public by a variety of publications. The New York Times quoted the Southern Lumberman, which interpreted the "encouraging growth" of southern cities reported in the census as a sign that the South was at long last recovering from the devastation of the Civil War.

New York Times, 1 September 1890

GROWING SOUTHERN CITIES

The census returns will show a most encouraging growth of Southern cities, and will be substantially as follows: Louisville has grown from 123,000 population in 1880 to 180,600, Memphis from 33,000 to 64,000, Nashville from 43,000 to 75,000, Atlanta from 43,000 to 65,000...and the growth of all other towns has been equally as great. It is safe to say that the Southern towns, taken on the average, have almost doubled in population within the last ten years and have increased fourfold in wealth.

The active development of the mineral and timber interests in the South has been one of the chief factors in promoting the growth of the towns, and has added no small share to the general prosperity.

The population in northern cities had also grown, but this was seen as troubling, for as the population swelled, living conditions often deteriorated and crime increased. Many of the new city dwellers in the North were immigrants, and many were poor or unemployed. Some pointed to the direct correlation between the size of their cities, the number of inhabitants in each home, and the rise in crime and poverty. The New York Times in particular paid attention to bulletins that related to life in urban areas. When the Census Bureau issued a report on housing and then related those statistics to the crime and mortality rate for various cities, it appeared that New York was the "costliest, wickedest and deadliest city in America." In an editorial commenting on these findings in which it cited Jacob Riis as an authority, the Times published a table showing the numbers for five cities. While the national average showed something less than 5 persons in a family and almost a whole house for each family, approximately 16 persons per dwelling were reported in New York City, resulting in its "leadership in immorality and disease." The Times used these statistics to condemn the prevalence of tenement housing in New York City and call for action by the city's Board of Health.

New York Times, 8 May 1892

FAMILY LIFE IN AMERICAN CITIES

Cities	Dwellings	Families per Dwelling	Death Rate per thousand	Arrests per hundred
New York	81,828	3.82	28.6	4.92
Chicago	127,871	1.72	21.1	3.63
Philadelphia	187,052	1.10	22.6	4.78
Brooklyn	82,282	2.08	25.5	3.52
London (Police District, 1881)	645,818	*	21.6	—

*Persons per dwelling, 7.4

The full measure of the cause [of immorality and disease]—viz. the hiving of humans like bees—does not appear in the table. In New York only 12.02 percent of all the families have a house to each and 82.08 percent live in tenements which are 42.77 percent of all dwellings. It is nothing to say that civilization presents no parallel for such unnatural and demoralizing conditions of life. It is not only the maximum crowding known, it is the actual maximum possible and the proof of it is the decline of population in the congested districts.

The bare bones of the facts given in the table shown can best have the breath of life breathed into them by citing in testimony men of undoubted experience and authority. Prominent among such observers is J. A. Riis, who says in "How the Other Half Lives": "It is these tenement nurseries of death, pauperism, and crime that fill our jails and police courts; that throw off a scum of 40,000 human wrecks to the Island asylums and workhouses, year by year; that turned out in the last eight years a round half million beggars to prey upon our charities; that maintain a standing army of tramps, with all that implies; that, above all, touch the family life with deadly moral contagion." Testifying before a legislative investigating committee the Secretary of the New York Prison Association declared that "80 per cent of crimes against persons and property are perpetrated by individuals who have either lost connection with home life, or never had any, or whose homes have ceased to be sufficiently separate, decent, and desirable to afford what are regarded as ordinary wholesome influences of home and family. The younger criminals seem to come almost exclusively from the worst tenement districts." Regarding the death rate under the conditions of New-York's population, it will be sufficient to cite a single sentence from the annual report of Board of Health: "The death rate of the city is not excessive (!) considering the comparative density of the population in many localities...and New-York City can justly claim to be pre-eminent as a healthy place." "Considering" the facts, the Health Board seem to be an amiable and easily-pleased body of gentlemen. Evidently the alarm bell will never be rung by them, even though New-York's death rate exceeds any other large city's (the yellow fever districts not excepted) by several units, each of which stands for more than a regiment of human lives. But their authority will be enough to give to density of population and improperly housed families first rank among the causes of a mortality which, with their permission, we will characterize as alarming and disgraceful.

Questions

1. Why is a census necessary? What use can the government make of the information it gathers through a census? Why were newspapers concerned that Superintendent Porter was manipulating the numbers?
2. Why would people be alarmed to learn that the foreign-born population was increasing? What foreign-born groups would the native-born population be concerned about? How was this population represented differently in Riis's description of the sweatshop workers and in the *Boston Traveller*'s editorial, "The Immigration Rate"? Although Riis's description of the garment workers is basically sympathetic, how does he reveal some stereotypes about Jews? How might these stereotypes be turned against Jews in later years?

3. If you were a manufacturer looking for a city in which to establish your business, how might your decision be influenced by statistics from the census? Would newspaper coverage of those statistics influence your decision?
4. What role did partisan politics play in the census of 1890? How might a newspaper's political allegiance affect its coverage of the census?
5. Many people view a statistical survey like the census as a purely scientific tool for measurement in which the information gathered is objective and in which "numbers don't lie." How could scientific data like results of the census be manipulated? How did the newspapers cited in this chapter reveal their distrust of such purportedly scientific methods?

NOTES

1. Jacob A. Riis, *How the Other Half Lives* (New York: Charles Scribner's Sons, 1890; reprint, New York: Dover Publications, 1971), p. 9.

2. Riis, pp. 100–101.

3. Untitled editorial, *Boston Transcript*, 1 October 1892, p. 14.

4. "A Census Bulletin," *Boston Transcript*, 18 July 1892, p. 4.

5. "The New Census," *New York Times*, 23 September 1890, p. 4; "The City and the Census," *New York Times*, 22 October 1890, p. 4.

6. "Faked Census Figures," *New York World*, 5 May 1892, p. 1.

CHAPTER 2

The Death of Sitting Bull and the Battle of Wounded Knee, December 1890

Afficulter two centuries of war and conquest, most of the Native Americans tribes in the United States had been either subjugated or exterminated by the Europeans who came to settle the New World. In an effort to placate those tribes willing to fight to the death for their land, the American government had signed successive peace treaties that defined vast expanses of land as Indian territory. Their provisions were violated quickly, however, and the treaties themselves were revoked as the needs of white settlers called for more land. Thus, by 1890 most of the West had been claimed by settlers and transformed into states and territories divided into tracts of land to be used for farming, ranching, mining, or development. The surviving Native Americans had been forcibly moved to reservations in the most inhospitable lands in the West, where they were deprived of guns and game, lived in poverty, and were completely dependent on federal agents for food and shelter.

Some bands of Indians refused to accept the terms set by the federal government and continued to raid homesteads in the hope of reclaiming their right to the land. Others, driven by hunger, desperation, and hatred, acted more like bandits and attacked wagon trains, cavalry units, and the railroad. When the threat became great enough, U.S. Cavalry units were dispatched to police the area, and their appearance often led to skirmishes that in some cases developed into full-scale battles.

In 1890 two events occurred that have become part of modern America's memory of the Indian wars. In December of that year, a number of Sioux bands gathered on the reservation in Grand River, South Dakota, to celebrate the Ghost Dance. This was a ceremony of fasting and dancing in which braves communed with their ancestors in the belief that they might resurrect them and the hope that this would strengthen their tribe.

Concerned that the ceremony might lead the bands to unite, the federal government sent Sioux police to arrest the tribal leaders and break up the gathering. When the Indians resisted, shooting started and one of the Sioux's greatest chiefs, Sitting Bull, was killed along with several tribal police.

Fearing reprisals, many of the Indians fled in the bitter cold. One group, under Chief Big Foot, was intercepted and moved to a camp on Wounded Knee Creek. Days later, on December 29, when the Indians refused to surrender their weapons to the cavalry, fighting broke out. The cavalry fired cannons into the camp, and 153 Sioux were killed, half of them women and children. Only 25 U.S. soldiers died in what became known as the Massacre at Wounded Knee.

Though December 1890 saw the end of the Indian wars under Sitting Bull and Big Foot, disturbances continued to occur between Indians and whites. Squatters invaded Indian land, Indians raided white homesteads, and tribes gathered to celebrate the Ghost Dance to the consternation of white observers with some regularity during the final decade of the century. Newspapers continued to cover these stories with some avidity,[1] but the wild years of the American West were over. In white culture, Buffalo Bill's Wild West Show (launched in 1882) turned the desperate Indian wars into a form of entertainment, and small children dressed up as cowboys and Indians for an afternoon's play. In the new century, the stories of chiefs such as Sitting Bull and Big Foot and their desperate battles with the whites were further exploited to become the frequent subject of dime novels and silent films. On the reservations, instead, the survivors lived with the consequences of the Indian wars. They wove the stories of Sitting Bull and Wounded Knee into the legends of their tribes and passed them down to the generations to follow.

As early as the colonial period, newspapers had reported the often violent encounters between whites and Native Americans. When several occurred in succession, they referred to them as "uprisings," and when the uprising was prolonged, it became an "Indian war." When the uprising was put down, peace was considered to be restored, though from the perspective of the vanquished Indians, the harsh conditions imposed on them could hardly be called a "peace." In the second half of the nineteenth century, most of these encounters were in the West. Newspaper reports usually named the tribe involved, reported the name of the cavalry officer in charge, and included the name of the chief of the band if he was known. The Indians were often referred to in negative descriptive terms such as "savages," "brutes," "redskins," and "hostiles." Most stories dwelt on the number of whites killed and the amount of damage done to their property; only occasionally did these stories describe the conditions among the Indians that led to their uprising. When stories described the reservations, they typically attributed the poverty and disease that plagued them to the red man's laziness and sloth rather than the harsh conditions imposed by the federal government and its Indian agents.

The death of Sitting Bull and the Massacre at Wounded Knee were two events of Homeric significance and easily fit into the narrative style used by many newspapers during this period. Some portrayed these incidents as proof of the Indian's savagery and characterized the two events as further evidence of the inevitable march of progress and European-American civilization. For others, the death of Sitting Bull and the Massacre at Wounded Knee assumed the proportions of great tragedy. Here was a hero (Sitting Bull) betrayed by his own people (the Sioux Indian police). Here was the slaughter of the innocents (the women and children victims) caused by the warring men (the Sioux warriors and the U.S. Cavalry). Though the United States had proven its might in its victory over the Sioux, it had failed to show Christian mercy or compassion. These newspapers condemned the government policies that could lead to such tragedy.

Newspapers across the country covered the events leading from Sitting Bull's death to the Battle at Wounded Knee avidly. Their varied responses to these events are represented in the six examples quoted here. These range from the *New York Times*'s description of Sitting Bull as a cowardly and ineffective leader to the *Milwaukee Journal*'s bitter condemnation of government policies and public attitudes that could lead to the extermination of a race. These examples provide a rich sample of the language that was often used in describing Indians. They also reveal the underlying conviction held by most Americans that the country's destiny was that of the white man and that anything that might impede that destiny must be swept aside.

The readings in this chapter are organized in three sections. In the first, the selections describe Indians in negative terms and view them as a threat to whites. The readings in the second section are sympathetic, describing the Indians as victims of white greed and government policy. The *New York Times* editorial in the last section blames government policy for mismanaging the situation and losing control.

NEGATIVE PORTRAYALS OF INDIANS AS A THREAT TO WHITES

The New York Times *was merciless and dismissive in its response to Sitting Bull's death. In this editorial published the day after his death on December 15, the* Times *portrays him as a devious troublemaker who brought his troubles on himself and his people and who would have been better off if he had accepted the inevitablility of his domination by the white man. This editorial also reveals common racist stereotypes of the time that cast Native Americans as lazy, childish, and dependent. Though Sitting Bull had been revered by his own people, this editorial expresses only contempt.*

New York Times, 16 December 1890

EXIT SITTING BULL

There seems to be no doubt that one of the most mischievous and turbulent Indians in the United States has been killed in the person of SITTING BULL. It is a good many years since SITTING BULL began to trouble the souls of Indian agents and officers of the United States Army. Like a bumptious and bombinating journalist of this city, whom he much resembled in his character and career, the late BULL was distinguished for the impracticality and apparent motivelessness of many of his most conspicuous performances. It is impossible to account for his public course upon any other hypothesis than that of "pure cussedness." BULL would undoubtedly have been a much more comfortable old savage if he had settled down under the aegis of the United States to draw his rations and to lament loudly whenever he found them deficient in quantity, for it is inconceivable that the red man should reject anything edible on the score of its quality. He has been, however, persistently of the opinion that

> "One crowded hour of glorious life
> Is worth an age without a name,"

and in his time he has had many crowded hours in setting traps for the United States troops, or in fighting them, or in running away from them.

Like a great many of our leading local statesmen and Napoleons of finance, he has had seasons when seclusion on the Canadian side of the border seemed much more wholesome for him than exposure to process of law on the American side. For some years after he had led his people to defeat and starvation he preferred Manitoba to the territories of our own Northwest, and there openly practiced polygamy, free trade, and other revolting vices at which we were aiming moral and patriotic legislation. It appears that he was at the bottom, more than anybody else, of the recent disturbances and rumors of disturbance. The old reprobate was himself unavailable as a Messiah, but he was as well aware as any copper-colored inhabitant of the country of the political value of a Messiah, and of the extent to which a belief in him might be worked. The announcement of his death is not calculated to arouse any other emotions than those excited the other day by the slaying of a "rogue" elephant in Cincinnati, though no quadruped ever did so much widely extended and long continued mischief as SITTING BULL.

The situation for the Indians in South Dakota continued to deteriorate as the year neared its end. The fleeing bands of Sioux were suspected of plotting to avenge Sitting Bull's death and take white scalps.[2] Cavalry troops were dispatched to track them down and bring them under control, which was usually accomplished only after some fighting. Once captured, the Indians were given the ultimatum that if they wanted to receive food and shelter, they must surrender their arms.[3] Original reports of the conflict at Wounded Knee must have originated with reports from the U.S. Army and were then disseminated by the wire services. Most newspapers initially reported some variation of the following telegraphic story, published in the Chicago Tribune.

Chicago Tribune, 30 December 1890

BLOODY INDIAN BATTLE
Fierce Fighting Between Big Foot's Band and the Troops

REDSKINS ALL WIPED OUT
Fifty Soldiers Killed and Wounded at the First Fire

CAPT. WALLACE AMONG THE DEAD
Braves and Squaws All Slaughtered Indiscriminately

PINE RIDGE IN A STATE OF TERROR

RUSHVILLE, Neb., Dec. 29–[Special]–The particulars of a battle with Indians on Porcupine Creek have just been received here. Big Foot's band, which was captured yesterday under a military guard, was within eighteen miles of the agency when orders were received from Gen. Brooke to disarm them and send them at once to Fort Omaha. When the demand for a surrender of arms was made the Indians replied by opening fire. The soldiers returned the fire and a terrible slaughter took place. The entire band of Indians, consisting of 120 braves and over 150 squaws and papooses, was killed. The loss of the soldiers was comparatively small, but several were killed, including Capt. Wallace of the Seventh Cavalry, and large numbers were more or less seriously wounded. When the news of the fight reached the agency it produced intense excitement there, and a large number of the Indians left the agency. Others under Red Cloud determined to stay with Gen. Brooke and are now helping to repel the attack of the renegade Indians who are attempting to capture and destroy the agency. A camp of friendlies within sight of the agency was burned just before sundown this evening, and it is supposed the inhabitants were massacred by hostiles.

Eyewitness and secondhand accounts of the conflict began to add flourishes and imaginative touches. The San Francisco Chronicle *described how the U.S. Cavalry had trained its Hotchkiss guns (cannons) on the Indian camp and how the Indians threw down their blankets, whipped up their rifles, and began firing on the troops surrounding them without warning.[4] The* New York Times *described the "bloody and desperate battle" in which "the Indians were shot down ruthlessly and in which the lives of several soldiers were sacrificed."[5] The conflict was described in headlines by different papers as a "battle," a "fight," and a "massacre." When it was all over, newspapers tried to make sense of the event in their editorial columns. The* San Francisco Chronicle *lived up to the* Atlanta Constitution*'s assessment of western papers as being "not disposed to be friendly to Indian interests" in the following editorial.*

San Francisco Chronicle, 31 December 1890

TREACHEROUS SAVAGES

The innate treachery of the Indian character was well illustrated on Monday by the incident which occurred at the Indian camp at Wounded Knee. Colonel Forsyth and two companies of dismounted cavalry were there to receive the submission and surrender of the Indians of Big Foot's band. An order was given to twenty Indians to go and get their guns and give them up. They went, but returned with only two guns. A detachment of troops then began to search the village, finding thirty-eight guns. As this task was about completed, the Indians who were surrounded by the troops began to move, and all at once they threw their blankets to the ground, snatched up rifles and opened fire among the soldiers. The troops were at a great disadvantage, fearing to shoot their own comrades, and the volley from the Indians killed Captain Wallace of Troop K and Private Cook of Troop B and dangerously and probably fatally wounded a number of others.

The account proceeds to say that the soldiers are shooting down Big Foot's men wherever they can find them, and no one can blame them. The chief had voluntarily surrendered, that is, the proposition had come from him, and the disarmament was one of the terms of the surrender. Big Foot could probably have controlled his young men had he chosen to, and it is to be hoped that he may be captured and hanged, as shooting is entirely too good for such a treacherous scoundrel as he has proved himself.

Probably the members of the Indians' Friends Society will have some theory on which to account for this despicable piece of work, but it will be hard for them to convince the American people that the killing of Captain Wallace and his companions was not cold-blooded murder. If the war shall become one of extermination, the Indians will have only such acts of treachery as this to thank for it.

SYMPATHETIC PORTRAYALS OF INDIANS AS VICTIMS

The Milwaukee Journal, *instead, condemned the sentiments toward Native Americans that could allow something like the murder of Sitting Bull. In this editorial the* Journal *speaks of Sitting Bull with admiration but also with pity. Here, he is both a hero and a victim. The* Journal *is bitter in its condemnation of "Christian civilization" and the avarice of white men that allow the destruction of Indian chiefs and tribes. It reflects on the nature of history that dwells only on the victor and laments what appears to be the inevitable extinction of the Indian race as well as the passing of the frontier.*

Milwaukee Journal, 26 December 1890

OUR GREAT INDIAN WAR

Our model Indian war grows apace. We have already succeeded in the assassination of a brave old chief for the offense of being a counsellor and defender of his country and people. Of course the murder of his son and half a dozen special friends counts only under the head of heroic massacre. Those who fled before the gatling-guns [*sic*] have been captured, and the latest announcement is, that order reigns in the Sioux nation. The dead Indians are now good Indians, and the memory of their taking off will tend strongly to reconcile the tribe to the benign influences of Christian civilization.

The red man has no chronicler. His side is never written up. His wrongs meet no responsive sympathy. The white man wants his country, his lands and his property and does not want him. Hence, according to our historians, he is always the aggressor, no matter what he does or omits to do. To be brave is criminal; to resent outrage and injury marks him down as a dangerous savage to be put out of the way like a wolf or panther. As to justice in his case, even to mention the word is to burlesque.

To complete the triumph and add to national glory, the butchery wound up by stealing Sitting Bull's body, after scalping, and it is to go into an anatomical museum as evidence to the future of a race nearly as extinct as the buffalo. Indeed, the wild game, human or otherwise, is little more than a memory. A few samples of aboriginal man may for a while be preserved as stock to graft Indian wars upon, since they are a white necessity and we can't get on without them. By diligent care, a few may linger for some years, but the fate of the mound-builders [extinct tribes that had inhabited Wisconsin prior to white settlement] will be theirs. They will leave a name but the race that preceded did not achieve even that much. Whose fate is happiest is not worth discussing. Oil and water will sooner unite than a wild man and a tame one. We take the oil, and leave them to the waters of oblivion. Extermination would almost seem a law of nature. Since America was discovered it has known no pause. The hand of fate is in it. The Indian must go. His virtues and good traits are rarely or never mentioned. We are all good white men and sure of it.

In the days and weeks that followed Sitting Bull's death, reports began to filter out that the chief had, in fact, been assassinated by the tribal police.[6] Some newspapers began to call for a reexamination of government policy and the causes underlying the conflict between the Indians and the government. On December 24, the Atlanta Constitution *called for an investigation into Sitting Bull's "murder." Far from the position taken by the* New York Times, *the Constitution's editorial depicted Sitting Bull and the Sioux as human beings whose rights had been violated by the U.S. government.*

Atlanta Constitution, 24 December 1890

THE GOVERNMENT'S DUTY

The Indian question is a live issue with the press at this particular time. This is as it should be, for recent occurrences in the Indian settlements have been of too grave a nature to be dismissed with casual comment.

Changes in the government's present policy of dealing with the Indians are both necessary and expedient, and an investigation should be ordered, so that the real causes of the disturbances that arise among them may be known and remedies applied wherever such may be possible.

Even the Western newspapers, which are not disposed to be friendly to Indian interests, have recently spoken plainly in their behalf, being led to do so by a sense of justice and the knowledge that the Indians have suffered wrong at the hands of the government. It is clearly shown that the recent Indian outbreak was the result of the government's "starvation policy," and that the Indians were simply starved into revolt. The killing of Sitting Bull is denounced as a murder, and it is charged as such to the government.

The Indians have rights which the government must respect. It has penned them in the cold corners of the far west where, in many instances, they are at the mercy of unscrupulous agents, who are said to be directly responsible for much of the trouble reported. It is, therefore, the duty of the government to make a thorough investigation which, if honestly conducted, will result in a settlement of present, while it may prevent future, troubles.

GOVERNMENT POLICY TO BLAME

From the relatively settled security of New York, where memories of Indian wars were far in the past, the New York Times *now adopted a more sympathetic tone as it received reports of the massacre. It deplored the actions of the troops, and found the Indians' desperate actions to have been caused by bureaucratic mismanagement. In a long editorial that examined various causes of the incident, the* Times *found the whole affair to be the natural conclusion of misdirected government policies that allowed the mismanagement of the reservations.*

New York Times, 31 December 1890

AN INDIAN MASSACRE

It would be an abuse of language to describe as a battle the encounter that took place on Monday between United States troops and hostile Indians. The Indians were captives and were surrounded by four times their number of armed white soldiers....

It is proof of a high degree either of desperation or of fanaticism that the captives should have preferred to trust the chance of resisting an irresistibly superior force of whites. They must have known when they emptied the rifles they were required to surrender into the ranks of armed soldiers that surrounded them that they were sealing their own doom. They had no refuge, no way of fleeing without being pursued and overtaken, and no hope of mercy when they were overtaken.... The mad and reckless resistance of the captives is such an act of war as would have been celebrated if it had occurred in civilized warfare, all the more by reason of its madness and recklessness....

It is different with the wretched, copper-colored starvelings who have just thrown away their lives, even from their own point of view, for they took very much less than their own in number of white men's lives in exchange.... But the ultimate responsibility for the Indian war is the responsibility for the killing both of the whites and of the Indians, and that is not very far to seek. All the authoritative accounts agree that these Indians were starved into revolt, although nobody disputes that we pay enough to have them abundantly fed. Either the money or the food is stolen in transit by rascally agents or else the food is bought and distributed by incompetent agents so that the Indians do not get it. In either case the fault lies immediately with the Interior Department, and ultimately with the President of the United States. The points made by Gen. Mills in his paper on the Indian question on which we commented a day or two ago appear very conspicuously in the reports of this massacre. In the first place we starve those whom we pretend to feed. In the second place, we allow to be furnished with arms creatures whom we know to be capable of ruthless murder on the slightest provocation. How came Big Foot's Band to be in possession of the rifles they were ordered to surrender? An Indian does not need a Winchester rifle to shoot Government rations. It is desirable to him only in order to kill men and by preference white men. It is plain that we must feed the Indians and disarm them. It is at once shameful and silly to withhold their food and to permit them to bear arms.

QUESTIONS

1. What was the logic behind the government's policy of confining Indians to reservations? What was there about government policies that would cause Native Americans to revolt?
2. What was the significance of the Ghost Dance to the Indians, and why did government authorities perceive it as a threat?
3. Why might western newspapers be "less friendly to Indian interests" than those published in the East?
4. How was the *Milwaukee Journal* being ironic when it referred to the death of Sitting Bull as reconciling his tribe to "the benign influences of Christian civilization"?
5. What are some of the terms used by the newspapers to describe Indians? How do these terms indicate prevalent contemporary attitudes about Indians? How are these terms related to stereotypes still relevant today?

NOTES

1. See, for example, "Ghost Dance Begun," *Boston Transcript*, 18 November 1892, p. 1, and "Peace Pipe Broken/Civil War in the Choctaw Nation Probable," *Boston Transcript*, 16 September 1892, p. 10.

2. "To Avenge Bull's Death/The Dead Chief's Band Decide to Lift Some Scalps," *Chicago Tribune,* 20 December 1890, p. 2.

3. "Nothing But an Indian," *Atlanta Constitution,* 24 December 1890, p. 1, and "Surrender or Starve/The Alternative Given to the Indians," *Atlanta Constitution,* 26 December 1890, p. 1

4. "Indian Treachery," *San Francisco Chronicle,* 30 December 1890, p. 1.

5. "A Fight with the Hostiles," *New York Times,* 30 December 1890, p. 1.

6. See, for example, "It Was Murder/The Cowardly Assassination of Sitting Bull," *Atlanta Constitution,* 22 December 1890, p. 1.

CHAPTER 3

Nativist Fears Limit Chinese Immigration, May 1892

The prospect of employment in a rapidly expanding economy and the promise of freedom from religious and political persecution attracted millions of immigrants to the United States through most of the nineteenth century. In the last decades of the century, however, rather than being welcomed into the land of plenty, these newcomers found a nation riddled with social, economic, and political anxiety. Faced with the problems of industrialization, the unregulated growth of cities, labor uprisings, economic depressions, and the threat of anarchism and socialism, some Americans pointed to these immigrants as the reason for many of the nation's troubles.

Chinese immigrants, in particular, were targeted as alien. But that had not always been the case. Starting in the mid-1800s, the U.S. government was eager to attract Chinese immigrants, particularly to the West, which desperately needed laborers to build its towns and railroads and work in its mines and fisheries. Recruitment advertisements enticed young men to come to America where they could find steady work as mine diggers and railroad laborers. Steamship companies sailing from the ports of southeast China offered special rates and convenient payment plans that allowed the impoverished immigrants to pay off their passage through reductions from their wages once they reached the United States.

In 1852 the need for these hardworking, undemanding laborers was so great that California Governor John MacDougall called the Chinese the "most desirable of our adopted citizens."[1] In 1868, at the United States's instigation, the United States and China signed the Burlingame Treaty, which recognized the "inalienable right of man to change his home and allegiance" and recognized the mutual advantages of the free migration and emigration of their citizens. By 1870 some 63,000 Chinese lived in the United States, mostly in the western states and territories.

In the next decade the tide of immigration from the Far East quadrupled, and an average of 12,795 Chinese immigrated to the United States each year. Some of these returned to China after a few years, but many remained, and by 1880 there were an estimated 75,000 Chinese in California alone. Another 9,000 had settled in Oregon, 5,000 in Nevada, 3,000 in Idaho, and another 3,000 in Washington. In addition to working in mines and on construction projects, they were employed as laundrymen, cigar makers, farm workers, and domestic servants. Those who were more established or ambitious began to open their own businesses, which ranged from laundries to truck gardens to grocery stores.

The Chinese were willing to work long hours for low wages and often competed with whites for the most backbreaking jobs. They lived frugally and saved every penny to send home to their families or, in some cases, to bring their families to America. They lived in enclaves, often with countrymen from their native region or town. They continued to speak their native language and dressed in a distinctive fashion that marked them as foreigners. This very clannishness set them apart from earlier immigrant groups, and many Americans regarded them with suspicion.

Nativists, particularly those in the Pacific Coast states, resented the influx of Chinese and feared the influence they might exert on American culture. As early as 1850, anti-Chinese sentiment in California coalesced into cries of "California for the Americans," despite the governor's more tolerant view. In the next decades nativists in that state succeeded in enacting a series of state and local laws to discourage Chinese ownership of property, to levy special taxes on the Chinese, and to regulate their customs and living conditions. Most of these laws were struck down in the courts as unconstitutional or proved impractical to enforce, but mobs were also active in persecuting the Chinese when the law would not. During the 1870s and 1880s, mobs attacked Chinese, destroyed their homes and property, and organized to boycott their businesses. In the most violent incidents, anti-Chinese riots in San Francisco, Seattle, Los Angeles, and Rock Springs, Wyoming, led to the violent death of many Chinese and the destruction of the Chinese quarter in those communities.

White workingmen also united against cheap Chinese labor, which they feared would undermine their own position in the workforce. The Workingman's Party of California referred to the influx of Chinese laborers as the "yellow peril." In 1877 the party began to lobby Congress to halt further Chinese immigration and expel any Chinese who had not already been naturalized. The party's slogan was, "The Chinese must go."

In response to nativist pressure, Congress passed the Chinese Exclusion Act in 1882. This suspended immigration of all Chinese for a period of 10 years and forbade naturalization of those already living in America. (This was Congress's first act limiting immigration of a specific racial or ethnic group.) Although the act did not apply to professionals, merchants, or students, it drastically reduced the number of Chinese coming to the United States. Because many of those already in the country at the time of the Exclusion Act were unmarried or had left their families behind in China (and therefore would have no children), the number of Chinese in the United States actually *declined* between 1882 and 1892.[2]

Then, in 1892, under continued pressure from labor groups and nativists, particularly those in the western states, Congress passed the Geary Act, which extended the Chinese Exclusion Act of 1882 for another 10 years. In addition, it required all Chinese already living in the United States to register with authorities and obtain a certificate of residence. The Geary Act also included provisions for deporting Chinese who entered the country illegally or who failed to register.

Although the exclusion of Chinese might have been spearheaded by the western states, it had ample support in Congress. In 1888, for example, the Republican Party platform stated: "We declare our hostility to the introduction into this country of foreign contract labor and of Chinese labor, alien to our civilization and constitution; and we demand the rigid enforcement of the existing laws against it, and favor such immediate legislation as will exclude such labor from our shores."[3] In 1892, after the passage of the Geary Act, the Democratic Party concurred, stating in its platform: "We heartily approve all legitimate efforts to prevent the United States from being used as a dumping ground for the known criminals and professional paupers of Europe; and we demand the rigid enforcement of the laws against Chinese immigration and the importation of foreign workers under contract, to degrade American labor and lessen its wages; but we condemn and denounce any and all attempts to restrict the immigration of the industrious and worthy of foreign lands."[4]

Some, however, opposed the restrictions. Some did so on moral and ethical grounds, arguing that the restrictions were racist and inhumane. Others opposed them on more pragmatic grounds, fearing that they would endanger diplomatic and trade relations with China and result in retaliation against American missionaries and business interests in that country. Opponents to the immigration restrictions were generally from the eastern states, which had not yet experienced the yellow peril.

Despite difficulties in enforcing some of its provisions, the Geary Act successfully slowed Chinese immigration to a trickle. In 1904 the Exclusion Act was extended indefinitely and the precedent of setting immigration restrictions according to race or nationality was followed throughout the twentieth century.

Immigration not only of the Chinese—was a frequent topic of debate during the 1880s and 1890s, and newspapers participated fully in the discussion of its benefits and dangers through news stories, columns, and editorials. The Chinese were certainly not the only immigrant group being discussed: newspapers on the East Coast were more frequently concerned with the effects of the influx of destitute, illiterate, and diseased "detritus" flooding in from countries like Italy, Russia, and Poland.[5] Easterners didn't have any particular concern about Chinese immigrants, but they were concerned that American customs and institutions were being undermined by those immigrants who insisted on adhering to their old ways.

SUPPORT OF IMMIGRATION RESTRICTION

In 1890 the Boston Congregationalist, *a conservative weekly, expressed the fear that America was losing her identity to her foreign immigrants who did not intend to become Americans. This sort of message was particularly appropriate to discussion of the Chinese, who were known for their clannish and foreign ways. It was immigrants like these, the* Congregationalist *warned, who would undermine the unity of the nation.*

Boston Congregationalist, 10 July 1890

AMERICA FOR THE AMERICANS

The oratory of Independence Day has grown less florid but not less fervid with passing years. It has good reason to grow more deliberate and impressive. Greater victories than those by which our independence as a nation was won, which have since been achieved, deserve to be remembered. We face greater foes than Great Britain ever was. Our fathers won for us civil liberty; we have a greater task to keep it. It was easier to preserve unity among three millions on the Atlantic coast than to keep one national spirit among sixty-four millions of people spreading from ocean to ocean.

Much is said of the dangers which threaten us from immigration. But the nation is not imperiled by the influx of foreigners. There is room for all who wish to come....

Our perils are not from the number of those who come, nor from the diversity of their nationalities, but from those who seek, not to add to our national honor and wealth by sharing them, but to take from them; who come, not to accept our institutions, but to import others; not to adopt with pride and gratitude our history, but to substitute other histories in its place....

The only questions we have to ask of any immigrant are, Does he seek to become an American? and, Is he capable of becoming one?...If any prefer China to America, let them stay in China. They have no right to import into this country a section of China that they may enjoy our privileges without sharing our citizenship. There is no room in this country for a new Germany, a new Spain, or a new Ireland. American citizens ought to fight every effort to establish these countries within ours, with a patriotism as consecrated and determined as that with which our fathers fought England.... America is for Americans, and Americans from whatever nation are welcome to America.

Attitudes like those expressed by the Boston Congregationalist *set the scene for the introduction of a series of bills aimed at the Chinese in the early 1890s. In 1890, for example, a bill had been introduced in the House of Representatives that would prohibit any Chinese other than those in the consular or diplomatic service from passing through the United States. Though this had been defeated, it prepared the ground for the debate on the extension of the Exclusion Act of 1882. The* San Francisco Chronicle *was one of the act's strongest proponents. It applauded the section of the bill that called for registration of the Chinese already in the country, pointing out: "Nothing else can accomplish the work, for the Chinese are almost as much alike as a flock of sheep, and it is practically impossible to tell them apart if they want to conceal their identity."*[6] *The* Chronicle *attributed any opposition to the act to ignorance, explaining: "The East, as we on this coast have tried hundreds of times to convince them, has been dealing with an ideal and imaginary race, wholly unlike the Chinese whom we know, and in consequence would not look at the coolie as he really is."*[7] *When the Geary Act was approved by Congress without a hitch and immediately signed by President Benjamin Harrison on May 5, 1892, the* Chronicle *reported the event with satisfaction at the president's swift response.*

San Francisco Chronicle, 6 May 1892

THE BILL NOW A LAW
SIGNING OF THE EXCLUSION MEASURE

Sensational Reports About the
Withdrawal of the Chinese Legation

Special Dispatch to the Chronicle

WASHINGTON, May 5—The President to-day had a conference with the Attorney-General concerning the Chinese prohibition act. As the Attorney-General said it was a grave question whether all the existing restrictive legislation did not expire to-morrow, the President signed the bill to avoid possible legal complications.

Sensational reports are afloat as to the effect of the new law upon our commercial and diplomatic relations with China. It is said to-night that the Chinese Minister is so indignant that he has plainly intimated his intentions to ask for his passports and withdraw the legation from Washington....

When the original Geary bill was put through the House the Chinese Minister made it no secret of the fact that he regarded the act as not only unnecessary, but decidedly unfriendly and entirely unconstitutional and illegal, as being a plain violation of treaty obligations.... Whether his displeasure and indignation, however, will lead his Government to the point of severing diplomatic relations with the United States can only be conjectured....

DETROIT, May 5—Last night at 12 o'clock four Chinese took advantage of the supposed expiration of the exclusion act and crossed to this side, landing near the Wabash depot. After an exciting chase, in which an officer fired two shots, the fugitives were captured and taken to the police station. It is supposed that other Chinese crossed on Sunday night.

OPPOSITION TO IMMIGRATION RESTRICTION

One of the eastern papers opposed to the Geary Act was the New York Times. *In story after story about the proposed extension of the exclusion act, it referred to the Chinese in sympathetic terms. It referred to the laborers as "exploited," "patient," and "benighted." It characterized the immigration restriction as "harsh" and an unfriendly act toward a friendly nation. It described the campaign by "a few States on the Pacific side of the continent where the anti-Chinese prejudice is strong" as having succeeded in convincing other politicians, who "had more fear of offending this prejudice than they had regard for friendly relations with China."[8] When the Geary Act was signed by President Harrison, some business and religious organizations denounced his action, fearing that China might retaliate against missionaries and businesses in China. The* Times *used the concerns of the Methodist General Conference as an opportunity to blast Congress's action in this untitled editorial.*

New York Times, 8 May 1892

Congress Gave in to Pressure from Western States

The sentiment expressed in the Methodist General Conference on the subject of the Chinese Exclusion act is likely to be shared by all the religious organizations which maintain missions in China. No doubt the animus of the denunciation of the act may be largely a fear that it will be followed by retaliation, which will interfere with mission work, if not wholly break it up, in the Chinese dominions, but this, though not the strongest ground for condemning the action of Congress, is one which will excite widespread sympathy among an influential class of citizens. Should retaliation come, it will affect another influential class of more worldly-minded people, those who have some interest in trade with China, a trade which would be susceptible of a large development if friendly relations were maintained with that country. And who are to be the gainers of this act of bad faith? No class whatever, for the restriction previously existing was sufficient for all needed protection of the workingmen of the country against the competition of the Chinese, which is not really injurious with the limitation upon immigration which China has so far assented to. The act of Congress was one of political cowardice, inspired by a fear that the prejudices of a small class in a few States on the Pacific slope might work to the injury of the party which should oppose the wrong. It is one of the most humiliating acts of which any civilized nation has been guilty in modern times.

It was the additional provision that called for the registration of all Chinese residents, which was to go into effect May 5, 1893, that provoked the strongest opposition from Chinese already living in the United States. Some, especially those who had already become citizens, objected to the requirement that they register, arguing that this infringed on their constitutional rights. They formed the Chinese Equal Rights League and held meetings around the country to protest the Geary Act and to seek its repeal. Meetings in Boston attracted the attention of the Boston Herald, *which announced one of the meetings with a few paragraphs. Though the article is short, it lends distinction to the meeting with its identification of one of the Chinese speakers as a journalist and a reference to New England's famous abolitionist, William Lloyd Garrison.*

Boston Herald, 18 November 1892

THE CHINESE MEETING TONIGHT

The meeting to be held in Tremont Temple this evening, in protest against the oppressive injustice of the Chinese registration act, is worthy the encouragement of our citizens. A novelty attending it will be an address from Wong Chin Foo, a Chinese journalist of New York, and a naturalized American. An appeal will be made to Congress not to repeal the law forbidding immigration, but to remedy the injustice in some of the provisions of the registration act. Senator Sherman has denounced them in Congress, and Representative Hitt of Illinois has won much credit among those whose good opinion is worth having by his eloquent exhortations in the same direction. The son of [abolitionist] William Lloyd Garrison, who bears his honored father's name, and is active in originating this meeting, declares that "no such infamous enactment as this has disgraced the statute book of the nation since the fugitive slave law."

The agitation of the Chinese Equal Rights League also caught the attention of the Boston Transcript, *which called for the repeal of the registration portion of the law and denounced it as a defiance of the common rights of humanity and the constitutional rights of U.S. citizens. In this long editorial, the* Transcript *opposes the Geary Act on moral, humanitarian, legal, and constitutional grounds. Further, it points to the racist nature of the law.*

Boston Transcript, 15 November 1892

AN INFAMOUS LAW

The agitation started by the Chinese Equal Rights League for the repeal of the Geary Chinese registration law enacted at the last session of Congress ought to enlist the sympathy of all Americans who believe in preserving national good faith and in keeping out of our law extraordinary principles directed against Chinese that may yet be applied to others.

This Geary Chinese registration act, which was approved May 5 last and which goes into effect May 5, 1893, should not be confounded with the several laws which have been passed to limit or restrict Chinese immigration. It applies to Chinese resident in the United States by virtue of treaty at the time of its passage, and requires them to be registered, and tagged, at the same time setting up such requirements as will make their compliance with its provisions very difficult. Failure or inability to meet requirements is punishable by deportation, or imprisonment with hard labor. Independent of the objection to the law on the score of humanity, it is open to others from the standpoint of American institutions and national good faith.

In the first place it distinctly violates the provisions of existing treaties with China which accord to Chinese subjects resident in the United States the treatment given to the subjects of the most favored nation. Secondly, the common law principle that the accused shall be deemed innocent until he is proved guilty is set aside. The Chinaman must, under the provisions of the Geary Law, prove that he is legally in the United States. The burden of proof is thereby placed on the defendant, and failure may be punishable with imprisonment among felons. The spirit that dictated this requirement speaks throughout the bill. A Chinaman who has proved that he had the certificate called for, but has lost it, may yet be detained in custody until he secures a duplicate, and the "costs" of the detention may, at the discretion of the court, be thrown upon him. If language means anything, the bill unconstitutionally imposes a discrimination by excluding colored people from the witness box. Section 6 provides that the accused may prove inability to secure the required certificate by unavoidable causes "by at least one credible *white* witness." An attempt has been made, a lame and halting one, to explain that "white" doesn't mean "white;" that the law only seeks to exclude Chinamen from the witness box on behalf of Chinamen and that "white" means black. Nevertheless, there stand the words, and they certainly mean, if they mean anything, that a Negro is not a competent witness in such proceedings, or a man of African descent—"colored" in the usual sense of the term.

These are only some of the objections to the Geary law, which is a hodge-podge of abominations throughout. We are glad to note that the Chinese residents in the United States are agitating for its repeal, and that, not content with resting their case on legality, they appeal to the manhood of the American people. As they say in their appeal, they are "a mere handful of defenceless men." As such, they ought to move the sympathies of Americans. In their agitation, they can take comfort from recent events. The bill was signed to placate the sentiment of the Pacific coast. The signing was a mistake. It placated the people of the Pacific coast, it offended the humanity of the nation at large. The best sentiment for a man to placate, whatever be his position, is his own sense of humanity, his duty to do unto others as he would be done by. We hope these considerations will induce Boston citizens to cooperate with the Chinese Equal Rights League to make its meeting at Tremont Temple a most significant protest against the continuation on our statute books of a law that sets at defiance not only the common rights of humanity, but the common law of the United States, the constitutional rights of its citizens, and the plighted faith of the nation.

GEARY ACT A FAILURE

In the six months following Harrison's signing of the Geary Act, newspapers followed the reaction in the Chinese community closely. They reported rumors that various entities, from the Chinese Equal Rights League to the Chinese Six Companies to the Chinese government, were advising Chinese residents to refuse to register.9 When no concerted resistance seemed to coalesce, they began to report the country's progress in registering Chinese residents. By the deadline of May 4, 1894, for example, some 47,000 laborers and merchants had been registered in San Francisco, the Milwaukee Journal reported.10

The Geary Act was not the perfect tool for immigration restriction its creators had hoped it would be, however. It provided no mechanism for controlling Chinese immigration from Canada and Mexico, and Chinese intent on coming to the United States could easily bypass immigration control by coming through these entry points, something newspapers were quick to point out. In July 1892, for example, the Chicago Tribune *reported that at least three hundred Chinese had made their way from British Columbia to Toronto and from there into the United States in the past several weeks.11 Another major weakness in the law was Congress's failure to include a provision for funds to pay the considerable cost of enforcing it. In this editorial, published in May 1893, the* Boston Pilot, *a Catholic newspaper that championed Irish immigrants but had little sympathy for Chinese immigrants, declared the Geary Act was a failure because of the government's inability to enforce it.*

Boston Pilot, 27 November 1893

IS THE GEARY LAW DEFEATED?

The Geary law, requiring every Chinaman in this country to be registered and photographed before a given date in the present month, has become a dead letter. The object of the bill was to prevent a fraud frequently practiced by Chinese immigrants who misrepresented themselves as old settlers returning from visiting their native country. If the Geary law were enforced, every new arrival would have to prove his identity by indubitable evidence, or be denied admission to the country.

There was nothing degrading or harsh in the proviso. American and other travelers on the continent of Europe submit to similar regulations without complaining. The passport system embodies the same principal, and no law-abiding tourist objects to it. But the Chinese residents, or rather the Chinese Six Companies who control their every action, pretended to regard it as an insult and an outrage, and refused to comply with it. The penalty, clearly defined, was the deportation of every offender; but it was a penalty more easily prescribed than enforced; for it is estimated that the sending home of all the unregistered would entail an expense of not less than $6,000,000 and no provision has been made by Congress for any such outlay.

Therefore, the Geary law remains a dead letter and a subject of ridicule to Americans and Chinamen alike. The only alternatives are for Congress to repeal the law or appropriate money enough to enforce its penalties.

The fact that Congressman Geary is a cheap demagogue naturally prejudices his bill in the public estimation; but the government must look at it from the sole standpoint of law and right. There is no hardship or insult in the law requiring anybody to be lawfully identified, if the public welfare demand such as proceeding, as it certainly does in the case of the Chinese residents.

Some intemperate opponents of the measure declare that China will retaliate by expelling all American residents in that country; an assertion which is simply rubbish. China does not care a straw about her subjects in foreign countries. She tolerates Americans and other foreigners in her dominions for business reasons alone, or because she is bound to do so by treaty stipulations.

The Chinese registration question is a purely domestic one. It can be enforced if our Government care to enforce it. Nobody knows this fact better than the cunning Six Companies and their hired advocates like Mr. Joseph Choate. The people of the Pacific coast, who are the chief sufferers from the Mongolian plague, will not be deceived by the sophistry of paid attorneys or pseudo-philanthropists on a matter which so vitally concerns them and their posterity.

QUESTIONS

1. Why did the United States initially welcome Chinese immigrants? What would make them particularly valuable in the West?
2. What caused Americans, particularly in the West, to turn against the Chinese? What were some of the prejudices against the Chinese? How are these revealed in some of the language used in the newspaper articles and editorials quoted in this chapter?
3. Why is it understandable that the *San Francisco Chronicle* would support the Geary Act? Do you agree with the *Chronicle* that eastern newspapers could not understand the issue of Chinese immigration and the need for the immigration laws?
4. Some of the newspapers opposed to the Geary Act referred to it as "unconstitutional," "unjust," or "inhumane." What are some of the reasons for using these terms?
5. William Lloyd Garrison was an abolitionist who worked for years for the emancipation of slaves. Why did his son, of the same name, compare the

Geary Act to the Fugitive Slave Law? What would these two laws have in common?

Notes

1. "Chinese and Chinese Exclusion Act," in *Encyclopedia of American Immigration*, ed. James Clement, vol. 1 (Armonk, N.Y.: Sharpe Reference, 2001), p. 74.

2. The Chinese population in the United States declined from a high of 107,488 in 1890 to a low of 61,638 in 1920.

3. "Immigration Planks of Republican Party Platforms, 1860–1996," in *Encyclopedia of American Immigration*, ed. James Clement, vol. 4 (Armonk, N.Y.: Sharpe Reference, 2001), p. 1400.

4. "Immigration Planks of Democratic Party Platforms, 1856–1996," in *Encyclopedia of American Immigration*, ed. James Clement, vol. 4 (Armonk, N.Y.: Sharpe Reference, 2001), p. 1405.

5. "The Alien Mob," *Boston Traveller*, 20 December 1892, p. 4.

6. "Chinese Exclusion," *San Francisco Chronicle*, 3 May 1892, p. 6.

7. "The Exclusion Bill," *San Francisco Chronicle*, 5 May 1892, p. 6.

8. See, for example, "China's Earnest Protest," *New York Times*, 22 March 1892, p. 4; "The Patient Chinese Kick," *New York Times*, 21 March 1892, p. 4; "What Will China Do about It?" *New York Times*, 9 May 1892, p. 4.

9. "Chinese Will Not Register," *San Francisco Chronicle*, 24 November 1892, p. 1; "A Chinese Proclamation," *Boston Transcript*, 21 September 1892, p. 10.

10. "Registration of Chinese," *Milwaukee Journal*, 4 May 1894, p. 2.

11. "Chinamen Come to the United States," *Chicago Tribune*, 7 July 1892, p. 9.

CHAPTER 4

The Homestead Strike Pits Labor against Management, 1892

The 1890s saw a remarkable growth of manufacturing in the United States that meant more products for consumers and bigger profits for corporate investors and owners. While this growth might have meant more jobs and better pay for workers in previous generations, technological developments made factories increasingly mechanized. This undermined the position of skilled workers, many of whom belonged to labor unions and depended on those unions to negotiate better working conditions. In the volatile economic climate of the early 1890s, many factory owners attempted to lower salaries and impose longer working hours to increase their own profits. They were blocked in this if their workers were unionized. Unions meant strikes. Strikes meant decreased production. Some factory owners, however, were determined to prevail.

This is what happened in 1892 at the Carnegie Steel works in Homestead, Pennsylvania. In January, the company's negotiations for a new contract with the Amalgamated Association of Iron and Steel Workers reached an impasse. Carnegie's manager, Henry Frick, demanded an 18 to 60 percent pay cut and warned union workers that they could accept it or find work elsewhere. When an agreement had not been reached by June 23, Frick announced he would close the plant on July 1 and reopen July 6 with nonunion labor. Frick knew he could operate the highly mechanized plant with cheap unskilled labor and bypass almost entirely the skilled and higher-paid union workers. If he could break the union, it would mean complete control of the workforce by the company and bigger profits for the foreseeable future. Perhaps anticipating an attempt by the workers to take over the mill, he constructed barricades and fences around the property, earning it the nickname of "Fort Frick" from sardonic locals.

But as the shutdown loomed, the nonunion workers chose overwhelmingly to support the union in a walkout. As one of their first actions, the workers created a committee to organize the boycott and keep order. The committee formed a militia made up of the entire workforce of four thousand men, took over the mill, set up sentry outposts on the Monongahela River, blocked all roads, took over the town, and shut down all the saloons. When the county sheriff sent a dozen deputies to establish an official presence, they were sent packing. Frick secretly hired three hundred guards from the Pinkerton Detective Agency, a well-armed private police force that was notorious for using brutal tactics in subduing labor agitation.

On July 6 Frick tried to sneak the Pinkertons onto the property at dawn by bringing them in by boat and barge, but they were spotted by union sentries who opened fire on them with rifles. The sentries were soon joined by a mob of workers and townspeople who hurled rocks and fired in the air, warning the Pinkertons to turn back. The Pinkertons, armed with Winchester repeating rifles, attempted to drive the workers back, and the situation quickly escalated. Both sides fired on each other. Though they initially had superior firepower, the Pinkertons were driven back and trapped on the barges. As the day progressed, the workers hurled dynamite at them and at

"The Bloody Battle at Homestead, PA," Utica (New York), *Saturday Globe,* 9 July 1892, p. 1. *Striking workers confronted Pinkerton guards called in by the Carnegie Corporation to protect the steel mills in Homestead, Pennsylvania. The Pinkertons were known for their violence and were denounced as armed ruffians. In the Battle of Homestead in July 1892, however, the workers got the better of the Pinkertons and drove them off after a bloody confrontation.*

one point trained a cannon on one of the boats. The strike committee attempted to maintain control of the mob and to negotiate terms for surrender of the Pinkertons, but its members were greatly outnumbered by the angry workers. The Pinkertons surrendered to the committee late that afternoon, but were beaten and stoned by the mob as they made their way to comparative safety. By the end of the day at least a dozen men were dead, 60 wounded by gunfire, and at least 100 Pinkertons bruised and humiliated.

Though the strikers held the ground for the day, the Battle of Homestead was ultimately a defeat. The governor called out eight thousand state militia to maintain order. Frick rejected the union demands and announced that if the Carnegie workers did not return to the job by July 21, he would bring in outside workers—"scabs." Fearing the permanent loss of their jobs, nonunion workers slowly began to filter back so that by July 16, more than two hundred were back at their posts.

The strike suffered another blow on July 23, when a young self-professed anarchist attacked Frick in his office. The would-be assassin shot Frick three times and stabbed him another three times before being overpowered by the wounded Frick and his office clerks. The attacker, Alexander Berkman, was a Russian-born Jew who had emigrated to the United States in 1886. He had no ties to the Amalgamated Union, but said he had decided to take the opportunity to strike a blow against American capitalism. Frick capitalized on his near martyrdom by returning to work immediately and announcing that the attack would not change his position on the strike. The scabs he had hired were assured that under no circumstances would they be discharged to make room for the workers who remained on strike.

The Homestead strikers held their ground doggedly through the summer and fall, but by September the mill's workforce, now largely consisting of nonunion workers, was almost back to its full complement. The strikers were worn down. The governor recalled the militia in mid-October and a month later the local union leaders conceded defeat. The union workers who did succeed in getting their jobs back did so at reduced wages. The company blacklisted the members of the strike committee and barred them from work in the steel industry for the rest of their lives. Carnegie Steel adopted a policy of hiring only nonunion workers in all its plants This policy was quickly adopted by other steel companies, with the result that by 1893, the Amalgamated had lost some 10,000 members throughout the iron and steel industry. The strike leaders faced trials for murder and treason, but were all acquitted. Alexander Berkman was speedily tried, convicted, and sentenced to 21 years in the state prison.

Events at Homestead occupied the news from January until late November. Five major periods or events marked the 11 months of the affair—the failed contract negotiations, the shutdown, the Battle of Homestead, the attempted assassination of Frick, and the failure of the strike and its eventual end in November—during which sympathies for and against the strikers fluctuated wildly. As it developed, the story had all the elements of high drama—the struggle for power between the rich and the poor, the conflict between order and disorder, and the emergence of villains and heroes. Many newspapers sympathized with the workers early in the spring and summer as Frick rejected all their attempts to negotiate, but this sympathy quickly dissipated as visions of anarchy, chaos, and mob rule emerged. Sympathy returned as the strikers were forced to give in to Frick's conditions, and many were left destitute. Because so many issues were involved during the Homestead Strike, the following readings are organized in five sections: articles and editorials that support or are sympathetic to the strikers; those that criticize the failure of the owners and government agencies to settle the strike; those that blame the press for contributing to the atmosphere of violence; those that blame the strikers for inciting anarchy; and those that blame the mill owners for providing grounds for anarchy.

SUPPORT OF STRIKERS

When the strike began on July 1, the New York Times *was quick to tie the story into national politics and current congressional debates about the tariff. It also pointed out that the strike had begun because Carnegie had refused to come to terms with his workers while other mill owners had reached settlements with theirs. In this front-page description of the failed negotiations, the* Times *contrasts the powerful Carnegie Corporation, with its $25 million of capital, to the bitter workers who face severe pay cuts.*

New York Times, 2 July 1892

EIGHTY THOUSAND MEN OUT

THE BIG STRIKE AMONG THE
IRONWORKERS IN FORCE
CARNEGIES CLAIM THE TARIFF IS
NOT A FACTOR IN THE DIFFICULTY—
REPUBLICAN CHIEFS, HOWEVER,
ADVISE SPEEDY SETTLEMENT

PITTSBURG [*sic*], Penn., July 1–Eighty thousand iron workers and their dependents threw down their tools early this morning when the last "heats" were drawn. When they will take them up again, and on what terms, is a question which time alone can solve.

There are over 100,000 iron and steel workers west of the Alleghany [*sic*] Mountains. One-fifth of this number are employed in the sheet iron, tinned plate, and tube mills. The owners of these withdrew their proposition for a reduction in wages, and work in their mills has gone on. Perhaps 70,000 more men are employed in other mills throughout the country, where owners as individuals made terms with their workmen.

The manufacturers demand a reduction of from 20 to 40 percent in wages; the workmen insist on a continuance of the wages that have ruled for the past twelve months.

Some hopes of an early settlement were entertained to-day, the Pittsburg [*sic*] manufacturers having asked for a conference with the workmen, but these disappeared when, after a few hours talk, it was announced that nothing had been accomplished.

Another conference will be held next Wednesday. If neither side yields at the meeting a long and hard struggle may be expected. The workmen are hopeful that they will gain their point before long.

The several manufacturers who have withdrawn the demand for a reduction are situated in all parts of the West [areas west of the Alleghenies], and the products of their mills include every grade of iron. The workmen argue that if these manufacturers can afford to pay the wages that have ruled during the past twelve months, there is no reason for a reduction in other mills....

It is evident that there is no "bluffing" at Homestead. The fight there is to be to the death between the Carnegie Steel Company, limited, with its $25,000,000 capital, and the workmen.

The Carnegie Steel Company gave formal notice to-day, through its Secretary, that the Homestead mill is to be operated as a non-union plant and that no expense is to be spared in the hiring of new men....

In addition to this, Carnegie put forth a statement in justification of its position. In this it is claimed that the reduction [of wages] offered is due to trade conditions, and that with the improved facilities provided to the workmen they will be able to make as much money as under the old scale....

The statement of the Secretary has added to the bitterness at Homestead. That of the firm is regarded as a skillful juggling with figures. The workmen are convinced that an acceptance of the Carnegie scale means a reduction in wages of from 20 to 60 percent as well as the abolishment of their organization, and they are prepared to fight to the end....

The workmen have the mill and the whole town in a state of siege. Committees have been appointed to patrol the river stations and all entrances to the town....

The only counter-move thus far made by the Carnegies has been to increase the force of watchmen in the mills. It is reported to-night that an attempt will be made before morning to land 300 mechanics in the mill by the river entrance in order to make necessary repairs. The strikers, to prevent this, have the river bank lined with 600 men, and any attempt of the mechanics to land will provoke an ugly fight.

Newspapers watched the situation closely for the next five days, reporting that the workers were peaceful, vigilant, and unyielding. Everything changed, however, on July 6 when the battle between the workers and the Pinkertons took place. Newspapers that got the news in time for their deadlines that day ran their versions of the latest accounts under eye-catching front-page headlines. "BLOOD FLOWS / Pinkertons and Strikers in Conflict," shrieked the Boston Traveller. *"EXTRA! / 5:15 A.M. / RIOT AT HOMESTEAD / Five thousand Men Attack the Pinkertons," shouted the* Chicago Tribune. *The same day, the* St. Louis Post-Dispatch *provided a blow-by-blow account of the unfolding drama. Here, Pulitzer's* Post-Dispatch *is clearly sympathetic to the strikers in this colorful and dramatic description of the workers and their families under siege by marauding hordes.*

St. Louis Post-Dispatch, 6 July 1892

Blood Flows

Labor and Capital in Deadly Conflict at Carnegie Mills
Battle Between Pinkerton Guards and Striking Workmen
Five Men Known to Have Been Killed on Each Side
Twenty Others Carried From the Field Badly Wounded
Cannon and Winchesters the Weapons of Warfare
The Guards Driven Off But the Fight Continues

GOV. PATTISON REFUSES TO CALL OUT THE MILITIA

Perilous Position of the Pinkertons Penned Up in the Barges Between Two Fires—Strong Probability That the Homestead Mills May Be Burned to the Ground—A Truce Shot Down by the Strikers—Graphic Story of the Battles on the Bank of the Monongahela—Names of the Men Who Fell

HOMESTEAD, Pa., July 6—Capital and labor have clashed at Homestead, and the town is red with blood. Never in the bloody history of riots in this vicinity, save the great rail road [*sic*] riots of 1877, has there been such carnage and such a battle.

The 300 Pinkertons who came in a boat to Homestead in the early morning have desolated many a heart and their shots have aroused such desperation that it is safe to say that before the men would now allow the mill to be operated by non-union men they would burn it over their heads.

The story of this battle is hard to tell. In the dark mist of early morning, when the town was quiet, the rumor of the arrival of a boat-load of Pinkertons reached Homestead. The word was sent along the line and the streets in almost an instant were crowded with men, women and children, hurrying in the direction of the works landing. Some were only half clad. On the maddened mass rushed, some to return without even a tear in their eyes; others to part forever on the battle grounds. Mothers stood with babes in their arms wondering what would be the result if the Pinkertons made an attempt to land. The most horrible foreboding must have been realized and there are many homes are in distress, many mothers, fathers, sisters, brothers and sweethearts with tears running down their cheeks, mourning the loss of some one who fell by the bullets from that boat. The landing of that boat will ever be remembered at Homestead and for generations to come the fathers will tell their children of the bloody battle of Monongahela.

Newspapers followed the events spinning off the Homestead Strike through the summer and early fall, avidly covering the various investigations and trials involving the Pinkertons, the union leaders, and Alexander Berkman, as well as the many sympathy strikes called at other Carnegie factories. But coverage of the strike itself gradually decreased as Frick's policies wore down the workers' resolve and they slowly began to trickle back to work on his conditions. The headlines on the last weeks of stories signaled the strikers' defeat. When the strike was finally called off officially on November 20, many newspapers noted its futility and the havoc it had wreaked on the workers. Not only had they failed in their demands, they had lost wages as long as they remained out of work, and were allowed to return to work only if they agreed to leave the union. In an unusual move, some newspapers even called for aid for the destitute workers. On December 9, the Pittsburgh Press *launched a crusade to raise funds for the strikers' families. This effort was repeated in other cities, and on December 21 the* Boston Transcript *promoted an appeal for funds by a local committee of workmen and citizens.[1] Here is the beginning of the story in which the* Pittsburgh Press *launched its crusade for the workers:*

Pittsburgh Press, 9 December 1892

IN HUMANITY'S NAME
The Press Appeals for Aid For Suffering Homestead

EXTREME DESTITUTION IN THE UNFORTUNATE BOROUGH
What the Investigation of a Press Reporter Revealed

WOMEN AND CHILDREN WHO WANT FOR BREAD
The Work of Relief Far Greater Than the Local Committee Can Undertake

PRIDE SEALS THE LIPS OF STARVING MEN AND WOMEN
The Press Starts the Relief Fund With a Contribution of One Hundred Dollars

SOLOMON & RUBEN ADD ONE HUNDRED DOLLARS MORE

"The strike is over," familiar heading this to those who read of Homestead. Yes, it is over but the train of evil and misfortune which must follow in its wake has just begun.

What of those who took part in the disastrous effort to secure what they deemed their rights? Some—a comparative few—are back in their old positions, thankful they were not turned away with the cold answer "There is no work for you," but in Homestead there are today 1,800 men, most of them with families for whom no employment can be found. For many of them the Christmas prospect is an empty cupboard and a cheerless hearth. For many of them there is even now an empty cupboard....

Along the river banks, where the big mills are located, there is a scene of activity; the wheels are turning; the rolls are revolving, and above all the buildings and machinery can be seen the steam clouds, the smoke clouds. It is down in those yards, a lost paradise to the hungry men who stand outside and watch what they so well know is a positive reality—a successful resumption of work in the great steel plant which for months they tried to hold silent....

Around us in this prosperous city the heralds of a great anniversary are announcing "peace on earth, good will to men"; eight miles away mothers sit wringing their hands in a grief the sight of which effects [sic] you all the more because it is the grief of the proud, the grief that will not ask for alms, yet needing them.

For these unhappy ones, with the Christmastide bringing humanity closer together, there should be sympathy, practical sympathy. It will not do to say, "I am sorry for the poor creatures." Sorrow don't clothe children, don't feed the hungry.

Criticism of Owners and Government

The morning after the battle newspapers provided updated reports that included details about the workers' rout of the Pinkertons and names of some of those killed and wounded. All of them deplored the violence, and many held Carnegie responsible for failing to reach an accord with his workers. News-

papers were particularly critical of Frick's decision to bring in the Pinkertons and for days published stories decrying the private police force's methods and very existence.[2] The Catholic weekly, the Boston Pilot, *was particularly adamant. It called the conflict "labor's Battle of Lexington" and referred to the Pinkertons as "Hessians," "organized mercenaries," and a "lawless army." By contrast, it described the workers in heroic terms. "Like the farmers of Concord and Lexington," it rhapsodized, "they have entered into the present fight as much for the sake of a principle as because of the money interest at stake." The federal government "must forbid the very existence of the Pinkertons as an organization. The United States must deal with the treasonable usurpation of its powers by organized ruffianism," the* Pilot *demanded.[3] The* Chicago Tribune *condemned Carnegie for calling in a "private army" instead of negotiating an agreement with the workers and urged Carnegie to submit the dispute to arbitration: "A concern which employs 4,000 men, on whose conduct depends the peace and prosperity of the entire community, and which can by one rash act convulse a State and excite a nation...has duties and obligations towards society which it must not forget, and not the least of them is to do all in its power, and make all the concessions it can, to preserve civil and industrial peace."[4] In the following editorial, published the same day, the* Tribune *holds the city, county, and state responsible for the failure to maintain the peace.*

Chicago Tribune, 8 July 1892

SITUATION AT THE HOMESTEAD MILLS

The entire contest thus far at the Homestead steel mills between the Carnegie company and its striking workmen has turned upon the issue of Pinkertonianism. No property of the company has been destroyed, though in the absence of efficient protection the strikers were in a position to have done so had they been so disposed. None of the officials of the company have been menaced. The resentment of the strikers was directed against the Pinkerton detectives, so called, alone. It will be fortunate if things remain in this situation.

The first step by the strikers was to drive out the deputies sent to the works by the Sheriff of Allegheny County upon application of the company, and this was done without violence. The action of the Sheriff indeed was little less than farcical if he expected that eleven Deputy Sheriffs were going to cope with 5,000 enraged strikers and their thousands of sympathizers. The alacrity indeed with which the eleven deputies disregarded their duty and quit the premises at the first notification showed that they had no interest in staying there. Gov. Pattison therefore is right in his declaration that sufficient means had not been resorted to put down this trouble. The civil authorities clearly had not done all that was within their power.

The next step was to call in Pinkerton's mercenaries from other States. They were not citizens of Pennsylvania. They come mainly from Chicago, New York, and Brooklyn. They appeared there, not with police clubs but with loaded Winchester rifles. They were not at the Homestead mills as part of the police power of Pittsburg [sic], or as militia of the State of Pennsylvania, of the County of Allegheny, or of the borough of Homestead. They had not even been sworn in as deputies. They were the private army of the company—the iron and steel police, just as there are in that State railroad and coal police, entirely independent of the civil authority, responsible only to the Carnegie company, not to the burgees of the borough or to the Sheriff of the country and employed to execute its wishes.

The result was what might have been anticipated, considering the feelings of the community on the subject. Since, however, the State must have special policemen in these great coal and iron districts, where the population is of a turbulent, excitable, and aggressive character, the next Legislature, in view of public sentiment, undoubtedly will repeal the present law which compels only the county and State to guarantee manufacturers and corporations ample protection in the possession of their property and the exercise of their rights without resorting to these extra and illegitimate methods which have been condemned by other States. Meanwhile, the strikers having eliminated the element of Pinkertonianism and freed themselves from the presence of these offensive detectives, who, it goes without saying, have no desire to return to Homestead, all parties concerned can now begin where they should have begun in the first place and settle all matters at issue by a resort to proper agencies and methods under the law.

Sensational Press Responsible for Attack on Frick

Carnegie and Frick did not submit the dispute to arbitration, but did withdraw the Pinkertons in the face of broad outrage and criticism. The Pennsylvania governor sent in the state militia to maintain the peace, but violence exploded again when Alexander Berkman attacked Frick in his office on July 23. First reports of the attack were brief and inaccurate, with various newspapers reporting variations on Berkman's name and describing him as a Hebrew, as a German, and as a Russian anarchist. Most newspapers accepted Berkman's claim that he was acting without the knowledge of the Homestead strikers and stressed their belief that he was outside the norm, calling him "a frenzied maniac" (Boston Journal), a "crack-

brained" and "unbalanced" crank (New York Times), *and a "homicidal crank"* (Boston Pilot). *Further interpretations of the attempted assassination explored various themes, such as the relation between labor agitation and anarchism, the responsibility of government authorities in mediating labor disputes, and the role of the press in the affair. In the following editorial, the* Boston Traveller *suggests the press contributed to the lawless and violent atmosphere that led to the attempted assassination.*

Boston Traveller, 25 July 1892

RESPONSIBILITY FOR ASSASSINATION

The attempted assassination of Manager Frick was the foulest and most dastardly of crimes. It is a matter of congratulation that the attempt did not succeed, and also that the assassin has been in no way connected with the strike or the strikers at Homestead. Bergman [*sic*] is found to be an anarchist who accepts the teachings of John [Johann] Most, and who has what Most has not—the courage to carry his threats into practice. The strikers at Homestead, unjustifiable as many of their acts may be, are not to be held responsible for this foul crime. From the beginning of the trouble they have repudiated the ravings of the anarchists, and drove out of town the anarchist emissaries who came there. But we are not so sure that the responsibility of the crime rests with Bergman [*sic*] alone. The drunken, half-crazed John Wilkes Booth was no more responsible for the assassination of Abraham Lincoln than were the incendiary Copperhead [anti-Union] newspapers that had for four years incited to just such a deed. So in the present case, there have been since the Homestead troubles began, utterances on the part of many newspapers from which better things may have been expected, which really have been incitements to assassination. It is a dangerous thing to play with the passions of men who are possessed with a craze for notoriety and are moved by a thirst for revenge on their fancied enemies, and there ought to be some way of reaching those whose responsibility for this foul crime is hardly less than that of the monster Bergman [*sic*]."

STRIKERS RESPONSIBLE FOR ANARCHY

Other newspapers drew the conclusion that labor unrest led naturally to civil unrest. The New York Times, *which had been somewhat supportive of the strikers in their confrontation with the Pinkertons, now suggested that labor disputes were inherently dangerous. In the following editorial, the* Times *argues that Berkman's attempted assassination proves labor ac-*

tion can lead to civil disorder and eventual anarchy. Here the Times *comes down firmly on the side of law and order. No matter how bad the provocation, it seems to argue, violence is never the answer.*

New York Times, 25 July 1892

LABOR AND ANARCHY

The would-be assassin of Mr. Frick of the Carnegie Steel Company appears to have been a fanatical Anarchist seeking to strike down a man who to his disordered mind seemed to be a conspicuous enemy of the poor and the oppressed. His dastardly deed was probably the result of the labor trouble at Homestead only in the sense that this trouble made Mr. Frick stand out conspicuously for the time being as a representative of what Anarchists and Socialists are wont to denounce as the "capitalistic class," and that the excitement produced by the contest directed the attention of such wild fanatics especially to him as an enemy to be destroyed. These pestilent creatures have been fostering the notion that violence and destruction are justifiable in a warfare against what they prate about as the wrongs of labor, and have been breeding possible assassins in a class that hardly knows what honest labor means. There are no worse enemies of the workingmen of this country than those same ignorant and reckless Socialists and Anarchists of foreign origin who make so much noise about the rights and wrongs of society of which they have no intelligent comprehension.

But while the strikers of Homestead cannot in any sense be held accountable for the act of this crack-brained Anarchist, they have given an indirect encouragement to lawless notions of which such an act is always a possible outcome. They have set agoing impulses the consequences of which are beyond their control. When they met the Pinkerton men on the banks of the Monongahela River with weapons in their hands, and began to shoot them down as they attempted to land, they taught a lesson of violence and disregard of the restraints of law which carried with it all the possibilities of anarchy. The difference between the shooting of the Pinkerton men as the hired foes of organized labor and the shooting of Mr. Frick as the arch-enemy of all workingmen in the fevered imagination of the rabid Anarchist is a difference only of degree....

The spectacle of Homestead for nearly three weeks past has been the practical suspension of civil authority, due solely to the fact that the people had refused to submit to it. What is the essence of Anarchy but a refusal to submit to law and authority and a subversion of the constituted order of

Check Out Receipt

Franklin Lakes Public Library
201-891-2224
http://www.franklinlakeslibrary.org/

Friday, April 7, 2017 1:47:49 PM
GIANNAKAS, CAROLYN F.

Item: 39112092151610
Title: The Progressive era : primary documents on events from 1890 to 1914
Call no.: 973.8 BURT
Material: Hardcover
Due: 05/05/2017

You just saved $30.00 by using your library. You have saved $375.00 this past year and $375.00 since you began using the library!

Hours of Operation:
Mon-Thurs: 10 am - 9 pm
Fri: 10 am - 6 pm
Sat: 10 am - 5 pm
Sun: 1 pm - 5 pm

Closed Sun July-Labor Day

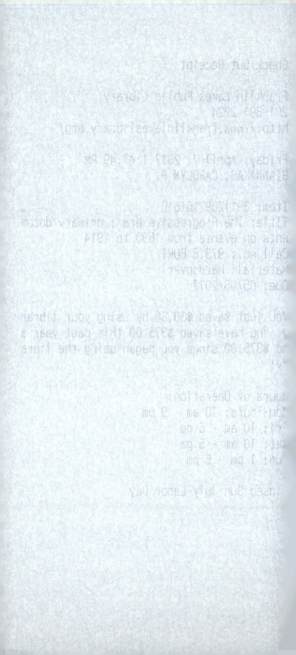

civil society? In these proceedings the people of Homestead have given encouragement to the worst enemies of the cause of honest labor....

Not until that normal state of things [in which military force is no longer
required to maintain order and the protection of the Carnegie property] exists can the workmen vindicate their claim of being law-abiding citizens and
free themselves wholly from the charge of giving encouragement to the
spirit of anarchy. Not until then can they regain the full sympathy of those
who regard the maintenance of law and order as the first condition of the
settlement of disputes between labor and capital.

MILL OWNERS RESPONSIBLE FOR VIOLENCE

The Boston Pilot *concurred in this opinion, but put the blame for Berkman's actions on his own fevered imagination. In this editorial, it absolves
the strikers from responsibility and maintains that once Frick ("the
haughty magnate") had introduced violence through the Pinkertons, more
violence was sure to follow.*

Boston Pilot, 30 July 1892

THE ASSAULT ON MANAGER FRICK

It is rank nonsense to speak of the attempted murder of manager Frick as
an injury to the cause of the workingmen. The workingmen are no more responsible for that crime than the Republican party was responsible for the
murder of President Garfield. A homicidal crank in each case undertook to
"remove" his victim, without the connivance or aid of anybody else.

The man who assailed Manager Frick last Saturday was not connected in
the remotest degree with the Homestead quarrel. He is a Russian anarchist,
living in New York, and only within a few years a resident of the United
States. If the Homestead workingmen had hired him to murder the manager of the Carnegie works, they would have been guilty of a crime as atrocious as that committed by Mr. Frick himself when he hired Pinkerton's
bravoes to shoot down his employees; but they did nothing of the sort. The
blood-guiltiness thus far is confined to Manager Frick, the Pinkerton
Agency, and the Russian lunatic who perpetrated last Saturday's crime.

The latest tragedy is a natural outcome of the graver one that preceded
it. When Mr. Frick engaged the Pinkerton thugs and sent them to Homestead armed and equipped for battle, he knew that bloodshed would surely
follow, as it did. He was the first to invoke force in the struggle between

Labor and Capital. The State of Pennsylvania was amply able and ready to protect the property of the Carnegie Company....

Such legal and peaceable recourse did not suit the haughty magnate Frick. He felt that the opportunity had come for crushing out the labor union. He had the millions of a great corporation at his back; the courts of the law-officers, the army itself, of a mighty Commonwealth stood ready to support his lawful rights; but he preferred appealing to private force. Anarchist Bergman [*sic*], with his disordered logic, goes a step further and constitutes himself a higher tribunal.

The law will teach Mr. Bergman [*sic*] to respect its prerogatives; for Mr. Frick, with rare courage and coolness, prevented the infliction of summary punishment on the would-be assassin. The experience, let us hope, may teach Mr. Frick the injustice of asserting even just claims by violent methods such as those of the atrocious Pinkerton guards.

QUESTIONS

1. Why did most newspapers (and people) condemn Frick's action of calling in the Pinkerton guards to protect the Carnegie mill? What did the Pinkertons represent?

2. Many people were sympathetic toward the miners during the spring. How did that begin to change after the Battle of Homestead? Can you find some of the words or phrases in the articles or editorials about the battle that reveal some criticism or fear of the union and the workers?

3. Why did the *Boston Traveller* criticize newspapers for being incendiary in their coverage of the conflict between the strikers and the Pinkertons, the strikers and the mill owners? What was some of the vocabulary used in the newspapers that might incite someone like Berkman to violence? Do you think newspapers are responsible when a sensational story they have covered is followed by violence? How can a newspaper cover incendiary events without being incendiary itself?

4. Why did public opinion turn against the union and the strikers after Alexander Berkman attempted to assassinate Frick? Note the use of the words "anarchism" and "socialism" in the articles and stories. How were these words used to evoke unconscious ideals of democracy and fears of change?

5. Some newspapers believed law and order would bring about justice. But how would this idea actually work against workers trying to defend

their rights from factory owners? Where do the various articles condemning the workers' (and Berkman's) actions miss this point?

Notes

1. "In Distress at Homestead," *Boston Transcript,* 21 December 1892, p. 5.
2. "Pinkerton Methods," *Boston Transcript,* 7 July, 1892, p. 1.
3. "Labor's Battle of Lexington," *Boston Pilot,* 16 July 1892, p. 4.
4. "Arbitrate the Homestead Strike," *Chicago Tribune,* 8 July 1892, p. 4.

CHAPTER 5

Lynch Law Terrorizes Blacks in the South

Although blacks were freed from slavery in 1863 and guaranteed the rights and protections of citizenship following the Civil War, those rights were gradually eroded in the South after the Reconstruction Era. By the late 1880s blacks were systematically prevented from holding office, voting, and using the same facilities as whites throughout the southern states. Segregation and discrimination became endemic to the region, protected by law, convention, and mob rule.

One particular practice, lynching, was a vicious form of social control used by whites to keep blacks docile and in their place. In the typical lynching, a black or blacks would be accused of sexually assaulting a white woman, captured by a mob of whites, and hanged from the nearest tree without the benefit of a trial. In the more violent cases, the black victims were beaten, tortured, cut up, shot, or burned before or after they were hanged. Sometimes the accused were tracked down by the lynchers and killed on the spot. In other cases they had already been arrested and were in custody of the authorities when they were forcibly taken by a mob and lynched. Some lynchings were performed in remote rural areas in the middle of the night with only the lynchers and victims present; others took place before large crowds of cheering spectators in public places.

Blacks were not the only victims of lynching—lynching was certainly a form of instant justice in the West and wherever citizens had no patience with the courts or legal process—but the majority of those lynched were blacks, and the majority of lynchings took place in the South. During the 1880s and 1890s, it has been estimated that more than 100 blacks were lynched each year. In 1892 the number of reported lynchings peaked at 241; of that number, 160 were of blacks, and 180 occurred in southern states.[1]

Most lynchings resulted from accusations that a black man had raped ("outraged") a white woman. Others occurred after a black man (or woman, on occasion) was accused of other offenses against whites ranging from alleged insult, insolence, or lack of respect to theft, assault, or murder. Many charges were apparently trumped up when a black simply stepped out of line. Many lynchings were carried out in the heat of the moment with little or no evidence and sometimes got the wrong man.

Many issues and perspectives were involved in the phenomenon of lynching, some of which are illustrated in the readings in this chapter. These news articles and editorials are organized in two sections. In the first, the selections condone lynching, either by implying that swift justice is required because of the bestial nature of the black man's crime or by defending the South's pressing need to control black rapists. In the second section, the readings oppose lynching on a variety of grounds: that lynch mobs make mistakes; that lynching represents a breakdown in law and order; and that lynching is a racist crime. The last three news articles in this section report and praise the results of the efforts of the *Chicago Tribune* to keep an annual record of lynchings as a method of reducing and eventually eliminating the practice.

CONDONING LYNCHING

Lynchings were reported on a regular basis in newspapers published in the North as well as the South. These stories typically reported the event in a few paragraphs that named the black who had been lynched, the details of the crime of which he had been accused, and the actions taken by the vigilantes. What is most notable about many of these stories is how routine they were. Furthermore, they almost always assumed the guilt of the lynch victim, as in this brief example from the Carrollton *(Missouri)* Journal *published in 1891.*

Carrollton (Missouri) *Journal,* 19 September 1891

WHITE AGAINST BLACK

Two Opposing Mobs Gathered In a Missouri Town

CARROLLTON, September 19—While May Betzenberger, 15 years of age, was returning home from school yesterday, she was accosted by Joseph Oliver, a negro boy, who attempted to assault her, and in the struggle which ensued, stabbed her in the shoulder.

Oliver was arrested, and after examination this afternoon a crowd of white men attempted to lynch him, but he was landed safely in jail. At midnight to-night a mob of whites assembled about the jail to secure the negro and lynch him, while opposing negroes are gathered to protect the prisoner. A fight between the two mobs is imminent. Both sides are well armed, and it is feared there will be much bloodshed.

On occasion, a lynching attracted widespread public participation. When it led to prolonged rioting and widespread damage to property, it attracted more attention and resulted in news stories covering several columns. The following story published in 1892 by the New Orleans Times-Democrat, *for example, covered four full columns. Though this story describes in great detail the violent atmosphere in the town, it also presents the actions of the "lynch committee" as if its members were carrying out their task in a democratic and responsible fashion. The* Times-Democrat *takes the guilt of the "black fiend" for granted and presents the lynching as a "warning to evildoers."*

New Orleans Times-Democrat, 1 May 1892

A MOB'S VENGEANCE

A FIENDISH NEGRO PAYS THE PENALTY OF HIS CRIME
HE IS SWUNG OFF A BRIDGE AND RIDDLED WITH BULLETS
THE FIRST EFFORTS TO BREAK INTO JAIL UNSUCCESSFUL
THE CROWD DISPERSED BY THE POLICE
TWO MEN SHOT IN THE COLLISION
THE JAIL FINALLY FORCED IN BROAD DAYLIGHT

Special to The Times-Democrat

Nashville, Tenn., April 30—This will ever be a memorable day in the history of this city, marked as it was by several desperate attacks upon the Davidson County jail, the shooting of two men while the mob was attempting to batter down the jail doors and the lynching of Eph. Grizzard, who had been arrested for criminally assaulting Misses Mollie and Rosina Bruce near Goodlettsville on Wednesday night. The same punishment that was meted out Thursday morning to his brother, Henry Grizzard, by the mob at Goodlettsville, was visited upon the wretch for whose blood a mob has clamored for two days and nights. The merited vengeance was wreaked by a large mob, in broad daylight, in the very heart of the capital city of the State, the authorities being powerless to resist. The terrible crime was avenged and that the lesson will prove a warning to evil-doers cannot be denied.

Last night was one of great excitement, but the excitement that prevailed to-day was intensified tenfold. The failure to secure Grizzard last night, the strong resistance made by the sheriff, the chief of police, and their officers, and the fact that two men had fallen in front of the jail with what were believed to be fatal wounds, infuriated the members of the mob and it was clearly apparent that they would take Grizzard from his cell and kill him and that continued resistance would result in bloodshed. There seemed to be no doubt whatever of Grizzard's guilt as was proved by the evidence of his own sister that he had attempted to burn his blood-stained clothing and shoes to destroy the damning proof of his terrible crime. This and other testimony fastened the guilt upon him and nothing but his death would satisfy the indignant people.

[A lengthy description of the mob's repeated attempts to break into the jail, the resistance by armed officers, and appeals from the governor follows. Finally, shortly before 2:00 in the afternoon, the crowd forced its way into the jail.] At 1:50 o'clock this afternoon Dr. Davis called the mob to order in the public square. He stated that a committee of three would be appointed to demand Eph. Grizzard. Who would volunteer? A dozen men stepped forward. Then the crowd started with a shout toward and down Front street. In the rear of the Brandon Printing Company building a halt was called, and a committee of three was sent to the jail. The lock on the immense gate had been broken the night before. Entrance was easily effected.... Jailer Willis had just come from the front corridor of the cage, where he had been dressing Grizzard

IN WOMAN'S CLOTHES

preparatory to spiriting him away, and men were due at 2 o'clock to take charge of the "woman."

After the keys had been secured, one of the committee told Jailer Willis that he...would go in and get Grizzard while the other two held him...and prevented other prisoners from escaping. Meanwhile, the men on the outside had crowded up to the jail, and at intervals during the wait of ten minutes cheers rose to urge those on who had gone within. Thousands of spectators crowded to suffocation every avenue leading toward the jail, but they kept at a respectful distance from the mob of about one thousand men, which crowded up against and hung on to the iron bars in front of the jail. Then the committee of three appeared, and between them was Eph. Grizzard. Not a shot had been fired and no sound, save intermittent cheering, had been made. But at the sight of the black fiend the mob and spectators alike cheered, until the sound must have been heard in all parts of the city. A wild rush was then made for the square, those about him slapping his head with open palms and Grizzard crying, "Quit hitting me; I'll go."

From the square the mob turned onto the bridge. From the time the negro was first brought from the jail until he was hanged the cheering never ceased.... [A detailed description of the hanging from the bridge follows. Grizzard was beaten, then dropped over the side of the bridge with a hemp rope around his neck; his nearly nude body was shot several times as it swung on the rope.]

The whole incident consumed only fifteen minutes, and at no time were the police able to withstand the heavy rush of the mob. At 4 o'clock, after thousands of people had gazed upon the body as it dangled from the great bridge, the body was pulled up and delivered to the coroner, who was instructed to hold an inquest as quickly as possible, as the crowd wanted to take it to Goodlettsville, and let the people of that place and vicinity see it.

An inquest was held and a verdict returned to the effect that Grizzard came to his death from gunshot wounds and strangulation at the hand of persons unknown to the jury. The inquest over, the body was placed in a cedar box and went to Goodlettsville by train. As the train passed the stations between Nashville and Goodlettsville people cheered, and when it arrived at Goodlettsville the box containing the body was taken to the public square, where the corpse was viewed by a large crowd.

Many northern newspapers criticized the lawless nature of lynching. They often described lynching as "southern barbarism," and in the process reinforced northern stereotypes of southerners as ignorant and backward. Southern newspapers responded defensively, arguing that liberal do-gooder northerners didn't know what southerners were up against. In 1892, when northern papers criticized Alabamans for lynching three blacks in Anniston, the Memphis Daily Commercial *responded in this editorial, which, in effect, holds black victims—"Negro scoundrels"—responsible for their own lynching.*

Memphis Daily Commercial, 17 May 1892

MORE RAPES, MORE LYNCHINGS

The lynching of three Negro scoundrels reported in our dispatches from Anniston, Ala., for a brutal outrage committed upon a white woman will be a text for much comment on "Southern barbarism" by Northern newspapers; but we fancy it will hardly prove effective for campaign purposes among intelligent people. The frequency of these lynchings calls attention to the frequency of the crimes which causes [*sic*] lynching. The "Southern barbarism" which deserves the serious attention of all people North and South, is the barbarism which preys upon weak and defenseless women. Nothing but the most prompt, speedy and extreme punishment can hold in check the horrible and bestial propensities of the Negro race. There is a strange similarity about a number of cases of this character which have lately occurred.

In each case, the crime was deliberately planned and perpetrated by several Negroes. They watched for an opportunity when the women were left without a protector. It was not a sudden yielding to a fit of passion, but the consummation of a devilish purpose which has been seeking and waiting for the opportunity. This feature of the crime not only makes it fiendishly brutal, but it adds to the terror of the situation in the thinly settled country communities. No man can leave his family at night without the dread that some roving Negro ruffian is watching and waiting for this opportunity. The swift punishment [lynching] which invariably follows these horrible crimes doubtless acts as a deterring effect upon the Negroes in that immediate neighborhood for a short time. But the lesson is not widely learned nor long remembered. Then such crimes, equally atrocious, have happened in quick succession.... The facts of the crime appear to appeal more to the Negro's lustful imagination than the facts of the punishment do to his fears. He sets aside all fear of death in any form when opportunity is found for the gratification of his bestial desires.

There is small reason to hope for any change for the better. The commission of this crime grows more frequent every year. The generation of Negroes which have grown up since the war have lost in large measure the traditional and wholesome awe of the white race which kept Negroes in subjection....

What is to be done? The crime of rape is always horrible, but [for] the Southern man there is nothing which so fills the soul with horror, loathing and fury as the outraging of a white woman by a Negro. It is the race question in the ugliest, vilest, most dangerous aspect. The Negro as a political factor can be controlled. But neither laws nor lynchings can subdue his lusts. Sooner or later it will force a crisis. We do not know in what form it will come.

The theme that southern lynch mobs were only protecting southern womanhood was reiterated in southern newspapers repeatedly. Some, paradoxically, used the high number of lynchings reported in the South to justify lynching, as did the Atlanta Constitution *in this brief untitled paragraph on the editorial page.*

Atlanta Constitution, 4 June 1892

VICTIMS OF NEGRO LUST

The New York Press says that 800 Negroes have been lynched in the south during the past ten years. This means that a thousand white women and girls have been made the victims of negro lust. These are eloquent figures.

Some southern newspapers also used examples of lynchings in northern states to justify southern lynchings. When a mob in Port Jervis, New York, lynched a black accused of raping a white woman in June 1892, the Atlanta Constitution *was quick to note it. In the following editorial, the* Constitution *argues that lynching is a natural response in human nature to the outrage of a particular crime—rape. It finds the South is no more prone to this response than the North and advises northern papers, in essence, not to cast the first stone.*

Atlanta Constitution, 4 June 1892

LYNCHINGS NORTH AND SOUTH

We referred not long ago to a very sensible editorial in The St. Louis Globe-Democrat relative to the lynchings that occur in the south. The Globe-Democrat, although a republican paper, wrote as if it had an interior understanding of the somewhat abnormal situation that exists at the south.

There are many reasons why the northern editors should repress their transports of rage when discussing the causes that lead to southern lynchings. There are many reasons why they should soften the epithets which they employ when referring to these unfortunate affairs. There are many reasons why they should take pains to inform themselves of the true inwardness of the situation of which these extra-judicial executions are the outcome.

The [Atlanta] Constitution has always denounced the appeals to mob law as a species of demoralization which no reputable social organization can survive. Yet we are bound to say that the lynchings which follow the outrage of women, girls, and even little children are as excusable as any result of mob law can be.

It is to be observed that these affairs are not confined to the south. At the north, whenever a negro barbarian assaults a white woman, the penalty of death is promptly visited upon him. At Campbellsville, O., a few days ago, there was a case of this kind, and the public sentiment of the community became at once judge, jury and executioner. Let it be borne in mind that in this instance the crime was not completed. The negro simply betrayed his intentions, and he was promptly swung up.

In yesterday's Constitution, there was a dispatch setting forth briefly the details of a spectacular performance at Port Jarvis [*sic*], N.Y., in which a white girl was the victim of a negro brute. The statement is that he was pursued, captured, brought back, and "strung up to a neighboring tree in the presence of a howling mob of over a thousand people." Nothing was wanting to make the affair a success, showing that climate and environment have little or no influence on human nature, which is pretty much the same everywhere under the sun.

We advise our northern contemporaries to deal as gently as they can with the manifestations of human nature which take place in the south and are duplicated in the north whenever the opportunity offers. That they are deplorable is not to be denied. But the cause that leads to them—the situation out of which they are developed—is more deplorable still. It is no light thing, may it please your honor and gentlemen of the jury, for the women and girls of the whole country side to live in practically a state of siege—to be afraid to venture to a neighbor's or to the school house lest some black beast leap from the bushes and give them over to a fate worse than death. Let us think of these things when we become critical enough to take on judicial airs.

OPPOSING LYNCHING

Stories describing lynchings were also published frequently in northern newspapers during the period. Though they might deplore the lawless nature of mob violence, few had sympathy for the black lynching victims and almost all considered them guilty. In this brief untitled editorial published by the San Francisco Chronicle *in 1893, however, the California newspaper also points out that mob action sometimes led to getting the wrong man.*

San Francisco Chronicle, 12 July 1893

LYNCHERS GET THE WRONG MAN

It cannot be pleasant for the people who lynched a Negro in Kentucky for the outrage and murder of two white girls to learn they hanged the wrong man. Yet this is an error to which all lynchers are liable, for in the heat of passion, men cannot weigh evidence carefully, and identifications are often made which afterward prove false. The lesson is that lynching should not be encouraged, for it does not deter criminals and it frequently leads to the cruel and shameful death of innocent men.

Even when northern newspapers condemned lynching, they often assumed the guilt of the black victim. In this editorial on the Port Jervis, New York, incident mentioned above, the New York Times *condemns the action of the crowd on three counts. First, its actions were an example of lawlessness and violence. Second, the mob very nearly got the wrong man. Third, the mob took action before it got evidence it could have used to indict a second man. But the editorial never once questions the black man's guilt. In fact, it refers to him as "the ruffian," "the perpetrator," and "a brute." It states, in fact, that blacks are more likely to commit rape than whites.*

New York Times, 4 June 1892

The Dangers of Lynching

A considerable number of persons, some of them possibly very worthy citizens in a general way and others pretty certainly nothing of the kind, united on Thursday in Port Jervis to hang a negro who had committed a criminal assault upon a white girl. The feeling that actuated the more respectable members of the mob was undoubtedly the same that is cited as a defense for like lynchings in the Southern States. It is that the penalty prescribed by law is not sufficient for the offense which is punished by lynching. It is not to be denied that negroes are much more prone to this crime than whites, and the crime itself becomes more revolting and infuriating to white men, North as well as South, when a negro is the perpetrator and a white woman the victim. Of this the law cannot take notice, but it is doubtful whether the general conviction that the crime is capital [punishable by death] ought not to be embodied in legislation. It is unlikely that such a change in the law would diminish the number of lynchings. These are commonly committed by crowds which are animated by so furious an indignation that they would not wait for the law to take its course, even though the punishment were capital and certain, but would insist upon themselves doing their prisoner to death rather than to wait for months, or even weeks, to have him done to death by the law. This lawless temper is not commendable, and it ought to be discouraged by the law. Although it is probable that the good citizens of Port Jervis sympathized with the mob when they first learned of its murderous work, it is also probable that they are by this time ashamed of it and of their sympathy with it, and regard the lynching as more of a disgrace to the town than the crime it avenged, for which only a single brute was responsible.

The dangers of lynching are made especially evident by this example. In the first place, it is admitted that the mob, misled by one of the rumors that spread in times of excitement, came very near hanging the wrong man, and this is a danger that always attends the unlawful execution of justice. If the mob had actually got possession of the wrong man, it is almost certain that they would have hanged him. His protestations of innocence would have been disregarded, and they would not have confronted him with his victim for identification. They did not do this in the case of the man actually hanged, who was undoubtedly the right man. They set out to do it, but their passions got the better of them and they killed him without waiting to have him identified. The only evidence available against him at the time when he was lynched was his own confession to his captors. If he had withheld this, the mob would have been without any plausible pretext for hanging him, but doubtless it would have hanged him all the same.

But the lynchers by their precipitation seem to have operated a defeat of justice almost as great as if they had hanged the wrong man. The negro not only confessed his crime, but declared that he had been instigated to commit it by a white man whom he named. His inculpation of this man is as valuable as his inculpation of himself, which was held to be valid enough to hang him on. If we accept it, the white brute seems to be even a baser wrench than the black brute. The law certainly does not provide an adequate punishment for the offense of the instigator of such a crime. If the instigation were fully proved, there would be a stronger case for lynching the white man than there was for lynching the negro. It would have been worthwhile to promise the negro some mitigation even of his lawful punishment for the sake of securing his evidence against a more dangerous villain. Yet there is now no evidence at all against him, nor is any likely to be produced. The word of a dead ruffian is all that the people of Port Jervis have to go by. It is enough, very likely. If it be accepted, the work of the lynchers is censurable for being incomplete, as well as on other grounds. They have no case at all in law against the accused white man, and the accusation is not well enough supported to furnish grounds for another lynching. The greater criminal, if he be a criminal at all, is likely to go scot free because the people of Port Jervis have hastily and carelessly hanged a man who, if he had been spared, might have proved a valuable witness. This is a danger of lynching that the lynchers have incurred which they themselves must confess to be a serious drawback to the success of their method of doing justice.

Few newspapers had the courage or insight to reveal the true nature of lynchings. A brave few argued that lynchings were not just the spontaneous response to a crime by an unthinking, unorganized mob, as they were often described in newspapers and public discussion. They were, instead, an orchestrated, ritualistic, socially acceptable act of terror perpetrated against blacks by whites in order to maintain power and control over them and to halt their social, political, and economic progress. Rather than using these terms, however, "lynch law" focused on the purported criminal—especially sexual criminal—acts of the accused. The underlying assumptions that allowed and encouraged this construct were that blacks were brutes, blacks hated whites, and blacks would do violence against whites unless kept under control. Two other underlying assumptions were that all black men wanted white women and that white women would never have sexual relations with black men willingly.

One writer—black journalist Ida B. Wells—began to attack these assumptions. A co-owner of the black publication Free Speech, *Wells began to gather statistics on lynchings in 1892 after three of her friends were unjustly accused and killed by a mob in Memphis, Tennessee. Two months after their deaths, she wrote an angry editorial in which she challenged the underlying assumptions concerning white women that allowed lynchings to take place in the first place. After the editorial appeared, several local papers responded with thinly veiled threats against* Free Speech *and its editors. The newspaper offices were ransacked and the equipment destroyed. Wells, who was in New York on business, learned that some white men in Memphis had threatened to torture and kill her if she ever returned. She remained in New York to become a reporter for the* New York Age *and did not return to the South for years. She encouraged southern blacks to migrate to the North and pursued her antilynching campaign in print and on the lecture circuit for the rest of her life. Here is her untitled editorial that caused such a violent response.*

Free Speech, 21 May 1892

Ida B. Wells: No One Believes Blacks Guilty

Eight Negroes lynched since the last issue of the *Free Speech,* one at Little Rock, Ark., last Saturday morning where the citizens broke into the penitentiary and got their man; three near Anniston, Ala.; one near New Orleans, and three at Clarksville, Ga., the last three for killing a white man, and five on the same old racket—the new alarm about raping white women. The same programme of hanging, then shooting bullets into the lifeless bodies was carried out to the letter.

Nobody in this section of the country believes the old thread bare lie that Negro men rape white women. If Southern white men are not careful, they will over-reach themselves and public sentiment will have a reaction; a conclusion will then be reached which will be very damaging to the moral reputation of their women.

Eventually, others began to share Wells's perspective that lynchings were racially motivated. When a black woman and her daughter and son were taken from jail and lynched in Carrollton, Mississippi, in 1901 after being accused of murdering a white couple, the San Francisco Chronicle *called the incident a disgrace to the nation. Its editorial on the event indicates a shift in the way some newspapers, at least, regarded these events. The victims were no longer assumed to be guilty and lynching was perceived as a racially motivated crime.*

San Francisco Chronicle, 3 August 1901

Lynch Law in the South

Lynch law appears to be on the increase in this country, and in the majority of the cases the victims are of the Negro race. In the Southern States we recall no recent instance of the lynching of a white man....

Lynching not only disgraces the community in which it occurs, but tends directly to the increase of crime. Especially is this true when the executioners are of one race and the victims of another. Swift and certain punishment under the solemn forms of the law is an effective deterrent of crime. Death at the hands of a mob has the opposite effect. A race numbering millions in one country cannot be subdued by the fear of lynching. They can be, and in the South, are being turned into wild beasts, reckless of their own lives and of the lives of others. The object of lawful punishment is repression of crime. The object of lynching is wild vengeance upon some one assumed to be guilty. Every negro in Mississippi knows that the three persons who were lynched on Thursday at Carrollton met their fate not because they were criminals but because they were negroes. Had they been white, they would have been duly convicted before punishment.

Perhaps inspired by Ida B. Wells's campaign against lynching, the Chicago Tribune *began compiling information on lynching and began to publish annual reports of lynching statistics. When it did so in 1901, some newspaper editors applauded the* Tribune's *efforts. These were quoted in an editorial page column in the* Tribune.

Philadelphia Press, 12 September 1901

The Tribune's Lynching Statistics

It is well to put this matter on record now. There are evidences in the South of an awakening moral sense and of an appreciation of the danger of the drift toward barbarism. There is no better teacher than history. And the history of lynching during the last twenty years, given by the CHICAGO TRIBUNE, should teach this country what it must avoid in future if it wishes to preserve its civilization.

New Orleans Times-Democrat, 12 September 1901

More on the Tribune's Lynching Statistics

The best work has been done through appeals to public opinion and the recognition by the people that lynchings not only do harm to a community by the bad reputation they entail but increase crime by suggestion, if not by encouragement, of violence. This is now becoming better recognized every year, and in the more advanced districts lynchings are growing less frequent. We may expect this view to spread over the whole country in time and lynching to die out. In spite of all appearances to the contrary, there has been a considerable improvement made in the last ten years; and we may hope for still greater improvement in the next decade, now that public sentiment is so pronounced on this subject, is no longer apologetic, but speaks out clearly and strongly against Judge Lynch.

In 1913, 21 years after Wells started her antilynching campaign, the Chicago Tribune *reported that the number of known lynchings had decreased from a high of 241 in 1892 to 64 in 1912. This was hailed by many as a great step forward for civilization. The* New York Times *reported the* Chicago Tribune*'s statistics and then asked a number of authorities what they meant. African American Booker T. Washington, known for his compromising promotion of "accommodationism," was quoted as saying that the underlying cause of lawlessness in the South was not racial antagonism but poverty and ignorance.[2] In a* New York Times *letter to the editor, statistical authority Frederick L. Hoffman deplored the continued occurrence of lynchings in the South, but pointed out that they were decreasing, not only in number but in proportion to the population. He predicted optimistically (but, alas, inaccurately) that lynchings would soon cease entirely. Lynchings did continue to decrease in number as Hoffman predicted, but they continued as a threat and a form of racial oppression in the South well through the Civil Rights era of the 1950s.[3]*

New York Times, 4 March 1913

Frederick L. Hoffman: Fewer Lynchings

Recent lynchings in the South have once more attracted public attention to a most deplorable phase of Southern life. There is probably no Southern problem more generally misunderstood in the North and more unduly exaggerated than the occasional outbreaks of mob violence chiefly against suspected or confessed criminals of the lowest possible type. No defense can be made of lynchings in a civilized community, nor can this wrongful procedure be explained on rational grounds. It is, therefore, of considerable importance that the facts of lynchings should not be misunderstood, if but in simple justice to the overwhelming majority of Southern people who neither encourage nor condone mob violence in any form. [Hoffman compares the numbers of lynchings per year to the size of the population and concludes that lynchings have decreased from 3.58 per million in 1892 to 0.67 per million in 1912.]...

It is no cause of satisfaction that there should have been sixty-four lynchings during 1912 in the United States, chiefly in the South; but the country may well be satisfied with the fact that, with a single exception, this was the lowest number of lynchings during the last twenty-eight years, and, without exception, in proportion to the population, the lowest rate of lynching during the period for which the historical record has been preserved. Since in all matters of social progress, the tendency is of most importance, it may safely be assumed that since the rate has steadily gone down, the time is not far distant when lynchings North or South will be practically a thing of the past.

QUESTIONS

1. How was lynching used as a form of social control in the South? Can you think of other ways in which a dominant group in society imposes control over a subjected group or groups?
2. What were some of the terms used by newspapers to describe the lynchers? The lynch victims? From the samples quoted here, how did these terms change over time? How do these terms reveal how these people were viewed by the newspaper writers?
3. The explanation that many lynchings were carried out to avenge women who had been assaulted and to protect women from future assaults reveals concepts about women's place and role in society. What are some of these concepts? How did lynching also victimize women?
4. Newspaper stories about lynchings revealed a social construct that defined black men, white men, and white women in a particular fashion. Identify some of these definitions. How did these social constructs permit and even condone lynching? What are some of the factors that contributed to a change of this construct that also changed views of lynching by 1920? How and why did the perception of lynching as a necessary evil in the 1890s change to the perception of lynching as a crime by 1920?

NOTES

1. "Fewer Lynchings," *New York Times,* 4 March 1913, p. 12. This article cited a report compiled by the *Chicago Tribune* of lynching statistics from 1885–1912. According to these figures, 1,646 lynchings occurred between 1890 and 1900.

2. "Statistics of Lynching," *New York Times,* 4 March 1913, p. 12.

3. Sixty-one lynchings were reported in 1920, 21 in 1930, 5 in 1940, and just 2 in 1950. During the mid-1950s there was a brief resurgence in the number of lynchings in the South during the Civil Rights and voter registration movements.

CHAPTER 6

Coxey's Army Marches on Washington, 1894

The last decade of the 1800s was a rough one economically, with ups and downs in the economy that often led to panics and economic depressions. In spring 1893 one such panic caused a stock market crash and the failure of banks nationwide. By the end of the year, some 600 banks had closed, 74 railroads had gone out of business, and more than 1,500 commercial enterprises had collapsed. The resulting depression eventually hit all sectors of the economy and trickled down through the ranks to the lowliest laborer. Workers in every part of the country found their jobs lost or wages severely reduced and their living conditions threatened. Even newspapers, which had been growing in size every year since the Civil War, stopped hiring new reporters and cut back on staff and expenses.

In December 1893 Jacob Coxey, a wealthy Ohio horse breeder and quarry owner, came up with a novel solution. He established the Good Roads Association and proposed that Congress appropriate $500 million for road improvement projects. The money would be raised through non-interest-bearing bonds to the states and localities, and the ensuing projects would provide immediate work for thousands of unemployed men. Though the plan anticipated the Works Progress Administration Franklin D. Roosevelt would inaugurate during the Great Depression of the next century, Coxey's idea was too visionary for his contemporaries. Conservative politicians and financial markets dismissed his ideas, fearing they would hurt rather than help the economy.

When he failed to win political support, Coxey decided to publicize his program with a protest march of unemployed men to Washington. Upon their arrival, he would read his proposal on the steps of the Capitol and then present his bills to Congress. He was joined in his plan by Carl Browne, a seller of patent medicines, a former journalist, and a religious fanatic. Coxey would put up the funds for the march, and Browne would publicize it. Thus, they quickly attracted notice as they addressed clubs and civic groups and mailed out promotional literature. News of their plans was picked up by the wire services and published in newspapers from New York to Minneapolis, which, unfortunately for Coxey, treated the planned march more as a joke than a legitimate political strategy. As the date of departure neared, newspapers began to count arrivals at the starting point in Massilon, Ohio, always comparing them with humor to Coxey's grandiose goal of 100,000 men. For example, when the first two recruits showed up on March 24, the *New York Times* could not resist poking fun with its headline on the story, "Two Now in Coxey's Army."

Despite the jokes, Browne and Coxey succeeded in amassing a contingent of about 100 men and, accompanied by a brass band and 44 reporters, embarked on the four hundred-mile journey on Easter Sunday, 1894. At the same time, men attempted to organize in other cities, departing in groups ranging from a dozen to a few hundred from Philadelphia, Baltimore, San Francisco, and Sacramento. The press still found the whole affair a joke and continued to ridicule the effort. The *New York Times,* for example, reported with tongue in cheek that 40 or 50 men had reported at a Baltimore saloon where they were fed by "philanthropic sympathizers of the Major General." The men were described as "presenting a woebegone appearance and seem to be of the 'Weary Walkers' class." And in Birmingham, Alabama, the *Times* reported, "John G. Townley, a seedy-looking old man," was reported getting off a train from Cincinnati with the plan of recruiting an Alabama brigade to join the march.[1]

Browne created a circus-like atmosphere around the march, devising a series of what would today be called "media events." But as the marching armies began to face resistance from local officials and railroad managers who refused them reduced fares, the circus-like atmosphere deteriorated into lawlessness and violence. In Montana, four hundred unemployed miners seized a train and headed east. A posse of federal marshals and deputies pursued them and President Cleveland finally called out federal troops to intercept the hijackers, who were eventually stopped and taken peaceably into custody at Forsyth, Montana.[2] In Terre Haute, Indiana, another contingent under a "General" Fry seized a freight train. And in Portland, Oregon, five hundred Coxeyites were foiled in their plan to seize a train when the engineer disconnected the boxcars from the passenger cars, leaving them in the train yard.[3]

Though the railroads refused to offer free or reduced transport to the men marching from the west and arrested those who attempted to seize boxcars, local farmers were more sympathetic. They provided food, shelter, and transportation by wagon along the marchers' route. At least one farmer offered jobs to the men he was transporting, but was turned down, according to the *Chicago Tribune*. When the farmer asked them what they would do if they failed to convince Congress to do something for them, one man was reported as saying, "Why, there'll be 2,000,000 of us there and if they don't give us what we want we'll take Washington, that's what we'll do."[4]

Publicity of this kind of defiance backfired, and had the opposite effect on Congress that Coxey had hoped for. On April 26 a number of Congressmen, including the Populists who had initially supported Coxey's plan, spoke out against the march. Some even labeled the march an act of anarchy. A few Populists continued to portray the Coxeyites sympathetically as "a persecuted set of beings," the *Chicago Tribune* reported, but Congress and the administration were determined to enforce the laws to preserve peace.

BROWNE'S CAPTURE.
(Drawn by one who saw it.)

"Browne's Capture," *New York World*, 2 May 1894, p. 1. *When Jacob Coxey marched to Washington with a band of unemployed men in 1894, he was ridiculed by the press and the public. His plan had been to attract attention to his proposal for a public roads project, but the march attracted more attention to the ragtag army and its antics than it did to Coxey's ideas. When he attempted to make his speech from the Capitol steps, he and his partner in the venture, Carl Browne, were arrested.*

Thus, when Coxey and his contingent of about four hundred finally reached Washington and he attempted to make his speech from the steps of the Capitol on May 1, he was prohibited from entering the grounds. In front of some 20,000 spectators, he and Browne attempted to push past a line of three hundred police blocking the entrance to the Capitol grounds, but were stopped after a tussle and escorted away. Both men were arrested and on May 9 were convicted of carrying banners on the Capitol grounds and walking on the grass. Both were sentenced to jail for 20 days. Coxey's address and his proposals for economic recovery were eventually read to Congress by a Populist legislator, but his ideas were dismissed as impractical. It was another year before the economy began to recover and the unemployed found work again.

Thus, Coxey's march was a failure in several respects. First and foremost, it failed to promote his plan for economic recovery. Second, though he succeeded through Browne's antics in attracting public and media attention, the attention focused only on the sensational aspects of the march rather than on either the plight of the unemployed or the merits of his economic recovery plan. Finally, even as newspapers devoted thousands of words to every aspect of the march, they never considered the larger questions that begged an answer: why a country of such wealth could have so many poor and unemployed, and why these poor and unemployed could not find relief through sanctioned political process but instead must resort to unconventional steps such as protest marches and mob action.

Because many issues were involved in the events surrounding Coxey's march, the following readings have been organized in five sections. The first two sections contain articles and editorials opposed to Coxey and his plan; of these, the first section contains materials ridiculing Coxey, the second contains material that considered his march a threat to law and order. The third section contains material that was critical of Congress's role in the affair. The fourth section contains two of the very few items that were *sympathetic* to Coxey and his men. The chapter closes with a selection from the *New York Times* that praises the American political system for its ability to withstand such passing "fads" as Coxey's movement.

OPPOSED: RIDICULING COXEY'S PLAN

From the beginning, Browne used all the techniques of the showman to dramatize the march and succeeded in attracting extensive newspaper attention at all stages of the march. He was so successful, in fact, that when it departed Massillon on Easter Sunday, the small army was accompanied by 44 reporters, 1 for every 3 marchers.[5] Most reporters, however, focused on the sensational aspects of the march. They ridiculed Coxey and his "army of tramps" and largely ignored his political and economic propos-als. In its report on Coxey's announcement of the march, the New York Times *was no different. In this article, that staid representative of the busi-ness community adopts a humorous, mocking tone. Though the* Times *is careful to quote Coxey's assurance that the march will not include any an-archists—and perhaps because it is careful to do so—the reader comes away with the sense that Coxey is a delusional fanatic.*

New York Times, 28 January 1894

LOOK OUT FOR 'IM, CONGRESSMEN!

Here's Mr. Coxey, Coming 100,000 Strong to Do Wondrous Things

MASSILON, Ohio, Jan. 27—When J. S. Coxey announced the other day that he would organize an army and march from Ohio to Washington to de-mand the issue of $500,000,000 of treasury notes, the declared purpose was looked upon as the whimsical idea of a rich man. It is a fact, however, that Mr. Coxey is spending a great deal of money in preparing this programme for practical execution. Mr. Coxey said today:

"You'll find that when we reach Washington on May 1, we'll have 100,000 men. We'll not take a dollar with us, and instead of muskets every man will carry a white flag with the words 'Peace on earth, good will toward men, but death to interest-bearing bonds.' No criminals or Anarchists will be allowed to mingle with us. We will depend entirely on the enthusiasm of the down-trodden people for the necessaries of life."

When asked what he would do with his army of 100,000 men when he struck some town of 10,000 people for the night, he declared in his belief that the town would provide.

Mr. Coxey prepared "Bulletin No. 2" last evening, and it is now in the hands of printers for promulgation next week. He says in it:

"We propose only the peaceable plan now. When that fails it will be time enough to talk about force. The line of march will be given in Bulletin No. 3 in about three weeks. We want 100 old officers, Union and Confederate, to volunteer as marshals of divisions. Horses will be furnished to most of them. It is expected that the farmers of Pennsylvania will furnish supplies for the procession in its patriotic mission of the salvation of the Republic."

Charles Dana, the colorful editor of the New York Sun, *also could not re-sist lampooning the ragtag army and its leaders in this brief untitled edito-rial as they embarked on their journey.*

New York Sun, 29 March 1894

A CRANK-ASS MOVEMENT

The Hon. Silica S. Coxey is a compound crank of 82,000 ass power, dragging an advertising cart, and the Hon. Carl Browne's head is a shell without partitions; but we are sorry for Stump Lushy. Stump was the only man in the whole army of three that had any sense, and Stump got an awful kick from a mule-car mule in Brimstone City in 1893. Still, Stump is the best man in the crowd; and we don't like to hear of his starting for Washington with no other means of transportation than the wheels in Boxey & Crowne's heads.

Opposed: Coxey's Army a Threat

As the marchers, particularly those traveling from the West and through the Midwest, began to have violent skirmishes with the railroads, some became concerned that "lawless elements and anarchists" would gain control over the movement. These fears gained some credence when "General" Charles Kelly announced he had learned there were several anarchists in his Sacramento contingent. In the following editorial, the San Francisco Chronicle *expresses the fear that the entire movement, "foolish" from the start, will become tainted by the actions of a few black sheep.*

San Francisco Chronicle, 26 April 1894

THE DANGER IN IT

Intrinsically there is no danger to the nation in the pilgrimage of the Industrials to Washington. They may be—nay, they certainly are—foolish and ill advised, for they can accomplish nothing by their mission, but if it could be conceded that they are simply so many hundreds or thousands of men out of employment, who have undertaken to petition Congress personally to assist them, the enterprise, though silly and quixotic, could not be harmful.

Unfortunately every such movement as this attracts to itself the idle and worthless, and even worse, and the danger is that this corrupt leaven may leaven the whole lump and array the people of the United States against a movement, which, in itself, could have no substantial element of danger to society in it.

At Atlantic, Ia., where one regiment of the Industrials is encamped, General Kelly, who is in command, has said that he had private information that there were several anarchists among the Sacramento contingent, and that it was his desire and intention to drive them out of the army at once. It need not have take private information to teach General Kelly that there were black sheep in his flock. If he be a capable leader of men he should have known that almost by intuition, and if not in that way, at least by common rumor.

Here then, as we say, is the danger that the scum and the riffraff may come to the top, and the man of honest though mistaken purpose be condemned for ideas, plans, and acts with which they have no sympathy and in which they have taken no part. There ought to be some winnowing process devised for the Industrials by which the wheat could be separated from the chaff, for unless this be done it will become the popular impression that it is all chaff, which certainly is not the case.

Coxey's main army reached Washington April 29, two days before the date he had set to speak from the Capitol steps and present his bills to Congress. They set up camp at Brightwood Riding Park, seven miles from the Capitol, after being forbidden the use of public land, and Coxey and Browne proceeded to Washington to attend to official matters. In the following front-page story, the Milwaukee Journal *was one of several newspapers to play up the danger inherent in the situation. Here it describes the nation's capital as a city under siege.*

Milwaukee Journal, 30 April 1894

CONGRESS IS IN FEAR
SOME CRANKS MAY THROW A BOMB FROM THE VISITORS' GALLERY

"GEN." COXEY CAUSES IT ALL

His Followers Not So Much Feared As the Swarm of Cranks and Thieves Expected at the Capital All This Month—It May Hasten Action on the Tariff.

WASHINGTON, April 30—Probably not since the war, when the confederate troops were menacing this city, have the Washington people been in such fright as is caused by the presence of Coxey's army, which went into camp at Brightwood park, in the outskirts of Washington, yesterday. Nothing else is talked about in the streets and public places, and preparation may be noted on every hand for security and protection. Government buildings are barred and bolted and all necessary entrances closed. Special police and deputy marshal are being sworn in by scores and arms and ammunition have been provided. From now until the "Army of Peace" shall again have disappeared, the great treasury building will have all its entrances but one closed and those going in and out there will be closely scrutinized. The vaults where the money is kept are now closed to visitors.

President Cleveland had intended to move out to his country seat on May 1, but has now given this up until the army has been dispersed.

In the capitol [*sic*] building, where the army will probably swarm in the greatest numbers, extraordinary precautions are being taken. All the sub-basement doors will be closed and no entrance can be gained except at the main doors, and these will be guarded by the police....

The main outward sign of preparation in the capitol [*sic*] today was in the erection of two large partitions with gates on each side of the main rotonda [*sic*]....

The senators and representatives are scared half to death for fear some crank may throw a bomb. This week will be an anxious one for all of them. They do not fear Coxey or his immediate followers so much as the great crowd of cranks and thieves who will be attracted here by the Coxey demonstration. The city is filled with strangers, and the house [*sic*] and senate [*sic*] galleries are thronged daily with a motley mass of people outside of the usual run of visitors.

Congressman Somers expresses the liveliest fear that some crank may develop who will destroy life and property by means of dynamite. He says the members of both houses fear such a casualty. He, like others, has been in receipt of threatening letters and circulars. From the mail he was just opening when seen he got the following circular, which is only one of the many abounding in all kinds of blood-curdling statements and threats daily received by members of Congress:

O FOOL PLUTOCRATS!
O FOOL CONGRESSMEN!
THE REVOLUTION IS ON.
SHALL IT BE A BLOODY ONE?
SHALL IT BE A PEACEFUL ONE?
YE "FIDDLE WHILE ROME IS BURNING."

The tramps are coming; labor is coming, to demand justice. Governors of states! Chiefs of police shed not one drop of blood, or you will be drowned in the blood of plutocrats. Feed the army of tramps; feed the army of labor; thousands are tramping to Washington. Five millions of labor-men are at home watching; they are ready to fight. Call out no gatling guns, for this reserve labor army can sweep away all plutocratic hordes. Abolish the tariff. Pass "a direct tax bill." Make land practically free by a tax on rental values. Let labor swarm onto vacant land. There is the only safety. Here is pure justice.

"PA" CHASE, St. Louis, Mo.

One senator has received a letter openly threatening a dynamite bomb to be thrown into the Senate unless the Coxeyites are given free admittance and a full hearing. Mr. Somers thinks there is danger in the air and is in favor of every precaution to be taken.

CRITICAL OF CONGRESS

Some newspapers were impatient with what they believed to be Congress's failure to take charge of the situation by issuing a definitive response to Coxey's plan. Though Washington was taking defensive measures, these papers believed Congress should play a more active role. In the following editorial, the San Francisco Chronicle *asks why Congress is not fore-stalling the army by clearly stating its inability to enact Coxey's proposals. The* Chronicle, *a politically independent paper, takes advantage of the situation to criticize the Democratic administration and Congress. It com-pares their slow reaction in this instance to their quick response in 1892 to indict Pinkerton violence in the Homestead Strike.*

San Francisco Chronicle, 16 April 1894

CONGRESS AND THE INDUSTRIALS

Although Coxey's Industrial Army has reached Maryland on its march to the national capital, Congress does not appear as yet to have heard of the movement, though as the CHRONICLE has pointed out, the first shot had hardly been fired at the Homestead Works before Democratic Senators and Representatives were demanding special committees of investigation to as-certain whether the policy of protection could not be indicted for murder.

It is the duty of Congress to declare itself at once on this question of the Industrials, and the plain and bounden duty of [Democratic] President Cleveland to call the matter to the attention of Congress in a special mes-sage. While it is certain that Congress can afford no immediate relief in any way to the Coxey army, unless by a purely charitable donation, it should in-form the misguided men who have blindly followed a few demagogues that their visit to Washington must be fruitless. Why should Congress wait until the Industrials assemble around the Capitol to tell them that their errand must be a bootless one? A resolution should be adopted and made public at once, directing the attention of Coxey and his followers to the true state of the case, and pointing out the futility of their visit to Washington.

Obviously the reason why this is not done is because Cleveland and his party have made so many mistakes that they have become afraid of their

own shadow, and alarmed at any and everything which presents any unusual or abnormal features. They do not know but that this Industrial movement may be a cunning device of [New York Democratic Senator David]
Hill's, or some deep-laid scheme of [Kansas Senator William] Peffer and
[Kansas Representative] Jerry Simpson and Pennoyer to bring the Populist
party into favor, or even a Republican move to still further discredit the
Cleveland Democracy, if such a thing be possible.

It is very well to prepare the militia of the District of Columbia in anticipation of possible trouble in Washington, but a joint resolution of Congress,
pointing out clearly and briefly the limitations imposed on Congress by the
Constitution and the utter impossibility of that body complying with the
demands of the Industrial Army, would bring very many people to their
senses and result in checking the advance on Washington. This will have to
be done very soon, and it would be better done now than after the Industrial Army has succeeded in locating itself in the capital of the Nation.

---

*Only a few newspapers looked at the causes of the situation—what had
moved Coxey to propose his economic plan and the march in the first place.
The* Chicago Tribune *traced the nation's economic crisis to Congress's acts
to destroy trade protection and lower wages and prices. In the following editorial, the* Tribune *points to Congress's failure to take appropriate action
in the economic crisis as being responsible for Coxey's march and the ensuing panic.*

Chicago Tribune, 27 April 1894

SENATOR MILLS' FALSE PREDICTIONS

Senator Mills tells the suffering wage-workers, farmers, and trades people that when the Wilson bill becomes a law the times will be prosperous,
the present business depression will pass away like a summer cloud, and
everything will be lovely once more, and the people of the United States will
recline peacefully on Mr. Cleveland's bosom.

The Senator seems to have borrowed his method of dealing with the
body politic from the quack who first threw his patients into fits because he
was "death on fits," and had no difficulty in dealing with sickness when it
took that form. The Senator and his fellow-Confederates first throw the
country into fits by their proposal to destroy protection and cut down wages
and prices. Then they proceed to administer their quasi free trade and income tax medicine to cure the fits they have caused by breaking down the
long-established system of high wages and ample protection to American
industries. The Confederate quacks are worse than the fits doctor, because

his patients had something the matter with them when he was called in. The Confederate quacks found the country in perfect health.

The remedy prescribed by Senator Mills will not work. The Wilson bill cannot cure the evils it has caused. The "hair of the dog that bit him" recipe will not do in this case. The McKinley high protection tariff law has been re-pealed practically and the Wilson tariff bill has been in force ever since the Democrats in Congress declared last fall that it was their intention to enact it into a law and to minimize protection. When they made known their pur-pose the business interests of the country began at once to prepare for the great change of conditions. As a consequence of the anticipation by the business community of the inevitable effects of the Wilson bill the country is suffering under it now. The poverty, disorganization, and demoralization of the labor element show clearly the evil influence of the Southern Con-federate measure upon the industries and prosperity of the country. The passage of the Wilson bill by the Senate and the signing of it by the Presi-dent will confirm and intensify, not undo the mischief wrought by its sub-mission by the Committee on Ways and Means to the House and its passage by that body.

The spontaneous movement towards Washington of masses of men who voted in 1892 for tariff changes, but who are deprived of employment now by the Wilson bill, is caused by their feeling that the authors of their misery should be compelled to provide for their wants. The unemployed see in Washington the very demagogue [President Cleveland] who eighteen months ago persuaded them to vote against protection and for free trade, promising them better wages, more work, and cheaper living if they would help put those demagogues in control of the government.

Finding themselves out of work and wages and in a deplorable state of destitution, while the demagogues who deceived them are in power and in the receipt of big salaries, they as a last wild resort, adopting Coxey's ideas, are organizing themselves into armies and are marching on Washington with some vague plan of compelling their deceivers to redeem the pledges of 1892 or at least to furnish the unemployed million of men with the means of subsistence at the public expense. Those befooled men turn naturally to the free trade demagogue whom they voted into power for relief in their dire distress. They offer their service, to make roads or dig irrigation ditches in the arid regions, or to do anything else their demagogues can find for them.

When Coxey reached Washington and attempted to make his speech at the Capitol, he was arrested. The San Francisco Chronicle *used this occasion to once again criticize the Democratic administration for letting the situa-tion get out of control.*

San Francisco Chronicle, 4 May 1894

COXEY'S ARREST

Though General Coxey made a blunder in fighting and struggling to secure a position on the Capitol steps from which to deliver an address, his folly was supreme wisdom as compared with the course of the Washington officials. Had the original Coxey plan materialized and he had appeared in Washington at the head of 50,000 men, his army might have been a distinct menace to the national capital, but when he marched down the street with a following of not over 300, many of whom were evidently looking for a chance to escape, he should have been ignored entirely.

Suppose he had taken his whole 300 into the House of Representatives, what of it? The galleries in that chamber will seat at least 2000, and Coxey and his whole army could have accommodated six or seven times over and have listened to Tom Johnson or some equally wild-eyed reformer pleading their cause on the floor of the House. Or if this did not comport with the dignity of the House, Coxey might very well have been permitted to make his speech before a committee and then present his petition for consideration.

It is always unwise to make a martyr of an extremist. If a Democratic President and a Democratic Congress in their united wisdom could find no way to keep Coxey and his forces out of Washington, the authorities of that city should have let them have their say and be done with it, especially as the crusade had dwindled down to such proportions as to be not only harmless but ridiculous. If anything more is heard from Coxey, the Washington officials and the Presidents and Congress will have to answer for it.

SYMPATHETIC TO COXEY

The New York World, *ever the champion of the underdog, was one of the few newspapers to be sympathetic toward Coxey and his army. When the army arrived in Washington, the paper downplayed the threat of violence and presented several story lines. In the following page-one story, the* World *presents Coxey as a latter-day David taking on Goliath but chastises him for apparently forgetting the needs of his followers. The* World *continues with a farcical account of Coxey's attempts to get official permissions to camp, to march, and to speak on the Capitol steps from a number of governmental bodies and their methods of frustrating him. The bureaucratic pettiness the "General" encounters in his round of government offices was an experience to which the* World*'s working-class and immigrant readers could surely relate.*

New York World, 30 April 1894

ALL EYES ON COXEY

Breathless Millions Wait to
See Him Beard the Solons in Their Den

HE MEETS REBUFFS ON ALL SIDES

Reminded that Officers Are Maintained
to Execute Laws, Not to Pass Upon Them

BUT HE WILL MARCH TO THE CAPITOL

And There Is No Reason Why He May Not if He Is Diplomatic, Deliver His Speech on the Capitol Steps

WASHINGTON, April 30—Gen. Coxey has revealed his plan of operations for to-morrow, and it looks very much as though he were going to get into trouble. There are some who say it would be only fair if at this stage of the proceedings Coxey were to undergo a few personal hardships, since the members of his army have encountered so many of them. A more miserably wornout and bedraggled set of men than the Coxeyites are at the present moment can scarcely be imagined. It seems incredible that they can be held together much longer if something is not done for their actual necessities, not to speak of their comfort.

Although hundreds of dollars must have been taken in at the driving park on Sunday, no portion of it, apparently, has been used for the benefit of the army. It was after 1 o'clock to-day before the poor fellows, many of whom had no bed other than the damp ground, got their breakfast.... It looks as if the entire morning had been spent by the driver of the commissary in hunting up and collecting free provisions from Coxey's sympathizers in various parts of the city, and had found more bread than anything else. Why, with plenty of money in the treasury, the army was not treated to at least one square meal of fresh meat and vegetables is hard to say....

General Coxey's excuse this evening for his and Browne's desertion of the men in their lonely quarters was that they were too busy with more serious matters to think of the personal comfort of their followers.

Coxey evidently believes he can do what he pleases with them. And he will probably be the most surprised man in America in the course of the next thirty-six or forty-eight hours, for the Commonweal is on the verge of a revolt and a collapse.

Coxey's Busy Day

There is no doubt that Coxey did have his hands full to-day. He finds that it is not so easy to carry out his intention of invading the Capitol as he had supposed. At 9 o'clock this morning, accompanied by a Mr. A. W. Cook, he made a call at the headquarters of the District Commissioners. The Commissioners were busy at the time, and, treating Coxey as they would any other citizen, did not accord him an interview until they had completed the business in hand. The knowledge that Coxey was waiting outside got to the ears of all of the clerks, however, and the result was that the leader of the Commonweal [Coxey] held a reception in the anteroom, cheerfully furnishing his autograph to all who asked for it, and looking as proud and haughty as the pictures of Washington crossing the Delaware. By the time the Commissioners were ready to receive Mr. Coxey he was in a frame of mind which led him to imagine that anything he might request would be granted.

The Commissioners arose and shook hands with him, eyeing him with much curiosity. He explained that he had called to obtain permission to change the site of his camp. He said that S. Bensinger had offered him the use of a lot on the north side of M. Street Southwest, between First and Second streets and that he would like to pitch the tents of the Commonweal on that side. He said this with the air of a man who is stating a purpose rather than asking for permission to carry a purpose out.

The Commissioners, who were still regarding him with curiosity, replied that they were not in the habit of permitting regiments to camp promiscuously in the District without regard to sanitary regulations....

The Commissioners assured Gen. Coxey that, although the lot he was speaking about might be an excellent place from a showman's standpoint, they would not permit it to be occupied as a camping place for an army of men unless a professional plumbing engineer was called in and adequate sanitary arrangements perfected.

"That'll be easy enough," said Coxey. "I will see that it is all fixed shipshape."

He evidently thought that permission to camp there would be given at once, but the Commissioners decided to appoint a committee to look more thoroughly into the matter, and with that, he had to be satisfied for the time being.

To-Day's Parade

Coxey's next thought was to arrange for to-morrow's parade, and to this end he called upon Major Moore, the Superintendent of Police. He has a breezy, airy way, has Coxey, but it "did not go" with Major Moore. That official pink of dignity and propriety informed him that permits for parades in Washington were not given to everybody, and could be obtained only from the District Commissioners.

Back to the office of the District Commissioners, therefore, went the General of the Commonweal, with the Superintendent of Police, and made a formal application for the privileges of marching his men, with banners and band, through the city of Washington, in the morning.

All these formalities, Mr. Coxey said, were very distasteful to him. He could not in the least understand why American citizens, in the capital of the nation, should be so hedged about with red tape.

But still worse was in store for him when he declared his intention of making an address from the steps of the Capitol. This, it was explained, was a matter outside of the jurisdiction of the Commissioners, and entirely in the hands of Congress; he would have to go to the Capitol to see about that.

Nothing daunted, off posted Coxey to the Capitol and sought an interview with Sergeant-at-Arms Dick Bright.

"I propose," said Coxey, in his chipper style, "to speak to-morrow from the east front."

"If you make an attempt," said Mr. Bright, "you will be arrested."

"But," said Coxey, "the Constitution guarantees me the right and privilege."

The Sergeant-at-Arms looked a little hot under the collar as he replied: "I would advise you, Mr. Coxey, to study the law. The regulations forbidding orations or harangues on the Capitol grounds are very plain, and persons violating them are likely to incur a $500 fine or six months in jail, or both."

"Well," replied Mr. Coxey, "I am not a law-breaking man, but I have a firm belief that it is my privilege to speak from the Capitol steps, and I propose to do so."

"All right," said the Sergeant-at-Arms, "you probably know your business, and the police probably know theirs."

That he will attempt to speak on the east front to-morrow is so evident as to give rise to the opinion that he has made several heavy wagers to that effect, and it is reported this evening that he has hit upon a plan by which he can not only carry out his declaration, but at the same time avoid the penalty of the law.

The programme as outlined by those who pretend to know exactly what this cheeky horse-breeder from Massilon, O., intends to do, is as follows: He will head the procession of the Commonweal down Pennsylvania Avenue to the Capitol and around convenient streets until he reaches the east front. There an order will be given to the Commonweal to break ranks. All the banners and curious devices in the way of transparencies carried by the army will be stored in one of the commissary wagons and the members of the

Commonweal will flock over into the Capitol grounds as individuals. Of course, there will be no way, or, in fact, any desire to prevent their being there. Mr. Coxey will then climb the steps of the east front and be met at the top either by Senator Allen of Nebraska, or some other member of Congress who sympathizes with the ideas which he is supposed to represent. To this member of Congress Mr. Coxey will deliver his little speech, and possibly follow it up by handing out a written document. It is doubtful the police will feel justified in interrupting any such proceeding such as this. Coxey may thereupon return to Ohio and boast that he did make an address on the steps of the Capitol, and his half-starved followers can shift for themselves as best they may.

As he had promised to do, Coxey led his ragtag troops into Washington and toward the Capitol, where a crowd of 20,000 spectators was waiting in anticipation of the confrontation that was sure to come. Though the march proceeded without violence, Coxey's attempt to circumvent the police surrounding the Capitol was a fiasco and ended in arrest and humiliation. Newspapers covered the day's events in great detail, almost with relish. Once again, the New York World *was one of the few to sympathize with the marchers, blaming Congress for refusing them the right to a hearing. Even in this untitled editorial, however, the* World *does not regard the march altogether seriously, referring to it as "the Coxey farce."*

New York World, 2 May 1894

Coxey Abandoned by Congress

The Coxey farce ended rather dismally yesterday, when its leaders were [chased down and arrested] by the police, while the rank and file, that had made a pathetically comical march through the streets of Washington, stood outside and waited with a vague and inarticulate notion that something was about to happen. "Gen." Coxey has had his first collision with the law, with the only result possible and which he might easily have foreseen. In the mean while the Republican senators and Congressmen are strangely silent at this refusal to grant a "hearing" to American citizens who had traveled to the capital to inform Congress what kind of legislation they wanted. The McKinleyites should not repudiate their offspring.

SUPPORT OF AMERICAN SYSTEM

Although it was another month before Coxey and Browne completed their sentences and the army of tramps disbanded to return home, Coxey's arrest and trial signaled the end of the movement. Never given any serious contem-

plation, his proposal for economic recovery was dismissed as an impractica-
ble scheme. Though the men who had joined his army did so out of despera-
tion, their plight was likewise dismissed as a temporary setback that would
soon pass. The New York Times *referred to the entire movement as a mere*
"fad," and sighed with relief when it ended and things returned to normal. In
the following editorial, in fact, the Times *is a bit smug in considering the*
moral that can be learned from the entire affair—that mob rule will never
prevail in a democracy ruled by consensus, where law and order is respected.

New York Times, **4 May 1894**

POPULISTS AND TRAMPS

Upon the whole, it is a very good thing that Coxey and the Coxeyites have been impelled to make their "demonstrations." The solid and respectable citizens have as good a reason to be grateful that they turned out "with boots on," in order to be looked at and counted.... There have been several beneficent sequels of this happy thought. One is that it has now become plain to everybody how extremely contemptible are in this county, even in very hard times, the forces that make for disorder compared with the forces that make for order. This is a demonstration that would not have been made if Coxeyism had been stopped in its initial stage by the intervention of the police. Some of us felt rather aggrieved that it was not, but such persons must now admit that they were in the wrong. The Coxeyites took their way through the rural parts, where there are no police, and thinly-settled States, where the militia is not very numerous or trustworthy, and in some of which cowardly or demagogic Governors were afraid to use the authority in them vested to disaffect the tramp vote; and we have no army. Now, it has been shown that we do not need any. It is plain to everybody that our society cannot be upset by its failures, and that even if all the poorhouses and insane asylums along the routes had been opened and the oppressed inmates allowed to go free and join the "armies" they would not have endangered public order. The single Washington policeman who gently led Coxey away by the ear for violating a police regulation was a far more impressive symbol of the strength of law and order in this country than a single brigade of troops would have been dispersing the Coxeyites.

QUESTIONS

1. What attitudes might have predisposed Congress and the press to consider Coxey's economic recovery plan impractical and "the whimsical idea of a rich man"?

2. The newspapers quoted here frequently used negative and derogatory terms to describe the marchers. Identify some of these. What are their connotations? How do they use and reinforce stereotypes? How did the use of these terms deny the legitimate purpose of the marchers?

3. The leaders of the contingents, from Coxey to Frye, were all given the title "General," even though they held no military position. Why did the newspapers, even the *New York Times,* observe this convention? Do you think this was a mark of respect, a sign that they were simply using the vocabulary adopted by those in the movement, or a sign of derision? Why is the decision to use one title instead of another (General Coxey, as opposed to Mr. Coxey or simply Coxey) of symbolic importance?

4. Can you think of previous instances in American history in which actions similar to the march on Washington have been proposed and carried out? Why is there a tendency for institutional figures and the press to label these protesters in a negative fashion as they did Coxey's army?

5. Some newspapers compared Coxey's march with the Homestead Strike, which was covered in an earlier chapter in this book. What similarities do you see in the two events? In the newspaper coverage?

6. What are some of the factors that contribute to the press's failure to cover issues like Coxey's economic recovery plan seriously? Why did newspapers focus on the more sensational events concerning the issue (such as the march, the character of the marchers, Browne's flamboyant tactics, and Coxey's eccentricity)?

7. If you were trying to promote legislation or a reform, what would you do to attract attention in such a way as to ensure that the media would focus on your ideas (and not your actions)? What might Coxey have done differently?

Notes

1. "Coxey's Army on the Move," *New York Times,* 26 March 1894, p. 1.

2. "Larceny of a Train," 25 April 1894, p. 1; "Fight with Deputies," 26 April 1894, p. 1; "Guard Go with Them," 27 April 1894, p. 1; all in *San Francisco Chronicle.*

3. "Fry's Men Seize a Train" and "Industrials of the Coast," both in *San Francisco Chronicle,* 26 April 1894, p. 1.

4. "Tired of the Tramp/Footsore Industrials Longing for Box Cars," *Chicago Tribune,* 27 April 1894, p. 1.

5. H. W. Brands, *The Reckless Decade: America in the 1890s* (New York: Thomas Dunne Books, 1995), p. 163.

CHAPTER 7

The Sinking of the *Maine,*
February 15, 1898

Just as the United States was pondering its role in the Western Hemisphere and redefining the Monroe Doctrine to include the Caribbean and Central America, insurrection broke out in Cuba in 1895. It was not the first time Cuban nationalists had attempted to free themselves from Spanish rule, for they had been defeated in the same purpose after a 10-year war with Spain between 1868 and 1878. At that time the insurgents had begged the United States for protection and financial assistance, but the United States had responded by merely admonishing Spain to treat its colonial subjects better.

Now, in 1895, the determined rebels launched a guerilla war against the Spanish, who responded with brutal measures. Rebels were executed, villages and crops were burned, and peasants were herded into so-called reconcentration camps, where many died of starvation and disease. Spain's military commander on the island who oversaw the suppression of the rebels, Captain-General Valeriano Weyler, was dubbed the "Butcher of Havana" by the American press. Amid reports of atrocities, which in some cases were exaggerated and even invented by sensational newspapers competing with each other for circulation, President Grover Cleveland offered to act as mediator. When his offer was rebuffed, American sympathies for the rebels increased. American businessmen with millions invested in Cuban sugar plantations also began calling for American intervention.

William McKinley, who succeeded Cleveland in the presidency March 1897, hoped to mediate for peace rather than intervene militarily. He sent an envoy to Cuba shortly after his inauguration to investigate the war zone and the condition of the *reconcentrados.* The resulting report of the island's deplorable state spurred him to condemn Spanish policy in Cuba and to demand that its suppression of the rebels be at least conducted according to the

103

military codes of civilization. Spain responded by recalling Weyler, who appeared responsible for the worst atrocities, but did little else to address McKinley's concerns.

In January 1898 McKinley requested permission from Spain to send a U.S. warship to Havana and invited Spain to return the gesture by sending her own ships to American harbors as a display of international friendship. When the U.S.S. *Maine* arrived in Havana Harbor in January carrying more than three hundred men, Spanish officials stationed in Havana greeted her with some pomp and circumstance. Not all Spanish officials were so respectful, however. On February 9, the *New York Evening Journal* published a private letter written by Dupuy de Lome, the Spanish ambassador to the United States, to a Spanish newspaper editor visiting Havana. The letter, which was leaked to an *Evening Journal* reporter by a Cuban nationalist, described McKinley as "weak and catering to the rabble, and besides, a low politician."[1] Though Spain issued a formal apology and de Lome immediately resigned from his post, the incident rubbed feelings raw. Then, on the night of February 15, the *Maine* blew up, killing 266 of the crew. Two separate blasts tore through the seven-thousand-ton warship, and within minutes she had sunk to the bottom of the harbor.

Although no one knew the cause of the explosions, many suspected that the *Maine* had been deliberately blown up by a bomb, torpedo, or mine. McKinley ordered an inquiry, and at the end of March his commission reported that the explosion had been caused by something external to the ship. It was not clear what this had been nor who had been responsible, but rumors suggested both the Spanish hoping to get rid of the Americans and the nationalists hoping to get America into the war on their side.[2]

Calls for U.S. military action increased the moment the *Maine* exploded. McKinley, however, hoped to avoid outright hostilities and instead ordered a naval blockade of Cuba on April 22. In response, Spain declared war on the United States on April 24. The United States declared war on Spain the next day, and McKinley called for 125,000 volunteers for the army in this, the country's first major conflict since the Civil War. "Remember the *Maine*" became the battle cry associated with the Spanish-American War.

Much has been said about the role of the press, particularly the yellow press, in the Spanish-American War. In the 14 months preceding the explosion on the *Maine*, many newspapers had called for American intervention in Cuba to protect the Cubans as well as American interests. Those that have been most identified as jingoes are William Randolph Hearst's *New York Evening Journal* and Joseph Pulitzer's *New York World*, which at that time were locked in a circulation war. Other newspapers, such as the *San Francisco Chronicle* and the *New York Times*, adopted a wait-and-see attitude and seemed more concerned about the effects a war with Spain would have on American trade and ocean commerce.[3]

The explosions on the *Maine* took place shortly after 9:45 p.m. on February 15, and accounts of the event were telegraphed to the United States almost immediately. Newspapers published the next morning reported

"Maine Explosion Caused By Bomb or Torpedo?" *New York World,* 17 February 1898, front page. *When the U.S.S.* Maine *blew up in Havana Harbor on February 16, 1898, sensational newspapers leaped to the conclusion that she had been blown up by the Spanish. An investigation concluded soon after that the explosion had been caused by something outside the ship, but did not determine if it had been a mine, a bomb, or a torpedo. The investigation also never uncovered who had been responsible for the explosion. Nevertheless, newspaper articles and illustrations like this one were later blamed for driving the United States into war with Spain.*

WAR HAS BEEN DECLARED
The Fearless Yellow Journals Open Up Operations on the Enemy.

"War Has Been Declared: The Fearless Yellow Journals Open Up Operations on the Enemy," *Minneapolis Journal,* 25 February 1898, p. 1. *Critics attacked the yellow press for its sensational coverage of the sinking of the* Maine. *Some even appropriated the figure of the Yellow Kid, which had first appeared as a comic strip in the* New York World *(hence the term "yellow journalism"), to lampoon the sensational journals. Here, the Yellow Kid gives a lesson in warfare using a rolled up newspaper as his cannon and typeface as his ammunition.*

whatever details they had at that time, including the text of the telegraphed report of the incident by the ship's commander to the secretary of the navy, the names of the ship's officers, and technical descriptions of the ship. They published illustrations of the *Maine* before the explosions and sketches of Havana Harbor and nearby Morro Castle, where rebel prisoners were held, as well as a portrait of ship commander Captain Sigsbee. They printed comments and speculations from a variety of purported experts, administration officials, military officials, and international political leaders.

Between February and the end of August, news of the Cuban situation, the ensuing Spanish-American War, and, ultimately, the American victory, consumed the American press. Newspapers sent more than five hundred reporters, photographers, and illustrators to cover events firsthand. They paid exorbitant fees to get their stories transmitted by telegraph, and published dozens of extras a day when the competition was hot. Hearst's *New York Evening Journal,* which actually published as many as 40 extras on one occasion, was said to have spent as much as $50,000 a week to cover the war. James Gordon Bennett, Jr.'s *New York Herald* was said to have spent as much as $40,000 a week. Some newspapers increased their size to accommodate the many stories on the developing situation with Spain; most increased their circulation. The public was hungry for news, and, apparently, the more newspapers published, the more the public wanted. Ironically, when it was all over, many critics, including those within the press, condemned the yellow press for pushing the United States into war.[4]

The articles and editorials below are divided in two sections: those that promote military intervention and those that urge caution and demand more information before taking military action. In some cases, the same newspaper appears to take different positions. For example, while the *New York World* initially urged caution on its editorial page, its sensational and alarmist stories could be said to *promote* military intervention. Each of these selections is included in the appropriate section.

PROMOTING MILITARY INTERVENTION

The New York Evening Journal *had been calling for U.S. intervention in Cuba for more than two years. In its coverage of the* Maine *explosion it was quick to quote any source that pointed to foul play by the Spanish. All the headlines on its front-page stories on the day following the explosion point to the Spaniards' culpability, though the facts given in the stories do little to support such claims. This front-page article appeared in the newspaper's ninth extra of the day under scare headlines stretching the full width of the page. While the article provides little evidence against the Spanish—and, in fact, quotes authorities saying the cause of the explosion is still undetermined—the writer does his best at the end to play up what he describes as "the general belief in Spanish treachery." This alarmist and, some would say, irresponsible interpretation of facts, as well as the sensational headlines on the story, was surely aimed at promoting military intervention by the United States.*

New York Evening Journal, 16 February 1898

CRISIS IS AT HAND

CABINET IN SESSION; GROWING BELIEF IN SPANISH TREACHERY

DE LOME, IN PANIC, FLEES

253 KNOWN TO BE LOST

Maine Destroyed by an Outside Attack,
Naval Officers Believe
Censored Dispatches From Havana
Say a Shot Was Heard Before
the Ship's Magazine Blew Up

Washington, Feb. 16—The President hurriedly called a special meeting of the cabinet at 11:30 a.m.

While the Cabinet was in session the following cable dispatch from Captain Sigsbee was handed to the President:

"Advise sending wrecking vessel at once. The Maine is submerged except debris. It is mostly work for divers now. Jenkins and Merrit still missing. There is little hope for their safety. Those known to be saved are: Officers, twenty-four; uninjured crew, eighteen; wounded now aboard steamer, city hospital, and at St Mascotte Hotel number fifty-nine, as far as known.

All others down on board or near the Maine. Total loss of missing, 253. With several exceptions no officer nor man has more than part of a suit of clothing and that wet with harbor water....

Damage was in compartment of crew. Am preparing to telegraph list of wounded and saved.... Will send all wounded men to hospital at Havana."

After the Cabinet had been in session an hour and a half, [Secretary] Long sent this reply:

"Sigsbee, U.S.S. Maine, Havana: The President directs me to express for him and for the people of the United States his profound sympathy with the officers and the crew of the Maine, and desires that no expense be spared in providing for the survivors and in caring for the dead."

Secretary Long also announced that an unsigned dispatch from Havana reported the number of dead at 275.

Vice-President Hobart was in the Senate chamber at noon when he received a message from the president calling him to the White House.

The President and members of the Cabinet were still in conference, but the Vice-President was at once admitted.

A dispatch was received from General Lee this afternoon, saying: "All quiet. Great sorrow expressed by authorities. Sigsbee has telegraphed details to Navy Department. Not yet prepared to report cause of explosion."

Public opinion in Washington is rapidly changing. It is now believed that the destruction of the Maine could not have been due to an accident. There is a strong belief in Spanish treachery.

General Blanco has cabled Senor Du Bose, the Cuban Charge d'Affairs, that a dynamo boiler on the Maine blew up, causing the explosion of the magazine.

Admiral Sicard of the North Atlantic squadron will be communicated with at once respecting the sending of another battle ship to Havana.

The lighthouse tenders Fern and Mangrove have arrived at Havana. The coast survey steamer Ericsson has been dispatched from Key West with orders to Rear Admiral Sicard at the Dry Tortugas.

Rumors of Dynamite

Vague rumors reached New York at noon to-day that the Maine had been blown up by the bumping of a small boat filled with dynamite or other explosive against the battle ship's bows.

The press censorship at Havana has suppressed all but the most meager news.

Newspapers and private corporations having Cuban interests have made every effort to get dispatches through a plausible cipher.

From a complicated dispatch received by the president of a coastwise steamship company at noon to-day the news of a dynamite plot to destroy the Maine was deciphered.

Ironically, the Spanish warship Vizcaya *was scheduled to arrive in New York harbor the day after the explosion on the* Maine. *This was part of the friendly exchange between the United States and Spain proposed by McKinley, but both the* New York Evening Journal *and the* New York World *viewed the battleship's impending arrival in the unprotected harbor with alarm. The* World *published the following story accompanied by a fanciful illustration of the* Vizcaya *in New York harbor firing artillery shells onto Manhattan, the Bronx, Brooklyn, and Queens. The cutline reads: "Range of the Guns of Spanish Battle-Ship,* Vizcaya, *whose arrival in New York harbor is expected to-day."*

New York World, **17 February 1898**

THERE ARE SUSPICIONS THE MAINE WAS TORPEDOED

VIZCAYA STILL AT SEA

Spanish Ship Did Not Arrive Yesterday as Expected

NO VESSEL TO RECEIVE HER

Rear-Admiral Bunce Will Send His Representative Down the Bay in a Tug

CRUISER BROOKLYN MAY ARRIVE

Belief That She Will Accompany the Spaniard to Port in the Guise of a Protector

The, Vizcaya, the Spanish man-of war, was due to arrive in New York bay yesterday. Instead came the news of the blowing up of the Maine in Havana. The Vizcaya had not been sighted up to a late hour last night.

The exclusive publication in yesterday's World of the unprotected condition of New York harbor at the time when the Spanish armored cruiser Vizcaya is due here was widely discussed by businessmen yesterday, and it was generally declared that the Government should take immediate steps to keep some of our ablest fighting ships within reach of the Spaniard during her stay in these waters.

The fact that there is no warship in the Brooklyn Navy-Yard, not even a torpedo boat, fit for active service, was a surprise to most people. It is the first time that New York harbor has been in such defenseless shape in many years.

At the Brooklyn Navy-Yard, the various officers on duty eagerly awaited news of the sighting of the Spaniards. They declared that the catastrophe to the Maine would not affect the recognition which would be given the visitors.

Bunce Has Made Preparations

Rear-Admiral Bunce, commandant of the yard, will send a number of his aides in one of the departmental tugs to extend the customary welcome to the Vizcaya.

The belief was general in naval circles that the cruiser Brooklyn, which has been lying off Hampton Roads, will pick up the Vizcaya at sea and escort her to this port.

The presence of the Brooklyn will be explained as a precautionary measure to prevent any harm which might happen to the Vizcaya as a result of the bitter feeling among the Cuban population of New York against everything Spanish.

Well-informed naval men assert that if war were declared while the Vizcaya were in port, the cruiser Brooklyn would not be able to dispose of the Spaniard.

As reporters collected information from any and all sources, the evidence against Spain seemed to mount. The New York Evening Journal *rose to the heights of yellow journalism two days after the explosion, when it plastered its front page with enormous scare headlines and an imaginative illustration showed a mine floating below the hull of the* Maine. *It threw itself into the fray as an active and nearly hysterical participant by offering a $50,000 reward for "the detection of the perpetrator of the Maine Outrage!" and the "conviction of the criminals who sent 258 American sailors to their death." The following story stretched in a single bank across the full width of the page below the illustration of the* Maine *anchored over the hypothetical mine.*

New York Evening Journal, 17 February 1898

NAVAL OFFICERS THINK THE MAIN WAS DESTROYED BY A SPANISH MINE

George Eugene Bryson, the Journal's special correspondent at Havana, cables that it is the secret opinion of many Spaniards in the Cuban capital that the Maine was destroyed and 258 of her men killed by means of a submarine mine or fixed torpedo. This is the opinion of several American naval authorities. The Spaniards, it is believed, arranged to have the Maine anchored over one of the harbor mines. Wires connected the mine with a powder magazine, and it is believed the explosion was caused by sending an electric current through the wire. If this can be proven, the brutal nature of the Spaniards will be shown by the fact that they waited to spring the mine until all the men had retired for the night....

Hidden Mine or a Sunken Torpedo Believed to Have Been the Weapon Used Against the American Man-of-War—Officers and Men Tell Thrilling Stories of Being Blown Into the Air Amid a Mass of Shattered Steel and Exploding Shells—Survivors Brought to Key West Scout the Idea of Accident—Spanish Officials Protest Too Much—Our Cabinet Orders a Searching Inquiry—Journal Sends Divers to Havana to Report Upon the Condition of the Wreck. Was the Vessel Anchored Over a Mine?

By Captain E.L. Zalinski, U.S.A.
(Captain Zalinski is the inventor of the famous dynamite gun, which would be the principal factor in our coast defense in case of war.)

Assistant Secretary of the Navy Theodore Roosevelt says he is convinced that the destruction of the Maine in Havana Harbor was not an accident.

The Journal offers a reward of $50,000 for exclusive evidence that will convict the person, persons, or Government criminally responsible for the destruction of the American battle ship and the death of 258 of its crew.

The suspicion that the Maine was deliberately blown up grows stronger every hour. Not a single fact to the contrary has been produced. They are taking the course of tactful men who are convinced that there has been treachery.

Washington reports very late that Captain Sigsbee had feared some such event as a hidden mine. The English cipher code was used all day yesterday by the naval officers in cabling instead of the usual American code.

President McKinley's response to the incident in Cuba was complicated by political intrigues in Washington. According to the New York Evening Journal, *at least, political boss Mark Hanna was the man behind McKinley and dictating his decisions. Here, the* Journal *chastises Hanna (and therefore McKinley) for lacking the gumption to hold Spain responsible for the explosion on the* Maine *It also accuses McKinley of giving into Wall Street interests, which opposed war because it would be bad for business. When the* Journal *demands that McKinley address the Cuban situation, it is, in effect, asking him to take actions that can only lead to war.*

New York Evening Journal, 17 February 1898

HANNA IN THIS, TOO

Mark Hanna, in a dispatch from Washington, declares he has no doubt whatever that the destruction of the Maine was an accident. And then comes his real utterance. He says:

"Even if it should prove not to have been an accident we could not hold the Spanish Government responsible for the act of a Spanish Guiteau."

So the man who elected McKinley and now controls him is the author of our cowardly attitude toward Spain.

We owe to Mark Hanna the disgrace put upon the country. It is Mark Hanna who feels that the murder of a few sailors is not to be considered sufficiently important to risk hurting the Stock Exchange.

The first thing to do is to attend to Spain. After that it will be in order to attend to Mark Hanna.

The Situation

This is the situation to be faced to-day. Not all the supineness of the supinest of administrations can dodge the facts any longer.

The United States has been insulted in various ingenious ways. Men and women have been butchered at our doors for months. That has had no effect.

A heroically plucky little people has fought steadily on against overwhelming odds, occasionally turning its face pleadingly toward us. That has had no effect.

This nation has been browbeaten by Spain, and our president has been called a low trickster by Spain's minister. That has had no effect—even on the President.

Now, as a final and finishing touch one of our big ships is sent to the bottom of the sea in the harbor of Havana and more than two hundred American sailors go down with her.

It seems to us that that MUST have some effect. There MUST be a limit to our willingness to submit. There MUST remain somewhere in us some slight touch of the spirit that threw the tea overboard and welcomed a fight with power that seemed bound inevitably to annihilate us.

Mr. McKinley MUST feel he is responsible for this great calamity. He MUST realize that in shirking his duty as the guardian of the Nation's honor he has indirectly brought about this catastrophe.

He cannot longer deter action. He MUST demand of Spain full reparation, and get it. He MUST prohibit peremptorily wholesale murder at our doors in Cuba. He MUST teach the moral bankrupts who murder women and scuttle ships that they have gone too far.

These things he MUST do, and at once, though he should jeopardize the fortune of every Wall Street man who paid to get him elected. The United States is really tired of sitting still to be kicked.

URGING CAUTION

The New York Evening Journal*'s archrival, the* New York World, *was equally sensational in its treatment of the* Maine *affair and the stories spinning off it. On its editorial page, however, the* World *urged that all the evidence be gathered and the facts be known before any action—either diplomatic or military—be taken.*

New York World, 18 February 1898

FIND OUT THE FACTS

Was the Maine designedly blown up by a torpedo? Or was her destruction accidental? Was it fate or malice that sent 250 of our brave bluejackets to their death?

These are questions that can be answered definitely, and they should be answered quickly. Upon the answer given to them depend the future relations of Spain and the United States. Upon it may hang the issue of peace or war, with the fate of the brave Cuban people as the stake.

If the explosion was within the ship and accidental, there is an end to the matter so far as Spain is concerned. But if it was external and of malicious design, then Spain will be held responsible by outraged civilization for one of the greatest infamies recorded in history.

For whether a torpedo was exploded under or in the ship by Spanish authority, or whether it was done by treacherous Spanish partisans without authority, or whether it was the work of Cuban insurgents anxious to precipitate a conflict between Spain and the United States, Spain is clearly responsible.

The Maine had gone to Havana on a legitimate mission, at a time of peculiar stress and irritation. She and her officers had been received with every show of courtesy.

Spain controls Havana and its harbor. Her authority there is absolute. Her power to police the harbor is without limit. She is responsible for any act of hostility within that harbor, no matter by whom committed.

The thing now to do is to find out whether or not this fearful catastrophe was brought about by any act of hostility. If it shall appear that it was, not only must our Government exact the penalty, but all governments, for the sake of civilized intercourse itself, must hold Spain to be an outlaw among nations.

Find out the facts! That is the duty of the hour.

The San Francisco Chronicle, *which for two years had opposed intervention in Cuba because of the negative effect a war with Spain would have on trade, also warned against jumping to conclusions. In the following editorial, the* Chronicle *aims its criticism at the McKinley administration, which it admonishes for sending the* Maine *to Havana in the first place.*

San Francisco Chronicle, 18 February 1898

THE MAINE DISASTER

If it is true that the harbor of Havana is thickly sown with torpedoes connected by wires with electric stations on shore—all of which is probable—the sending of the Maine there to protect Americans was an act of bad judgment. A vessel rendered by her position unable to save herself could not save others; and an act of hostility on her part could have been nothing less than the signal for her complete destruction This would follow in the Maine's case even if mines and torpedoes had not been planted, because the vessel was surrounded by forts, the high-powered guns of which could have visited her with a plunging fire.

This lesson of the disaster, so far as it relates to the dispatch of ships into a semi-hostile and well-defended port on an errand like the Maine's, is rightly interpreted by Senator Long. We will send no more vessels to Havana unless to make war. It would be a challenge to fate to do so, for it is probably true that Spain could blow up the whole American Navy unawares providing it could first corral the vessels among the Havana torpedo nests. That is a risk the Navy Department has no business to run. As for Americans living in Havana, they take their lives in their hands if they stay there during a time of strained relations, and instead of calling upon the home Government to safeguard them should protect themselves by going away from the island.

We speak of the peril which any American war ship runs in Havana harbor now by way of laying down a general proposition rather than a specific admission that the Maine was destroyed by Spanish agencies. Upon that point, nothing is yet clear. It is going to be difficult, we surmise, until the ship has been raised, and possibly even then to determine the facts....

Unless it can be clearly shown that the battle-ship was destroyed by the garrisoned Spaniards or with the knowledge and connivance of the authorities we do not look for war. Mines may be set off or torpedoes used by private conspirators of the class of the Fenians [Irish nationalists], who once threatened to blow up an English cruiser in New York harbor. Such men are anarchists, for whom no government can be held responsible. Had the British ship been thus destroyed England would have demanded and received the apology of this Government, indemnity for the loss of property and life and the punishment of the convicted parties. The question of war would have been secondary to that of reparation. Upon the same principle if the United States finds and proves that the Maine was sent to the bottom by Spanish dynamiters, who acted in secret and without the knowledge of Captain-General Blanco and his military and naval commanders, then Spain will be called upon for damages. Certainly there would be no offhand declaration of war, and none would be justified. What might come of the direct inculpation of Spain and her refusal to accept responsibility for the act of a subject is another matter.

The New York Times *also counseled caution and urged its readers to suspend judgment until an inquiry could be undertaken. Ever true to its respect for legitimate government, it declared that even if some fanatical Spanish partisan had done the deed, "nobody is so foolish as to believe that*

the Maine *was destroyed by Spaniards with the knowledge and connivance of her Government."*[5] *In response to the sensational accounts of
events by papers such as the* New York Evening Journal *and the* New
York World, *it attacked the "freak press" for seasoning the news to "make
it 'bite' at all upon the jaded palates of their habitual readers."*[6] *In the following editorial, the* Times *praises the Spanish for their response to the incident and lashes out at the continued "frothings" of the yellow press.*

New York Times, 19 February 1898

THE SPANISH CONDUCT

Whatever may finally be found to be the cause of the destruction of the
Maine, the conduct of the Spanish officials and of the Spanish people at
home and in Cuba has been such as to strengthen the bonds of sympathy
between them and us and to give to the world a new reason for faith in
human nature.

In this statement we put aside as unthinkable the wild supposition that
the Maine was destroyed by the order or by connivance of the Spanish Government or any of its responsible officials. No one whose opinion is worth
quoting has entertained such a supposition, nor would we entertain it on
our part unless forced to do so, and, despite the forced frothing of one or
two journals, no one on the Spanish part has accused us of such a suspicion.

The situation as it has actually developed has been one of serious tension.
When our battleship was ordered to Havana there was a very general feeling
in both countries that, though her visit was friendly in form, it was closely related to the condition of affairs in Cuba. To the Spaniards in the island and at
home she was necessarily the embodiment of that power which at any moment might be launched against them. The insurrection which, rightly or
wrongly, they regard as we of the North regarded the rebellion of the Southern States, has been largely sustained by means secured from this country.
While our Executive has, by the acknowledgement of the Spanish Government, been active in suppressing all unlawful efforts to furnish such means,
there has been in our Congress a party crying aloud for intervention in the
Cuban trouble. And two successive Presidents have declared plainly that, if
the conflict were not settled otherwise, intervention was a question of time.
Such a declaration, "mutatis mutandis," [a Latin phrase meaning "the necessary changes have been made"] would not be accepted by the United States
Government or people as other than hostile—contingently and remotely, perhaps, but in effect and in spirit hostile. For all these reasons, the Spanish people had no cause to love us as Americans, and they did not.

Then came the destruction of the Maine in the Harbor of Havana. The first boats to reach her in the attempt to rescue those not killed came at the same moment from the Spanish cruiser, bearing the name of the child-King, Alphonso XII, and from an American merchantman. When Capt. SIGSBEE stepped into his boat—the last man to leave the sinking ship—it was to the Spanish cruiser he repaired, to thank in person the Spanish sailors whose aid had been so swift and courageous. From the Queen Regent and the Premier in Madrid, from Gen. BLANCO and the Municipal President in Havana, from the Navy of Spain, and from every official source expressions of profound sympathy poured in upon Washington. In the Havana hospitals the wounded were tenderly cared for, and the Spanish authorities instantly took steps for funeral honors, at once imposing and touching, to the dead. The royal and local Government, the army and the navy, the Church and the people of Havana, from the most fanatical of loyalists to the most wretched concentrados, joined in the demonstration of sorrow. And in this hour of deep emotion the Spanish Government seizes occasion to send to Washington a manly, emphatic, and comprehensive disavowal of all the utterances of its late minister [de Lome] to which we had any right to object—not merely his offensive references to the President, but even more earnestly the expressions justifying suspicion as to the good faith of Spain with reference to reciprocity and autonomy.

This is the record to the present time. It is honorable to the Spanish Government and people. It is deeply gratifying to all rational Americans and to those of any nationality who love manliness and rejoice to see it shown in times of sudden trial.

QUESTIONS

1. What in particular was inflammatory in the way the *New York Evening Journal* reported the explosion of the *Maine*? Consider the use of headlines, typographical characteristics, words, and sources. How could this information have been reported in a noninflammatory way? Try rewriting this story in a neutral tone.

2. Do you think it was ethical for the *New York Evening Journal* and the *New York World* to publish illustrations of what might happen if the *Vizcaya* were to fire on New York? Why is this an example of yellow journalism?

3. How much of the reporting in the *New York Evening Journal* was self-promotion? Do you think this kind of behavior is ethical behavior for a news organization? Do you see examples of this kind of self-promotion in the news media today? If so, give examples.

4. In its attack on the yellow press, which it called the "freak press," the *New York Times* accused it of trying to season its stories with exaggerations so as to appeal to its readers. Why was it believed sensationalism in newspapers like the *New York Evening Journal* would increase circulation? What kind of readers would be attracted by this style of journalism? Why?

5. Even though the *New York World* urged caution in its February 18 editorial, it revealed attitudes toward the Spanish and the Cubans that were not conducive to peace. What are the words and phrases that reveal these attitudes?

6. Many critics later blamed the yellow press for inciting America to war. Do you think it's possible for the press to have such an effect? What other factors play a role in affecting public opinion?

Notes

1. "The Worst Insult to the United States in Its History: Spain's Minister Calls President McKinley a 'Low Politician, Catering to the Rabble,'" *New York Evening Journal,* 9 February 1898, p. 1.

2. Two investigations were conducted in later years. One conducted in 1911 agreed with the 1898 finding that the explosion had been external. A second, conducted in 1976, suggested that the explosion had been internal and had perhaps originated in a fuel bunker.

3. "Our Cuban Policies," *San Francisco Chronicle,* 22 December 1896, p. 6.

4. "The Year's Record," *Fourth Estate,* 12 January 1899, p. 2.

5. "The Maine," *New York Times,* 17 February 1898, p. 6.

6. "The Maine and the Freak Press," *New York Times,* 18 February 1898, p. 6.

CHAPTER 8

The Treaty of Paris Launches America as an Imperialist Power, December 10, 1898

It took the United States three years to go to war with Spain over Cuba (see Chapter 7), but once it declared war on April 24, 1898, it did so with great fervor. Whipped up by sensational news accounts of atrocities against the Cuban insurgents and the terrible destruction of the U.S.S. *Maine*, volunteers swamped recruiting offices. Theodore Roosevelt resigned from his position as under-secretary of the navy to volunteer for the army and helped organize a dashing cavalry unit called the Rough Riders. Newspapers rushed to get their own men and even a few women to cover every aspect of the war.

The war was not limited to Cuba alone and quickly engulfed the other Spanish colonies in the Caribbean and the Pacific—Puerto Rico, Guam, and the Philippines. The Spanish fleet in the Philippines was destroyed in Manila Harbor by Admiral John Dewey on May 1, and the Spanish fleet in the Caribbean was destroyed by the U.S. Navy on July 3. The U.S. Army won major battles in Cuba and Puerto Rico and took possession of both islands by the end of July. The Philippine Islands were taken in August and an armistice with Spain was signed on August 12. By its terms, Spain was to grant Cuba complete freedom and the United States was to keep Puerto Rico indefinitely. In the Pacific, the United States was to hold Manila until the fate of the Philippines was decided. The armistice was to be considered a suspension of hostilities rather than a definitive end to them. America's "splendid little war" cost only 289 American lives in battle, but due to poor sanitary conditions and sweltering humid heat, more than four thousand troops were lost to typhoid, yellow fever, dysentery, and food poisoning.

It took another four months—longer than the actual war—to hammer out a peace treaty acceptable to all parties, not the least of which were the U.S. Congress and the American public. The Filipinos, who had been conducting their own insurgency against Spain, now wanted complete independence. McKinley instead proposed annexing the Philippines on the grounds that the Filipinos were unprepared for self-government and self-defense. Though his arguments for annexation were couched in paternalistic terms, they were largely motivated by the United States's commercial and military interests in retaining the islands and their control of the trade routes to Asia.

The fate of the Philippines was debated widely, with much of the argument centering on self-interest, democratic principles, expansionism, and imperialism. Those in favor of annexation used four basic arguments. First, as the victor, America had the right to claim the spoils of war (the former Spanish territories). Second, control of the Philippines would ensure protection of U.S. trade routes to China and the rest of Asia. Third, if America didn't claim the Philippines, a European power would. Fourth, the Filipinos were not ready to govern themselves and needed American protection and guidance.

"A Long Reach, But His Arms Are Equal to the Emergency." *Chicago Tribune*, 2 August 1898, p. 3. *Anti-imperialists were concerned that America was taking on more than it could handle by annexing the Philippines as part of the treaty ending the Spanish-American War. Opponents feared that America's standing army would have to be increased in size and that the country's resources would be stretched too thin. Imperialists, however, believed the victor should get the spoils. This cartoon, which first appeared in the* Boston Globe, *was reprinted in the* Chicago Tribune.

Those who opposed annexation had three basic arguments. First, they maintained, the United States would join the league of imperialistic colonial nations—including Spain, which it had just defeated—if it were to annex the Philippines. Second, annexation would be antidemocratic and would violate American principles. Third, the United States would be required to commit military resources to protect the Philippines, which would overtax its resources. If the United States were to annex the islands, they argued, the country would have to increase the size of its standing army at considerable expense.

The imperialists prevailed and the Treaty of Paris was signed on December 10. By its provisions, the United States annexed the Philippines and paid Spain $20,000,000 for the privilege of doing so. One of the immediate results of the treaty was that on December 21 the United States established military rule on the Philippine Islands. Another result was that a month later, Filipino rebels under Emilio Aguinaldo proclaimed an independent republic. In February 1899 hostilities began between the insurgents and American troops. The ensuing Philippine war for independence from the United States, which was as bloody and costly to the Filipinos as had been their rebellion from Spain, was to last another three years. It ended in 1902 with the defeat of the insurgents. The United States governed the Philippines directly until the mid-1930s and indirectly until 1946, when it finally granted the island nation its independence.

During the debate over the fate of the Philippines, newspapers were torn between pride in America's quick victory in the war with Spain and concern that a just and manageable treaty be made that would be in keeping with American democratic principles. The editorials and news articles in this chapter are organized in three sections: the first section provides readings urging thorough and open debate and consideration of all sides of the issue before a decision is made; the second section provides examples that support annexation; and the third section provides examples that oppose annexation.

Urging Consideration of All Sides

While many newspapers, politicians, and members of the public already had strong opinions about how the United States should treat its conquered territories, the New York Times *represented the voice of reason and caution. Throughout the Spanish-American War, the* Times *had provided a relatively rational and accurate account of events in comparison with its more sensational peers like William Randolph Hearst's* New York Evening Journal *and Joseph Pulitzer's* New York World. *Here, also, the*

Times *attempted to maintain that tone of rational analysis. In the following editorial, by presenting the various issues that would be involved in the annexation of the Philippines, the* Times *sets the stage for the debates to follow.*

New York Times, 13 August 1898

THE FUTURE OF THE PHILIPPINES

Senor Sagasta semi-officially announces the position of the Spanish Government regarding the Philippines: "The Government is of the opinion that the most critical period of the peace negotiations has now arrived, as it depends on the arrangement of details as to whether the peace will be more or less advantageous. Spain wishes to preserve her sovereignty over the whole of the Philippines to which she proposes to accord all political and administrative reforms consistent with the maintenance of her sovereignty." This is obviously a question that will come fairly and fully within the discretion of the peace Commissioners acting under the instructions of their respective Governments. The summary of the reply of President McKinley to the overtures of Spain, given out to the public on Aug. 2, contained the following broad statement, which is repeated verbatim in the protocol: "The United States will occupy and hold the city, bay, and harbor of Manila pending the conclusion of a treaty of peace, which shall determine the control, disposition, and government of the Philippines."

It will be seen that this leaves to the negotiators of the treaty of peace the consideration of "the control, disposition, and government of the Philippines." It also provides, however, for the evacuation by Spain of the only important city, fortified place, and adequate bay and harbor in the islands, and for their occupation by the United States. In other words, the United States, as victors in the war, practically take possession, with the assent of the defeated Government, of the key to the Philippine group. Whatever modification of this arrangement may be made will be in the nature of concessions by the United States. Not only is Spain, as the result of her defeat, generally incapacitated to dictate terms, but she specifically surrenders all means of disputing by force the control of the islands.

This does not imply that our Government will make indefinite use of the advantage given by the fortunes of war. It means only that we have taken ample security that whatever policy we may finally decide upon can be carried out with freedom and according to our judgment. It is our clear duty to make such provision as we can for a stable, just, and orderly government of the islands, for our own advantage, for the protection of the present population, and, still more, to secure the development of the region and its opening to the influences of modern civilization. What that provision can be and should be is a large question, and will tax the ability and sagacity of the statesmen to whom its solution is to be entrusted.

Once the McKinley administration and Spain reached an agreement over the conditions of the treaty in early December, it was handed over to Congress for ratification. Rather than debating the conditions of the treaty in open session, the Senate conducted its debates in closed sessions. This meant that neither the public nor the press knew what was actually being said on the Senate floor and could not, therefore, form an opinion on the arguments being made. Several anti-imperialist senators objected to this, and their cry was quickly taken up by the press. For newspapers, this was not just the principle that the Senate should be providing information about all sides of the debate; this was a First Amendment issue of freedom of the press. In the following editorial, the New York World *takes up the demand for open debate. Here, it reiterates the fundamental democratic principle that a free press, open access to information, and an informed citizenry are essential to self-government.*

New York World, 12 December 1898

THROW THE DOORS OPEN

Senators Hoar, Hale and Caffery will lead the Senate opposition to the ratification of a treaty that commits the country to a policy of expansion and imperialism.

They insist that this whole matter shall be discussed in open session of the Senate. They rightly contend that so radical a change in the national policy and practice should not be "made in the dark." They justly say that for the information and enlightenment and education of the public the arguments that are to be made for and against the proposed policy ought to be heard through the newspapers by all the people. They demand an "open door" of discussion, so that the public may hear and consider the arguments, so that the press may comment upon and supplement them, and so that the people may sit as a court of last resort upon this question.

It is the people's right to decide.

Publicity! Publicity! Publicity! That is the watchword of self-government. Throw open the doors! Let nothing be done in the dark!

SUPPORTING ANNEXATION

As the politicians debated the future of the Philippines, some newspapers saw no need for deep thought over the matter and considered the annexa-

tion of the Philippines to be a logical resolution. The Chicago Tribune, *which during this period published on its editorial page a picture of the American flag under the slogan "One Flag, One Cause, One Country," saw this as a historic moment in which the nation was entering upon its "imperial career." In the following editorial, the jingoistic* Tribune *states its impatience with "mugwumps" and "Bryanites"—party independents who would vote their own conscience rather than tow the party line. The* Tribune *does not mince words in its basic argument for annexation—"to the victor go the spoils."*

Chicago Tribune, 12 August 1898

THE WAR IS OVER

The Spanish Cabinet, after due consideration of the terms of the peace protocol, yesterday decided to accept it.... Virtually it was an ultimatum. It recognized none of Spain's attempts at evasion or diplomatic trickery, but went straight to the point, showing the superiority of "shirt-sleeve" diplomacy, and forced the usually wily, tricky Spaniards to take action....

The government is now in a position to proceed to the negotiations of terms of peace, and the next step will be the appointment of peace commissioners, who, in compliment to the French government, will meet in Paris. Under the protocol which Spain has accepted Porto [*sic*] Rico will be ceded to the United States, Cuba will be freed, and Spain at the earliest practicable day will evacuate all its West Indian possessions.... Manila Bay, with the city and surrounding territory, will be retained by the United States, and the future government of the Philippine Islands will be determined by the commission. There is nothing in the latest proposition which debars the United States from retaining the whole of the islands, and if the commissioners are live Americans and not mugwumps or Bryanites, and if they are in sympathy with the spirit of the American people, they will decide that this country shall permanently hold the territory which it has cost so much to take. The United States is the victor in this war and it has just the same right to hold the Philippines that it has to hold Cuba and Porto [*sic*] Rico. No permanent peace can be made which is not based upon their possession. To give these islands back to Spain or to leave them in such a condition that they become the property of other nations would be a violation of the national honor and a cowardly shirking of responsibility....

The war has been shorter than even the most sanguine anticipated. Since April 21, the date fixed by Congress as the beginning of the struggle, Porto [*sic*] Rico, Cuba, the Ladrones, and the Philippines have passed into our possession, two Spanish fleets have been destroyed, one Spanish army has been captured, and in every engagement the enemy has been defeated in the face sometimes of overwhelming obstacles. The valor, endurance, skill, and discipline of American soldiers have been fairly tested, and they have compelled the admiration of the foreign military observers. The navy has covered itself with glory and challenged the plaudits of the whole world. In these few weeks the United States has taken position as one of the strong naval nations and a military power which must hereafter be taken into account in world movements. The country has entered upon its imperial career. The Maine has been remembered. Spain will never forget it.

Another newspaper to support annexation was the San Francisco Chronicle. *In this article, published as Democrats were maneuvering to frame a position regarding expansionism on their party platform, the* Chronicle *equates expansionism with inevitability, patriotism, and the American spirit. In this paean to Manifest Destiny, the West Coast paper evokes the spirit of "virile yeomanry" espoused by presidents Thomas Jefferson and Andrew Jackson.*

San Francisco Chronicle, 12 August 1898

DEMOCRACY AND EXPANSION

It does not now look as if the Democracy [Democratic Party] would agree upon the general anti-annexation platform which Bryan, Jones and Bailey are urging it to adopt. Many Democrats and perhaps some Democratic organizations cling to the hermit policy of Cleveland, but the influence of earlier and better Democratic traditions sways the mass of the party. Besides, the history of Democratic efforts to stem the tide of advancing national sentiment does not encourage the wiser leaders to oppose the vastly popular doctrine of a Greater America. It is politic as well as patriotic in this case to go with the flood.

But few state conventions of either party have as yet passed upon what Bryan is pleased to call "imperialism," but those that have left but a meager heritage of comfort to the contractionists....

Mr. Bailey's plea [to the Texas State Democratic Convention] that no territory should be admitted to the Union which will necessitate an increase of the standing army would have excluded Texas and California from the sisterhood of states. No doubt the Texans argued as did the American of 1846 that it is better to have a few more regiments of our own to hold strategic outposts than to have them occupied by the armies of a possible enemy. A standing army is an undoubted evil, but when it comes to one at our own doors we had better control it instead of leaving the matter to a rival power or to a commerce-wrecking and trade-smashing junta of guerrillas....

While bloodless pedagogues of the Mugwump stripe are remembering Sumner and Cleveland, the virile yeomanry of the Democratic party are thinking of Jefferson and Jackson. They do not object to the spread of American civilization and the increase of American strength and prosperity.... Nor do they doubt the wisdom of acquiring outposts and trade preserves. It is this sentiment which leaders of the Bryan and Bailey sort...have tried in vain to contend with, and which is bound in the long run to force them to the rear of the column. Whatever they may undertake they cannot, we believe, induce their party to make even a brief trial of strength against manifest destiny.

A good number of the American public accepted reductive arguments that presented the Philippine situation in terms of either-or solutions and left no room for recognition of the Filipinos as capable of self-determination. This misleading dichotomy was aptly captured by the Chicago Tribune *in a brief editorial as Congress prepared to ratify the treaty in December. The editorial also captures the evangelical and progressive spirit expressed in many of the arguments for the so-called salvation of the Philippines.*

Chicago Tribune, 8 December 1898

Save the Philippines for Civilization

To give these islands up to barbarism, into which they would revert if left to themselves, or to give them up to Spain to be harried, or even to give them over to some European power, to please Senator Hoar [who opposed annexation], is something the American people will not tolerate.

OPPOSING ANNEXATION

The New York World, *which had been criticized for urging the country into war with its yellow tactics, showed remarkable restraint in its response to the conditions of the protocol. From the beginning, it had supported war against Spain as a fight for freedom and democracy in Cuba. When the war ended in August, the* World *hailed America's victory, declaring, "It is a peace with honor, because it secures its sole object on our part—freedom for the oppressed [in Cuba].... The settlement extends the area and the blessings of freedom, rids this hemisphere of the last remnant of tyranny and oppression, enlarges the boundaries, and greatly enhances the prestige, power and influence of the United States."[1] The* World *quickly changed its tune, however, as the annexation of the Philippines became a prominent part of the negotiations in Paris. When those opposed to annexation formed the Anti-Imperialist League, the* World *gave members like industrialist Andrew Carnegie, reformer Jane Addams, author Mark Twain, and labor leader Samuel Gompers generous coverage, frequently boxing articles about them and reproducing letters written by them. It also gave prominent coverage to others opposed to imperialism and the annexation of the Philippines, such as Senators George Hoar and George Vest, former presidential candidate William Jennings Bryan, and former Secretary of State John Sherman. The following page-one article captures some of the major arguments of the anti-imperialists. Based on a letter by Sherman, the arguments made against imperialism are largely pragmatic and smack of more than a little cultural ethnocentrism.*

New York World, 8 December 1898

JOHN SHERMAN SAYS REJECT THE TREATY

Declares Annexation of Philippines Would Be Degrading to Present States

LET THE ISLANDS BE FREE

To Hold Them as Conquered Territories a Departure from Our Established Policy

UNITED STATES AND WEST INDIES

No Entangling Alliances, but Needed Coaling Stations and Facilities for Our Commerce

(Special to The World)

BOSTON, Dec. 7—A letter from John Sherman, ex-Secretary of State, taking strong ground against the annexation of the Philippine Islands, was read at a meeting of the Executive Committee of the Anti-Imperialistic League to-day.

Bishop Potter and James C. Carter, of New York, were added to the list of vice-presidents of the league.

Mr. Sherman's letter is a long one. In part, he said:

"I concur with you in opposition to the acquisition of the Philippines as a part of the United States.

"The harsh and cruel despotism of Spain over the inhabitants of Cuba fully justified the intervention of the United States to drive out Spanish soldiers from that island. This has been my desire for thirty years and more.

"No Entangling Alliance"

"Here the Spanish war ought to have ended. Cuba will be free and will have the hearty support of the United States. The other islands of the Caribbean Sea are wisely governed by foreign powers. The friendly influence and example of a great nation like the United States will always be of value to these islands. Our Government should make no entangling alliance with any of them, but it can easily obtain from them coaling stations and other facilities for our commerce.

"This, I believe was the desire of the President, but the eager greed of some of our people to extend our territories to remote parts of the earth has apparently led him to acquiesce in the seizure of the Philippine Islands on the opposite side of the globe in the tropical zone, near the equator.

"These islands are said to contain ten million people, composed of Malays, Japanese, Chinese, and of many nations and tribes. They are now at war with the Spaniards, and will be at war with us if we undertake to govern them. It will be necessary to maintain an army and a fleet to hold them in subjection.

Increasing the Public Debt

"What good can come of such an acquisition? We already feel the evil result of our threats to occupy and hold the islands. Our debt is already on the increase at a time when we had a reasonable hope for its full payment.

"The United States now embraces the better part of a great continent in a compact form with a population of seventy million people speaking the same language, increasing annually nearly 3 percent, with ample territory for several million more.

"Our flag is the token of friendship wherever it is unfolded. Why then should we seek to acquire and govern the Philippine Islands?

Annexation Degrading to Us

"Will we allow them to be represented in Congress? Will we form them into States? The general voice will be against either proposition.

"There are special objections to the acquisition of the Philippine Islands by the United States. The great body of the inhabitants do not speak our language and are inferior in intelligence and education to any part of the people of Europe or of the American Continent. To annex them as States in the Union would be to degrade all the States. To hold them as conquered territories would be a departure from the established policy of the United States. Nor is it certain if we pay Spain $20,000,000 for her disputed title to the Philippines that we can get peaceful possession.

"The geography of the islands alone should condemn their acquisition by the United States. They number 1,500 or more and lie between the fifth and twentieth degrees of north latitude, a latitude that begets sloth and feebleness, and has never in the history of the world produced a strong, virile people or nation.

Give the Islands Independence

"My hope is that the Senate of the United States will reject the treaty and leave the people of the Philippine islands free from the shackles of Spain and the distant domination of the United States.

"I sympathize with [Philippine insurgent leader Emilio] Aguinaldo in his ambition to found a republic in the China Sea near the equator, and hope he may become the Washington of a new nation, absolutely free from European and American influence."

More than five hundred petitions protesting against an imperialistic policy regarding Spain's conquered possessions have been received, each petition bearing many signatures, and it was decided to-day to begin immediately the presentation of the petitions to the Senate.

One of the anti-imperialist arguments was that although the United States had conquered Spain, it had not conquered the Philippine people and had no right to treat them as chattel. Anti-imperialists argued that since the Filipinos had already been attempting a revolution against the Spanish, it would be logical to assist them in obtaining that independence rather than annexing them. In the following brief editorial comment, the Louisville Post *contrasts the situation of the Filipinos to that of the American colonists at the conclusion of the Revolutionary War.*

Louisville Post, 7 December 1898

Buying People Like Merchandise

In their unwillingness to be sold to the United States, the Filipinos must feel as George Washington and his followers would have felt if France had claimed the right to govern this country after the Revolutionary War. After all, it appears that we have agreed to pay $20,000,000 to Spain for a rebellion.

The Monroe Doctrine, first put into words in 1823 and then reinterpreted in 1845 and every decade thereafter, had established the principle that the affairs of the New World should be left to those people who had by that time settled and supposedly civilized it. While this effectively barred European nations from further colonizing North, Central, and South America, it at the same time established a de facto sway of influence by the United States in the Americas. As expansionists eyed territories to the west of the continental United States, anti-imperialists argued that the United States should stay within her own hemisphere. She should stay out of the Pacific, even though she had already ventured into it with the overthrow of the Hawaiian monarchy in 1892 and then the annexation of Hawaii earlier that year. In this brief editorial comment, the San Francisco Call *warns that by annexing the Philippines, the United States would undermine her own position forbidding European excursions into the Americas.*

San Francisco Call, 7 December 1898

Abandoning the Monroe Doctrine

The purchase of the Philippines, if that folly be ratified by the Senate, will be the final, formal, and official abandonment of the Monroe Doctrine by the United States. It is the consummation of an act of aggression against a European state, concluded outside of our own hemisphere. Having broken out of our own hemisphere we can no longer oppose the breaking into it by any power that has strength.

The Filipinos' desire for independence served as a strong argument for anti-imperialists who opposed annexation. One option that did not fit the either-or mold that limited the possibilities to either complete independence or annexation was to make the Philippines a protectorate. This would be a temporary measure to remain in effect only as long as the island nation needed it. This solution was attractive to some, for it would let the United States maintain her principles as a democratic nation that had gone into the war only to protect the oppressed. In the following news story, the New York Times *presents the position of the Filipino leader, someone who was often ignored in the debate regarding the islands' future.*

New York Times, 8 December 1898

FUTURE OF THE PHILIPPINES

Filipinos Desire Independence with This Country's Protectorate

WANT FREEDOM FIRST OF ALL

Aguinaldo And His Followers Realize that the Islands May Be a Prey of Other Nations

MANILA, Dec. 7—The native press continues to advocate independence and a reimbursement to the United States Government of the amount to be paid to Spain for the Philippines. It insists that the Filipinos have aided the Americans solely because they believed they were fighting for independence. The paper quotes liberally from President McKinley's last speech in Chicago to support its contention that the Americans are pledged to give the Filipinos independence.

Chief Aguinaldo and his principal advisors fully recognize the importance of a strong protectorate in some form. One of the latter has even ventured the assertion that if the Filipinos were granted independence, in accordance with the demand of the leaders, the United States would be immediately asked to establish a protectorate, as otherwise the Philippines must sooner or later become prey of a less liberal-minded country.

Despite the arguments for Philippine independence or the establishment of a protectorate, President McKinley committed the United States to the annexation of the Philippines in the final version of the treaty. According to the New York Times, *McKinley failed in his role as leader of the nation, for he had failed to listen to public opinion, which opposed this move. Above all, according to the* Times, *the president failed to make his case to the public in such a way as to bring about consensus.*

New York Times, 9 December 1898

TELL THE PEOPLE

Without a word to the people or the slightest attempt to explain and justify his policy, the President has committed the country to the policy of expansion and has contracted an obligation to pay twenty million dollars. The Peace Committee at Paris were his agents, they did what he bade them to do. It is to him that the people look for some announcement of what he has done and of the reasons which have prompted him to spend this money and add to their domain. He is silent. He treats them as if the acquisition of the Philippines were none of their business. We think he has made a serious mistake. The taking over of this remote territory and our appearance among the nations of the earth as a colony-holding power are changes of momentous importance in our national policy. The raising of our flag over millions of aliens who are to be governed by us without their consent is a sudden and wide departure from the fundamental principles and established traditions of the Republic. A great part of our people, including many of the wisest, look with grave misgivings on these new imperial fashions. Some of the leading men of the President's own party condemn the policy to which we stand committed by his act. The contract to pay twenty millions to Spain is not to be passed lightly by even in these times of great expenditures. It is the people's money he is spending—the President must not forget that.

President McKinley would have been wise to devote a great part if not the whole of his message to the new policy. These are stirring days of great events, but he gives us a perfectly humdrum message. The people do not care for a recital of the perfectly well-remembered events of the Spanish war; they turn with impatience from a rehash of department reports. History is making before their eyes, but their servant who is making it with their money, renders no account of his work. It cannot be urged in defense of the President that the public interest would have suffered or that the success of the diplomatic negotiations would have been put in jeopardy by an official revelation of our policy. The whole world knows it. The President's Peace Commissioners at Paris have given to the press practically a full report of all their important proceedings. We knew weeks ago that we were to take the Philippines. We knew that we were to pay Spain twenty million dollars. Why did not the President tell us his reasons for taking the islands, and for what we are to spend the twenty millions?

We hope President McKinley will presently repair this omission by sending to Congress a special message on imperialism. The people want to know what he has to say for his policy. They want to know what reason he can show for adding $20,000,000 to the heavy cost of the war. The treaty will go to the Senate for discussion in secret session. The President ought not to work in the dark. He should take the people into his confidence to the extent of discussing their own affairs with them.

The Treaty of Paris was ratified by the Senate by a narrow margin of 57 to 27—just one vote more than the necessary two-thirds and was signed December 10. This act formalized the United States's abandonment of its former official policy of isolationism and set it formally on the path to becoming a world power it was to pursue for the next century. In the following editorial, the New York World *expresses dark forebodings of what this act will signal for the nation's future.*

New York World, 11 December 1898

THE TREATY AND THE PEOPLE

The treaty of peace with Spain was signed last night at Paris. The American Commissioners will sail home on Saturday next, bringing the document with them. No treaty in the past fifty years has wrought such a change as this will make in the political geography of the globe, or has been fraught with ultimate consequences so important to the race and to the cause of free government.

The treaty alienates from Spain and puts in the possession or under the protection of the United States more than 2,000 islands with nearly 200,000 square miles of territory and 10,000,000 of inhabitants. It makes changes in the map of the world as it has stood for hundreds of years. It will, if carried to its logical length, effect changes in the fundamental principles and the traditional system of our Government such as those who founded and those who have developed it into the greatest power on earth never dreamed of.

It is likewise the first treaty in the history of the world, so far as we are aware, which not only does not exact one cent for indemnity to the victors—who spent $200,000,000 in the war—but which pledges $20,000,000 to the vanquished for territory which they could not have retained and possession of which they are not asked to guarantee.

Equally remarkable is the treaty for the fact that it contains, as the result of a war undertaken in behalf of freedom and independence for an oppressed colony of Spain, a title to the sovereignty, the land, and the people of the Philippine group, with their 8,000,000 inhabitants, on the other side of the globe. This ends a war for freedom with a peace of subjugation. We set out to free the Cubans. We end by taking Spain's place as the master of the Filipinos.

In sending this extraordinary treaty to the Senate it is to be presumed that President McKinley will make good the omission in his message and give to the people who must pay the bills and assume the burdens of these new ventures his reasons for "expansion" and his plan, if he has any, for the disposition of government of the new possessions.

QUESTIONS

1. Why did so much of the debate about the annexation of the Philippines revolve around the concepts of freedom and democracy, tyranny and oppression? Why would these concepts be particularly resonant for American newspapers?
2. At least two of the newspapers cited in this chapter compared the Philippine insurgency to the American Revolution. What are the names, words, and phrases used to evoke this comparison? Do you think this was an effective rhetorical device to influence public opinion at that time? Would it be as effective today?
3. What were some of the strategies (rhetorical, editorial, typographical, and journalistic) used by the newspapers cited in this chapter to support or promote one side or another in the debate?
4. The *New York World* was criticized by many contemporary newspapers for being a yellow journal that sensationalized events and partly respon-

sible for pushing America into the war with Spain. Yet it opposed annexing the Philippines at the end of the war. Why does this seem contradictory? What arguments can you use to explain why it would not be contradictory?

5. Many of the terms and phrases used to describe the Filipinos (and the Spanish) in the stories and editorials reveal cultural ethnocentrism and racial and ethnic stereotyping. What are some of these words and phrases? What attitudes do they reveal? How might these stereotypes have served as persuasive devices? How might they have undermined the explicit arguments being made regarding democracy and freedom?

NOTE

1. "Peace with Freedom," *New York World*, 13 August 1898, p. 6.

CHAPTER 9

The Turn of the Century Brings Hopes and Fears

The arrival of the twentieth century served as a marker for people the world over, but particularly so for Americans, whose nation had grown from infancy to adulthood in the span of the last one hundred years. They greeted the twentieth century with a combination of optimism and trepidation. Looking back on the changes that had occurred during the nineteenth century and how they had affected every aspect of life, they attempted to predict what developments they could expect in the future and how those would affect life as they knew it.

The nineteenth century had been a period of massive change during which geographic, political, social, economic, and technological developments had affected every American citizen and every aspect of life. The nation had grown from a cluster of 16 states crowded between the Atlantic Coast and the Alleghenies to a patchwork of states and territories that stretched to the Pacific. Its influence had spilled over its own shores to envelop Hawaii, the Philippines, and Guam in the Pacific and Puerto Rico in the Caribbean.

The small-town rural and commercial economy favored by Thomas Jefferson at the close of the eighteenth century had been transformed by the Industrial Revolution so that by 1900, the nation was largely driven by an urban-industrial economy. The country's resources—land, timber, coal, iron ore, water—seemed limitless and allowed for expansion and development, providing work for the many and vast wealth for a few. Science and technology had brought developments in transportation so that travelers could travel coast-to-coast by train in less than a week. Developments in communication, including the telegraph, the telephone, photography, and motion pictures, allowed the instant transmission of vast amounts of information in a variety of formats over great distances. Advances in medicine were curing diseases and lengthening the average life span. The end of the nineteenth century and the beginning of the twentieth fell in the middle of the Progressive Era, and true to the ideology of the period, many of these developments were lauded as the positive and inevitable progress of civilization.

Some of these developments, however, had a dark side. The expansion of the United States had decimated the Native American peoples and subjugated the Hawaiians and Filipinos. As Americans looked toward the twentieth century, some feared that imperialism and expansionism would undermine the essential nature of American democratic institutions. Others feared that the country's transformation from a rural-agricultural to an

Father Time—"My! My! But it looks more like 1900 B. C."

"Father Time—"My! My! But it looks more like 1900 B.C.," *New York World,* **1 January 1900, p. 6.** *At the turn of the century, many praised the scientific, economic, and political advances of the nineteenth century and predicted a future of peace and prosperity. The* New York World, *however, was a bit more skeptical as it considered the various wars and revolutions going on in all parts of the globe. In this cartoon, the anti-imperialist* World *depicts two wars of oppression going on as the new century dawned—the oppression of the Philippine revolution by American business interests and the suppression of the Boers in South Africa by the British. Both wars were being fought in the name of progress.*

urban-industrial society would destroy the traditional democratic and participatory nature of the citizenry. Resources that had appeared limitless one hundred years earlier were now being decimated without provision for their replacement. Some asked if there would be enough water, lumber, and land for everyone in another 50 years. As for science and technology, people saw danger there, also. Life-improving inventions were all well and good, but some scientists were devoting their energies to inventions of destruction. Technology did not only provide faster trains, it also produced more lethal weapons to be used in the destruction of life.

As the new century approached, these were some of the issues being debated as Americans tried to define who they were and where they were going. The significance of the transition from the nineteenth to the twentieth century became the topic of countless books, lectures, and sermons. Naturally, it also became the topic of discussion in newspapers, which published a variety of news stories and editorials devoted to the topic. Many also published turn-of-the-century supplements that provided the space for a range of commentators to expound their views.

Ironically, one of the first issues to be dealt with was exactly *when* the twentieth century was to begin—January 1, 1900, or January 1, 1901. This was not a new debate, and, in fact, had occurred at the turn of the previous century. Nevertheless, many newspapers debated the point and, in true Progressive Era fashion, relied on a combination of historical precedent, religious authority, and scientific deduction to pinpoint the exact moment the new century was to begin. Naturally, they reached different conclusions.

Once the debate of *when* was over, newspapers devoted themselves to the twofold task of analyzing the significance of the nineteenth century and predicting what was to come in the twentieth. They published articles, columns, and editorials—not only by their own writers, but also by social, religious, reform, political, military, scientific, educational, and financial leaders—that summarized past developments and predicted what the future might hold. The majority of these looked at the developments of the past century as triumphs over political tyranny, social unrest, ignorance, poverty, and disease. Others, however, were more skeptical and even critical. They feared the direction mankind was headed and warned against a possible future of overpopulation, warfare, class conflict, and loss of traditional comforts and values. Some even used the turn of the century as an occasion to grind a particular axe, such as their opposition to the McKinley administration or the nation's recent emergence as an imperialist power. Because so many issues and so many writers with varying viewpoints were involved in discussion of the turn of the century, these conflicting views sometimes appeared in the same newspaper over a period of time or even side by side on the same day.

The readings in this chapter are organized in two sections. The first contains editorials and columns that are basically optimistic. These hail the nineteenth century as one of unrivaled progress and enlightenment and predict that such progress will continue in the twentieth century. The second section contains selections that are more critical or skeptical of mankind's supposed progress. Some of these selections criticize specific developments or conditions; others simply express a foreboding that progress can in some cases be negative or even harmful.

OPTIMISTIC VIEWS OF THE NINETEENTH AND COMING CENTURIES

Many newspapers chose to enumerate the many accomplishments and developments of the nineteenth century as a way of commemorating the turn of the century. The New York Times *chose to do this on the last day of 1899 in a full-page editorial in which it described the advance of freedom around the world, the great advances in scientific discovery, the expansion of the United States and its international influence, and the growth of the national wealth. Since the editorial faithfully enumerates the many wars, uprisings, and revolutions of the century, it might well have called this "the Bloody Century." Instead, the* Times *frames these conflicts almost as a necessary means to an end—the triumph of progress, civilization, popular or representative rule, and Protestantism over despotism, tyranny, and superstition. Here are excerpts of this lengthy interpretation of the history of the nineteenth century, which ends with a quote from Tennyson's "Locksley Hall."*

New York Times, 31 December 1899

THE NINETEENTH CENTURY

Tomorrow we enter upon the last year of a century that is marked by greater progress in all that pertains to the material well-being and enlightenment of mankind than all the previous history of the race; and the political, social, and moral advancement has hardly been less striking.

The century opened with all Europe in a state of war, and after the delusive and short-lived peace of Amiens (1802), Napoleon as First Consul and then as Emperor of France, was for thirteen years in almost continual conflict with the great powers....

After the Napoleonic disturbances of boundaries in Europe the Congress of Vienna, in which Russia, Austria, Prussia, and England had the prevailing voice, undertook to reconstruct the nations nearly upon their old lines and to restore the ancient forms and methods of government.... But the subject peoples, who had borne the cost and suffering of twenty-five years of conflict were no longer submissive to the old order of things. The lessons of American independence, the French Revolution, and Napoleon's subversion of ancient traditions were bearing fruit, and a struggle began for constitutional liberty and representative government.... [Describes various revolutions that succeeded in overthrowing foreign or tyrannical powers and establishing popular rule, including those in Argentina, Mexico, Brazil, Greece, Italy, and Egypt.]

Other wars in the last half of the century have been waged mainly to force civilization forward. The revolt of the Christian provinces against the cruel oppression of Turkey brought on the conflict between Russia and that nation in 1857.... England's contests in India, and with the fierce peoples beyond its borders had their serious episodes.... After the fierce battles by which the consequent insurrections were quelled, the Government of India was for the first time placed under the British Crown direct.

The history of the United States since the early years of the century has consisted mainly of territorial expansion, industrial and commercial development, and the settlement by political agitation and the conflict of arms of the problems entailed upon the Republic by the heritage of slavery.... When Lincoln was elected in 1860, and the ordinances of secession were adopted, the passions of the people were wrought to such a pitch that only war and the destruction of slavery could save the Union. When the Republic had passed through that fiery ordeal her face was set in a new direction. The nation was reconstructed with new guarantees of freedom and equal rights, and with new difficulties to overcome. They are not all surmounted yet, but the movement has been steadily forward....

But what characterizes the nineteenth century more than all else is the vast strides in scientific discovery and the application of the forces of nature to the service of man. The wave theory of light, the nebular hypothesis, and the discovery of spectrum analysis have made new revelations in the heavens and exalted our conceptions of time and space....

Attending the wonderful advance in the use of labor-saving and product-multiplying machinery and in the means of transportation and interchange, has been the growth of corporations, by which the productive power of capital has been massed, and the development of a vast system of credit and banking whereby 95 per cent of the exchanges is effected without the use of money, although the volume of currency in use has enormously increased. The creation of wealth during the present century has been prodigious and goes on with accelerating pace, and in spite of complaints of unfair distribution, its benefits are irresistibly diffused, so that the condition of the mass of the people is immensely improved and continually improving. There is much to do, but the forces that enlighten and elevate humanity have gained tremendous power in the century and are dispelling ignorance, degradation, and misery as never before.

We step upon the threshold of 1900, which leads to the new century, facing a still brighter dawn for human civilization. Through agitation and conflict European nations are working toward an ultimate harmony of interests and purposes, and bringing awakening Asia into the sweeping current of progress. Light has been let into the "Dark Continent" beyond the ancient borders and is rapidly spreading. America is facing westward and beginning to take its part in carrying the regenerating forces of popular government to the uttermost parts of the earth. Notwithstanding the bloody conflicts through which some of the steps of progress must still be made, the "vision of the world" grows clearer toward the time when—

> The war-drum throbbed no longer, and the
>   battle-flags were furled
> In the parliament of man, the federation of
>   the world.
> There the common sense of most shall hold
>   a fretful realm in awe.
> And the friendly earth shall slumber, lapt in
>   universal law.

Some parts of the nation had not fared so well during the nineteenth century, specifically the South, which was still struggling at the turn of the century to recover from the devastations of the Civil War. The Atlanta Constitution, *under the leadership of managing editor Henry Grady in the 1880s, had sought to create a "New South." In its role as advocate for the New South, the* Constitution *promoted industrial development in the southern states, particularly Georgia, and sought to dispel the South's image as a provincial and undeveloped region, which was widely held in the North. Some of these themes are picked up in the* Constitution *'s tribute to the nineteenth century, published in the last days of 1900, but the article also reveals a certain provincialism in the author's worldview. The article, which covers three-quarters of a page, begins with the unabashed acclaim of the white man's domination over much of the globe and the United States's growth in international influence. Later in the article, when the author extols the benefits of equality, he completely ignores the prevailing reality of blacks in the South and women and people of color throughout the country. When he praises the effects of industrial organization, he also ignores the many conflicts that had erupted between labor and management throughout the latter half of the century.*

Atlanta Constitution, 30 December 1900

George Torr: 1800–1900
A REVIEW OF ONE HUNDRED YEARS OF PROGRESS

Whatever the future may bring, the nineteenth century must be looked upon as a turning point in the history of the world. In material achievement it has surpassed every century that preceded it; it has been an age of scientific investigation and discovery, followed at once by practical applications to the uses of man; an age of marvelous mechanical inventions, which have completely changed the habits as they have added immensely to the powers of mankind; an age of unparalleled expansion in territory and increase in numbers for the white races which have been the bearers of civilization. The temperate regions of the globe, on the American continent, in Australia and New Zealand, in southern Africa, in northern Asia, save only in the extreme east, are all in the white man's hands, and all, too, in his sole possession, for the sparse native population has everywhere died away at his approach. He alone has the land on which to multiply and divide, and science may yet give him the power to master the climate of the tropical regions he has seized on.

In this new conquest of the world the first and most marked factor has been the growth and development of the United States of America, the spread of its free institutions and their reaction on the political system of western Europe. The young confederacy with its 5,000,000 inhabitants between the Alleganies [*sic*] and the sea, shut off from the Gulf of Mexico, and with the Mississippi for its western boundary, has become in a hundred years a compact nation of 76,000,000 souls, stretching from ocean to ocean, equal in strength and resources to any European power, with every prospect of becoming within a measurable time equal to all Europe combined. The growth has been rapid, steady and unchecked. In the half century of bondage to absolute governments in which the greater part of Europe was held for half the century, the prosperous existence of the American republic, the sole example of peaceful government by a free people, served to keep alive the hope of liberty in the old world.

GROWTH AND INFLUENCE OF THE UNITED STATES IN THE CENTURY

The frame of government devised to hold together weak and disjointed colonies proved adequate for all the needs of a great nation. It became impossible to keep out the liberties demonstrated to be beneficial, and now all western Europe enjoys in substance representative government, freedom of speech, freedom of the press, equality before the law, freedom to migrate, public education, religious toleration, popular suffrage and the right for every one to pursue any suitable calling, regardless of class or sex. None of its hereditary rulers can regard his [*sic*] power seriously as derived from divine right, but must base it on the will of the people and the observance of a constitution....

IMPROVED CONDITIONS OF LIFE FOR RICH AND POOR ALIKE

A remarkable result of the flood of inventions [described in previous section] on social life has been the establishment of practical equality among men. It was inevitable that their products or their effects should become common and within the reach of all. The average of welfare and of comfort throughout the civilized world is incomparably higher than in any earlier century, and the improvement consists mainly in what has been added to the power of each individual. Little distinction between persons is possible in the use of rapid transportation, of abundant and cheap clothing or fuel or food, of public and private sanitary arrangements, of books, of the discoveries of medical science, and so on. It is an equality that has been made by raising the weaker, not by lowering the stronger. An equally noticeable result is the extraordinary development of organization among large bodies of men, and the spirit of discipline, without which it would be impossible to carry on any large industrial undertaking. The working of a railway depends as much on every employee doing his allotted task at the right moment as it does on the action of every piece in the mechanism of the locomotive. Men work together for a common purpose as they never did before.

The optimists would not hear some of the gloomy doubts expressed by less enthusiastic commentators. In fact, to the optimist, doubt and gloom were distinctly un-American, for optimism and the can-do spirit were an integral part of the American character. In the following editorial, the San Francisco Chronicle, *which represented not only this can-do American spirit, but the unbridled energy of the American West, greeted the new century with high hopes. The editorial begins with a brief reference to the foolishness of the controversy over the exact year in which the new century was to begin (1900 or 1901), then moves on to dismiss the fears of the pessimists before finally addressing the future.*

San Francisco Chronicle, 1 January 1901

THE NEW CENTURY

We begin the new century every day and never think of it, but once in a hundred years those living at the time make much of the fact that the earth has completed a particular century whose number is expressed in even hun-

dreds, reckoning from a date in the remote past which is not so definitely settled as to be beyond controversy, and the habit has become fixed, if that can
be called a habit which no one can do but once and multitudes can never do
at all. That we reckon and celebrate by cycles of 100, instead of 144, 49, or
some other number of years, is doubtless due to the invention of the Arabic
system of numerical notation, which makes 10 and its multiples the most
convenient divisors of time. The year is as natural a division of time as the
day, for both are based on natural phenomena, while the century is a purely
arbitrary cycle whose close we celebrate from convention, and because there
are always uneasy souls who must celebrate something. The beginning of the
New Year is a joyous occasion. We can be exhilarated for a few hours by the
idea that we shall really keep the good resolutions which we have made, and
when our friends wish us a "Happy New Year" we can cheerily respond with
the wish for "many returns," and all in good faith, not doubting that we at
least shall all be together again a year hence; but no one since the days of
Methusaleh would think of wishing his friends a "happy new century."

Roughly and not very accurately we are accustomed to think of certain
characteristics as attaching to each century of the past, and it is natural that
standing upon the threshold of the twentieth century, we should seek to
peer into the darkness of the inclosure [*sic*] before us, and which we must
enter whether we will or no, to ascertain what our footing and environment
will be, and whether, upon the whole, it is to be a comfortable century. We
see little, and it may be as well that we cannot see. The pessimist is very sure
that we should not like what is before us if we could see it. Lowell—usually
pessimistic—gives a gloomy touch to things, both past and future, when
he says:

No mortal ever dreams
That the scant isthmus he encamps upon
Between two oceans, one, the Stormy, passed
And one, the Peaceful, yet to venture on,
Has been the future whereto prophets yearned
For the fulfillment of earth's cheated hope,
Shall be that past which nevertheless poets moan
As the last opportunity of song.

But there is nothing in history to justify gloomy views of the future. On
the contrary, the story of the race is of constant uprising through strenuous
endeavor to better things. There is no period of the past to which any man
who knows the past would willingly be set back. It is not likely that there
will be any period in the future which will not bring to those who live in that
day more comfort than we now enjoy. Each age has contributed something
to the improvement of human existence, and there is no doubt that the

contribution of the twentieth century will be as valuable as that of any which it has passed. Just now society is moving by the employment of force for commercial ends. This does not seem good, and yet it is certain to increase the aggregate of human comfort. But the marked feature of the age, after all, is the increasing power of the moral sentiment which opposes the employment of force for such purposes. This sentiment is not yet strong enough to control, but it is stronger every day than it was the day before, and, so far as we can see, will in the end prevail. In earlier ages there was scarcely a sign of this sentiment. Its growth through the past hundred years has been the most noticeable and least noticed of social phenomena. It may be that the twentieth century is destined to behold the triumph of Peace. Or it may be some other century.

Some editorials and columns focused on very specific advances, reforms, discoveries, or inventions of the past or predictions for the future. In the following editorial, the New York World *focuses on the abolition of slavery, which it claims has been overlooked in retrospectives of the century. Despite the general positive tone of this editorial, its writer could not resist the temptation to insert a barb against the McKinley administration, which, after it had taken control of Hawaii, permitted there a "modified" form of slavery.*

New York World, 31 December 1899

THE EXTINCTION OF SLAVERY

The crowning glory of the century now drawing to a close, which strangely enough, is not noticed by any of the historians of the epoch, is the fact that it has abolished human slavery.

A hundred years ago the idea that one man might own another and make merchandise of him was everywhere tolerated and almost everywhere sanctioned. Religion itself searched Holy Scripture for justification of the hideous atrocity, and professed to find it.

Even Denmark's decree against this wrong did not take effect till the end of the year 1802, and French legislation did not finally abolish slavery in the colonies until 1818. It was not until 1834 that England decreed emancipation, and not until 1840 that the decree took effect. The ukase of Alexander II abolishing the Russian serf system was proclaimed in 1861, and our own emancipation was not effected until 1865.

To-day the very thought of slavery is discarded and it exists nowhere under the flag of any great civilized nation, except in Salu and in a modified form in Hawaii, under toleration of the great Republic [the United States] that bases its very existence upon the doctrine of the "unalienable right" of every human being to liberty.

For a single century this development of the idea of liberty is achievement enough. It would make the century the greatest in all history if nothing else had been recorded concerning it. It has marked the birth of real and actual civilization, for it is impossible to reconcile the idea of true civilization with the "barbarism of slavery."

Though the blacks had been freed from slavery in 1865 and then granted citizenship and the right to vote after the Civil War, by the turn of the century women had not yet won that right in the majority of the states. In fact, by 1900 they had full suffrage, which meant they could vote in the presidential and all other elections, in only three states (Colorado, Utah, and Idaho) and the territory of Wyoming. One of the most prominent leaders of the woman suffrage movement was Susan B. Anthony, who had been campaigning for the reform for more than 40 years, and whose articles were widely sought for "new century" editions. In the following column published in the Brooklyn Daily Eagle, *she reiterates her frequent argument that women have much to offer society, if only they are given a political voice through the right to vote. Then she expresses her conviction that this will inevitably come about in the twentieth century.*

Brooklyn Daily Eagle, 30 December 1900

Susan B. Anthony: WOMAN TO HAVE THE BALLOT

Final Working Out of the Great Principles of Justice and Equality Will Result in Something Vastly Superior to the Present

The woman of the twentieth century will be the peer of man. In education, in art, in science, in literature. In the home, in the church, the state; everywhere she will be his acknowledged equal, though not identical with him. We cannot begin to see the good of this recognition.

It is impossible to foretell the exact conditions that will exist in the house; but we may be sure that they will be more in accord with enlightened manhood and womanhood than any now known. The children will be better fed and clothed and schooled when the father, together with the mother, remains at home and takes part in their training.

The transition period from absolute subjection inevitably has many crudities, and many mistakes will be made; but we must have faith to believe that the final working out of the great principles of justice and equality into woman's perfect freedom with man will result in something vastly superior to the present. Man himself will be greatly improved when he finds at his own fireside an equal in the person he calls wife.

And this cannot be until she holds in her hand that right preservative of all other rights—the ballot. So the sooner man takes the adjective "male" from all of his creeds, codes and constitutions, and leaves woman to feel her responsibility equally with himself in making and executing all the laws that govern society, the sooner will we begin to reap the harvest of the seed sown in the woman's rights agitation of the nineteenth century.

The Twentieth Century will see man and woman working together to make the world the better for their having lived. All hail to the Twentieth Century.

CRITICISM AND SKEPTICISM TOWARD THE COMING CENTURY

One of the major reasons for criticism of the supposed progress of the nineteenth century and pessimism about what the future might hold was America's emergence toward the end of the century as an imperialist nation. Many prominent figures had formed the Anti-Imperialist League in 1899 in response to the annexation of the Philippines, and one of the best-known members was satirist and former journalist Mark Twain. Mark Twain could always be counted on to make a pithy statement about just about anything. When he was asked to provide a "greeting for the twentieth century," he responded with a cryptic salutation that was quoted in a number of newspapers, including the Springfield *(Massachusetts)* Republican. *Here it is in its entirety.*

Springfield (Massachusetts) *Republican,* 31 December 1900

Mark Twain on the Twentieth Century

I bring you the stately matron named Christendom, returning bedraggled, besmirched and dishonored from pirate raids in Kiaochow, Manchuria, South Africa and the Philippines, with her soul full of meanness, her pocket full of boodle and her mouth full of pious hypocrisies. Give her soap and a towel, but hide the looking glass.

The New York World, *which had also opposed the annexation of the Philippines and the United States's emergence as an imperialist nation, used its twentieth-century supplement to present several views condemning imperialism in the United States as well as in several European nations. A guest article by anti-imperialist Edward Atkinson attempted to tally the cost of America's "criminal aggression" in the Philippines, including the cost of "buying" the islands from Spain, the cost of putting down the revolution (which was not suppressed until 1902), and the eventual cost of "civilizing" the islands inhabitants. Here Atkinson notes the irony that while America had fought the Civil War at great cost to itself to "free our own 'niggers,'" it had fought the Spanish War at even greater monetary cost to enslave the Filipinos. Atkinson's repetitive use of the term "niggers" to describe the Filipinos here is more a form of rhetoric to condemn America's imperialism than a racist term.*

New York World, 31 December 1899

Edward T. Atkinson: COST OF CRIMINAL AGGRESSION TO DATE

It is not possible to set off the exact items of the money cost of the William McKinley war upon the inhabitants of the Philippine Islands. We are obliged to use his name as the title of the war, although he may be merely the puppet worked by the jingoes whose motives are to get big [trade opportunities] out of China. It has been well said by an English writer that "when you scratch a jingo you find a pirate"—an axiom which fits the jingoes of this country as well as those of England, only the English jingoes fight themselves, while our type do the dangerous part by deputy.

One item of the criminal cost of criminal aggression may be named and measured. The representative of the administration bought the Spanish title to the Philippines for $20,000,000.... Our Commissioners are also assumed to have bought eight to ten million "niggers" at about $2 per head. This is a very low price. Mr. McKinley has admitted in the treaty with the Sultan of Sulu that "niggers" are worth $20 a head, and may buy themselves of us at that rate through the agency of the Sultan; but even that rate is too cheap. The common estimate of the number of "niggers" in these islands is 10,000,000. In our effort to enforce our title to them we have already spent more that $20 each, and we have not yet established our claim. Ten million "niggers" at $20 each comes to $200,000,000. We spent that amount last year....

How did Mr. McKinley and the jingoes behind him make such a bad mistake? It cost the North and the South about $1,500 each in cash and property debt to free our own "niggers" in the civil war.... The total, up to final payment of debt and pensions, will come to just over $12,000,000. Liberty has cost that sum of money and 300,000 lives. How much is it costing us to subjugate and deprive 10,000,000 "niggers" of their liberty? How much money? How many lives?

The New York World *was also unhappy with President McKinley, whom the paper characterized alternately as a despot or as a puppet controlled by Wall Street interests. In this brief editorial it contrasted the hopes and potential of the common man standing on the threshold of the new century with the destructive power yielded by the tyrannical McKinley, to whom it refers as "the uncommon man."*

New York World, 1 January 1900

UPON THE THRESHOLD

The last year, let us hope the best year, of the Wonderful Century.

The common man entered The Wonderful Century a slave to ignorance and her grinding, unthinking, uninspiring toil. To-day machinery has taken his place, has emancipated him, has given him the leisure and the opportunity to think, to learn, to free himself, to attain to the stature and erectness of manhood.

The common man is not free, but he is being freed. The heaviest of his shackles have fallen from him, the worst of the obstacles that beset his path have crumbled. To say that he will not go forward, is like saying that there is danger lest a vigorous, clear-headed youth of twenty may in his twenty-first year be compelled to turn back and cut teeth and learn to walk and talk.

In this last year of the Wonderful Century the common man, standing upon the threshold of the twentieth century ought to do a great deal of thinking about himself and about the causes of his present estate. And he ought not to neglect to think also of the uncommon man—the fellow with the "divine commission" to rule and to set his fellow-beings on to murder and rob one another. That uncommon man has been the common man's worst enemy through the ages. Is it quite certain that he is now his friend?

Another cause for pessimism was the political crisis engulfing the nation at the turn of the century. This was a period during which the ideological differences between the two major parties—the Republicans and the Democrats—were deep and wide. In this brief editorial, the New York World *mourns the nation's lack of a leader of the stature of a Thomas Jefferson to mend the rift and bring the nation to consensus. Clearly, in the* World's *opinion, President McKinley does not fit the bill.*

New York World, 1 January 1900

1800–1900

In this country a hundred years ago to-day two political parties were preparing for a "crisis campaign."

The one believed in an aristocratic republic, the other in a democratic republic. The one believed that public officials are rulers, the other that public officials are servants. The one believed in privilege, the other abhorred it.

Through the genius of Jefferson the issue between the two theories was squarely joined and the verdict was clearly rendered.

Today the issue again presents itself. But where is the man?

While most newspapers greeted the invention and diffusion of new technologies from the telephone and electricity to the steamship and airplane with naive enthusiasm, a few were a bit more skeptical about the dangers such innovations could bring about. After all, not all change is automatically good, even though that tended to be the general belief of the Progressive Era. C.M. Skinner, a writer for the Brooklyn Daily Eagle *and a master of irony, took advantage of all the positive prognostications for the future written for the* Eagle*'s twentieth-century supplement and turned them topsy-turvy. He wrote a sort of Rip Van Winkle tale, a fantasy of what it would be like if he were to be put to sleep for a hundred years and then awakened. Here, he first, he summarizes the "accomplishments" of the nineteenth century, not all of which—such as the United States's interventions in the Philippines and the Chinese Boxer Rebellion—he sees as unqualified progress. Then he takes all the predictions made by the contributors to the supplement to produce a frightening vision of the future. His tale is a lengthy one and fills half the front page of the supplement. Here are some excerpts:*

Brooklyn Daily Eagle, 30 December 1900

C.M. Skinner: THINGS WILL BE SO DIFFERENT A HUNDRED YEARS HENCE

WELCOME and goodby! Hail to the new century and long memory to the old! In our short sight no century to come can be as important as the one that is drawing near its end. So let's get a long sight.

This century has surpassed all others in material progress, and a spirit has grown out of it that means more than that. The rights of men have supplanted the rights of man. Schemes for the advancement of the race were never so many and so delightfully impractical as now, and were never studied so solemnly. Civilization was never so rampant, for the civilized are determined that the uncivilized shall share their advantages whether they want to or not. We are putting morality into the Philippine islanders and Chinamen with bullets, and are having a merry time with dwellers in the slums, dragging them up to the stools of repentance, no matter how little they think they may have done to merit the obloquy of the folk in brownstones, or of their consciences.

Future generations will judge us by the material achievements of this century, yet it is the moral advance that counts. Moral advances are insidious, like measles, and are neither understood nor appreciated at the time, whereas there is something definite and to be dated in the invention of the dynamite gun or a quinine pill.

And surely in the matter of guns and pills we have beaten the Romans and several other history makers.... We never quite appreciate periods in which we live. We see them in their true relation when we have outgrown them. And, of course, we must outgrow a lot of things after next Tuesday [January 1]. And how would you like to turn in this evening and awake in 1999? I think it would be larks.

I can say that the Eagle is preparing a surprise for itself and the public....Special arrangements have been made [to put a reporter to sleep for the next hundred years.] It is believed he can be kept in the proper condition to furnish amusement and instruction for the public when he awakes on the eve of the next century....

It is hardly necessary to inform you that life in those times will be as nearly a holiday as it is possible to make it. Work will be reduced to a minimum by machinery. Everything will be brought to your hand by deaf and dumb waiters and sliding shelves operated by electricity supplied to the entire country by the power of the sea. A force of billions of tons is going to waste along our coast every minute. We shall utilize the surf to drive trolley cars along overhead viaducts and through underneath tunnels. The servant girl problem will be automatically solved. We shall have wooden girls then. This will be an immense improvement. There will be no labor unions and no strikes, because there will be no labor worth mentioning, and such as is done every man can do for himself. Just press buttons and things will come out and do things for you, and there you are. Isn't it easy? And why is it you waited to have me suggest it, before you took out a patent on them.

I can guess a few more things before I awake. We shall discontinue steam. It will not be worthwhile, and beside, with the disappearance of coal, steam will be too expensive. Electricity will do the work and do it more safely and quietly, without kicking up such a bobbery and dust. One of the things it will do will be to drive submarine boats, not for purposes of destruction, for killing will be all out of fashion among the nations, but for study and exploration of sea depths, and the avoidance of collisions in crowded waters. Then it will run the fans, propellers and steering gear of the air ships. Nobody who is anybody a hundred years hence but will have his automobile and his air yacht, whether he has a boat or not. He will not be a sportsman, because there will be no sport. At the present rate of killing the wild animals, except the New Jersey mosquitoes, will have disappeared by 1950, and such a thing as a bird will be found only in histories. Farming will be carried out in large glass houses, and those in them will be careful not to throw fits. For in the open air, the insects, encouraged by the disappearance of the birds, will devour every green thing, except the men who live in western Kansas, and the once forests and gardens will be as dreary as in the middle of Fulton Street....

What used to be called the home will have disappeared. We shall all live in fifty-story flats, with modern improvements in each room and buttons all over the place. The open hearth before which our grandfathers used to sit will have gone with the woods that used to provide the fuel, and we will hold the family meetings around a hole in the floor. While we shall not be communists...we shall belong to all sorts of trusts which will provide us with the necessities, and some luxuries at cost, and the laborers and clerks will draw more pay than the presidents, because the latter will want to escape their taxes. New York City will have 50,000,000 inhabitants and will need taxes. These thoughts should make us glad to have lived in a backward age, for we now know what is before us, and rejoice in our ability to push along the millennium.

Questions

1. What are the basic Progressive Era ideals expressed in these editorials, even in those that spoof or criticize the advances of the nineteenth century and predictions of the twentieth?
2. The *New York Times* editorial is basically optimistic toward the future and seems to believe the resolution of class and national divisions is inevitable in the coming century. The *New York World*'s editorials about McKinley and Mark Twain's "Salutation" are far more pessimistic. Find the passages that indicate their respective positions. Which do you think was being more realistic, given the national and international political situation at the time?

3. Edward Atkinson's column in the *New York World* criticizing McKinley's actions in the Philippines uses the word "nigger," a word that is culturally offensive today, but was widely used in 1900. Furthermore, he uses this as a *rhetorical* term rather than a *racist* word to make a point (note that he repeatedly puts the word in quotation marks). What is the point? What two groups of people is he talking about when he uses the word? Why does his use of the word make this criticism of McKinley's policies more powerful?

4. Several Progressive Era authors wrote novels in which they fantasized about time travel or the discovery of societies locked in time in order to critique the present and propose utopian societies. These include Edward Bellamy's *Looking Backward* and Charlotte Perkins Gilman's *Herland*. How did the *Brooklyn Daily Eagle* adopt this theme to critique the supposed achievements of the nineteenth century and predictions of the future described by the other contributors to the supplement? What are some of the underlying concerns the author of this piece might have? Do you think his skepticism and concerns were matched by society at large? With the advantage of hindsight, do you think his concerns were valid?

CHAPTER 10

President William McKinley Is Assassinated, September 6, 1901

O n September 6, 1901, President William McKinley was shot while attending a reception at the Pan-American Exposition in Buffalo. His attacker, a self-proclaimed anarchist, was captured immediately. He was identified as Leon Czolgosz, the 28-year-old son of Polish-Russian immigrants. He declared he had planned the assassination on his own, but had been inspired by the lectures and writings of anarchist Emma Goldman.

While the nation waited for updates of McKinley's condition, police around the country focused their attentions on rounding up known and suspected anarchists, including Goldman and newspaper editors Abraham Isaak (the *Free Society,* published in Chicago) and Johann Most (*Freiheit,* published in New York). Though those detained and questioned told police that anarchists had no reason to kill McKinley, that they had no connection with the assassin, and that Czolgosz was either a crank or insane, suspicion continued to focus on them.

McKinley lingered eight days while doctors issued conflicting reports, the cabinet prepared for emergencies, the police contemplated the possibility of revolution, and the nation prayed. Blame for the attack was parceled out liberally to anyone who had ever criticized the president or his administration. These included radical socialists, anarchists, immigrants, former Democratic presidential candidate William Jennings Bryan, anti-imperialists, labor unions, and even sensational newspapers and their editors.

One newspaper editor to be singled out was William Randolph Hearst, who throughout the years of the McKinley presidency had characterized him alternately as an imperialist despot or a bumbling fool following the orders of Wall Street business interests. Following the shooting, some recalled that the *New York Evening Journal* had published two particularly suggestive editorials on assassination the previous spring. One, published in April, had discussed recent murders of officials by Russian revolutionists and asked the rhetorical question of whether such murders were justified, suggesting they were.[1] A second editorial published in June asked if assassinations had changed the world. Here, it listed the great leaders who had risen *because of* the assassination of their predecessors and the great events that had been made possible *because* some great leader had been swept aside.[2] Though the *New York Evening Journal* never named McKinley in either editorial, it was commonly believed that both were aimed at the president as part of the *Journal*'s unceasing campaign against him.

McKinley died on September 14, and Vice President Theodore Roosevelt was sworn in as the nation's 26th president. Leon Czolgosz was quickly brought to trial and found guilty on September 23. He was executed by electrocution October 29, just six weeks after the president's death.

Newspapers covered all aspects of the unfolding drama avidly. Bulletins were published daily on the president's improving or worsening condition, complete with medical explanations and interviews with his physicians. The detention of numerous anarchists and "reds" was accompanied by dozens of stories describing the anarchist movement, its goals, and its leaders. The history of political assassinations, from the stabbing of Julius Caesar in ancient times to the shooting of King Humbert of Italy in 1900, was reviewed. Past police investigations of anarchist groups and plots were dredged up and presented as evidence that these political dissidents were in some way responsible for Czolgosz's action. At the same time, connections were made between immigrants and anarchists, and, inevitably, demands were made for stricter immigration restriction and regulation. As arrests of anarchists and other radicals proliferated, some groups began to fear that civil liberties and the right to free speech would be violated. Only a few mainstream newspapers took this issue seriously enough to cover it as a legitimate issue; some, in fact, supported the idea of censoring anarchist speech and press.

Heroes and villains emerged. McKinley, who during his presidency had been rigorously opposed and viciously lampooned by some of his critics, was now portrayed almost universally in glowing terms. He was described as a good and fair man, a "representative" American, a great leader who had led the country to a position of international and imperialist stature, and a martyr to the cause of social order. Theodore Roosevelt, his successor, was portrayed as a dashing adventurer, the swashbuckling hero of the Spanish-American War who would rescue the nation in this moment of peril. Much was made of the fact that when McKinley finally died, Roosevelt had to be tracked down in the Adirondack Mountains of upstate New York where he had gone for a hunting trip.

Czolgosz was described in less generous terms. He was portrayed as insane, a crank, and a loner. Emma Goldman, who Czolgosz claimed had inspired him, was described as a menace to democracy. Anarchists, as well as anyone who had ever associated with them, from socialists to union leaders to immigrants, were painted with the brush of suspicion. Cartoons and illustrations portrayed anarchists as bearded, wild-eyed fanatics.

When McKinley died, newspapers published his portrait on their front pages, draped with funeral wreaths and the American flag. Many outlined the columns on their first several pages for several days in heavy black lines. During his presidency he had been criticized as an imperialist, an instrument of the trusts and, by some, a tyrant. But at his death, most newspapers eulogized him. Some, like the *San Francisco Chronicle* in its editorial, "He Died for Civilization," even described him as a martyr to the cause of social order.

Regardless of their previous opinions about McKinley and his policies and performance as president, newspapers were united in their condemnation of the attempt on his life. They were also unanimous in their call for the discovery of any conspiracy and their demand that Czolgosz and any other guilty parties be punished appropriately. Where they differed was in the tone they adopted. Some newspapers framed events in terms of democratic law and order overcoming evil, while others focused on the elements of fear, crisis, danger, and violence in the situation. Though some newspapers, such as the *New York Times*, were fairly consistent in their tone and approach, others changed from day to day or story to story, depending on the unfolding events or even the particular reporter writing the story. The readings in this chapter, therefore, are organized in two sections. Those in the first section are articles and editorials that promote confidence. These selections tend to adopt a dispassionate tone in the discussion of events. Through their use of scientific, medical, and legal facts and opinions, they promote the idea that despite the turn of events, the United States's democratic and constitutional form of government, law, and order will prevail. The readings in the second section, instead, arouse fear that the nation is in danger. Rather than inspiring the public's support of a democratic and representative solution of the problem, these articles and editorials would encourage tyranny and oppression. Because individual newspapers were not always consistent in the tone or themes they adopted, selections from the same newspaper may appear in both sections.

PROMOTING CONFIDENCE

On the day following the shooting, most newspapers devoted dozens of articles to the different angles of the story, including the attack and Czolgosz's arrest, the president's condition, Mrs. McKinley's reaction to the news,

Roosevelt's reaction and his immediate departure for Buffalo, steps being taken by the cabinet, and reactions in Washington, New York City, and London. They also published recaps of McKinley's career, histories of previous assassinations of leaders of state, and explanations of the chain of command in the event of presidential disability or death. The New York Times covered its front page with reports on the attack, McKinley's condition, and various angles to the story. The lengthy article reporting the attack and the president's condition is remarkably detached and adopts the unemotional tone and language of the physicians reporting on the president's condition, complete with reports of his vital statistics. This can be interpreted as an example of the age's supreme confidence in the triumph of reason and science over chaos. It can also be interpreted as the Times's attempt to reassure the public that despite the attack, all is under control.

New York Times, 7 September 1901

PRESIDENT SHOT AT BUFFALO FAIR

Wounded in the Breast and Abdomen

HE IS RESTING EASILY

One Bullet Extracted, Other Cannot Be Found
Assassin is Leon Czolgosz of Cleveland, Who Says He is an Anarchist and Follower of Emma Goldman

BUFFALO, Sept. 6—President McKinley, while holding a reception in the Temple of Music at the Pan-American Exposition at 4 o'clock this afternoon, was shot and twice wounded by Leon Czolgosz, an Anarchist, who lives in Cleveland.

One bullet entered the President's breast, struck the breast bone, glanced and was later easily extracted. The other bullet entered the abdomen, penetrated the stomach, and has not been found, although the wounds have been closed.

The physicians in attendance upon the President at 10:40 o'clock tonight issued the following bulletin:

"The President is rallying satisfactorily and resting comfortably. 10:15 P.M., temperature, 100.4 degrees; pulse 124; respiration 24.

"P.M. RIXEY,
"M.B. MANN,
"R.E. PARKE,
"H. MYNTER
"EUGENE WANBIN

"Signed by George B. Cortelyou, Secretary to the President."

This condition was maintained until 1 o'clock A.M. when the physicians issued the following bulletin:

"The President is free from pain and resting well. Temperature, 100.2; pulse, 120; respiration 24."

The assassin was immediately overpowered and taken to a police station on the Exposition grounds, but not before a number of the throng had tried to lynch him. Later he was taken to police headquarters.

The exact nature of the President's injuries is described in the following bulletin issued by Secretary Cortelyou for the physicians who were called:

"The President was shot about 4 o'clock. One bullet struck him on the upper portion of the breast bone....

Leon Czolgosz, the assassin, has signed a confession, covering six pages of foolscap, in which he states that he is an Anarchist and that he became an enthusiastic member of that body through the influence of Emma Goldman, whose writings he had read and whose lectures he had listened to. He denies having any confederate, and says he decided on the act three days ago and bought the revolver with which the act was committed in Buffalo.

He has seven brothers and sisters in Cleveland, and the Cleveland Directory has the names of about that number living in Hosmer Street and Ackland Avenue, which adjoin. Some of them are butchers and others are in other trades.

Czolgosz is now detained at Police Headquarters pending the result of the President's injuries. He does not appear in the least degree uneasy or penitent for his action. He says he was induced by his attention to Emma Goldman's lectures and writing to decide that the present form of government in this country was all wrong, and he thought the best way to end it was by the killing of the President. He showed no sign of insanity, but is very reticent about much of his career.

While acknowledging himself an Anarchist, he does not state to which branch of the organization he belongs.

The New York Times *continued in this moderate tone and in its faith in the strength of Western rationalism. It picked up this theme again the next day in the following editorial in which it describes the assassination attempt as an act hearkening back to the Old World and that has no place in a modern democratic nation. The individual violent act of an individual against the government has no lasting effect when the government has been chosen democratically, organized rationally, and secured in stability, the* Times *assures its readers.*

New York Times, 8 September 1901

THE CRIME AND ITS EFFECT

It is one of the elements of wanton atrocity in the crime attempted upon the President that, had it been successful, it would and could have made no change of importance in the course of the national life. Had the desire of the assailant been to secure a change in the Government, it would have been absolutely futile, and must have been known to be so to any person of even low intelligence. While this fact makes the crime more inexplicable, it is one of immense significance for the American people. It makes plainer than ever the essential stability of our Government and the degree of completeness with which it serves its original purpose.

The President may die, and the land will mourn with deep and sincere grief, but any vacancy in the office, however it may occur, whether it be temporary or final, is provided for. The Vice President is chosen for precisely that emergency. Whatever may be the opinion of a critical minority as to the excellence of the choice made last Fall, it was the choice of the legal majority of the voters, made with full knowledge of the ultimate purpose of the Vice Presidency, and of the fact, that for seventeen Presidents who have served out the term of their election there have been four Vice Presidents who have succeeded to the office of President. The election of Vice President is definitely a contingent election to the Presidency. If the possible contingency occurs, the incumbent enters on his duties and powers with the full and explicit authorizations of the popular will duly expressed. There can be no serious interruption. And the law has taken care that no interruption shall exist even if the Vice President is also disabled. The head of each of the important departments is designated to assume in turn the office that may be left vacant.

Nor does the admirable stability of our Government depend solely on the forethought with which possible accidents have been provided for. It rests on deeper foundations. Its peculiar basis is the representative character of the Government itself. The power lodged therein is not an inheritance, and follows no line of personal succession. It is derived from the popular will, and it is distributed between the Legislature and the Executive. The share of the latter is great, but it is substantially subordinate and delegated. The immediate repository of the National will is the Legislature. Both together are but the temporary agents of the real principal, the people. Year by year, sometimes blindly and foolishly, but always in the stern school of experience and responsible freedom, the people live their own life, develop their own character, find their way through the complex conditions of National growth. The passing of the greatest of their servants, even by atrocious violence, cannot deeply disturb, cannot at all disable their vigorous and steady institutions....

Another feature in the effect of the crime attempted on the President is to be noted. The feeling that has found universal expression among all classes is, to a remarkable degree, as much personal as patriotic. It is not the possible vacancy in the office of the Chief Executive that is in the general mind. There has been hardly a trace of apprehension as to consequences. There has been a deep sense of sorrow over the suffering and danger of a brave and blameless citizen. There has been an outpouring of affection for the public servant who had endeared himself to the people and was so un-affectedly one of them in heart and thought. But the calm, sustained confi-dence of the Nation in itself has not for a moment been shaken. Nor, even, if the worst should come, need it be!

Another newspaper to use this occasion to make comparisons between dis-order and order was the Chicago Tribune. *In this selection, the* Tribune *celebrates the public's restraint in the heat of the moment and the American legal system that would see to it that the assassin got his just deserts. This was much in keeping with the* Tribune's *general attitude toward mob vio-lence, for it had been conducting a vigorous campaign against the lynching of blacks in the South for the past decade. For the* Tribune, *Czolgosz's or-derly arrest—despite the enormity of his crime—is a vindication of Amer-ica's form of government and the rule of law.*

Chicago Tribune, 8 September 1901

PUNISHING THE ASSASSIN

The feeling among law-abiding people everywhere—after the moment of blind sorrow and anger—will be one of satisfaction that the man who at-tempted to assassinate President McKinley was not killed by the excited crowds at Buffalo. The first and natural impulse in such a case is to slay the offender as summarily as one would crush a venomous insect. If the mob had leaped upon the assassin and taken his worthless life on the scene of his deed the first impulse of the nation would have been to exclaim that he de-served it. But this would have been followed almost instantly by a sober sec-ond thought of regret. It is best that the law should punish lawbreakers. The greater the crime the more necessary is it that the proper punishment shall be inflicted in accordance with the dignity and majesty of the law.

If the President should die of his wounds the assassin will be tried ac-cording to the just forms of law and will be put to death as he deserves. If the President recovers, as the whole nation devoutly hopes, then the criminal will suffer a corresponding punishment in the form of a prison sentence. In either case, the law will be vindicated and justice will be done. The dignity and self-restraint of this orderly procedure in a trying crisis are in themselves a vindication of the splendid system of government whose Chief Executive has been stricken down. President McKinley himself would have been the first to deplore the lynching of his assailant. One of his first thoughts amid the confusion that followed the shooting was to ask that no violence be done to the assassin.

The moral effect of the orderly trial and deliberate punishment of such a criminal is worth infinitely more than the momentary gratification of the savage instinct of self-preservation which suggests that he be killed on the spot. Lynching at best is the avenging of one crime by another. It tends to multiply lawbreakers rather than to decrease their number. For the mob to have torn the assassin limb from limb would not have undone any of the harm inflicted by his bullets, but would simply have added a new cause for regret. It would have been a temporary lapse into the anarchy which this criminal stands for and which is the enemy of all government except that of brute force. Even the excited crowds that called for the assassin's death realized this fact the moment their reason had a chance to assert itself.

Even when McKinley died on September 14, some newspapers were able to promote a sense of confidence in the system. The San Francisco Chronicle*'s description of a peaceful and forgiving McKinley at the hour of his death quoted here might be trite and might even be a complete fabrication. However, it does succeed in promoting a certain confidence that all will be well.*

San Francisco Chronicle, 14 September 1901

DEATH STILLS THE HEART OF PRESIDENT M'KINLEY IN THE EARLY MORNING HOURS

Mrs. McKinley With Him During His Last Conscious Moments—Touching Incidents at the Deathbed

BUFFALO, September 14—President McKinley died at 2:15 this morning. His last breath passed calmly and almost imperceptibly. Peace and forgiveness were written on his white face. He had been unconscious for several hours before the end came, and his death was free from pain.

Secretary Cortelyou made the announcement. He came out of the Milburn house and walked slowly down to the newspaper men, who were congregated behind the rope barrier.

"The President died at 2:15 o'clock," said he, in an even address.

He then turned and walked back to the house, maintaining even after all was over, the calm demeanor which has characterized all his actions during the anxious days and the sleepless nights which have passed since the President was shot.

All night the President battled with death. At 10 o'clock he was alone in the combat. Science, skill, infinite tenderness, were beaten and hopeless. Surgeons and physicians measured his brief span by moments. They had no hope and offered none. Mystified, baffled and defeated, they stood aside and left William McKinley alone to face the inevitable.

Meanwhile the nation—the world—stood watching for the final word. Buffalo, where the President was assassinated, stood agape with horror and rage. Doctors of known and heralded cunning were summoned from all available quarters. They came by special trains, and were rushed into the presence of death and its unyielding victim. The wires were hot with summonses for the Vice-President, for the Cabinet, for the friends nearest to the dying man, and they came.

From all quarters men who have known the dying man as a man first and then as a leader of his people came rushing, pale with sad-eyed and hopeless grief....

AROUSING FEAR

Not all newspapers were quite so sanguine in addressing the national crisis, and even those quoted in the previous section could become emotional when it came to reporting on the hunt for anarchists. Even though there was no evidence linking Czolgosz to any anarchist group, these stories instilled a fear that anarchists were everywhere and ready to wreak havoc. The New York World *splashed headlines over its stories that promoted this idea, even though the information provided in the stories did not always support it. On September 8, for example, the* World *plastered page three with articles devoted to the anarchist angle below these headlines: "Anarchist Says Woman's Speech Inspired Him to Kill"; "Assassin's Only Regret is That M'Kinley Lives"; "Will Crush Paterson Reds by Imposing Death Penalty"; "Avowed Anarchist But a Great Coward"; "Twelve Rabid Chicago Reds Locked up as Accomplices"; and "Anarchists to be Kept on the Move Hereafter." At the top of the page is a large headshot of Emma Goldman—looking more intellectual than violent—headed by a caption, "Emma Goldman, Anarchist, Who Moved Czolgosz to Murder." The Chicago anarchists, whose arrests are described in this selection, were later released when no evidence was found to connect them to the shooting.*

New York World, **8 September 1901**

TWELVE RABID CHICAGO REDS LOCKED UP AS ACCOMPLICES

While in that City Following Emma Goldman, Czolgosz Visited and Conferred With
Them—They Say They Thought Him a Spy

(Special to the World)

CHICAGO, Sept. 7—Nine men and three women are under arrest at Police Headquarters charged with conspiring to kill the President.

The warrants were issued and served today. The prisoners are:

CLEMENTS, PFUETZNER
ABRAHAM ISAAK, SR.
ABRAHAM ISAAK, JR.
ALFRED SCHNEIDER
HIPPOLYTE HAVEL
HENRY TRAKAGLIO
JULIA MECHANIC
MARIE ISAAK, SR.
MARIE ISAAK, JR.
MARTIN FOX
MICHAEL BOS
M. RASIRAKE

Last night the chief of police received this telegram from Superintendent of Police Bull of Buffalo: "We have in custody Leon Czolgosz, alias Fred C. Nieman, the President's assassin. Locate and arrest E. J. Isaak, who is editor of a Socialistic paper and a follower of Emma Goldman, from whom Nieman is said to have taken instructions. It looks as if there might be a plot and that these people may be implicated."

The office of the Free Society was found at No. 515 Carroll avenue. Capt. Colleran and four men found the first floor, used as publication office, dark and silent. From the second floor came the sounds of voices.

"Up there is where they held their meetings," said one of the policemen. The door to the hall was locked. It was quickly forced and six men, three women and a child were discovered.

Were Discussing the Shooting

The men were talking loudly. The subject under discussion was the shooting of the President. The police heard two of the men say it was wrong while the others indorsed [*sic*] and gloried in the crime. No resistance was offered.

One of the Anarchists cursed the police during the drive to headquarters and predicted a day when men would be allowed freedom and not be molested by authorities. The entire building was seized by the police and all correspondence is now under examination. It is a two-story brick cottage and the tenants have been a mystery to neighbors.

On the walls of the publication office are portraits of the hanged Haymarket Anarchists and quotations from their speeches. None attracted more attention than this:

"The dragon of despotism is not slain by decapitation, for where one head called by the name of king has been cut off, another called president has grown in its place."

This afternoon, the police of the Maxwell street district made a descent on the house No. 100 Newberry avenue and captured Bos, Fox and Rasirake. They were discussing the crime and drinking beer.

A Rendezvous for Reds

The place was a rendezvous of Anarchists, and like the Carroll avenue place, was plentifully supplied with "red" literature. Abraham Isaak, Sr., who occupied the cottage at 515 Carroll avenue, and who is editor of Free Society, came here last January from Portland, Ore., where he conducted a sheet called the Fire-Brand. He was prosecuted by the Federal authorities for illegal use of mails and moved to San Francisco. He has been nine years in America and is a Russian Pole. All the prisoners are foreign-born.

Upon establishing Free Society here Isaak jumped into leadership among the local Reds. He entertained Emma Goldman when she was here in July. Following her about at the time was a man believed to be Czolgosz. Isaak says he was known both as Nieman and Czolgosz. [An account of Isaak's encounter with Czolgosz follows, in which Isaak says the Chicago anarchists denounced Czolgosz, who was not a member of any known group, and warned others of him because of his statements that he wished to organize attacks on authorities.]

"The deed was foolish, but I do not condemn it [Isaak told the police]. As long as we have free speech and a free press, and as long as we are not imprisoned for the sake of our principles. There is no reason to assassinate people who happen to be on top."

Isaak is a tall, heavy man, with a good-natured face and has no resemblance to the typical Anarchist. Smooth of tongue and address he impresses one favorably. His son, who is a prisoner with him, resembles his father. The youth is scarcely out of his teens.

The other male prisoners are clearly of a lower intelligence. Clements Pfeutzner is a rabid Anarchist who has been in trouble with the police before. He has a shoe shop at Wabash avenue. Hippolyte Havel is a canvasser. He was convicted in Pilsen, Bohemia, of speaking and writing against the Government and was sent to prison for two years. He has grown more radical than he was at home. Henry Trakeglio is an Italian and looks like a typical brigand.

Though Isaak and his friends were probably doing nothing more than any other working-class Americans might be doing that day after the attack on the President—drinking beer and talking about the attack—the inflammatory nature of their literature made them an easy target. The San Francisco Chronicle, *which was particularly venomous in its attack on anarchists, published a series of editorials in the following days that referred to them as "fiends," "devils," and "bloodthirsty conspirators." It called for political, police, and legal action against anarchists and anyone who encouraged them. Because anarchists did not respect the laws of the United States, it argued, they should expect no protection under those laws. In the following editorial, the* Chronicle *supports suppression of anarchist speech and press and suggests that anarchists from other countries be barred from immigrating into the country.*

San Francisco Chronicle, 10 September 1901

EXTERMINATE ANARCHY

Our present hopes for the recovery of the President should not beguile us into any abatement of the public determination to put a final end to all open approval of anarchy in this country and to either expel, imprison or exterminate all anarchists found within our borders. Measures for adequately dealing with these wretches require modification of that provision of the Constitution of the United States which forbids any state to deny any person the equal protection of the laws. Anarchists should be put outside the pale of the laws, whose authority they denounce and to whose protection they should have no claim. They should be driven from the country and, if need be, imprisoned until some other country is ready to receive them. This applies to the so-called "peaceful wing" as well as to the "violent" groups. The former are, in fact, the more dangerous. Composed of the more cowardly and contemptible of the clan, they are merely preparatory schools where the minds of the weak and vicious are fitted for final instruction in the schools of murder. Women anarchists should receive less mercy than any others. None is so low as a fallen woman, and the devilish malignity of these unsexed hags surpasses human conception and would be impossible to a male of the species.

But pending Constitutional amendment permitting adequate treatment of anarchists, much can be done under the ordinary police powers of the state and Nation. It may be assumed that we shall have statutes fixing the penalty for attempts or conspiracies to do political murder equal to that of the completed crime. But we may go further than that. Society has the rights of self-preservation. Public utterance of anarchistic sentiment may be punished under the general police power by which we punish obscene display. Anarchistic writings and publications may be suppressed in the same way, and all commerce in them stopped. Anarchists can be listed and the use of the mail denied them as it is denied common swindlers. Lists may be published for common information. They may be denied entrance to the United States and affirmative evidence of innocence required of intending immigrants in suspicious cases. Secret assemblies of listed anarchists may probably be made prima facie evidence of criminal conspiracy. They may, of course, be denied the elective franchise, a restriction mainly useful in assuring a constant watch for them by all classes of the community. All these and other restrictions which may be devised are thoroughly justified and must be enforced with no more pity than is observed in the extermination of rattlesnakes. When the human form is the mere cover of a fiend it need give no protection to its wearer. We deprecate the lynch law which some advocate. Not even anarchy justifies that. It is itself anarchy. But we do not wish to cherish devils in our midst. No anarchist has any claim to live in a country whose people desire government, and if all peoples desire government, they have no right to live anywhere. They should be made to get off the earth, and if the American people, warned as it now is, rises to the exigencies of the occasion, they will be made to get off our part of it.

But while we inflict only upon avowed or convicted anarchists the extreme penalty of the law, we are by no means to forget that as the anarchist groups are responsible for their tools, so those who deliberately foment general class hatred are responsible for the anarchist groups. The fundamental remedy for anarchism must be a public sentiment so sane and virile that fomenters of class hatred and wrath shall no longer dare to raise their heads in our midst.

The idea that individuals opposed to American institutions should be denied the protection of those institutions might appear logical, but it was in contradiction to democratic constitutional principles. It was especially strange to see newspapers, which normally championed the First Amendment, suggesting that anarchists be denied freedom of speech and of the press. Even the New York World, *which frequently attacked government and corporations alike for trammeling the people's right to know and*

*speak, abandoned that principle in this case, proving that nothing is
absolute.*

New York World, 10 September 1901

THE SNAKES' NESTS

The best way to deal with a snake's nest is to "stamp it out"—first being
sure that your boots are thick and high!

Since the utterly causeless and dastardly assault upon President McKinley by an avowed Anarchist the impulse of the American people, as manifested in the utterances of sober-minded Governors, cool-headed lawyers,
intelligent workingmen and usually benevolent clergymen, is to "stamp
out" the nests of Anarchism in this country.

Against this natural impulse there is cited the provision of the Constitution forbidding Congress to make any law "abridging the freedom of
speech or of the press, or the right of the people peaceably to assemble."

But various States have passed, and the courts have sustained, laws declaring incitement to violence and disorder by spoken or printed words to
be an "overt act" of a criminal nature. Under such a law the Chicago Anarchists were condemned and hanged for having caused the murderous
bomb-throwing [in the Chicago Haymarket riot of 1889]. It has been held
that some of those convictions were procured without insufficient evidence,
but the principal of the law stands.

Under a similar statute, the notorious Emma Goldman was convicted
and sent to Blackwell's Island in this city, John Most was silenced and the
"Red" Anarchist meetings were broken up.

There must be power in this nation and in the State to put all necessary
restraint upon those forms of political anarchism and social insanity which
deny the authority of all government, defy its laws, and applaud if they do
not openly counsel the assassination of rulers and public servants as a
means of "changing the existing order" and bringing in a fool's and lazy
man's millennium. To deny the existence of such a power is to repudiate for
the Government the "first law of nature"—self-preservation.

Just what measure of repression is safest and best is a matter for our social scientists and lawmakers to consider. But in view of this latest crime, and
of the public temper concerning it, it is plain that something must be done,
and that quickly.

---

*Several newspapers focused on the prominent role immigrants played in the
anarchist movement and used the attack on the president as a pretext for de-*

manding stricter immigration regulations. One of these was the Buffalo Times.

Buffalo Times, 12 September 1901

KEEP OUT THE SCUM

We must not, in pursuance of our policy of absolute freedom of immigration, permit the scum of creation, the foul teachings of the cast-off of Europe, to pollute our institutions and to make the American Republic a mockery in the mouths of Anarchists and all others that are evil loathsome, and base.

Nativists seeking to limit immigration had long focused on keeping out the "criminal element." This label, unfortunately, was frequently attached to anyone who was poor, uneducated, from southern or eastern Europe, or who held unconventional (non-American) political ideas. Furthermore, by obliquely referring to anarchists as criminals rather than political activists, as in the following brief editorial comment by the New Orleans Times, *the critic deprives them of their political identity.*

New Orleans Times, 12 September 1901

KEEP OUT THE CRIMINAL ELEMENT

By keeping a little better supervision of immigration we can hope to shut out the dangerous criminal element, and by the enforcement of very simple laws preventing the teaching or encouragement of crime we can very soon get rid of the propaganda which turns out assassins like Bresci and Czolgosz.

In the search for someone to blame, some critics focused on sensational newspapers that had pilloried McKinley during his presidency. They accused the "yellows" of stirring up the ignorant and discontent, the uneducated and politically susceptible—exactly the class of people most often receptive to political agitators. This kind of argument was a dangerous one for the general circulation press to make, for if the campaign to muzzle the anarchist press was pursued in the current climate of hysteria, any publication critical of the government could become a target for the censors. One of the newspapers to attack the sensational press was the San Francisco Chronicle, *no stranger to occasional sensationalism itself. In this editorial the* Chronicle *blames the sensational press for preparing the ground of hatred for the seeds of anarchy.*

San Francisco *Chronicle,* 8 September 1901

THE SEEDS OF ANARCHY

Every street corner agitator, every unbalanced pamphleteer, every sensational newspaper is a joint worker in undermining the foundation of civilization, and preparing the world for a campaign of wrath. In those utterances and publications which inspire envy of the thrifty, the able or the prosperous, and set one class in anger against another, lie those seeds of anarchy whose first fruits we now see, but whose full harvest is too terrible to contemplate.

Society is placing the responsibility of the assassination of President McKinley where it belongs. The wretch who will suffer for it is not even mentioned. The cowardly group of which he proclaims himself a member is too insignificant to have produced such a result, except as it is set in the baleful atmosphere of falsehood, intrigue, envy and hate created by the sensational press. It is in such atmosphere, thus created, that the foul spores of anarchy take root in the human soul and turn it to a mass of festering corruption. Except by the constant pandering to the passions of the brutal, which disgraces a portion of the journalism of the period, the seeds of anarchy could no more take root in America than a water plant bloom in the dry plains of Nevada. It is the black gospel of hate proclaimed for money, by sleek cormorants who live daintily by the debasement of the wretched who would be spurned from their doors that is responsible for the crime at Buffalo, and upon the heads of those guilty of spreading that gospel an outraged Nation is now invoking the wrath of God.

QUESTIONS

1. Newspapers reported information about McKinley's shooting and the arrest of his attacker by the next morning and provided updated reports of his condition each day. How would this sort of reporting serve the public? Would it calm the public and prevent panic or stir up unrest and fear? Look at each of the stories or editorials quoted here and identify those that might calm the public. Identify those that might cause panic. Why?
2. Once Czolgosz announced he was an anarchist, police quickly began to round up anarchists in a number of cities. Why were newspapers so

quick to focus on this angle of the assassination story? Was their extensive coverage of anarchists, anarchism, and anarchist arrests necessary? Do you think it contributed to a general climate of panic?

3. How did some of the stories and editorials quoted here reveal social attitudes toward foreigners and immigrants? What was the logical connection between Czolgosz and immigrants? How did people make the logical (or illogical) leap from the assassination to a need for stricter immigration regulation?

4. Some newspapers supported the idea of censoring the anarchist press. Why would this be acceptable in an industry and profession based on the concept of freedom of the press? Consider the role of the press during periods of crisis (such as wars, revolution, and social unrest). Can the nation afford freedom of the press at these times?

5. Was it reasonable for critics to hold newspapers that had criticized McKinley responsible for the assassination? How can newspapers draw the line between responsible criticism of public officials and the kind of criticism denounced by the *San Francisco Chronicle*?

Notes

1. Untitled editorial, *New York Evening Journal*, 10 April 1901, editorial page.

2. "Assassination Never Changed the History of the World," *New York Evening Journal*, 1 June 1901, editorial page.

CHAPTER 11

America Backs the Panamanian Revolution, November 1903

In 1868 satirist Mark Twain happened to pass through Panama on his way from California back to his home in Hartford, Connecticut. His ship, the *Montana*, enjoyed "smooth waters and cool breezes" all the way to the isthmus, he wrote in a letter to the San Francisco *Alta California*. Then the passengers disembarked from the *Montana* to cross the isthmus by rail, and begin the Atlantic leg of their journey north on a second ship. Twain, who was an inveterate traveler, had gone this route before. "We found Panama in the same place," he quipped. "It has not changed perceptibly. They had no revolution while we were there. I do not know why, but it is true that there had not been a revolution for as much as two weeks. The very same President was at the head of the Government that was at the head of it a fortnight before. It was very curious. I suppose they have hanged him before this, however."[1]

What Twain wrote in 1868 could easily have been written 30 and even 40 years later, for Central and South America were famous for political instability, coups, and revolutions. That he was writing it about Panama and the Isthmus of Panama was of particular significance, for the isthmus—the travelers' shortcut between the Atlantic and Pacific Oceans—was to become the focal point of political and economic maneuvering for much of the latter part of the nineteenth century. And the focal point of that attention was the dream of building a canal across the isthmus.

Interest in building a canal across Central America to link the Atlantic and Pacific Oceans existed as early as 1523, when Charles V of Spain ordered a survey of the isthmus. In the next three centuries, several projects were proposed and abandoned, first by the Spanish government, then by various international and American business groups. Between 1876 and 1894 several companies were formed, and routes were proposed in both

Panama and Nicaragua. In 1880 a French group of investors formed the Panama Canal Company. This company hoped to build a sea-level canal across the isthmus, but failed in 1889. In that year a U.S. company began work in Nicaragua, but failed during the depression of 1893. In 1894 the Panama Canal Company was reorganized but was limited in its progress because of insufficient funds.

The U.S. government, which had not yet played an official role in any of these ventures, was nevertheless interested in controlling any canal that might be built across the isthmus for both trade and military reasons. Following its annexation of Hawaii and the Philippines and its emergence as a world power after the Spanish-American War, that control became mandatory. In 1899 Congress created an Isthmian Canal Commission to examine the possibilities and recommend a route. After the Panama Canal Company offered its assets to the United States for $40,000,000 in 1902, the commission recommended that the route be built across Panama.

Proponents of a canal plan included shipping lines, U.S. business interests, investors, developers, and both the Nicaraguan and Colombian governments. Opponents included isolationists and anti-imperialists who opposed America's expanding domination over other countries. The canal was also opposed by U.S. railroad companies and their backers, who had a lock on transcontinental and transisthmian transportation.

In late 1903 the United States entered into negotiations with the Colombian government to lease a strip of land six miles wide across Panama for the canal project. When the Colombian senate refused to ratify the terms of the concession contained in the resulting treaty, the Panama Canal Company launched a revolution on November 3. Pledged by an earlier treaty to protect neutrality in the region, the United States dispatched armed and naval forces to prevent the suppression of the uprising by Colombian troops and quickly recognized Panama as an independent state. All this transpired within days.

The new republic immediately granted the United States a 5-mile-wide and 10-mile-long strip across the isthmus. By the terms of the Hay-Bunau-Varilla treaty concluded on November 18, the Republic of Panama granted to the United States in perpetuity the use, occupation, and control of the canal zone for the construction, maintenance, operation, sanitation, and protection of the canal. In return, the United States agreed to pay the new republic $10,000,000 and provide it with military protection. In addition, it would assume the assets of the Panama Canal Company for $40,000,000.

From this point, the dream of building a canal across the isthmus quickly became a reality. The plan for the construction of the Panama Canal, which was to use a system of locks, was approved in 1906, and in 1907 President Theodore Roosevelt put the project under the U.S. Army Engineers. Construction began immediately, and the canal was opened for traffic in August

1914, just as Europe became engulfed in war. The first commercial steamship to use the canal shortened its voyage between San Francisco and New York by one month and eight thousand miles, and the project's completion was hailed as a triumph of engineering, administration, and statesmanship.[2]

At the time of the Panamanian revolution, however, there was little consensus about the validity of the so-called insurgence and the future of the region. Far from being a democratic revolution of the people, the 1903 uprising was clearly engineered by officers of the Panama Canal Company, headed by Phillippe Bunau-Varilla and supported by President Theodore Roosevelt, for financial and political reasons. Anti-imperialists denounced U.S. involvement in the revolution and feared the next step would be for the United States to annex Panama as it had annexed Hawaii and the Philippines just a few years before. Expansionists and business interests in support of the Panamanian route hailed the revolution as a triumph for democracy and American influence. Even a number of progressives saw the

"The annexer'll git you ef you don't watch out." *New York Times,* 20 **December** 1903, p. 16. *Uncle Sam looks like a hungry insect here, ready to snatch up any hapless victim that strays in his path. He has already collected the Philippines, Guam and Hawaii, and it looks like Panama will be his next victim. American-backed business interests in Panama staged a coup and then called for American assistance in their supposed revolution against the Colombian territory. The successful revolution resulted in providing the United States with the land for the construction of the Panama Canal, much to the dismay of anti-imperialists.*

success of the revolution and the triumph of the plan to build the canal in Panama as opportunities to use developing technology and science to civilize a backward people.

These arguments were played out in newspaper stories and editorials about the revolution and the impact it might have on plans to build the canal. Thus, newspapers focused on the rapidly unfolding military and political conflict as well as the specific issues of the United States's political and economic self-interest and the impact the revolution would have on plans to build a canal. Many of these news stories and editorials also incorporated the broader themes of freedom and revolution, tyranny and imperialism.

The readings in this chapter have been organized in two sections. The first set of readings supports the revolution and U.S. military support of the revolution. This support may be clearly expressed in arguments put forth in editorials. It may also be inferred from news stories and editorials alike in their frequent use of emotionally and ideologically loaded terms, such as "freedom," "democracy," "order," and "protection of the people's rights." The second set of readings opposes the revolution and the United States's support of it. The *Chicago Tribune*, for example, argues that the revolution is not a real movement for liberation but is instead a political coup organized by a group of businessmen. The *New York Times* opposes U.S. intervention and support of the revolution on the grounds that the next step might be annexation.

SUPPORTING REVOLUTION AND U.S. INVOLVEMENT

The San Francisco Chronicle *was typically an enthusiastic supporter of Roosevelt's aggressive expansionist policies. In this report on the beginning of the revolution, the* Chronicle *presents the news of the revolution in terms of freedom and independence. This story describes the revolution as a popular uprising with more than three thousand men and a number of political parties participating. No mention is made of the businessmen who instigated the coup.*

San Francisco Chronicle, 4 November 1903

PANAMA SECEDES FROM COLOMBIA

Revolution on the Isthmus Stirs United States to Action—
War Ships Ordered to Scene

PANAMA (Colombia), November 3—The independence of the Isthmus was proclaimed at 6 P.M. to-day. A large and enthusiastic crowd of all political parties assembled and marched to the headquarters of the Government troops, where General Tovar and General Amaya, who arrived this morning, were imprisoned in the name of the Republic of Panama. The enthusiasm was immense, and at least 3000 of the men in the gathering were armed.

The battalion of Colombian troops at Panama favors the movement, which is also thought to meet with the approval of at least two of the Government transports now here.

WASHINGTON, November 3—The following cablegram was received at the Navy Department to-night:

"An uprising took place at Panama to-night. Independence was proclaimed. The Colombian army and naval officials were made prisoners. A government was to be organized, consisting of three Consuls and a Cabinet. It is rumored at Panama that a similar uprising was to take place at Colon."

Later a cablegram was received reading as follows: "A number of confused and conflicting dispatches have been received from the Isthmus indicating rather serious disturbances at both Panama and Colon. The Navy Department has dispatched several vessels to these ports with direction to do everything possible to keep order along the line of the railroad."

The sensational advices from the Isthmus were not entirely unexpected, in view of the other reports recently received. The news caused a sudden outburst of activity in the Navy Department, and at once on President Roosevelt's return he was made acquainted with the situation.

Secretary Hay, Assistant Secretary Darling and a number of others were summoned to the White House, and measures were at once taken for the protection of American interests on the Isthmus.

By the next day, the San Francisco Chronicle *was reporting that the insurgents had asked for American recognition. It continued to ignore the role of economic interests, instead playing up the political nature of the rebellion. When the United States did send in troops, the* Chronicle *stressed the idea that America was intervening only because it had been asked to. The administration's motive was to preserve order, protect Americans, and keep the transisthmian railway open, the* Chronicle *explained. Underlying this was the assumption—bolstered by the ideology of the Monroe Doctrine—that it was perfectly natural for the United States to intervene in Central American affairs. The idea that the United States has gotten involved for altruistic reasons is repeated in this editorial. Here also, the* Chronicle *links the revolution to the plan for a canal and notes that America's "guardianship" of any canal to be built is sanctified by European governments.*

San Francisco Chronicle, 6 **November 1903**

THE PANAMA REVOLUTION

It is not at all unlikely that the Panama revolutionists will succeed. They have declared their independence and asked from our Government the recognition of Panama as an independent nation. By the treaty of 1846 [with Colombia] this country positively and efficaciously guarantees the "neutrality" of the Isthmus, which, being interpreted, seems to mean that there shall be no fighting there. A Washington dispatch states that our naval officers on the spot are to "take any necessary measures to prevent bloodshed," and as revolutions are seldom suppressed by any other means—at least Central American revolutions—it may be safely assumed that this one will be successful. It does not, in fact, appear that means are available to Colombia to suppress the insurrection under any circumstances. Her gunboats could bombard and destroy the coast towns, but that would not suppress the rebellion, nor does modern warfare recognize such bombardments except after ample warning, nor would our Navy permit it to the hindrance of peaceful travel over the Panama Railroad, which we have promised Colombia to guarantee. Colombia apparently has no means of subduing the insurrection by land forces. If it could land them it could not maintain them. All the inhabitants of the Isthmus are said to be, and probably are, in sympathy with the revolution.

In Europe the situation is regarded with about the same concern which we have for the disturbances in the Balkans. That is a European affair. This is an American affair. We should not be welcomed in the Balkans. Europe would expect no welcome should she interfere on the Isthmus. In fact, Europe has plainly turned over that peppery spot to us and seems delighted to be rid of responsibility. The maritime nations recognize us as the proper builders and guardians of an isthmian canal, and only wish we would get to work and build it, incidentally, protecting their citizens resident in those parts. There is little doubt that European governments expect and desire that the revolution in progress shall result in the formation of a new republic virtually, if not formally, under the protection of the United States. It is not unlikely that this may be the result.

The Atlanta Constitution, *instead, concentrated more on the conflict involved—between Panama and Colombia and between the United States and Colombia. Its headlines and stories during the first few days of the revolt described the Panamanians as downtrodden, Colombia as a bully, and the United States as a benevolent protector. In the following editorial, the* Constitution *succeeds in combining the romantic notion of freeing the Panamanians from a corrupt tyrant (Colombia) with the pragmatic argument that a successful revolution will permit construction of the canal.*

Atlanta Constitution, 6 November 1903

THE PANAMA SECESSION

The revolution in Panama is the logical outcome of the rascally proceedings of the Colombian government. It is a revolt that ought, in the justice of things, to be successful, either in establishing an autonomous government in Panama, or in compelling Colombia to deal in honor and in decency with the canal question.

The people of Panama, as we believe all the people of Colombia do, desire the isthmian canal built by the United States over the Panama route and in full sympathy with existing treaties. The adjournment of the Colombian Congress after rejecting the Hay-Herran treaty and sending to this country an outrageous hold-up proposition, left the people of Panama the alternative of revolution or the almost sure loss of the canal. They chose to revolt and it only remains to see if they can win their fight.

Colombia is bankrupt and unless some other interests, such as our American transcontinental railway trust, cashes her war bills she will have a hard job coercing the Panama revolutionists. Those latter are at home, fighting over their own ground and inspired to sacrifice in arms without pay for the sake of the weal of the future. It is not at all probable that any one will try to intervene in the fight and the odds now are on Panama to win her independence.

The United States is bound to preserve peace along the canal route and at the termini, so that free transit may be had between Colon and Panama. This she can do with ships and soldier-manned trains without taking sides between the warring factions. That policy of neutrality is the right attitude of the hour, however much inclined Americans generally would like to back up the Panama rebels.

If the outcome shall be the freedom of Panama, promptly recognized by the world powers, the negotiation of the canal business would be swift and sure. It is a good guess, too, that before the canal could be constructed the Panama people would ask annexation to the United States, which, if granted, would strengthen our everlasting hold on that waterway of gigantic moment to the world.

President Roosevelt prided himself in his ability to come to swift decisions and take immediate action. He dispatched troops to the Isthmus of Panama, ordered them to guard the transisthmian railroad, and by swift action undercut any significant opposition. The New York Herald *notes this in the following editorial in which it calls for the nation to stand behind its man.*

New York Herald, 10 November 1903

THE PANAMA CASE

The die is cast. President Roosevelt has decided to virtually recognize the independent existence of the new Republic of Panama.

As patriots, as practical men, Americans of every shade of opinion should accept the accomplished fact and support the government. The question whether Mr. Roosevelt be right or wrong is one that concerns the future. The people at the polls, perhaps, indeed, the delegates at the next republican convention, will render a verdict on that point and will pronounce upon his decision, either indorsing [*sic*] it as just, prudent, and statesmanlike or condemning it as iniquitous, shortsighted and reckless.

One fact is indisputable—Mr. Roosevelt has the courage of his convictions. No more striking contrast with his predecessor [William McKinley] could be imagined. The one by throwing down the reigns to a jingo congress under the influence of a jingo press made possible the Spanish-American war; the other, with excessive self-confidence, voluntarily accepts the heavy responsibility of a Central American policy that may yet involve the United States in foreign complications.

For the moment, however, the prospect is very smiling....

As an independent newspaper, and therefore as one without political prejudices or obligations, The Herald frankly admits that the time has gone by when controversy about the superiority, respectively, of the Panama and Nicaragua [canal] routes could be profitable. Such a controversy in fact is no longer possible. The latest uprising on the Isthmus and the attitude of the Washington administration toward it have at least the merit of settling the canal question. The waterway is to be constructed along the Panama route.

Today then it is of vital importance that opposition to it should cease. Neither The New York Times nor Senator Morgan can undo the events of the last few days or hope to change the attitude of the government, now that it is pledged to a certain line of action. At such a moment there can be neither democrats nor republicans, neither supporters of the Panama project nor advocates of the Nicaragua route—there are only Americans, and it is their duty to support the government, right or wrong.

This fatalistic attitude of "my country right or wrong" combined with admiration for a decisive president and national self-interest to win support of a treaty that recognized the independence of Panama and to assure the United States's control of the canal to be built. The treaty was signed with the new government on November 18 and was quickly ratified by Congress. The vic-

tors in the debate concluded that despite some quibblers who argued that Roosevelt's actions were illegal or that the United States was trampling the rights of a sister republic, this was the inevitable result of natural selection—survival of the fittest—and Manifest Destiny. In this chilling presentation of that proposition in this editorial, the San Francisco Chronicle *repeats the age-old justification for colonization—and even genocide—and foreshadows an argument that was to become one of the assumptions underlying American foreign policy in third-world countries for the next century. The* Chronicle *bolsters this position by stating that it is shared by many others, including other newspapers. To prove this point, the* Chronicle *quotes a brief excerpt from the* New Orleans Picayune *in which the* Picayune *states its conviction that the United States will eventually annex the new republic to allow it "all the advantages of being part of the great American republic."*

San Francisco Chronicle, 18 November 1903

THE PANAMA INCIDENT CLOSED

It may be assumed as a settled fact that the Panama Canal will be built by the United States through territory whose sovereign is nominally the Republic of Panama but really the Republic of the United States of America, and that it will be done with the approbation of the people of this country and the civilized world on the same grounds upon which we justify wrestling this continent from the possession of a nomad race which did not and could not make use of it. The doctrine is becoming firmly established in the modern mind that communities in possession of land must make use of it, permit others to do so on reasonable terms, or get out of the way. Mankind has the right to be born to live and to do business by economical methods, and the land of the world must be so used as to afford those opportunities so long as the land lasts. Within civilized countries there is the law of eminent domain. Since there is no international law of that kind, we must of necessity revert to what, anterior to civilization, was universal law—the will of the strongest.

That all this is true is made evident by the expressions of opinion and feeling which find their way into the public press of this and other countries. Perhaps as clear and unvarnished a declaration of this kind as can be found is the following from the *New Orleans Picayune....*

Panama as an independent nation is too small in extent and too weak in population to maintain herself, and the most obvious ending to the situation which now exists will be in due time to annex the country and give it all the advantages of being a part of the great American republic and enjoying its powerful protection.

In the foregoing excerpt there are no evasions and no illusions. It is a robust justification of exerting the power of the strong for the progress of civilization, regardless of the wishes, the feelings, or the apparent rights of the ineffective. The world must move. It is an age of power. The weak will be protected, but they will not be permitted to obstruct, whether on the continent of America, the Isthmus of Panama, the isles of the Pacific, the plains of Manchuria, or the valleys of the Ganges and the Indus. It is manifest destiny.

OPPOSING THE REVOLUTION AND U.S. INVOLVEMENT

The Chicago Tribune, *instead, rejected arguments that this was a people's revolution or that its success would bring about political freedom of the Panamanians. It described the revolt as being all about the canal and the competing business interests. In its reports on the unfolding events, it focused on how they would affect the laws and treaties negotiated thus far. It also examined the United States's obligation to prevent anything that would jeopardize the prospect of the canal and how the debate over the canal route would play out in the U.S. Senate. In this front-page story by a writer identified only as "Raymond," the* Tribune *provides an astute analysis of the maneuvers of various financial interest groups and the bribery and corruption that had led up to the revolt.*

Chicago Tribune, 6 November 1903

PANAMA REVOLT SETS BACK CANAL

If New Government Is Set Up in Isthmus It Will Be Necessary to Pass Fresh Laws And Treaties

MEANS ROW IN CONGRESS

Friends of the Nicaragua Plan, Headed by Senator Morgan, Declare President Must Select That Route

[BY RAYMOND]

Washington, D.C., Nov. 5—[Special]—Of course all the difficulty on the isthmus of Panama is caused by the canal project. It has been the burning question there for a generation, and now, in the middle of an apparently successful revolution, the status of the Panama canal is even more curious than ever before. People here are in a quandary as to what the effect on the canal and its ownership—by the United States—will be.

While at first sight the revolution seems to be in the interest of the United States, there are legal questions involved to say nothing of diplomatic ones, which may have the effect of postponing the settlement of the question for years to come. If Panama becomes an independent nation, new legislation by Congress will become necessary before any treaty can be negotiated with the infant republic, and it is also within the range of possibility that a new agreement with the Panama company will have to be made.

All Work Must Be Done Over

In any event it is likely that the whole canal question will have to be thrashed over in congress this winter with the result that the old fight between Panama and Nicaragua will be renewed. This will be good news to the transcontinental railroad interests, which are opposed to the construction of any canal.

There have been frequent rumors afloat here that these same railroad interests were responsible for the opposition in Colombia to the ratification of the canal treaty with the United States. However this may be, it is at least suspicious that there was a sudden change of front on the part of the Colombian government, which began to make exorbitant demands of the United States.

There was really little cash-interest in the canal for the United States of Colombia. It had milked the canal company of all it could hope to expect and the amount to be received from the United States was comparatively insignificant. The American transcontinental railroad could easily have formed a pool to buy out the corrupt government of Colombia and pay more for the failure to ratify the treaty than the total amount mentioned to be paid by the United States as a bonus to Colombia.

Revolt Chokes Off Bogota Greed

Apparently the creation of a new republic on the isthmus of Panama by means of a successful revolution was the only means of circumventing the greedy officials at Bogota, who were always willing to sell themselves out to the highest bidder. It has been freely alleged that the United States officials on the isthmus, while they did not actually participate in the revolution, allowed it to be understood that the United States would be friendly to a revolutionary move and would preserve the neutrality of the Panama railroad so completely as to prevent the Colombian government from forwarding troops and munitions of war along that line. Such a charge is a serious thing from an international standpoint, and President Roosevelt's administration will not be anxious to pose as the receiver of stolen property or as having aided and abetted a revolution to secure to itself personal advantages.

Canal Influences Behind Revolt

There is an understanding here that the real influence behind the revolutionists at Panama has been the canal company itself. The stockholders in the French corporation cannot get a cent of their forty millions until the treaty is signed by Colombia as well as by the United States....

The local sentiment on the isthmus is, of course, favorable to the canal, and the people there have at last realized that if any money is to be paid by the United States it is much better that it should go to the government along the line of the canal than into the official financial rat hole at Bogota.

A variety of critics opposed U.S. support of the revolution and the establishment of a republic under the canal investors. These included those who still promoted the plan for a canal in Nicaragua, anti-imperialists who opposed further territorial expansion, Democrats critical of Roosevelt's Republican administration, and anyone opposed to Roosevelt's bellicose stance in international policy. One of those concerned about the repercussions of U.S. involvement was the New York Times. *It took the position that because of the terms of its treaties with Colombia, the United States could not ethically support the revolution while it continued to promote the Panama route for the canal. In this strongly anti-imperialistic editorial it suggests that the ethical and practical solution to the dilemma would be to adopt the Nicaragua route for the canal. The* Times *likens the situation in Panama to the role of business in the overthrow of the Hawaiian government and the subsequent annexation of the Hawaiian Islands.*

New York Times, 5 November 1903

THE PANAMA DANGER

Our entanglement with the Panama Canal undertaking has somewhat swiftly brought us to the point where we must either withdraw at once from the miserable business, or, shutting our ears to the voice of conscience and to the reproaches of civilized mankind, plunge on the path of scandal, disgrace, and dishonor.

The revolt of the Isthmian States against the Government of Colombia and the setting up of a little republic there has been altogether too openly encouraged and foreshadowed in this country to permit any further dalliance on our part with the abandoned Panama Canal unless we have come to such a pitch of shamelessness that we are willing to give the world the right of say that we have for our own selfish ends despoiled a sister republic of a part of her territory. The overthrow of the Hawaiian Government was accomplished under American guns, as a consequence of intrigues carried on with American help and encouragement openly given. That transaction put a stain upon our name, a blot upon our reputation for international fair dealing won by a century of honorable neutrality. A situation of like nature and involving a like measure of infamy has been created on the Isthmus.

The successive steps in our policy which have betrayed us into this position will be readily recalled....

We cannot in honor and with safety take part in the fighting unless we promptly proclaim, as we ought on other grounds to proclaim, our intention to have nothing further to do with the Panama Canal. In our treaty of 1846 with New Granada [which became the United States of Colombia], we guaranteed "positively and efficaciously to New Grenada...the perfect neutrality of the...Isthmus, with the view that the free transit from one to the other sea may not be interrupted or embarrassed in any future time while this treaty exists; and in consequence the United States also guarantees in the same manner the rights of sovereignty and property which New Grenada has and possesses over the same territory." The occurrence of a revolt and the steps to put it down would inevitable interrupt transit over the Panama Railroad. In performance of our guarantee we must interfere. We have already interfered by protesting against the bombardment of Panama. Our marines will be landed, force will be employed. Whatever professions of neutrality between the contestants we may make, our interference actually does prevent the suppression of the revolt by the Colombian Government. We in fact give almost the greatest possible aid and comfort to the rebels. All the world will say that we got up the revolution, that we procured the establishment of the little republic because of Colombia's refusal to give us the right to build the canal. Our most solemn assertions of disinterested motives would be laughed at. We should be held guilty of an act of sordid conquest, of splitting the Republic of Colombia in two to carry out our canal policy. Were the Isthmian republic established, declared independent, and the canal constructed, we should then become charged with responsibilities for its existence and its conduct, which would threaten our peaceful relations with other nation.... If any nation across the sea were seeking a cause of quarrel with us they would have it ready at hand. Moreover, we should infinitely deepen and intensify the distrust with which all the Spanish-American republics now regard us. What face could we put on against their charges of selfishness if they could point to the spoliation of Colombia as an exhibition of our National spirit and purposes? Our interference on the Isthmus to prevent war and bloodshed is a matter of right and obligation. But we can interfere with clean hands and unsuspected motives only after disclaiming any purpose to proceed further with the Panama Canal.

Scandal, vexation, and delay have aided every step of our procedure in the ill-advised Panama Canal undertaking.... The American people prefer the Nicaragua route, they believe it to be superior, they want the canal constructed across the Isthmus at that point. Under the law of Congress it is probably the duty of the President, it is evidently within his discretion, to adopt definitively the Nicaraguan route and consign the Panama Canal to oblivion. Scandal has beset it throughout its history. That scandal now involves our Government. We must protect our good name.

Despite opposition, the U.S. government proceeded to support the rebels through "enforced neutrality." On November 6 it recognized the new republic as a de facto government and began immediate steps to negotiate a treaty that would allow it to construct and control the canal. As the proposed treaty came up in Congress, a few anti-imperialists attacked it vehemently on the Senate floor and accused the president of promoting the treaty to enhance his own reelection prospects. Further, one critic suggested that the Roosevelt administration had made plans in advance of the outbreak of hostilities to support the revolution, and, in fact, had played a part in starting it. The Chicago Tribune *captures the spirit of the opposition in the following news story.*

Chicago Tribune, 18 December 1903

BEGIN ATTACK ON PANAMA TREATY

Senators Hoar and Gorman Open Warfare on Isthmian Canal Compact

FORAKER TO DEFENSE

Ohio Senator Upholds Action of President Roosevelt in Recent Affair

Washington, D.C., Dec. 17–[Special.]–The fight in opposition of the isthmian canal treaty with the new republic of Panama began in the senate today in earnest, although the treaty itself was not up for discussion.

Senator Hoar opened the debate with a speech of several hours duration in which he sharply criticized the part the United States played in the recent uprising on the isthmus. He compared the conduct of the United States on the Isthmus to a policeman who would manacle and hold a person about to be attacked for robbery, and then would insist on having the spoils of the theft delivered to himself.

Senator Gorman made a political issue of the isthmian question, declaring that President Roosevelt is endeavoring to involve the United States in war, for the reason that a war party candidate has never been defeated in this country.

Senator Foraker resented the remarks of Senator Hoar, construing them as an attack on President Roosevelt. This view Senator Hoar repudiated, and there was a warm exchange of words between the two men in which there was some little display of bitterness.

Senator Hoar's Attack

The senator from Massachusetts spoke on his resolution calling for information on events leading up to the Panama revolution. He spoke from manuscript, having prepared his speech carefully in advance. He began by saying that no man in the country desired more eagerly than himself to support the administration and act with his party associates in the senate chamber. He also was favorable to the isthmian canal, and moreover he was anxious the construction of the canal should be accomplished in his life and by the republican party. He also was desirous that the present president of the United States should build the great waterway. But anxious as he was for the accomplishment of all these ends, he was even more anxious that the canal should be built "without taint or suspicion of national dishonor." He continued: "What we want to know, did this government knowing that a revolution was about to take place, so arrange matters that the revolution, whether peaceable or otherwise, should be permitted to go on without interruption, and whether our national authorities took measures to prevent Colombia from stopping it?"

Mr. Hoar quoted the correspondence bearing upon the revolution, and asked: "Why this great anxiety before any disturbance had occurred?" It was, he said, clear that if the correspondence so far printed included all the information possible to give on the subject, from twenty-four to forty-eight hours before the revolution broke out this government had instructed a man-of-war [to proceed to the area]....

Mr. Gorman then discussed the president as a "second Napoleon," which title, he said, had been assigned to him by some.

"A second Napoleon, indeed," he exclaimed. Had it come to this, that the United States must have a Napoleon to shape its destinies and to distort the presidential office from its proper functions?

Mr. Gorman intimated, in conclusion, that the situation on the isthmus had been invited for political purposes, and on this point said:

A war party, it may be said, is in this country never defeated. Can it be in the mind of any man that a desperate political chance, growing out of the depressed conditions, makes it necessary for a political success that the flag and the armies of the country may be exhibited in some foreign land to strengthen the party and secure party power?"

The New York Times *also opposed the treaty on the grounds that its approval by the United States would violate the preexisting treaties with Colombia. In this editorial, the* Times *accuses the president of usurping the power invested in him by the Constitution. The* Times *calls on the Senate to reject the treaty and check the president in the "path of madness and danger" on which he had embarked. This selection ends with a litany of the many evils the United States will call down upon itself if it proceeds to ratify the treaty.*

New York Times, 23 November 1903

THE PRESIDENT

It rests with the Senate of the United States to check the President in the path of madness and danger which he is following, with a visibly increasing disregard of law. He has hurt the good name of the Nation by a flagrant breach of treaty obligation. He now intends a dangerous executive usurpation of power. For the injury already done, to ourselves and to the victim of our wrong, but an imperfect reparation can be made. It is in the power of the Senate to avert the graver mischief of the wrong in contemplation.

The President, aided by the Secretary of State, has planned to carry through to the end his policy of territorial aggression and canal building upon the Isthmus of Panama without further authority from Congress.... If the Hay-Varilla treaty is ratified by the Senate the President can snap his fingers at the House and at the country.... We have made this new republic. We have broken treaty faith with Colombia and have gone to the very verge of war with her in making it. We treated her once as a friend, we have now made her our enemy. In Bogota there is talk of war to reclaim the Isthmus. Our treaty guarantees Panama against assault. If we ratify it as it has been drawn, we shall sooner or later become involved in war with Colombia, if not with other South American republics....

If the Senate has not become drunk with the heady wine of territorial adventure that now fires the blood of the Administration it will so dispose of the treaty that the House of Representatives will have the opportunity to review and sanction or arrest the policy of the President.... The House of Representative may [well] have reached the conclusion that we are paying much too dear for our canal. A smirched reputation, the possibility of wars, the loss of trade, the responsibilities not to be measured which we shall assume by our guarantee of the sovereignty of the new republic set up by our own acts of bad faith and exposed to rapacious assault by other treaty-breaking powers—these are not matters to be overlooked in our rush and recklessness.

Questions

1. What were the various issues complicating the progress of plans to build a canal between the Pacific to the Atlantic Oceans? What were the arguments for and against the United States's building such a canal? How are these identified by the various newspapers quoted in this chapter?
2. How did the issue concerning the construction of a canal become more complicated when the revolution began in Panama? How is that complication described by the various newspapers quoted here?
3. This chapter states that different newspapers approached the revolution from different perspectives and this can be interpreted from their headlines. Describe the three major perspectives taken by these newspapers. How are these perspectives supported by the choice of words or facts included in the headlines and text of the selections?
4. What is unusual about the November 6 article in the *Chicago Tribune*, "Panama Revolt Sets Back Canal," that makes it stand out from the other newspaper articles cited? How is this more like an editorial than a news article?
5. Identify some of the basic points of the Monroe Doctrine and the concept of Manifest Destiny. How do these various articles and editorials support the ideology of the Monroe Doctrine and Manifest Destiny?

Notes

1. Mark Twain, "Letter," *Alta California*, 6 September 1868, p. 4.

2. "Canal Saves Month in Pleiades Voyage," *New York Times*, 28 August 1914, p. 7, and "The Contrast," *New York Times*, 16 August 1914, p. 14.

CHAPTER 12

The Socialist Party Challenges
the Status Quo, 1904

Miss May Goelet was the richest young woman in New York City when she married in 1903. Her father's real estate holdings were worth $25 million, and her own personal property was said to be worth $5 million. It was no wonder, therefore, that her wedding in St. Thomas's Church on 53rd Street was attended by only the best members of society. The guest list was made up of the cream of the American industrial nobility and included names—Astor, Vanderbilt, and Belmont—familiar to any contemporary American. As their carriages made their way along 5th Avenue to the church, the wedding guests were mobbed by a crowd of more than eight thousand women eager to see the ladies decked out in satin and silk; their arms and necks bedecked with diamonds, pearls, and rubies, and their shoulders draped with furs.[1]

The contrast between May Goelet and her wedding guests and the women crowding the streets to catch a glimpse of them couldn't have been greater. Though some in the crowd surely were middle-class women, the vast majority must have been from the poor and working classes. Some of them, in fact, could have been the wives or daughters of the city's striking house builders who that very day were trying to win union representation.[2] Most of these women wouldn't earn in a dozen lifetimes the value of the clothing and jewels Mrs. Astor wore to the wedding that day.

May Goelet's wedding wasn't the first and would not be the last society wedding to act as a showcase for the wealthy. Anyone picking up a newspaper and turning to the society pages on any given day in any city would be smitten by the number of announcements of such weddings. One rector of a wealthy Baltimore parish was so concerned by the apparent callousness of these displays that he advised "those who have everything to set the example of a quiet, unostentatious religious service."[3]

The scene at the Goelet wedding was emblematic of the deep fissures that had developed between the classes by the turn of the twentieth century. Although the United States had become one of the richest nations on earth toward the end of the 1800s, the gap between the rich and the poor became wider every year. In 1890 more than half the nation's wealth was owned by just 1 percent of the population; in 1900, 90 percent of the nation's wealth was owned by only 10 percent of the population. Laborers who worked 10-hour days and six-day weeks for a pittance read in the newspapers about their employers living in high style, building mansions, traveling to Europe for vacation, and attending society balls. Workers' attempts to unionize and make conditions better often brought brutal reprisals instead of improvements. For unskilled workers, immigrants, and the unemployed, the situation was bleak.

Socialism, which advocated an end to capitalism and the public ownership of factories, utilities, and transportation systems, appeared to many as a solution to these economic injustices. The ideology began in Europe with the writings of Karl Marx and Frederick Engels, who proposed the complete abolition of capitalism and private profit by violent revolutionary means. The version of socialism to be adopted in the United States advocated change through democratic reform at the ballot box and legislative and *evolutionary* rather than *revolutionary* methods.

The first socialist party to be formed in the United States was the Socialist Labor Party, established in 1877. In 1901 it joined with a dissenting faction, the Social Democratic Party, to create the Socialist Party of America (SPA). Among the more prominent members of the party were Milwaukee Socialist Victor L. Berger and labor leader Eugene V. Debs. Though Socialists were active in union organization, labor and political reform, and the woman's movement, the party never gained a significant foothold in national politics. The party nominated candidates for public office in every election and succeeded only occasionally in winning seats in local and state government; in the national elections, they won only a tiny fraction of the overall vote.

The Socialists nominated Eugene Debs for president in 1900, 1904, 1908, and 1912, when he received more than 900,000 votes, causing more than a little alarm in some circles. In that year, the party's membership peaked at 118,000 and more than 1,000 of its members held public office. Then, with the beginning of World War I, the party began to suffer a decline. It denounced the war as an imperialist conflict and urged resistance to restrictions on freedom of speech and the press, and the right to strike. Its offices were raided, many of its publications were suppressed, and members were harassed and arrested. Debs was sentenced to 10 years in jail for speaking against the war. Despite these setbacks, Debs remained so popular with his supporters that when he ran for president in the 1920 election—from his prison cell—he received more than 919,000 votes.

Mainstream newspapers tended to ignore the Socialists as a viable political party, and rarely covered the party's conventions and elections in any depth. When they did cover speeches by prominent Socialists or candidates, they often dismissed or ridiculed their ideas as ridiculous, impractical, or even dangerous. When they listed the election results for Socialist candidates—along with those of other third parties such as the Prohibitionists and the Populists—they did so almost as an afterthought at the end of stories about the (conventionally) legitimate candidates for the Republican and Democratic Parties.

The mainstream press did, however, frequently bring up socialism and socialists when it reported stories on social unrest. Socialists were suspected of riling up the striking workers at the Homestead Strike, for example, and were thought to be behind the acts of anarchists. The more radical feminists in the woman's movement and labor organizers were also accused of having socialistic tendencies. The mainstream press often used the words "socialism" and "socialists" like shibboleths laden with negative connotations. Sometimes a newspaper story would gratuitously throw in the word "socialist," almost as boilerplate to indicate antisocial or violent tendencies, as in the assertion, "There are no worse enemies of the workingmen of this country than these same ignorant and reckless Socialists and Anarchists of foreign origin."[4]

In 1904 the Socialist Party captured more serious news coverage than usual when Eugene Debs ran for president on the party ticket for the second time and captured enough votes to become a significant statistic. The readings in this chapter, which are all about the 1904 election, are organized in three sections. The news articles and editorials in the first section dismiss the Socialist Party as a legitimate political organization by a variety of methods. These include ridiculing the party's ideas or candidates, ignoring it in its discussion of issues particularly salient to the party, and pointing out that the party is too small to matter. Readings in the second section, instead, treat the Socialist Party as a legitimate political organization, reporting about its platform, candidates, and election results as they might any other political party. Finally, the two news articles in the third section treat the Socialist Party as a danger to society. One of these indicates the unease aroused among businessmen and industrialists by the Socialist's election results; the last selection uses Debs's own words to predict a political shift along class lines.

SOCIALIST PARTY NOT A LEGITIMATE POLITICAL ORGANIZATION

Eugene Debs had some news value because of his background as a labor organizer and the notoriety he had earned for his leadership in the Pullman

Strike of 1892. His nomination for the presidency by the Socialist Party received three paragraphs on page three of the New York Times, *where a number of other political news items were published.*

New York Times, 6 May 1904

DEBS FOR PRESIDENT

Socialist Party Puts Him Up—Platform Favors Labor Unions

CHICAGO, May 5—The National Socialist Convention to-day nominated Eugene V. Debs for president of the United States. Benjamin Hanford of New York was nominated for Vice President. Neither of the candidates has any opposition.

The platform says capitalism and private ownership of the means of employment "grinds society in an economic slavery which renders intellectual and political tyranny inevitable."

The plank in the platform favoring labor unions, which caused several heated discussions during the convention, was adopted by a vote of 107 to 53.

The New York Times, *which was known for its staunch support of business interests, would have naturally opposed any Socialist candidate proposing the overthrow of capitalism and private ownership. But rather than debating the issue, it chose to dismiss the Socialist Party's candidate and platform as insignificant and irrelevant. In the following editorial, the* Times *describes Debs as marginal within his own party. The editorial also gets in a few jabs at the party, which it reduces to the status of a mere "mischievous element."*

New York Times, 7 May 1904

FOR PRESIDENT, EUGENE V. DEBS

There is something quite logical in the nomination of Mr. DEBS as President by the "National Socialist Convention." He stands and has from his first appearance in public agitation stood for the Socialist phase of trade unionism though he has not always professed Socialism, and the kind that he does profess and tries to put in practice would be repudiated by many Socialists.

DEBS represents the appetites of Socialism without the sense of real justice underlying the creed in many of its devotees. He and his followers believe in the division of the property of those who are in possession, but have little sympathy with the notion of the common obligation to produce and to share the product of labor which the more generous of the Socialists enforce with sincerity. The higher type of Socialism is as much opposed to the strict and selfish monopoly of the trades union as DEBS conceives it as it is opposed to the monopoly of wealth not acquired by manual labor, or its equivalent. While there is such a thing as constructive Socialism, in which mutual obligation is emphasized, DEBS'S policy is one of destruction on the one hand and greed on the other.

But it should not be forgotten that there is an ideal of trades unionism also that is free from the injurious and corrupting spirit of the DEBS sort, as is witnessed by the railroad unions over which he never, in his most fortunate period, obtained any influence. It is unfair and unwise to class all unions with the worst, as it is to class all employing corporations with the worst. It is ten years since DEBS was at the zenith of his remarkable career. At that time it seemed to many probable that he and his organization would not be suppressed until after a prolonged and severe struggle. The struggle was severe, but it was short, and to-day he is hardly more than an example to be avoided. His policy was, and was seen to be, as disastrous in his own class as to the people generally. That fact is encouraging. It is an evidence that in our country and under our institutions any large body of Americans can be trusted in the long run to cast out mischievous elements.

While the Republican and Democratic candidates in the 1904 election got plenty of coverage throughout their campaigns, the Socialist Party and its candidates, like most third parties before and since, rarely appeared in the mainstream press. (The Prohibition, People's and Socialist Labor Parties also had candidates in the 1904 election but received even less coverage than the Socialist Party did.) The San Francisco Chronicle, *which was an avid supporter of Republican candidate Theodore Roosevelt, could barely bring itself to mention the party. In this editorial exhorting labor to vote Republican, it studiously avoids even naming the Socialist Party, though it does refer obliquely to socialists as "agitators." This is a startling omission, given that the Socialists aligned themselves first and foremost with labor interests. This is the most negative editorial possible vis-à-vis the Socialist Party, for in not even mentioning the party, it denies its very existence.*

San Francisco Chronicle, 5 November 1904

THE "LABOR" VOTE

The Santa Fe and Southern Pacific railroads compete very vigorously with each other for business. If you do not believe it, go from one office to another and try to buy tickets to New York for a party of ten. But when it comes to securing legislation for the benefit of the railroad business they work as heartily together as though they never disagreed. If you don't believe it go to Sacramento next winter and watch the railroad lobby. It is the same with the corporations. However they may disagree about the division of business, or about other matters as they affect their profits as between each other, they labor and contribute alike for measures affecting the common welfare.

It would seem that wage-earners ought to show equal wisdom. That they sometimes disagree with their employers on matters arising between them is inevitable. In such cases the feeling may become as bitter as that between two corporations engaged in a competitive fight. It could be no worse. Nevertheless, the prosperity of the iron trade…and all other industries is as vital to the employed as to employers…. Considering all our industries, the interests of employers and employees are identical. It is silly beyond conception for working men to permit any temporary feeling of hostility toward employers to in the least affect their voices on political questions. An industry that is divided is in danger.

The natural cleavage of electors is along the lines of the interests of the occupations by which they live. Whatever promotes the prosperity of the Union Iron Works means more bread and butter for all employed there. The [Socialist] agitator who seeks to divide voters on the lines of their class instead of the lines of their industries is a social criminal. To the extent of his influence he is responsible for misery. There is no California industry which would not be injured by an impairment of the protective policy through fake reciprocity or otherwise. The Republican party stands for protection. The Democratic party stands for its abandonment. The California workingman who votes for any other than a Republican on the national ticket votes to reduce his chances of steady employment. They ought to see it. The men who would suffer most by giving union labor votes to Democratic candidates are union laborers. Think it over.

Even when Debs and the Socialist Party showed an impressive increase of votes at the polls over those in the previous presidential election of 1900, some newspapers dismissed the significance of their victory. In the following editorial, for example, the New York Times *attempted to put everything in perspective by first pointing out that the number of votes gained by the Socialists was relatively insignificant and then by arguing that the reforms sought by the party were no longer as radical as they had once seemed. Though the* Times *does not use the term, this editorial predicts that the goals of the Socialists are gradually being coopted by the established Republican and Democratic Parties and that the Socialist Party will soon find itself redundant.*

New York Times, 18 December 1904

SWALLOWING THE SOCIALISTS

We have not shared the alarm which the Debs vote has produced in the minds of some of our contemporaries. In the first place, the vote of Mr. DEBS' Socialist party was not 600,000 as first reported. THE TIMES'S figures of the total votes published last week show 392,857 votes for DEBS. The Rev. Mr. SWALLOW, the Prohibitionist candidate, polled 248,411. We have not heard that the distillery interests are alarmed by the Prohibition vote. There is little reason to be disturbed by the DEBS vote.

In the second place, it seems to us that the Socialist Party is in no little danger of being entirely swallowed up by the two great political [Democratic and Republican] parties.... What is going to happen to the Socialist Party is foreshadowed by Mr. W. J. BRYAN in The Commoner:

> The President, in his message, warns the Republicans that they must regulate railroad rates if they would prevent the growth of sentiment in favor of "more radical" legislation. This is a clear reference to the growth of the Socialist Party. When the Populist Party entered the political arena it favored the income tax, the election of Senators by the people...bimetallism, the issue of non-redeemable legal-tender Treasury notes, the Government ownership of railroads, a Sub-Treasury system for the storage of farm products, and the loaning of money to the people directly at a low rate of interest. The Democratic Party took up the income tax, the election of Senators by the people, direct legislation, and bimetallism. The Populist contention for an irredeemable currency...is not now discussed as much as it formerly was. The increased volume of money has lessened the interest in all phases of the money question, while the Democratic advocacy of the right of the Government to issue the paper money has narrowed the issues for which Populism distinctly stands.

The fate of the Populists, who are a crude and half-baked variety of Socialists, awaits the followers of DEBS. Many articles of the Socialist creed have been adopted into the Bryan confession of faith made at St. Louis last Summer. Mr. BRYAN says that "it requires no prophet to foresee the day when the people will prefer to risk whatever dangers may be involved in Government ownership (of railroads) to a continuation of private ownership under prevailing conditions." In principle that is pretty much the whole body of Socialism. For if it once be granted that the railroads must be owned and operated by the Government, there is no stopping place short of Government ownership of telegraphs, telephones, mines, and everything else in the DEBS category.

On the other hand, Mr. ROOSEVELT has laid a predatory hand upon the Socialist covenant in his recommendation that railroad rates be fixed by a

Government commission. The active Socialists are keen minded. They instantly saw that the President's doctrine of an always increasing Government control over interstate commerce advanced the President, and with him the Republican Party, sure and not short strides toward their own position. The end of continuing a constantly more detailed and intimate control of railroads by the Government is ownership. Private capitalists would in time decline to own them. They would make all haste to get their money out of such perilous investments. The roads would naturally fall into the hands of the Government. President ROOSEVELT must foresee all this if he has diligently and logically thought through the project.

So what is there left for the Socialists to preach and to do? In the slang of the day, "things are coming their way." When the Bryanized Democrats upon the one hand and the Republicans upon the other lay hold on the principles of DEBS, it is time for DEBS himself to be looking around for another job. There is too much competition for his faith and his flag.

SOCIALIST PARTY A LEGITIMATE POLITICAL ORGANIZATION

Debs and the Socialist Party got more serious coverage in Milwaukee, where Socialists had played a role in state and city government since 1898. The Milwaukee Journal, *for example, ran a regular Social Democrat Column, which was written by party leader Victor Berger. Though this often read like the minutes of a meeting, it did have the advantage of providing a full account of party activities and positions on issues. It also gave the various party leaders a chance to have their say. The column's announcement of Debs's nomination, for example, ran to a quarter-page, compared to the* New York Times*'s three-paragraph story. Far from dismissing Debs as a has-been, the* Milwaukee Journal*'s column describes him as a kind of hero whose nomination is greeted with enthusiasm and applause.*

Milwaukee Journal, 7 May 1904

Victor L. Berger: SOCIAL DEMOCRAT COLUMN
THE NOMINATIONS
(Conducted under the auspices of the state executive board
of the Social Democratic party, by Victor L. Berger.
Send all correspondences for this column to 344 Sixth-st.)
Never were candidates for the presidency and the vice presidency nominated with more enthusiasm and with less delay than Eugene V. Debs of In-

diana and Ben Hanford of New York by the Social Democratic party in its convention held in Chicago.

Thursday afternoon, upon the adoption of the platform, the chairman announced that the order of business now reached was the nomination of candidates for president and vice president of the United States. Prof. George D. Herron took the platform and nominated Eugene V. Debs for president in an enthusiastic and well-worded speech, which called forth rounds of applause from the delegates and the visitors in the galleries.

Professor Herron said that he would go away from the Chicago convention an optimist for the working class. Here in America the struggle between capital and labor has intensified more than one could have prophesied twenty years ago, and beyond anything in any other part of the world. He had no doubt that the great world struggle would be precipitated here in America. There was no doubt that the sun of the co-operative common-wealth would rise first rise upon the republic of America. There is no man who more faithfully embodies the struggle of the working class for its emancipation or more surely voices that struggle than Eugene V. Debs. The speaker counted it as the greatest joy in his life to stand before the convention and nominate Eugene V. Debs as the candidate of the Socialist party of America....

Delegate Titus of Pennsylvania then took the platform and nominated for vice president Ben Hanford of New York. Hanford, the speaker stated, was a man truly representative of labor. He struggled for the movement and he suffered for it....

Mr. Debs was not present at this stage of the proceedings, but Ben Hanford being in the hall, was escorted to the platform...and made a speech of acceptance. He said that whenever the Socialist party wanted him to do anything, he did it whether he liked it or not. He did this more readily because the Socialist party had done more for him than he had ever done for the Socialist party.... So far from having made sacrifices, the speaker believed that but for the Socialist movement he should not be living today. Some ten years ago a type-setting machine was introduced in to the office where he worked which threw out of employment himself and many of his fellow workmen.

He then saw men whom he had known for years...driven out into the street, into enforced idleness for the lack of work. He saw these men go into the ginshop and go down into a drunkard's grave.... [T]he reason he did not go down with them was that about that time the truths of Socialism dawned upon him, and while they became despondent and went to the saloon, he was always busy with some Socialist book, or some Socialist meeting, or went out on the streets to speak for the Socialist principles, and what was despair for others was the dawn of hope for him.

"Let your hearts be true as steel and we shall have Socialism—yes, and we shall have it in our time."

The convention adopted the following resolutions in regard to the Russo-Japanese war.... [The resolutions express solidarity with the working people of Japan and Russia, condemn the war, and invite the working people of Japan and Russia to join the International Socialist movement in its struggle for world peace.]

Many newspapers were taken aback when, at the conclusion of the 1904 elections, it became apparent that the Socialist Party had collected a respectable number of votes at the polls and that, moreover, these showed a significant gain over the previous election. One of the well-recognized news values is change, and any increase in votes for a marginal party was news. The party's gain in California was notable, and the San Francisco Chronicle *could not refrain from pointing out that this was "surprising."*

San Francisco Chronicle, 10 November 1904

SOCIALIST VOTE IS INCREASING

Several Counties of the State Gave Debs, Presidential Candidate, Surprising Support

PARTY QUITE STRONG IN LOS ANGELES

In That City Its Electors Received Nearly Half as Many Ballots as Democrats—Other Sections Gave Fair Returns

Special Dispatch to the "Chronicle"

Much interest has been aroused in California as well as throughout the country by the unexpectedly heavy vote cast by the Socialists. No effort has yet been made to secure complete tabulations, but special reports obtained by the "Chronicle" from various counties of the State give a fair idea of the increase in the Socialistic vote as cast for Debs, the Presidential candidate of the party. In Los Angeles city, Debs received nearly half as many votes as [Democratic candidate Alton B.] Parker and three times as many as the Prohibition candidate.

This proportion was not maintained throughout the country, as there are many strong Prohibition towns. But that the Socialists have gained strength is demonstrated by Debs receiving 290 votes to 243 for Parker in Pasadena. San Joaquin gave Debs 322 votes, while Swallow, the Prohibitionist, received only 93. Sacramento county contains 1055 Socialists and Santa Clara has 740 residents who have been attracted to the party, a notable increase in both counties. [Bulletins from Los Angeles, San Joaquin, Sacramento and Santa Clara follow with details.]

Those gains were reflected across the nation, with Debs winning the most votes in Illinois. This was noted by the Milwaukee Journal, *which, using estimated results of the election, provided a table contrasting the results of 1900 and 1904. Though this table is incomplete, with dashes representing unavailable numbers, it clearly indicates a substantial growth in the party's popularity.*

Milwaukee Journal, 10 November 1904

GREAT INCREASE IN SOCIALIST VOTE

Record made by Debs Second Only in Interest to Great Republican Pluralities

The notable increase in the Socialist vote in Tuesday's election is second in political interest only to the avalanche of votes for Roosevelt. Four years ago Debs, as the presidential candidate of the Socialist party, received 87,769 votes in the entire United States. Last Tuesday, Debs, as the candidate of the same party, received more votes in the state of Illinois alone than he did in the whole country four years before, and in the United States, his vote may touch the 500,000 mark.

State	1904	1900	State	1904	1900
Alabama	300	......	Nebraska	4,000	823
California	......	7,554	Nevada	1,700	......
Colorado	1,800	654	N. Ham.	......	790
Connecticut	3,000	1,029	N. Jersey	......	4,603
Delaware	......	57	New York	......	12,569
Florida	......	602	N. Dakota	1,500	518
Georgia	80	......	Ohio	35,000	4,847
Idaho	4,000	......	Oregon	22,000	1,466
Illinois	100,000	9,687	Penna.	5,000	4,831
Indiana	12,000	3,374	Rhode Isl.	789	......
Iowa	10,000	2,742	S. Carolina	50	......
Kansas	8,000	1,605	S. Dakota	7,000	176
Kentucky	......	760	Tennessee	750	410
Louisiana	1,500	......	Texas	50,000	1,846
Maine	1,500	873	Utah	3,000	720
Maryland	2,300	903	Vermont	100	......
Mass.	12,000	9,595	Virginia	200	......
Michigan	......	2,826	Washington	......	2,006
Minnesota	10,000	3,063	W. Virginia	2,500	288
Mississippi	300	......	Wisconsin	35,000	524
Missouri	......	6,128	Wyoming	500	......
Montana	5,000	708			

Early newspaper reports on the election results varied on the number of votes Debs had received. Early reports stated that the Socialists had polled 600,000 votes; this was later reduced to 327,857. The significant fact recognized everywhere, however, was that the party had grown in strength. In the following story summarizing the election results, the New York Times *(at that time, a Democratic paper) characterized this growth as remarkable—only after it first reported on the electoral triumph scored by the Republican candidate, Theodore Roosevelt.*

New York Times, 10 November 1904

343 ELECTORAL VOTES 1,766,400 PLURALITY

Roosevelt Presidential Figures The Greatest Ever Known

MAJORITY IN CONGRESS 100

Missouri in the Republican Electoral Column, but Folk Elected Governor—Adams Wins in Colorado—Socialists Polled 600,000 Votes

Revised election returns from the forty-five States serve but to accentuate the fact that Theodore Roosevelt has achieved the greatest personal triumph ever won by a candidate for President. Great as were the pluralities recorded for him Tuesday night from every State which had been classed as doubtful, they were increased by additional and completed returns yesterday. No such pluralities have ever been known in a Presidential election. They far exceed those given to William McKinley in the election of 1896. Mr. Roosevelt's net plurality in the whole country is 1,700,400.

The high-water mark established by Mr. McKinley on the Electoral vote is completely submerged by the great Roosevelt tidal wave. Mr. Roosevelt is certain of 343 votes in the Electoral College. He obtains the eighteen Electoral votes of Missouri, giving him 343 Electoral votes in all, or fifty-one more than Mr. McKinley had when four years ago he beat all records existing up to that time.

One of the remarkable features of the election was the unexpectedly large vote polled by the Socialists. Eugene V. Debs, the Socialist candidate for President, received over 40,000 votes in the city of Chicago alone, being nearly double the vote polled by the Socialists in that city two years ago. Everywhere the Socialist vote was largely increased.

National Secretary William Mailly of the Socialist Party in a dispatch sent to a Socialist organ [newspaper] in this city, last night estimated the total vote cast for Debs and Hanford in the entire country at 600,000. He stated that the party's vote was increased in every state except Massachusetts. Two members of the Assembly were elected by the Socialists in Illinois.

Socialist Party a Danger

Though Debs certainly had fallen far short of the presidency with only 3.5 percent of the popular vote, local Socialist candidates won seats in everything from city councils to state legislatures. This alarmed everyone from Republican and Democratic Party officials to local merchants and industrialists, who began to organize against the threat a successful Socialist Party might pose to their equilibrium. In Milwaukee, for example, some manufacturers began to collect statistics on party membership.

Milwaukee Journal, 10 November 1904

EMPLOYERS INQUIRE INTO SOCIALISTS' GROWTH

Reports from Chicago are that an inquiry is being quietly conducted in Milwaukee, as well as other points, to obtain statistics on the strength of the Social Democratic party. The defeat of Parker by Debs in Milwaukee County by several votes in the race for president is considered phenomenal, even among the party workers in Milwaukee, who are familiar with conditions.

In Chicago, the Socialists claim 50,000 votes and some manufacturers see in this growth the adoption by union men of the Social Democratic party as a means for organized movements for legislation. The information received in the inquiry now in progress is to be presented to Employers' Association officials in New York Nov. 23 and 25.

These words were used by Debs in a written statement shortly after the election describing what he believed to be the new political alignment of voters along class lines, with the Republicans representing the capitalist classes, and the Socialists representing the working classes. Debs's choice of words may have had a faintly threatening tone, but this is certainly accentuated by the Milwaukee Journal's *use of the phrase in its headline on the story.*

Milwaukee Journal, 10 November 1904

"MUST RECKON WITH SOCIALISM"

TERRE HAUTE, IND., NOV. 10—Eugene V. Debs, candidate on the Social Democratic Ticket for the presidency, writes as follows:

"The Socialist vote in every part of the country has been enormously increased. My advices are that Cook county, Illinois, will give us at least 50,000
votes. The state of Illinois alone will probably cast a larger Socialist vote this
year than was cast in all the United States four years ago. It is too early to
make an estimate of the total national vote, but enough is known to warrant
the statement that from this time forward the Republicans will have the Socialist party to reckon with and that the coming alignment will be between
the Republican party representing the capitalistic interests, and the Socialist
party representing the working classes. As for the Democratic party, the
eastern capitalists hit harder than they intended, and it can hardly be pulled
together again to serve as a twin to the Republican party to divide the working classes."

QUESTIONS

1. Why would mainstream newspapers tend to ignore the interests of third
    parties such as the Socialists? Why would the platforms, issues, and can-
    didates of these parties be considered irrelevant?
2. By 1904 newspapers were developing the modern concept of newswor-
    thiness, which identifies certain events and issues as being of interest for
    a newspaper. Some of the characteristics in a story that have been iden-
    tified as newsworthy are conflict, unusualness, prominence (of an indi-
    vidual or individuals in a story), significance, and impact. In what ways
    would a story about Eugene Debs winning the Socialist nomination be
    considered newsworthy? In what ways would it NOT qualify as news-
    worthy? How were these qualities of newsworthiness related to the way
    in which his nomination and election were treated by the newspapers
    quoted here?
3. What were some of the words and phrases these articles and editorials
    used to describe the Socialists that identified them as legitimate or ille-
    gitimate political players?
4. What is the difference in tone used in the three types of items cited here
    (news article, editorial, and party column)? How does each perform a
    specific function? Which of these is most truthful and informative?
5. How is it possible for an article or editorial to be negative or dismissive
    if it doesn't even mention the Socialist Party (like "The 'Labor' Vote"
    quoted in this chapter)?

NOTES

1. "Duke of Roxburghe Marries Miss Goelet," *New York Times,* 11 November 1903, pp. 1, 2.

2. "No Aid for Local Union," *New York Times,* 11 November 1903, p. 2.

3. "Criticises Society Weddings," *New York Times,* 17 November 1903, p. 7.

4. This appeared in a *New York Times* editorial after the arrest of a self-proclaimed anarchist for the attempted assassination of Carnegie plant manager Henry Frick during the Homestead Strike in 1892. There is no indication the would-be assassin was a socialist. "Labor and Anarchy," *New York Times,* 25 July 1892, p. 4.

CHAPTER 13

The Triangle Shirtwaist Factory Fire, March 25, 1911

Both Annie Altman and Antonetta Pasqualicca had jobs by the time they were 16 years old.[1] They, like thousands of other immigrant women, found work in New York City's garment industry, where they worked as many as 59 hours a week during the busy season for as little as $4 per week. Contrary to the fondly held belief that women were sheltered and cosseted in their homes by protective male relatives and worked only to earn "pin money," these women worked because they had to. They worked because their brothers and fathers did not earn enough to support their families, or they worked because they *had* no male relatives to support them.

Far from being cosseted, women like Annie and Antonetta—as well as many immigrant men who worked in the garment industry—labored in miserable, exploitative, and dangerous working conditions. They were locked in the sweatshops during the long working day so they couldn't pilfer bits of cloth and thread and so they couldn't step outside for a breath of fresh air. They were harassed by employers and shop foremen to speed up their work. They were charged for thread, the rental of their equipment, and any mistakes they made. They were shortchanged in their pay envelopes, and the time clocks were frequently set back so that they never got a full lunch break or would work an hour extra in the evening without realizing it. When they protested conditions, they were bullied and even beaten by hired thugs.

In the early 1900s garment workers attempted to unionize and instigated several walkouts and strikes. A walkout at the Triangle Shirtwaist Company—one of the city's many shirtwaist factories—in the fall of 1908 ended unsuccessfully after only three days, for the workers had no union to represent them and could not afford to stay out. The next year the Triangle workers joined the Uprising of Thirty Thousand, which resulted in a strike that lasted for three months between November 1909 and February 1910.[2] The strikers demanded union shops, weekly instead of biweekly pay, a 52-hour work week, and the discontinuance of workers being charged for electricity and materials. They also called for improved safety standards, including adequate fire escapes and unlocked doors.

The women who picketed the garment factories during the uprising were harassed and beaten by thugs hired by the factory owners and were then arrested by police for disturbing the peace, loitering, prostitution, and assault. They found little sympathy in the courts, and many were sent to the workhouse to serve sentences ranging from a few days to several weeks. Despite some financial assistance from wealthy New York society women sympathetic to the cause, the strikers could not outlast their employers, who refused to give in to their demands. The strike was called off in mid-February. While concessions were made by some employers, between one thousand and three thousand workers, including those at the Triangle Shirtwaist Company, went back to work with no gains.[3]

A year later, on a Saturday afternoon in late March, Annie Altman and Antonetta Pasqualicca, were among the five hundred workers at the Triangle Shirtwaist Company getting ready to finish their work and leave for the day. The girls worked in the top 3 floors of the 10-story building, where the rooms were crowded with equipment, the floors were littered with piles of fabric, and the air was filled with lint. It was just a few minutes before closing time when someone smelled smoke. Panic broke out immediately, and workers rushed for the stairs and elevators only to find them blocked and filled with smoke. The next half-hour was a disaster.

The building did not have a sprinkler system. Its staircases were narrow and blocked with litter; it had only one fire escape that led to a dead end in an inner courtyard, and it had only two exit doors, one of which was locked. When the fire companies arrived, their ladders only reached to the sixth floor. The workers had never been trained how to evacuate the building in case of emergency, and those who did not get out of the building in the first few minutes either died in the flames and smoke or leaped to their deaths from windows to the pavement below. By the time it was all over, 146 workers, most of them women, had died. Annie Altman and Antonetta Pasqualicca, 16, were among them. It was the worst industrial fire in American history.

The Triangle fire caught public attention quickly, partly because it took place in broad daylight in front of hundreds of witnesses, including newspaper reporters. Newspapers gave it front-page coverage for days and illustrated their stories with gripping photographs of police and firefighters piling charred and broken bodies in the street. Reporters interviewed stunned and grieving survivors and relatives and wrote heartrending ac-

"FIREPROOF!"

"Fireproof!" *New York World,* 27 March 1911, p. 10. *The* New York World *was outraged by the unsafe working conditions and unenforced safety codes that resulted in the death of garment workers in a devastating fire in the Triangle Waist Company in March 1911. The factory owners were tried for negligence, but got off with a slap on the wrist. Building codes, however, were tightened and new regulations required free access to exits, stairs, and fire escapes. Here, Death looks over the New York City skyline from the charred remains of the factory.*

counts of their ordeal. Most New York newspapers immediately called for an investigation of the building's owners as well as a full investigation of the city's inspection of building and safety codes. Some of the more sensational papers peppered their demands for an investigation with charges ranging from official incompetency to bribery. Newspapers in other parts of the country questioned the broader issue of worker safety and asked if this could happen in their own factories.

As the families claimed the victims, newspapers gave extensive coverage to the funerals that followed. A funeral parade organized by the International Ladies Garment Workers Union and the Women's Trade Union League was attended by more than half a million people. Newspapers captured the grim photographs of the mourners walking down Fifth Avenue with their heads staunchly bowed in the rain. In the more descriptive stories, some newspapers dwelled on the fact that many of the workers were immigrants and that many still spoke their native tongue. At a time when nativist sentiment was strong and many newspapers were hostile toward immigrants, these stories were remarkably sympathetic. They described the victims and their families as in-nocent, hardworking people—a far cry from xenophobic descriptions of im-migrants as ignorant, criminal, and the "scum of the earth."

The story developed into one of even broader implications when the Women's Trade Union League publicized the fact that the Triangle Waist Company had been 1 of the 13 companies to deny workers better working conditions in the Uprising of Thirty Thousand of the previous year. Ironically, one of the rejected union demands had been for adequate fire escapes and exit doors. When some of the survivors reported that one of the factory's two doors had been locked to keep out union agitators and to prevent workers from taking unauthorized breaks (the other had been blocked by fire), some newspapers focused on the struggle between labor and management.

The ensuing criminal investigation quickly led to charges of negligence and first- and second-degree manslaughter against the company's owners, and their trial was concluded in December. Though owners Isaac Harris and Max Blanck had already been tried, convicted, and hanged by public opinion and the press, the jury acquitted them. It could not be proven beyond a rea-sonable doubt that either of the two men was aware one of the factory's two doors had been locked and it could not be proven that its being locked had caused the deaths. The verdict was greeted with shock by a mob of sobbing and distraught relatives, some of whom shouted "Murderers! Murderers!" as the defendants were rushed from a side door of the court building.[4]

Thus, Harris and Blanck escaped the weight of the law. They started up the production of shirtwaists at another building within five days of the fire and were quickly found to be in violation of safety codes there also. They appar-ently didn't learn their lesson, for two years after that, Blanck was fined $20 for locking the door of his factory with a chain while 150 women were at work in the shop.[5] Nevertheless, the Triangle victims had some kind of vindication in that the publicity generated by the fire, the criminal investigation, and the trial led to the formation of the New York Factory Investigation Commission and, eventually, new safety codes in factories.[6] The story also attracted atten-

This Is One of a Hundred Murdered
Is any one to be punished for this?

"**This Is One of a Hundred Murdered**," *New York Evening Journal*, 27 March 1911, p. 1. *Many of the victims to die in the Triangle Waist Company fire were young women between ages 16 and 22. They worked for meager wages in crowded sweatshops where there were inadequate fire escapes, blocked stairways and exit doors, and no sprinkler systems. The* New York Evening Journal, *which called the deaths "murder," shows a pay envelope lying near the outstretched hand of this victim.*

tion to the miserable working conditions in garment-district factories and the hardships faced by the women who worked 59 hours a week in sweatshops like the Triangle factory. (Perhaps as a result of this publicity, their work week was reduced to 54 hours by state law in 1913.)

The most prominent issue to be debated in the aftermath of the Triangle fire was the question of who was responsible for the tragedy. Many pointed the finger at the factory owners who had failed or refused to install certain safety features, such as fire escapes and water sprinklers, and had blatantly violated safety codes by locking one of the two exits to the stairs. But some also found the city at fault for its failure to institute and enforce safety codes that would have prevented the tragedy. These perspectives can be found in many of the editorials, news stories, and editorial cartoons about the fire, even though their subject may be quite different. The readings in this chapter have been organized in two sections, reflecting the two sides to this debate. The selections in the first section cover a number of developments in the Triangle fire and the ensuing investigation, but at some point indicate the belief that the owners are responsible for the tragedy. Those in the second section, instead, focus more on the city's responsibility, asking why the building had not been inspected, why the existing, if inadequate, building code had not been enforced, and why a more vigorous code had not been in place. In some of these selections, specific city officials are blamed for corruption and inefficiency.

OWNERS RESPONSIBLE FOR THE TRAGEDY

The fire broke out late Saturday afternoon, March 25, and received prominent coverage the next day on page one in most Sunday papers. The usually sober New York Times *filled half its front page with an alarming four-column headline, a succession of 13 subheads in which it summarized major points of the fire, a three-column photograph of the top floors of the burning building, and the beginning of its lead story. The next four pages were devoted to stories about the fire that included interviews with witnesses, survivors, and relatives of the victims, descriptions of rescue workers' efforts, a list of those victims who had been identified, a statement from the factory's owners, and a report that the district attorney was launching an inquiry. Each page was illustrated with dramatic photographs. These stories were remarkably colorful for the* Times. *They included personal observations from its reporters—which was unusual in the* Times, *though practiced by many of its New York competitors—and came close to being emotional in their descriptions of the tragedy. In the following story, the* Times *describes the horror of the fire and the victims' fate before briefly reporting that the owners had escaped unharmed. The contrast between the owners' escape and their workers' deaths is startling.*

New York Times, 26 March 1911

141 MEN AND GIRLS DIE IN WAIST FACTORY FIRE; TRAPPED HIGH UP IN WASHINGTON PLACE BUILDING; STREET STREWN WITH BODIES; PILES OF DEAD INSIDE

The Flames Spread with Deadly Rapidity Through Flimsy Material Used in the Factory

600 GIRLS ARE HEMMED IN

When Elevators Stop Many Jump to Certain Death And Others Perish in Fire-Filled Lofts

STUDENTS RESCUE SOME

Help Them to Roof of New York University Building, Keeping the Panic-Stricken In Check

ONE MAN TAKEN OUT ALIVE

Plunged to Bottom of Elevator Shaft and Lived There Amid Flames for Four Hours

ONLY ONE FIRE ESCAPE

Coroner Declares Building Laws Were Not Enforced—
Building Modern—Classed Fireproof

JUST READY TO GO HOME

Victims Would Have Ended Day's Work In A Few Minutes—
Pay Envelopes Identify Many

MOB STORMS THE MORGUE

Seeking to Learn Fate of Relatives Employed by The Triangle Waist Company

Three stories of a ten-floor building at the corner of Greene Street and Washington Place were burned yesterday and while the fire was going on 141 young men and women—at least 125 of them mere girls—were burned to death or killed by jumping to the pavement below.

The building was fireproof. It shows now hardly any signs of the disaster that overtook it. The walls are as good as ever; so are the floors; nothing is the worse for the fire except the furniture and 141 of the 600 men and girls that were employed in its upper three stories. Most of the victims were suffocated or burned to death within the building, but some who fought their way to the windows and leaped met death as surely, but perhaps more quickly, on the pavements below.

All Over in Half an Hour

Nothing like it has been seen in New York since the burning of the General Slocum. The fire was practically all over in half an hour.... The victims who are now lying at the Morgue waiting for someone to identify them by a tooth or the remains of a burned shoe were mostly girls of from 16 to 23 years of age. They were employed at making shirtwaists by the Triangle Waist Company, the principal owners of which are Isaac Harris and Max Blanck. Most of them could barely speak English. Many of them came from Brooklyn. Almost all were the main support of their hard-working families.

There is just one fire escape in the building. That one is an interior fire escape. In Greene Street, where the poor unfortunates crowded before they began to make their mad leaps to death, the whole big front of the building is guiltless of one. Nor is there a fire escape in the back....

Leaped Out of the Flames

At 4:40 o'clock, nearly five hours after the employees in the rest of the building had gone home, the fire broke out. The one little fire escape in the interior was never resorted to by any of the doomed victims. Some of them escaped by running down the stairs, but in a moment or two this avenue was cut off by the flames. The girls rushed to the windows and looked down at Greene Street, 100 feet below them. Then one poor, little creature jumped. There was a plate glass protection over part of the sidewalk, but she crashed through it, wrecking it and breaking her body into a thousand pieces.

Then they all began to drop. The crowd yelled, "Don't Jump!" but it was jump or be burned—the proof of which is found in the fact that fifty burned bodies were taken from the ninth floor alone.

They jumped. They crashed through broken glass, they crushed themselves to death on the sidewalk. Of those who stayed behind it is better to say nothing—except what a veteran policeman said as he gazed at a headless and charred trunk on the Greene Street sidewalk hours after the worst cases had been taken out:

"I saw the Slocum disaster, but it was nothing to this."

"Is it a man or woman?" asked the reporter.

"It's human, that's all I can tell," answered the policeman....

Messrs. Harris and Blanck were in the building, but they escaped. They carried with them Mr. Blanck's children and a governess, and they fled over the roofs. Their employees did not know the way, because they had been in the habit of using the two freight elevators, and one of these elevators was not in service when the fire broke out.

The New York World *played up its own role in covering the tragedy by presenting one of its reporters as a participant in the headlines on this story, though the fact of the locked doors had been quickly established on the day of the fire and had already been reported by most newspapers. This was a self-promotional gimmick used by many sensational newspapers, including the* World's *rival, Hearst's* New York Evening Journal, *and these stories were often headed by the reporter's byline. This story, which does not carry a by-line, instead uses the* World *reporter's supposedly exclusive interview with survivors of the fire as the source of his information. It also uses his observations made during a tour of the ruined building to describe the crowded and unsafe working conditions that made the factory a veritable deathtrap.*

New York World, 27 March 1911

WORLD REPORTER FINDS INDICATIONS THAT LOCKED DOORS CAUSED BIG LOSS OF LIFE IN FIRE

Inspection of Burned Section of Asch Building Reveals Evidence Tending to Show that Exits to Stairway Leading From Eighth and Ninth Floors Were Fastened— Girl Survivor Says She Found Two Locked—Proprietor Harris Denies It

WE NEED DEATHPROOF BUILDINGS AS WELL AS FIREPROOF, SAYS CHIEF

Iron Shutters Swinging Outward Blocked Fire-Escape Landing, Just as They Did in Iroquois Theater Horror—30,000 Buildings of the Same Class Here, of Which 7,000 Are Defective in Equipment and Safety Devices, Declares Commissioner Waldo—Walls Rubbed by Girls' Bodies and Clawed in Frenzy to Escape, Mute Evidences of Stampede— Total List of Dead 144

A Search of the Asch Building at Nos. 23–39 Washington place and correction of the lists at the morgue last night fixed at 144 the number of those who lost their lives in the fire which swept the factory of the Triangle Waist Company on Saturday afternoon. Included in that total is a skull whose torso has not yet been found and two bodies reported by the police in the flooded sub-cellar of the building.

An all day investigation by the authorities brought them to the conclusion that the fire was caused by the ignition, if not the explosion, of gasoline used for heating pressing irons in the finishing room on the eighth floor of the building. Fire Chief Edward F. Croker believes that the spark which fired this gasoline came from a cigarette, the saltpetre in which kept it burning long after it had been carelessly flung away.

The day brought, too, clues of the most important bearing on the circumstances which brought about this frightful loss of life. Reporters for The World got the evidence of two survivors of the horror that the doors leading from the floors occupied by the Triangle company were locked when the mad rush by the operatives began. Annie Ullo of No. 437 East Twelfth street said that a forewoman in the factory protested that the door leading from the eighth floor to the stairs on the Greene street side was locked. Freda Vilakowsky of No. 639 East Twelfth street said she found that the door leading to the Washington Place stairs from the same floor was similarly fastened.

Fannie Sinsher, now Secretary to Frances Kellor, Chief Investigator at Ellis Island, but for a long time employed in the Triangle, offered her testimony that during her work there it was the habit to keep only certain exits unlocked at certain times.

Against these positive statements came this from Isaac Harris, a member of the firm: "It's an absolute lie that the doors were locked."

This vital fact was uncovered in the course of an examination which took in the three topmost floors of the building, all occupied by the Triangle Company either as offices, work rooms or stock rooms. In them they employed 700 people, three out of five of them girls or women. One of every five who died was a woman.

Workers Packed Together at Machines

The examination showed that these three floors contained nothing but charred ruins of the furniture and machinery they had contained. Six ranks of twenty sewing machines each were on the eighth and ninth floors, 240 altogether, none of which yesterday was more than a twisted and melted mass of metal. But even in this condition they offered evidence that they had been so close together the chair of an operative at one machine would touch the chair of the one who sat behind her. Nothing more was needed to show why the deaths had been so numerous on these two floors once the flight before the flames had been started.

What followed the flight was still to be seen yesterday in the eloquent conditions about the doors leading from these floors and in the hallways outside. An inspection of the passenger elevators at the front of the building indicated, twenty-four hours later, that only one of them was in use. One of the doors leading to the elevator shaft is closed. The other is partially open, but this may have been done by persons attempting to jump into the shaft or to slide down the elevator cables.

The main stairway of the building is just at the side of these two elevators. This stairway is a narrow, ill-lighted affair, built in the form of a square. At the hour when the fire started it was probably so dark that a person would have to grope his way. In addition to this the stairs were not quite so wide as the length of an ordinary walking-stick. One who speculates on such affairs, when cause for danger is all over, might easily ask, despite the condition of this stairway, why more girls on the eighth and ninth floors did not make it the means of their escape.

From the mass of light ashes that are spread over every inch of the floor surface the light inflammable substance with which the rooms were piled probably caused them to become veritable blazing furnaces in scarcely any time, and in addition the long rows of machines made an effectual barrier to the dozens of frightened girls who worked on the opposite side of the room....[T]he girls who could not make it to the stairway or the airshaft were forced the only way possible to go—the windows—from which they jumped.

New York City building and fire inspectors quickly focused their attention on who was to blame for the fire, perhaps in an attempt to deflect attention from their own shortcomings. Though the fire chief criticized the city building inspector for not demanding stricter building codes, the building's owners and the factory owners become the obvious culprits to be punished in this story.

Chicago Tribune, 27 March 1911

TRY TO FIX BLAME FOR FACTORY FIRE; RUINS YIELD DEAD

Pitiful Scenes Occur at Pier Morgue, When Thousands Seek to Identify Victims

KNOWN SLAIN NOW 141

New York Officials Promise to Punish Every One Guilty of Criminal Neglect

PERILS IN MANY OTHER BUILDINGS

New York, March 26—[Special]—While firemen and police today searched the scorched ruins of the Asch building for more bodies and grief stricken relatives thronged the temporary morgue to claim their dead, grand jurors and other officials began work to fix the blame for the fire which yesterday cost 141 lives.

That there is blame somewhere is self-evident. The Asch building was only one of many buildings in Greater New York where yesterday's holocaust might have occurred.

"There are many buildings in this city where even worse conditions prevail," declared Fire Commissioner Waldo. "On the Asch building there was only one outside iron balcony fire escape with treads eighteen inches wide, and so constructed that persons entering on the fire escape by windows would have to close the iron shutters before they could escape. There were two enclosed fireproof stairs, only wide enough for one person to descend at a time and with winding steps at the turns. Entrances to the stairs were blocked by partitions. From indications gates and doors appear to have been locked at the time of the fire...."

When the coroner and the grand jurymen began their investigation they touched shoulders with the district attorney's men, building department agents, with Fire Chief Croker, Fire Commissioner Waldo, and their helpers. District Attorney Whitman, after his inquiry, said:

"If what Chief Croker tells me is correct, then some one is criminally liable, and whoever it is, whether it be one or a dozen, shall be prosecuted."

Locked Doors Kill Many?

Mr. Whitman's assistants found that the three doors leading to the stairways—one on each floor—opened inwardly and that all of them were locked. Firemen told them that they found bodies piled in front of these doors, showing that dozens of girls had rushed for these exits, tried unavailingly to get out, and perished. The state law provides that such doors shall open outwardly "when practicable." It is left to the discretion of the building department apparently, to decide what is "practicable."

As the city's investigation focused on the role of the building's owners in the fire, the New York Evening Journal *called for retribution. In this long and rambling editorial, it suggests that greed motivated the factory owners to lock the doors, and that they held property more dear than the lives of their workers.*

New York Evening Journal, 28 March 1911

The Murdering of Those Unhappy Girls on Saturday

These are Points for Citizens, the Public Prosecutor and
the Grand Jury to Bear in Mind

Through great carelessness and criminal neglect almost one hundred and fifty humans were killed in the horrible factory fire. One or more men were primarily responsible for those abominable murders. Those responsible must be identified and punished. Fortunately, evidence of criminal neglect is plain. The proofs are there in the narrow dark staircase, in the weak, twisted and inadequate fire escape; above all, in the iron doors that kept the girls locked in, deprived even of the slightest chance to save their lives.

There are some questions that grand jurymen and the public prosecutor should ask, and to which they should force definite answers to be followed by the severest punishment—such punishment as manslaughter, based on brutal neglect and more brutal greediness, deserves.

The fire chief found fifty bodies of girls and young women piled inside an iron door through which they could not pass. Well might Chief Croker say that in all his years of fighting fire he had never seen such horror, such dreadful suffering, such needless death and pain, as were revealed in that mass of twisted, tortured bodies.

Who fastened that iron door? Who gave the order that the girls should be locked in, to be searched for stolen materials before leaving the shop?

Who was the man that gave the order to keep those iron doors locked—he is guilty of manslaughter. Equally guilty were those who obeyed his orders, and especially guilty were the public servants, building inspectors and factory inspectors, that, for the usual bribes, presumably, permitted the outrageous conditions to exist.

Some one wanted to make sure, even at the daily risk of life, that no girl would steal an hour of the working day or a yard of tick or muslin. So he, whoever he was, had the girls daily locked inside iron doors, and he murdered more than a hundred of them when the hour of the fire arrived.

Who was he? Whose business is it to identify him? Will he be identified, convicted, and punished in a way that will deter others from such murders, or is this another case of five minutes of public indignation and five years of doing nothing until the next killing shall occur?...

In that dreadful fire everything was insured and protected except the bodies of those girls burned alive.

There was insurance on the building, insurance on the inflammable material that made up the bonfire, plate glass insurance, casualty insurance to protect the owners if anyone got hurt in the elevator, employers' liability insurance to protect from damages the man that hired the girls in case one of them should get a hand caught in one of the machines.

Everything was well safeguarded there except the working girls and their families. They were left unprotected and the girls were killed.

How long are men to be allowed to put hundreds of girls to work in a fire trap, insure the trap against loss, and leave the girls to their fate?...

If those girls were locked in, as they were, and deprived, as they were, of all chances to save their lives, the owners of the building, the employer of the girls, and the city that did not give them protection, should be made responsible. Damage suits resulting in verdicts of a few million would be welcomed in this case, and the more the city might have to pay the better. Such a tax might impress on taxpayers the importance of interesting themselves in city government and of electing competent and honest city officials.

More than a hundred young girls, nearly one hundred and fifty human beings altogether, were trapped and killed. Will anything be done? Will anybody be punished?

INADEQUATE CITY REGULATIONS RESPONSIBLE FOR TRAGEDY

These same newspapers were also quick to place blame on the city for its failure to demand and enforce safety codes. While it was the worst industrial fire to date, the Triangle fire was certainly not the first. Just a year before, a factory fire in New Jersey had taken scores of lives. In this editorial, the New York World *asks why the city had not amended its building regulations following that deadly lesson. These questions were supported by Fire Chief Croker's statement that his recommendations had been ignored by the city building department.*

New York World, 27 March 1911

MURDERED BY INCOMPETENT GOVERNMENT

After the disastrous factory fire in Newark last November, [Fire] Chief Croker said:

There are buildings in New York where the danger is every bit as grave as in the building destroyed at Newark, and a fire in the daytime would be accompanied by loss of life. We can see that the law is complied with, but that is as far as we can go. What we should have is an ordinance requiring fire-escapes on every building used for manufacturing purposes. Take, for instance, some of the large loft buildings below Twenty-third Street. The employees go up to their work in the elevators and many of them do not even know where the stairways are. I have appeared before many committees trying to have the ordinance amended so that fire-escapes would be required on these buildings. The absence of fire-escapes on the buildings where persons work subjects them to a risk which they should not be compelled to take.

The World and other newspapers seconded Chief Croker's demand but nothing was done to prevent in New York a calamity greater than that in Newark. Saturday it came; and more than 150 [*sic*] persons died horrible deaths in the worst disaster since the burning of the General Slocum, victims of official negligence and incompetency in the face of the clearest warning.

Because the building where the fire occurred was of the approved "loft" type, "partly fireproof but not death-proof," as Chief Croker well describes it, there was but one narrow, flimsy fire-escape. It led not to the street and safety but to a courtyard below the street level from which at that hour there was no exit. This building is one which the Fire Department had "recommended" should be equipped with escapes, but the department has no authority to order fire-escapes put on.

A ten-story loft building, no matter how nearly fireproof it may be, is commonly filled with inflammable material. It should be equipped with automatic sprinklers on every floor. This building was not. It should have broad and ample stairwells with wide treads and low risers, inclosed [*sic*] in a fireproof well. This building had two stairways, each no wider than those in a private house, and on the fatal ninth floor a door opening inward prevented quick access to one of them. The doors of a public-school building open outward. That is the law. Loft buildings should be subject to the same rule....

Loft buildings by the dozen are being built to-day in New York which are legal death-traps. An enormous army of working men and women must starve, or in the law phrase "assume the risk" of working in them.

By what the Washington Place building had not and was not we know what a loft building should have and should be. If already constructed, it should be equipped at once with ample fire-escapes to the street—not steep and flimsy, but substantial, wide, easy to use. It should have automatic sprinklers, doors opening outward, compulsory fire-drills, placards of instruction, arrows on the wall pointing to stairways and windows, free access to the roof at all times. And no new building of this type should ever again be erected in New York without broad inner stairs, inclosed [*sic*] by fire-proof walls within a well in which nothing that can burn is permitted.

Against such reasonable safeguards we may expect architects to protest lest their designs be "disfigured" and owners and tenants to raise objections of expense. But if such arguments outweigh the mute appeal of those rows of charred bodies in the Morgue, of the yawning holes in the sidewalk through which young girls crashed to the vaults below, of the shafts in which the dying wretches flung themselves on top of the halted elevators—then what is to-day New York's sorrow will live and last as its shame.

We do not think so ill of the city as to suppose that this is possible. Safer buildings must come. Unendurable indeed would be the thought of a catastrophe so horrible and so excuseless if we might not expect from its example a great and lasting improvement of the condition in which men and women must earn their daily bread.

The New York Evening Journal, *which easily matched the* New York World *in its outrage, was more specific in assigning responsibility. It named names, pointing the finger at the city's superintendent of buildings, Rudolph Miller. The following story about Miller's extracurricular junket to Panama appeared below the sketch of a gallows. From the gallows hangs an empty noose; under it is the question, "This Ought to Fit Somebody; Who is He?"*

New York Evening Journal, 27 March 1911

MAN RESPONSIBLE FOR HORROR AWAY ON PLEASURE JAUNT

The death list in the Washington place and Greene street fire was swelled today to 145, a majority of the victims being young girls.

Seven of the unfortunate victims of the death trap have already been buried. To-day eleven more bodies, so badly charred that all hope of identifying them has been abandoned, will be laid to rest by the Hebrew Free Burial Society, of No. 245 Grand street.

With the beginning of the official investigation at Fre Hall, an attempt was made to fix the responsibility for the disaster.

The burden of opinion to-day places the responsibility for the conditions which resulted in the frightful loss of life upon Rudolph P. Miller, Superintendent of the Bureau of Buildings, and upon George McAneeny, President of the Borough of Manhattan, who appointed Miller to office and is his immediate chief.

Mr. Miller went to Panama March 1 with a delegation from the American Society of Civil Engineers to inspect the work upon the canal. Some of them have returned, but Mr. Miller is not expected back until April 1. This jaunt is not for the benefit of the taxpayers....

Fire Commissioner Waldo made a thorough inspection of the building and his official statement is a terrible indictment against the responsible city officials.

The tragedy of the Triangle fire resonated in other industrial cities, where newspapers featured the story for the first few days on their first page and followed the investigations sporadically thereafter. The Chicago Tribune, *published in the manufacturing capital of the Midwest, focused on the issue of safety regulations and asked if conditions were any better in Chicago. In this editorial, the* Tribune *places responsibility for the tragedy on indifference and negligence. It reminds its readers that government is only as good as the civic conscience and that it is the people of the community who are ultimately responsible for good government.*

Chicago Tribune, 27 March 1911

AGAIN

How many more chapters are to be written in the blood of the innocent before the American conscience makes an end of our heedlessness of human life?

The New York fire is sickening in its horror. But it is more hideous in its awful irony. It is the specter of needless anguish that hangs grinning over the charred and broken bodies of these fellow creatures—poor, useless sacrifices to the inefficiency, the indifference, the sloven negligence of our city governments and the backwardness of our social consciousness.

It is terrible to read of this tragedy. But it is far more terrible to find that it is all familiar, the same facts, the ghastly stereotype of our carelessness and folly.

"There are plenty of fancy fronts around here," was the bitter comment of one of the firemen, "but no fire escapes." Men, women, and girls huddled into rooms high in the air, with the constant threat of fire and panic hanging over them, the secret, invisible fate of agonized death among them—and no fire escapes, no adequate exits, no fire drill, no real fire protection.

This is the old story, and it is one that may be written again—now, before the smoke has blown away from the ruins of the Greene street fire. It has been written before in Chicago. It will be written again whenever the civic spirit of a community is not sufficiently alert to demand good government, to insist upon municipal efficiency. When these tragedies happen there is a brief outcry and a momentary response by the authorities. But what we need is the enforcement of law and the establishment of a public service which shall be as permanent and as thorough as disciplined duty in the army and navy.

What are the factory conditions in Chicago today?

Are men and women working in this city under conditions similar to the victims of the Triangle Waist company? Is any employer gambling with death to save a little money? Is the public inspectorship strict, or is it winking at law evasion, or is it inadequate and overworked, or is it incompetent?

We, the people of this community, are our brothers' keepers. It is for us to see that they who toil each day for that day's bread shall be safeguarded from these wholly unnecessary perils. In many cases, the workers cannot protect themselves. The community, if it is civilized, will do it.

How is it with Chicago?

When the owners of the Triangle Waist Company finally went to trial on charges of first- and second-degree manslaughter in December, their conviction appeared certain. The public, therefore, was bewildered when they were acquitted. In the following editorial, the New York Times *attempts to explain how such a verdict had been reached. Here, the* Times *holds the prosecutor responsible for the failure to convict Blanck and Harris.*

New York Times, 29 December 1911

Meaning of an Acquittal

Whoever reads with care the charge of Justice Crane will not only understand why the jury in the Triangle fire case brought in the verdict it did, but will also see that it would have been extremely difficult, if not impossible, for it to reach any other conclusion.

The acquittal does not mean, as too many will assume, that in the opinion of the jurymen nobody was to blame for this hideous disaster—that it was an unavoidable accident, or what used to be called more often than nowadays "a mysterious dispensation of Providence," and as such to be accepted with resignation. What the verdict really means, as we understand it, is that the two men, HARRIS and BLANCK, were not guilty as charged.

Between this and not guilty at all there is much more than a technical difference, and for what a large part of the public unquestionably considers the unsatisfactory termination of the trial it is at least possible to place the responsibility not on the court or the jury, but on the mistake of the prosecution in indicting the proprietors of the Triangle Company for a crime which they obviously had no intention to commit. The natural inclination, after a fire that cost 146 lives, was to seek the imposition of a commensurate penalty upon those who, obviously, were more to blame for it than anybody else, but in this case, as in so many of an analogous character, the attempt to do more than the circumstance, as viewed by the law would warrant, resulted in the doing of nothing and a complete miscarriage of justice.

To convict HARRIS and BLANCK as indicted it was necessary to prove that the fatal door was locked by their orders and that they were personally connected with and responsible for the death of the one particular victim who had been selected from many as the basis of the manslaughter charges. This was not done. Yet the result of the fire is in itself conclusive proof that the conditions in the factory were desperately bad—that necessary precautions had been habitually neglected. For this the proprietors were clearly to blame, and had they been merely accused of violating the factory laws, either they would have been sent to jail or heavily fined, or else the inadequacy of those laws to serve their intended purpose would have been so plainly demonstrated as to have brought about immediate reform.

QUESTIONS

1. What were some of the characteristics of the Triangle shirtwaist factory fire that made it so newsworthy at the time? Are these some of the same characteristics that make it a significant event in social history?

2. Why would the issue of factory safety be one of particular concern when the workers were women? How did the different newspapers describe the women workers at the Triangle shirtwaist factory? How did the language used to describe them reveal social attitudes toward women during this period?

3. How does the story of the Triangle fire capture many of the issues of the Progressive Era? How is the spirit of reform and progress captured in the language and underlying tone of these stories and editorials?

4. At a time when few newspapers used reporters' bylines in stories, the *New York World* frequently used them as a form of self-promotion. The *World* also promoted itself by claiming its reporters had gotten the scoop on a story. How would this serve to promote a newspaper? Do you see evidence of this type of self-promotion in the media today? What are some of the ethical issues involved in this practice?

5. Do you think newspapers' calls for justice, investigations, and new laws had an effect? Would public opinion have demanded this anyway? Would officials have taken these steps anyway? How effective do you think the press is in spurring government into action and change?

NOTES

1. Annie Altman and Antonetta Pasqualicca were among the 141 fatalities identified in the Triangle fire. "Death List Shows Few Identified," *New York Times*, 26 March 1911, p. 4.

2. This was also referred to as the Uprising of Twenty Thousand. Between 20,000 and 30,000 garment workers went on strike.

3. "Garment Workers Return to Work," *New York Call*, 15 February 1910, p. 1.

4. "Triangle Owners Acquitted by Jury," *New York Times*, 28 December 1911, p. 1.

5. Barbara Mayer Wertheimer, *We Were There: The Story of Working Women in America* (New York: Pantheon Books, 1977), p. 315.

6. Meredith Tax, *The Rising of the Women* (New York: Monthly Review Press, 1980), pp. 234–36.

CHAPTER 14

The *Titanic* Disaster, April 14, 1912

O ne of the great technological advances of the Progressive Era was the improvement of transoceanic travel, made possible by the development of high-powered steam engines, the production of lighter, stronger steel, and improvements in ship design and construction. Steamship companies vied with each other to build bigger and faster ships that could provide both luxury for first-class passengers and economy for steerage passengers. Because they could pack in more passengers and complete round-trip voyages in shorter periods of time, these companies were able to offer one-way steerage fares to immigrants traveling from Liverpool and Dublin for as little as $16.50 by 1891. Luxurious first-class cabin fares ran between $60 and $100.[1]

In that same year, ocean liners were making the crossing between England and New York in just under six days, and this time was gradually shortened by minutes and hours over the next 16 years. Steamship companies raced their liners against each other to establish and hold the record for the fastest crossing, and passengers on the competing ships actually bet on which one would make the best time. The companies then publicized their accomplishments and were greeted by the press with wide-eyed admiration and sporting enthusiasm. "The fastest passage ever made across the Atlantic was that of the White Star Line steamer Majestic, which arrived in New York on the 5th instant. She made the run from Roche's point, Queenstown Harbor, to Sandy Hook [New Jersey] in exactly five days, eighteen hours and eighteen minutes, an average speed of a little over twenty knots an hour," announced the Catholic weekly, the *Boston Pilot*, in August 1891.[2] But less than two weeks later, that record was beaten by the *Majestic*'s sister ship, the *Teutonic*. "August has been a red-letter month for the White Star people. Never before in the history of ocean racing has a line won such unexpected and repeated triumphs within so short a time," reported the *New York Times* on August 20. "Before the Majestic's brilliant performance in wresting the championship from the crack flier of the Inman Line has ceased to be a wonder, her sister ship, the Teutonic comes rushing over the ocean with a record of 5 days 16 hours and 31 minutes. This remarkable run displaces the Majestic and her hard-won record of 5 days 18 hours and 8 minutes from the front rank, and relegates the City of Paris, the former champion, to third place."[3] The race for the fastest crossing continued, and by 1907 the Atlantic crossing had been reduced to four days, ten hours and forty-one minutes by the Cunard Line's *Mauretania*. It held this record until 1929.

Newspapers served as great boosters for the steamship companies and ran several columns of their advertisements every day. Despite some collisions, mishaps, and the occasional loss of a ship, newspapers only occasionally warned of the dangers of such competition. In 1891, for example, the *Boston Pilot* questioned the wisdom of steamship racing in an editorial about the *Majestic's* record crossing. "Critics have raised the question whether such record-making and record-breaking are not dangerous experiments, no matter who be the winner.... Suppose, say the critics, that this enormous ship, plowing the seas at a rate of twenty knots an hour, had collided with another craft, an iceberg, or a derelict hulk, how many of her 1,366 passengers would have reached port?" the *Pilot* asked. "The fact that the voyage was made without a single accident, and the greater fact that loss of life and property has been reduced to a minimum on the fast ocean lines, may be a sufficient answer; but let a single ocean greyhound go to the bottom while speeding in fog or mist at twenty knots an hour, and the praises will be turned into a chorus of anathemas."[4]

Offsetting the dangers of fog, mist, and icebergs, new inventions in steamship construction and communication technology were introduced to ensure safety and reassure the public. The first wireless was installed on a steamship in 1900 by the North German Lloyd Line, and by the end of the decade the wireless had become a standard on most passenger lines that was advertised as a feature of their service.[5] "S.O.S." was introduced as the international distress call in 1910 to eventually replace the more common "C.D.Q." call for assistance. Marconi's wireless compass for triangulating a ship's exact position was introduced in 1912.

This was an age enamored with technological advances, and each of these innovations received ample press coverage. In 1910, for example, the *New York Times Sunday Magazine* devoted a full page to a story on the first use of the "S.O.S." call and the history of the wireless. Though the story certainly revealed the dangers of sea travel and enumerated many of the ships that had sunk in just the last year, it focused on sea *rescues* and the triumph of technology. "Less than two weeks ago W. G. Maginnis, the wireless operator, stepped to his key on the sinking steamship Kentucky and sent out the signal 'S.O.S', the international wireless distress call," effused the *Times*. "Before the water reached the dynamos his cry for help was heard. The Mallory liner Alamo, guided by information furnished by the operator, located the Kentucky and rescued her company just before the steamship went down. This happened near Diamond Shoals, and before morning came the story of the rescue was told ashore, and 'S.O.S', the new ambulance call of the sea, was made famous."[6] In 1912, when Marconi introduced his wireless compass, the *Times* was just as enthusiastic. "Within a few months, with a new type of wireless equipment, which is Guglielmo Marconi's latest invention, steamships caught in a dense fog need have no more fear of it than they have now of the starlight or the morning sunshine," reported the *Times*. "'The days of terror on account of fogs is about over on the sea,' declared Mr. Marconi.... 'The dread of the fog is the last remaining anxiety of seafarers.'"[7]

Another factor that reassured the public was the very *regularity* of ocean travel. As steamship companies reduced the time of the Atlantic crossing and became able to predict within a few hours how long it would take, they were able to establish regular weekly schedules. One liner could depart New York as a sister ship departed Europe, maintaining a constant, predictable flow of paying passengers. This reassuring aspect of ocean travel was picked up by the *New York World* in March 1912, when it likened passenger liners to ocean ferries. "Ocean travel between New York and the ports of Western Europe has long been so regular and so safe as to have fairly earned the title of 'ferry service,'" the *World* observed. "It now seems probable that in the near future it will have the form and substance of such service as well as the title. Efforts are being made to bring the steamship companies so to arrange their sailing dates that a boat will leave New York for Europe every day in the week."[8]

It was in this climate that, in 1912, the British White Star Line launched its latest ocean liner, the *Titanic*. Vaunted as the largest vessel in the world, the *Titanic* was more than four city blocks long and taller than some of the skyscrapers in New York City. Newspapers, especially those in New York and other port cities, covered the *Titanic*'s short existence thoroughly, from the first plans to build her to details on her construction, trial runs, speed tests, and departure from Southampton. Newspaper advertisements and company brochures promised her first- and second- class passengers all the luxuries of a vacation resort—a French à la carte restaurant, a "verandah" café and palm court, Turkish and electric baths, a swimming pool, a gymnasium and squash racket court, and four elevators. She could carry 835 first-class passengers and more than 1,500 second- and third-class passengers and crew. Hailed as the latest ocean greyhound, she was expected to bring her full speed to 23 knots.[9] In addition, she boasted the latest improvements in ship construction and was said to be unsinkable because of the watertight compartments in her hull.

The *Titanic*'s departure on her maiden voyage from Southampton, England, to New York on April 10 was attended by great celebration, due partly to her list of passengers that included such society notables as millionaires Benjamin Guggenheim, Colonel and Mrs. John Jacob Astor, Ida and Isidor Straus, the owners of Macy's, and J. Bruce Ismay, chairman and managing director of the White Star Line. Her departure was marred, however, when she suffered a near collision in Southampton Harbor. The suction created by the giant liner's departure broke the mooring hawsers of the American liner *New York* and set it adrift so that the two ships nearly collided. As crowds looked on from the piers, tugboats raced to the rescue and secured the *New York*. The *Titanic* steamed out of the harbor majestically, leaving only a few critics shaking their heads over the dangers posed by such enormous liners.[10]

The *Titanic* never reached her destination. On April 14, at 11:40 P.M., steaming at 22 1/2 knots, she struck an iceberg in the North Atlantic. Despite the miracles of modern technology, her supposedly watertight compartments were breached and she began to sink. Her calls for help over the wireless, using the "C.Q.D." signal, were not heard by a nearby ship, whose wireless operator had gone off duty. They were, however, picked up by the Allan liner *Virginian*, more than 170 miles and 11 hours from the *Titanic*. The *Virginian* transmitted the message to the wireless station at Cape Race, Newfoundland, and it was then transmitted to several other ships in the area. These immediately steamed to the rescue, but the closest, the *Carpathia*, did not reach the location of the collision until daybreak. In the meantime, the *Titanic*'s crew attempted to load as many passengers as possible onto the ship's lifeboats. She carried only 20, however, sufficient for less than half her passengers, and in the panic that ensued, only a fraction were loaded safely into the lifeboats. Within less than three hours, the *Titanic* had sunk into the icy sea. Of her 2,227 passengers and crew, only 705 were saved.

When news of the *Titanic*'s sinking reached shore, it was sped by wireless from city to city and thus to newspapers across the country. The story made the front page everywhere. The first stories reported whatever was known about the disaster, with constant updates on the rescue efforts and the number of survivors and victims. Many focused on the rich and famous aboard the liner, providing brief biographical sketches and even listing their net worth. In the week that followed newspapers attempted to clarify what had happened. They regularly revised the number of casualties, interviewed naval and engineering experts, and provided technical drawings and scientific-looking lists of statistics in an attempt to explain the factors leading up to and contributing to the tragedy. They interviewed survivors and witnesses, often focusing on the personalities involved. Heroes were created and demolished, depending on who was telling the story. Many of the male victims were hailed as heroes for having yielded places on the lifeboats to women and children, but according to other accounts, some of the male steerage passengers had panicked and rushed the boats in their attempt to escape. Captain Edward J. Smith, who went down with the ship, was first described as a hero for taking that romantic action, but later criticized for hitting the iceberg in the first place. J. Bruce Ismay, the managing director of the White Star Line, found himself in some disgrace because he had *not* gone down with the ship and because he later blamed Captain Smith, who could not defend himself, for maintaining speed despite reports of icebergs. Other stories focused on the technologies involved, questioning the adequacy of the systems in place for using the wireless, the supposedly watertight compartments that had failed, and the number of lifeboats on board.

Investigations were launched immediately in an attempt to find the causes of the collision and who, if anyone, was responsible. The *Titanic* story remained in the news well into the beginning of May and developed into a Senate inquiry and proposals for legislation. On May 18, the Senate investigation concluded that the British Board of Trade was overly lax in its shipping regulations, particularly those regarding the number of lifeboats on ocean liners. It also concluded that the White Star Line had been negligent in its failure to test lifesaving gear and establish drills. The Senate recommended that more stringent international regulations be established for commercial shipping and for the use and regulation of the wireless.

The major issue to be debated in newspapers was who or what was responsible for the disaster. Some simply described the collision as an accident, an example of man vanquished by nature and bad luck. Then, as details of the collision came out, some blamed the individuals involved—Captain Smith or J. Bruce Ismay—for recklessly speeding through the ice field. Others blamed the traveling public, which put pressure on the steamship companies to accomplish faster and faster crossings, despite the dangers involved. But most found the responsibility lay with the technologies involved. Ironically, the very advances in the wireless and in steamship construction had led to a false sense of security and even a state of hubris. Many of these stories focused on the inadequate number of lifeboats on the *Titanic* and the failure of the crew to train itself and its passengers in how to respond to an emergency.

The readings in this chapter are organized in four sections. In the first section, the selections assign the responsibility for the disaster to bad luck. In the second section, the readings begin to identify the individuals—Captain Smith and J. Bruce Ismay—whose actions or poor judgment led to

THE PACEMAKER.

"The Pacemaker," **New York World, 20 April 1912, p. 12.** *Death sets the pace here for an ocean liner racing across the Atlantic. When the "unsinkable" Titanic collided with an iceberg in the North Atlantic and went down with more than 1,200 passengers aboard, critics asked why ocean liners were in such a hurry. Many of the Titanic's passengers drowned because the ship did not carry enough life rafts.*

the collision. In the third section, an editorial from the *Hartford Courant* blames the tragedy on the general public and its heedless desire to travel ever faster despite the dangers. In the fourth section, the news stories and editorials assign responsibility to the failures of technology.

DISASTER DUE TO BAD LUCK

Most newspapers reported the same basic facts in their first stories about the disaster, though details varied: that this had been the Titanic's maiden voy-

age; that she had collided with an iceberg and was sinking; that the news had been received by wireless; and that other ships alerted by the wireless were rushing to her rescue. In this front-page story by the Atlanta Constitution, *the iceberg and the frigid North Atlantic are the villains.*

Atlanta Constitution, 15 April 1912

WITH 1300 SOULS ON BOARD, LINER TITANIC HITS ICEBERG AND IS REPORTED SINKING

Giant of the White Star Line Plunges Into the Arctic Terror on Her Maiden Trip Across Atlantic

MAJOR ARCHIBALD BUTT ONE OF MANY NOTABLES ON STRICKEN TITANIC

"C.Q.D." Call Sent by Wireless and Several Steamers Are Hurrying to Assistance of the Titanic—The Liner Collided With the Iceberg Shortly After Midnight—The Titanic Is the Largest Vessel Afloat

Montreal, April 14—The new White Star liner Titanic is reported in advices received here late tonight to have struck an iceberg.

The news was received at the Allan Line offices here in a wireless message from the captain of the steamer Virginian of that line. It was stated that the Virginian had been in wireless communication with the Titanic, that she had reported being in collision with an iceberg and asked for assistance.

The Virginian reported that she was on the way to the Titanic.

The Virginian sailed from Halifax this morning and at the time of the wireless was sent she is reckoned to have been about abeam of Cape Race. She has 900 passengers aboard, but can accommodate 900 of the Titanic's passengers should their removal be necessary.

The message from the Virginian's captain was sent by wireless to Cape Race and relayed to Montreal.

Titanic Reported Sinking

Cape Race, N.F., April 15—At 10:25 tonight the steamship the Titanic called "C.Q.D." and reported having struck an iceberg. The steamer said that immediate assistance was required. Half an hour afterwards another message came reporting that they were sinking by the head and that women were being put off in the lifeboats.

The weather was calm and clear, the Titanic's wireless operator reported, and gave the position of the vessel 41.46 north latitude and 50.14 west longitude.

The Marconi station at Cape Race notified the Allan liner Virginian, the captain of which immediately advised that he was proceeding to the scene of the disaster.

Rushing to Rescue

The Virginian at midnight was about 170 miles from the Titanic and expected to reach that vessel at about 10 o'clock a.m....

The last signals from the Titanic were heard by the Virginian at 12:27 o'clock a.m. The wireless operator on the Virginian says these signals were blurred and ended abruptly.

Largest Vessel Afloat

The White Star liner Titanic, the largest vessel afloat, left Southampton April 10 on her maiden voyage. She is a vessel of 46,328 tons, is 882 feet 6 inches long and displaces 66,000 tons.

The Titanic carried about 1,300 passengers of whom 350 were in the first cabin. Among those are F. D. Millet, the artist and president of the Consolidated American Academy of Rome; Major Archibold Butt, military aide to President Taft; C.M. Hayes, president of the Grand Trunk Railway; J. Bruce Ismay, chairman and managing director of the White Star Line; Henry B. Harris, the American theatrical manager; W.T. Stead; Mrs. Isador Straus; Mr. and Mrs. John Jacob Astor; Mr. and Mrs. G.D. Widener; Benjamin Guggenheim; and Mr. and Mrs. Widener.

By the next day, newspapers had more of the details, including the number of casualties and some details about the more prominent passengers. The Wisconsin State Journal, *published in landlocked Madison, Wisconsin, devoted most of its front page to stories on the tragedy. Its lead story was highly emotional, attributing heroism to the men who had died in the disaster and hailing the "Sea's Code of Honor." Here, too, it appears that the disaster is due to bad luck and an act of nature.*

Wisconsin State Journal, 16 April 1912

1,492 ARE LOST; 866 ARE RESCUED; TITANIC'S GRAVE IS 2 MILES DEEP

ALL HOPE IS GONE WHEN WORD IS RECEIVED FROM TWO LINERS NEARBY

Survivors Are Now Being Brought to New York on Board the Carpathia Which Went to Aid

ONLY 20 LIFE BOATS

Small Vessels Crowded to Limit With Women and Children;
Sea's Code of Honor is Observed

BOAT IS DUE FRIDAY

Stories of Experiences to Eclipse All in Fiction; Ice Floes Encircle Survivors' Boats

SEA'S CODE OF HONOR

"Save the women and the children."

In every disaster the great code of honor of the men who sail ships at sea has placed the safety of the weaker and the more helpless first.

And faithful to this code a thousand men gave up their lives in the sinking of the Titanic.

The list of survivors is made up largely of the women. And a great part of them were in the steerage.

Under the leveling touch of danger, even the men of the first cabins seem to have stepped aside to place in the hazardous safety of the life boats, the women of the immigrant parties.

For the code is a greater thing than life itself.

New York, April 16—Unable to sustain the wound she received yesterday when she crashed into a tramp iceberg, the giant Titanic today lies in a watery grave two miles down in mid-ocean.

When she gave up the fight and sank into her last resting place, the mammoth liner carried 1,492 souls with her. Speeding toward New York on the Carpathia are 866 persons—survivors of the most terrible tragedy recorded in oceanic history. Of these 886 are scores of wives and daughters of men—REAL MEN—men who followed to their death the unwritten code of honor of the seas: "Save the women and children first." When the big trans-Atlantic greyhound went down into the sea, helpless women and children strewn about in tiny lifeboats saw their fathers and husbands swept from their sight forever.

DISASTER DUE TO POOR JUDGEMENT AND IRRESPONSIBILITY

As newspapers learned that ships in the area had been warned of icebergs, people began to wonder why the Titanic's *captain had not heeded the warning and slowed his vessel. This editorial in the* New York Times *gives a hint of the deluge of criticism that was soon to follow regarding the steamship lines' unrelenting competition for speed. Toward the end of the editorial, the* Times *notes that Captain Smith must have been aware of the danger of speeding through the ice fields.*

New York Times, **16 April 1912**

The Appalling Disaster

The sinking of the Titanic, with some 1,450 of her passengers and crew still on board takes rank as one of the greatest disasters of the sea. In the annals of passenger traffic between this port and England or the Continent there have been many recorded, when ships classed as fine and first in their time have gone down, with the loss of three hundred or four hundred human lives, and 500 perished when the Bourgogne went to the bottom fourteen years ago after a collision off Sable Island, but this surpasses them all and holds a dread supremacy as the most deplorable and afflicting calamity that has ever befallen seaborne passenger travel.

Grief for the lost and sympathy for the bereaved are first in all hearts, but everywhere there is a feeling of amazement that this great, new ship could be so soon lost, and lost in that way. We have come to believe that our great modern liners, with their water-tight compartments, safeguarded by unceasing vigilance and rigid discipline, are secure against loss by collision, that even after the most violent shock they will be kept afloat. But here was the newest, the largest, the most completely and luxuriously appointed of all the ships that Ocean has ever borne on its bosom, and in four hours after colliding with an iceberg she goes to the bottom. Among her passengers were persons of great prominence, well known in both hemispheres who, inspired with a feeling like to that which makes men eagerly seek a place among first-night audiences at a theatre, had taken passage on the Titanic on her maiden voyage. That there was peril involved never occurred to them or to their friends. The ship was in command of a Captain of forty years experience, fully trusted by his company, and holding the place of highest honor and responsibility in its employ. Every circumstance conduced at once to inspire confidence in the fortunate issue of the voyage and to intensify the shock that its dreadful ending has caused. Nothing is wanting to make the disaster of the Titanic long memorable and conspicuous among the tragedies of the sea....

The region of icebergs is evidently too dangerous, with all possible precautions much too dangerous, for the fast liners of the Atlantic. We have been warned by many railroad accidents that speed and weight of trains have overpassed the limits of rail endurance. One or two days added to an ocean voyage are not too much to pay for the greater security of life. The Titanic must have run head on at high speed into a great berg, so crushing and twisting her frame that the water-tight bulkheads were a futility. When that can happen there is no safeguard save in avoiding the lurking-place of the icy peril.

The North Atlantic is not commonly invaded by icebergs from the arctic so early in the year as mid-April. Yet dangerous floating ice has been seen by all incoming ships in the last few days, and the Carmania was compelled to steer southward to avoid contact with a tremendous berg. Warnings of this danger had been transmitted to other ships equipped with wireless. It seems that Capt. SMITH, in command of the Titanic, must have known of the peril existing in his course.

Newspapers quickly picked up reports that Captain Smith had been warned of the icebergs in the Titanic*'s path but had proceeded with speed nevertheless.*

Atlanta Constitution, 17 April 1912

TITANIC WARNED OF THE ICEBERGS

Havre, April 16—The French liner La Touraine, which arrived here last night, reports that at midnight on April 10 she announced a huge field of ice with the tops of the bergs slightly above the water. La Touraine slowed down and emerged from the ice fields after an hour's steaming. Next morning she passed other icebergs.

La Tourraine was in communication with the Titanic on the afternoon of April 12.

The Presse Nouvelle quotes the captain of La Touraine as saying that he sent a wireless dispatch reporting the presence of the icebergs to the captain of the Titanic, who acknowledged the message with thanks.

J. Bruce Ismay, the chairman of the White Star Line, was one of the survivors of the disaster. Reports that he had escaped on Lifeboat 1—dubbed "The Millionaires' Special"—with fewer than a dozen first-class passengers, while more than a thousand died because there was no room on the remaining lifeboats, earned bitter recriminations.[11] These mounted as passengers reported his response to the warnings of icebergs and his behavior during and after the rescue operation.

New York World, 20 April 1912

ISMAY IS GRILLED BY SENATE COMMITTEE; TITANIC OFFICER ADMITS SPEED OF 21 KNOTS

Major Peuchen of Montreal Says J. B. Ismay Told Woman Passenger Titanic Would Go Faster Because of Ice Warnings So As to Get Out of Danger Zone Quickly—"Don't Knock" Sign on Ismay's Door.

WHITE STAR LINE FAILS TO ISSUE PROMISED STATEMENT

Company Now Places Loss of Life At 1,635 and Number of Saved at 705—Crew
Will Be Shipped Home This Afternoon Unless Senate Committee Calls Them—
Carpathia Sails for Mediterranian With Fewer Passengers Than When She Started
Last Week, Some Giving Up Cabins.

The White Star Line did not, as had been promised on Thursday, issue
yesterday an official statement of the wreck of the Titanic and the causes
leading thereto.

Not a word of explanation could be obtained at the offices of the line
concerning the report that the great liner was proceeding at a speed of
twenty-one knots through a field of ice in which were bergs that her Captain had been warned against.

But from the mouths of survivors, came statements attributing the wreck
to a desire to make a record in speed for the maiden voyage of the big ship,
a record that would remove her from the "eight-day boat" class, in which
her sister ship, Olympic, had been ranked.

Major A.G. Peuchen of Montreal, said to a reporter for The World that
J. Bruce Ismay, managing director of the line, had laughingly told a woman
passenger that the ice warning, so far from keeping the Titanic back, would
only cause her to increase her speed, so as to get more quickly out of the ice
field.

Other criticisms of Mr. Ismay by survivors, by passengers on the
Carpathia, who observed his conduct after he was rescued, and by lands-
men, were numerous. It was learned that he occupied the doctor's cabin on
the Carpathia, denied himself to all inquirers and caused the report to be
spread that a sick woman was in the cabin on whose door appeared the notice: "Don't Knock."

DISASTER DUE TO PUBLIC'S DESIRE FOR SPEED

*Of course, no one ever complained about the speed of transportation until
something went wrong. Steamship companies had for years been competing with each other to establish the fastest run across the Atlantic to satisfy
the public and promote themselves. That the speediest route might also be
the most dangerous was blissfully ignored by passengers betting on crossing times and securing tickets on the fastest ships as a way of social one-
upmanship. In the following editorial, the* Hartford Courant *blames the
tragedy on the public's hunger for speedy travel and the law of supply and
demand.*

Hartford Courant, 18 April 1912

SPEED OR SAFETY?

Supply and demand had a good deal to do with burying the Titanic in the depths of the sea. Supply and demand is an ancient rule, and now and then it is thought that man can supplement it or supplant it with one of his contrivances; but in the end the old rule works itself out and shows its dominating power. The Titanic was built to go fast and to go luxuriously simply because to go fast and to go luxuriously is the sure way to do the most business in the traveling line. The man going anywhere by rail who should take a slow train when he could get a fast one would be thought to be upset in his mind. It is the same thing with travel on the sea. Ship-owners are trying desperately hard to reduce the time of passage between this country and Europe; and every fifteen or thirty minutes of reduction is hailed as a record, and set up as a standard, and lodged permanently in the back of the head of every captain having control of one of these large and rapid passenger vessels as something that he must outdo if he would please his employers and bring renown to himself. The captains are not fairly to blame, and neither are the ship-owners, although we do not see that their responsibilities are reduced thereby. Both are merely trying to give the best-paying people among those who travel exactly what they want. Those who wish to travel like a streak of lightning, and with all the luxurious appointments that they have in their own costly residences at home, make the demand for these ships that drive straight ahead and take their chances, and the ship-builder and ship-owner and captain combine to furnish the supply.

If we knew of all the things that just do not happen on the sea the love of travel would be reduced. Take dodging icebergs as an example. Twenty ships might have gone through where the Titanic failed. They might have gone through at full speed, too, it would be a piece of gambling luck, of course, in case they all got through safely, but there is nothing inconceivable about it. But gambling luck is not what the speed fanatics expect, and certainly not what more moderate and modest people who travel with them have the right to expect. When it becomes known that many of these rapid passages are more or less wagers with death the public get angry. Then, after the public have become pretty angry, the ship-owners can order their ships to take a more southerly and longer course, and so avoid that dangerous ice zone, exactly as the leading ship companies have now done. But if they had issued the same order two weeks ago they would have lost business by it. Precisely the same dangers existed before the Titanic went to her doom as on that dreadful Sunday night, and every ship captain and every ship-owner knew it. The more cautious commanders reduced these dangers by excessive prudence, but

Captain Smith, we regret to say, appears to have been over-confident, and, having a new and fast ship, decided that he could slip through and thereby make a good run. Nobody can measure all the pressure that he felt and that caused him to do this. Perhaps he was not wholly conscious of the desperate nature of the undertaking. He had the habit of coming through safely, and habit counts for something in such cases. But the event was fatal; and now that the dangers of that northern course are evident and palpable to everyone, those whose first idea has been speed clamor for safety, and so the ships are going to take a less dangerous course.

The men and women who pay large sums to sail in these fine ships can make them safer or more dangerous as they please. The choice is in their own hands. When they demand safety, so far as human skill and experience can furnish it, they will get it.

DISASTER DUE TO FAILURES IN TECHNOLOGY AND EQUIPMENT

As details of the disaster became known, it quickly became apparent that there had not been enough lifeboats for the number of passengers and crew and that this was a major contributor to the loss of life. While American regulations insured a sufficient number of lifeboats for passengers, British regulations did not. British steamship companies were operating under the assumption that modern steamships with watertight compartments could stay afloat long enough for other ships to come to their aid. They believed a ship in distress would have the time to ferry its passengers to safety aboard other ships in repeated trips. Unfortunately, several watertight compartments on the Titanic *were damaged in the collision and she sank before the nearest ship to hear her distress call could reach her. This story in the* Atlanta Constitution *linked together several telegraphic reports from a variety of sources.*

Atlanta Constitution, 17 April 1912

John Corrigan, Jr.: ONLY 20 BOATS ON TITANIC; JUST ENOUGH TO ACCOMMODATE HALF THE PEOPLE ON THE SHIP

Washington, April 16.—[Special]—"It was an outrage that the finest steamship afloat should have been sent on its maiden trip without a full complement of lifeboats sufficient to permit every passenger and member of the crew to leave the ship," said Senator Bacon, of Georgia, today in speaking of the Titanic disaster.

The Georgia senator has crossed the sea many times and is decidedly of the opinion that adequate provision for the safety of the passengers is more vitally important than luxurious finishings and sacrifices for speed. While lifeboats take up room, there comes a time, as in the case of the Titanic, when they are worth everything, he said.

To Force Carrying of Boats

Representative Hardwick, of Georgia, introduced in the house a bill to provide that no ship should be allowed to enter an American port that did not have an adequate number of lifeboats to take on the entire number of human beings on board.

Senator Martine of New Jersey, was bitter in his denunciation of the craze for speed which sent the ship on the northern route, where the danger of injury from icebergs was imminent, and had so been reported by the Titanic herself. He will introduce tomorrow a resolution requesting the president to call an international conference of all maritime nations to discuss an agreement new lanes of travel across the north Atlantic.

He would also make provision for safety appliances and particularly an adequate number of lifeboats....

NO SHIP REQUIRED TO CARRY BOATS TO ACCOMMODATE ALL

New York, April 16—Statistical information of the life saving apparatus of the Olympic, sister ship of the Titanic, was given out today by the bureau of information of steam vessels. Figures for the Titanic are not available, but as the two ships are almost identical in size it is not likely that their life saving equipment materially differs.

The Olympic has sixteen life boats and four rafts calculated to accommodate 1,171 people. This means about one-third of the total number of passengers and crew altogether, which is 3,447, can be accommodated. It was stated at the bureau that no ship is required to have sufficient boat room to accommodate all its complete passenger and crew list.

The Olympic carries 3,455 life preservers and forty-eight life buoys, and these equipments are made in compliance with the regulations of the British Board of Trade. The United States bureau has no power except to see that each steamship meets the requirements of its home government.

ONLY TWENTY BOATS CARRIED BY THE UNFORTUNATE TITANIC

London, April 16—In response to a telegram of inquiry as to the number of boats carried by the Titanic, and how many persons that would accommodate, the White Star Company at Liverpool sent the following message:

"The Titanic had twenty boats, which is in excess of the official requirements."

The question of the number of boats carried by steamers has been widely discussed. It appears the board of trade regulations permit a reduction by half in the number of boats, rafts and buoyant apparatus carried when the ship is efficiently provided with water-tight compartments, but this concession does not apply to life-jackets and other similar appliances.

According to some experts, it would be an impossibility to carry a sufficient number of boats to accommodate all on board the mammoth liners, or if carried, it would be next to impossible to man and provision them. It cannot be doubted, however, that the disaster will lead to a stricter inquiry by the board of trade into this matter, and a revision of the regulations....

The Titanic was fit with electrically controlled water-tight compartments. Therefore, these should have been immediately closed from the bridge unless, as surmised, the collision also so damaged the electrical apparatus as to render this impossible, or the vessel's side was torn away by an iceberg....

Captain Wanted More Boats

Chicago, April 16—That Captain Edward J. Smith, of the Titanic, believed the steamer was not properly equipped with lifeboats and other lifesaving apparatus and that he protested without success against lack of precautions was the statement made by Glenn Marston, a friend of the captain, here tonight.

Marston said that while returning from Europe on the Olympic in company with Captain Smith he remarked on the small number of lifeboats carried by such a large passenger steamer. It was then, according to Marston, that Smith spoke of the life-preserving equipment of the Titanic, then in course of construction. "If this ship should strike a submerged derelict or iceberg, that would cut through into several of the water-tight compartments, we have not enough boats to take care of more than one-third of the passengers," he said.

"The Titanic, too, is no better equipped. It ought to carry at least double the number of boats and rafts that it does to afford any real protection to the passengers. Besides there always is danger of some of the boats becoming damaged or swept away before they can be manned."

The inadequate number of lifeboats on the Titanic *was compounded by the reliance on the wireless, which only worked to save a ship if nearby ships were listening. This was not the case for the* Titanic*—one ship close enough to have arrived in time did not have a wireless operator on duty at the time of the disaster and the nearest ship to receive the call was 170 miles away. In the following editorial, the* New York World *attributes the loss of life to nothing less than short-sightedness and a misplaced faith in modern technology.*

New York World, 17 April 1912

BACK TO FIRST PROBLEMS

The Titanic was the fastest ship in a slow process of evolution in marine architecture. If it was built to make money, money was not spared in the building. If its life-boat equipment could not float more than one third of the ship's living cargo, it was because the last word of theory and science in ship construction had said that a full equipment had become unnecessary.

None of the great liners now carries life-boats and rafts equal to the passenger and crew list. They have all been built and are being operated on the theory that they are unsinkable or can be kept afloat until help arrives.

It is a theory which some governments have accepted as sound. The Titanic's life-saving equipment was within the requirements of the Board of Trade and the admiralty laws of the first nation of the earth in mastery of ocean navigation. It was dictated less by motives of economy than by what had come to be regarded as a full consideration of all practical requirements.

It was believed that with wireless telegraphy the time had passed when ships could founder before other vessels could be brought to their rescue, and years of experience had given support to the belief. The old idea of life-boats enough to take away everybody and send them adrift possibly for days on a sailless ocean had become obsolete under new conditions of a thickly travelled oceanway and the water-tight compartment which would keep a ship long afloat after the most violent of collisions. Life-boats to effect transfers to other ships in repeated journeys back and forth had come to be the theory, and not life-boats to take away all at once.

But again theory has been exploded by new experience. Ships are still sinkable. Collisions with icebergs, sunken rocks or other vessels can be violent enough to open many water-tight compartments at once. If the explanation is that the Titanic struck the iceberg sideways and was ripped open longitudinally, none the less true is it that other ships supposedly perfect in their bulkhead protection are exposed to the same danger. All that inventive genius and money could do to prevent such a catastrophe had been done, and it has failed.

In the presence of such an upsetting of expert ideas lay opinion shrinks from positive assertion. But the destruction of the Titanic is a refutation of all the fine-spun theories of modern ship-builders. Out of the wreckage emerges one clear and indisputable fact—*if 800 passengers could be saved with the insufficient life-boat equipment of the Titanic, all of them could have been saved if there had been enough boats to take them off.*

The Chicago Tribune *also focused on the shortage of lifeboats and called for regulations to dictate the number of lifeboats per ship. In this powerful editorial, the* Tribune *condemns "man's indifference to man" that would allow such a tragedy to occur, but also finds inspiration in the heroic acts of the men who sacrificed their lives for others on the sinking* Titanic. *This romanticized view of the heroic sacrifice of the victims was misleading, however, for many panicked and resorted to violence in the rush for the lifeboats. Many of the victims did not die willingly so that others could live.*

Chicago Tribune, 17 April 1912

THE TITANIC DISASTER

There were not enough boats.

In this anguished pause while the world waits for the story of the loss of the Titanic from the lips of the survivors, that sickening fact stands out.

There were not enough boats.

There never are enough boats.

The laws of seafaring nations do not provide that there shall be enough boats on these great ships that carry thousands of human lives into the perils of the deep.

The Titanic went down in a smooth sea. The report is that "all its boats are accounted for," and they were all full. Yet only 868 souls were saved, while 1,341 who should have been saved, and could have been saved, were lost.

Year after year these huge steamers sail with far more passengers aboard than can be taken care of in case of mishap, and never was the terrible irony of man's indifference to man more tragically disclosed than in the loss of the Titanic. It sank at 2:20 a.m. and at dawn the Carpathia was on the ground, three hours too late for thirteen hundred precious lives. There floated the Titanic's boats—all of them safe—and the still sea covering the thirteen hundred who need not have died.

Will England act upon this staggering lesson?

Will America and Germany, and France and Holland?

Laws should be passed before the impact of this horrifying revelation is lost. This at least should be gained.

Yet more is gained. Dark as the story is, as we now know it, a light shines out of it. Nothing that can be told will be more eloquent than the list of the survivors. There are men on the list, among them the president of the White Star line, J. Bruce Ismay. The captain went down with the ship. It is the noble tradition of the sailor, but it does not reach owners.

Yet most of those who were saved were women and children. That tells a story of discipline and self-control and heroic sacrifice. There was no beastlike scramble. The boats are all accounted for. None was swamped or overfilled. That means that men stood back and chose to die.

The world is better for that. And those of us who walk today in the light of the sun ought to walk the more erect because of those who lie in the sea depths—to go with stronger, cleaner, higher hearts to do our work in the world because of those who chose to die.

QUESTIONS

1. Why were newspapers so eager to report stories about new developments on ocean liners and ocean traffic? What economic interest might newspapers have had in promoting steamship lines? How might this have caused a conflict of interest in newspapers, according to modern concepts of ethics?
2. How did newspapers' fascination with developments in steamship travel reflect values of the Progressive Era? How did developments in ocean liners represent progress? How was this reflected in the newspaper stories quoted here?
3. What was there about the story of the *Titanic* that captured so much public interest? (In addition to the hundreds of newspaper stories published about the *Titanic* at the time, it later became the subject of several books and at least two Hollywood films and is mentioned in most histories of the period.)
4. How did the newspaper stories of the tragedy create heroes and villains? Who were they?
5. What role did the wireless play in the *Titanic* story? How did the wireless assist in the reporting of the story? How did it interfere with the reporting of the story?
6. What are some of the rhetorical devices used in the stories quoted here, particularly the *Wisconsin State Journal*'s April 16 story ("1,492 Are Lost") and the *Chicago Tribune*'s April 17 editorial ("The Titanic Disaster")?

NOTES

1. Warren Line advertisement, *Boston Pilot*, 24 January 1891, p. 8; Cunard Line advertisement, *Boston Traveller*, 17 December 1891, p. 10.

2. "The Fastest Ocean Trip," *Boston Pilot*, 15 August 1891, p. 4.

3. "Beats All Ocean Records," *New York Times*, 20 August 1891, p. 5.

4. "The Fastest Ocean Trip," *Boston Pilot*, 15 August 1891, p. 4.

5. "All Our Steamers Have Wireless Telegraph and Submarine Signals," International Mercantile Lines advertisement, *New York Times*, 2 April 1912, p. 19.

6. "'S.O.S.'—The Ambulance Call of the Seas," *New York Times*, 13 February 1910, p. 7.

7. "Wireless Compass Ends Sea Fog Perils," *New York Times*, 4 April 1912, p. 1.

8. "An Ocean Ferry," *New York World*, 25 March 1912, p. 10.

9. "The New Giantess Titanic," *New York Times*, 14 April. 1912, p. 6; International Mercantile Lines advertisement, *New York Times*, 2 April 1912, p. 19.

10. "Titanic in Peril on Leaving Port," *New York Times*, 11 April 1912, p. 1; "A New-Old Peril of the Sea," *New York Times*, 12 April 1912, p. 12.

11. "Rescue Ship Arrives—Thousands Gather at Pier," *New York Times*, 19 April 1912, p. 1.

CHAPTER 15

Women Demand the Right to Vote, 1911–1912

Olympia Brown didn't vote until she was 85 years old. She had wanted to vote long before that. In fact, she had traveled around Wisconsin in 1886 to promote a state law allowing women to vote in elections pertaining to school matters and had gone to jail when she tried to exercise that right in the next election. She had sued the state, established a monthly suffrage journal to "set the record straight," and served as the president of the state suffrage association for the next 26 years. She also lobbied state and national legislators, marched for suffrage in New York and Washington, and picketed the White House in 1917 and the Republican national convention in November 1920. When she finally voted in 1920, she probably thought it was about time.

Olympia Brown was just one of the thousands of women who became involved in the woman suffrage movement. Many, however, didn't live long enough to have the pleasure of casting their ballot. Lucretia Mott, Lucy Stone, Elizabeth Cady Stanton, and Susan B. Anthony, all renowned leaders of the movement, as well as many women whose names have been forgotten, died years before the passage of the federal woman suffrage amendment in 1919.

Women, who were denied the vote by the U.S. Constitution, first began agitating for suffrage in 1848. During the next seven decades, they organized on the local, state, and national level to argue for their right to participate fully in the nation's business. They petitioned and lobbied their elected officials, published suffrage newspapers, put pressure on newspapers and magazines to publish their publicity and endorse their arguments, and spoke in a variety of settings, from lecture halls to street corners. Slowly and gradually they won the right to vote in school board elections, municipal elections, and even in some territorial and state elections. In 1867 the

Wyoming territorial convention granted woman suffrage, and in 1870 the
Territory of Utah did the same (but revoked the right in 1887). The first
state to vote for general suffrage (which would allow women to vote in all
elections) was Colorado in 1893. This was followed by Utah (again) in
1895, Idaho in 1896, and Washington in 1910.

During that same 62-year period, suffrage was defeated in hundreds of
campaigns. Kansas and Wisconsin, for example, both defeated proposals for
a suffrage clause in their state constitutions in 1867; similar provisions were
lost in South Dakota in 1890, New York and Kansas in 1894, and Massachusetts in 1896. On the national level, woman suffragists presented petitions to Congress for an amendment to the U.S. Constitution dozens of
times. A few of these made it to congressional hearings and even to votes in
the Senate or the House, only to die in committee or be defeated.

Proponents of woman suffrage argued several points. First, they maintained, women who were American citizens had the *right* to vote. Second,
they argued, women must have a voice to represent their needs and concerns in the political sphere. When these points failed to convince, proponents developed arguments as to why the country would be better off if
women were to vote. They would purify politics. They would clean up corruption. They would promote social and educational reforms that were
needed to improve the country. They would be able to apply their motherly,
feminine, and nurturing skills to the nation's business. Eventually the more
militant suffragists argued that women were exploited by the social, political, and economic system and must have the vote in order to stand up for
themselves on equal footing with men.

As a national movement developed in the 1860s, many proponents organized into local, state, and national clubs and associations such as the
American Equal Rights Association (1867), the Wisconsin Woman Suffrage
Association (1869), and the National American Woman Suffrage Association (1890). Woman suffrage also eventually found support in a number of
other organizations and reform groups, including the Women's Christian
Temperance Union, The Populist Party, the Socialist Party, some labor
unions, the Anti-Saloon League, and the General Federation of Women's
Clubs. Supporters included men as well as women, but by the 1890s, the
movement was led by women and women's organizations.[1]

Antisuffrage arguments, however, reflected many of the prevailing notions about women and their proper place in society and thus were more
widely accepted. First of all, antisuffragists maintained, women's proper
place was in the home taking care of their family, and they should not be
distracted from this by political concerns. Second, women did not *need* the
vote, since their men—husbands, brothers, fathers, or sons—could vote in
their interests. Third, politics was a corrupt, dirty affair, and women would

GO TO YOUR MOTHER

"Women care for the child in the home and in the school. Why should they be forced to neglect the children in the city? Give them the vote."
—*Jane Addams. Hull House, Chicago, Ill.*

"Go to Your Mother," *Wisconsin State Journal,* 23 May 1912, p. 1. *Woman suffragists argued that they needed the vote to clean up government and society. Because their role as mothers was acceptable to society, suffragists often played on their conventional womanly image. Some of the reforms they called for were better schools, playgrounds for city children, and sanitary milk and food.*

only sully themselves by getting involved in it. Fourth, women didn't have the intellectual, emotional, or physical strength and ability to participate fully in politics, so it would actually be *harmful* to them to have the right to vote. Fifth, it would harm *society,* since women's participation in politics would undermine the strength of the family, which was built on the subservient and motherly role of women. Sixth, they argued, most women *didn't want* the vote, so it wasn't fair to thrust this unwanted burden on them just because a few were demanding it. Finally, it was considered *unwomanly* for a woman to become involved in politics, and especially unwomanly for her to demand the right to be included. The women who demanded suffrage, they concluded, were mannish, unnatural, and unsexed misfits who could hardly pretend to speak for *normal* women.

Antisuffragists ("antis") could be found in all social classes and equally among both men and women, particularly those of a conservative nature. Some ethnic groups that held an authoritarian and paternalistic view toward women, such as Germans and Italians, were naturally opposed to suffrage. Authoritarian religions, such as the Catholic and Lutheran Churches, also opposed women's rights in general and woman suffrage in particular. Many opponents organized into antisuffrage associations such as the Massachusetts Association Opposed to the Further Extension of Suffrage to Women (1896) and the National Association Opposed to Woman Suffrage (1911). These organizations received support from conservative church leaders, educators, and politicians. They also received substantial support from the beer and liquor industries, which feared that if women were to vote they would vote for prohibition. These industries, in fact, spearheaded and financed many vigorous campaigns against suffrage.[2]

"Sure I Voted," *Milwaukee Journal,* 6 November 1912, p. 13. *Woman suffragists argued that they were just as qualified to vote, if not more so, as uneducated and immigrant men, who could vote. Unfortunately, those very men were likely to vote against suffrage if it came up in a popular vote. This fellow is a caricature of the Irish immigrant—rough, unshaven, lower class, probably a bit drunk, and very likely paid by the local saloon to vote against the woman suffrage referendum in that year's election.*

During the period 1911–1912, these conflicting attitudes toward women and their role in society were put to the test as suffragists became increasingly visible and vocal in their demands for the vote. In those two years, suffrage was on the ballot in seven states—Arizona, California, Kansas, Michigan, Oregon, Ohio, and Wisconsin. Led by a combination of veterans who had been campaigning for decades and a new generation eager to adopt some of the militant tactics of the British suffragettes, these campaigns attracted attention from the press, the public, and the antis. Suffragists marched in New York and toured the countryside in new-fangled automobiles to reach voters in isolated villages. Antis also rallied their forces, and beer and liquor industry leaders conspired to bribe voters and public officials and buy newspaper columns.[3] By the end of 1912 suffrage campaigns had been won in Arizona, California, Kansas, and Oregon. They had been lost in Ohio, Michigan, and Wisconsin.[4]

In Wisconsin, dominated by a large ethnic German and Roman Catholic population, the campaign was prolonged and bitter. In spring 1911 the campaign sought to convince the state legislature to approve an amendment to the state constitution that would allow women full suffrage. When that was passed, however, it then had to be approved by a popular referendum and was put on the ballot for the November 1912 election. That referendum was defeated by more than two to one of the popular (male) vote. Despite these defeats, suffragists considered 1912 a breakthrough year in the larger perspective. They now had full suffrage in nine states with a combined population of about six and one half million and 45 electoral votes. Reenergized by these victories, they continued their fight for suffrage, state by state as well as in Congress.

In the early years of the suffrage movement, mainstream newspapers were notorious for ridiculing suffragists, their goals, and their arguments in both their news and editorial pages. Olympia Brown wrote in her suffrage journal, the *Wisconsin Citizen*, that in the early years the mainstream press had often referred to female suffragists as "mannish women" and "persons belonging to the third sex," whose arguments were "blatant assumptions" and "wild vagaries."[5] Although most newspapers had come to mask this ridicule by 1911, the prevailing coverage still tended to be negative toward woman's rights. Newspapers expressed this negativity in a variety of ways— from jokes, fillers, and cartoons that portrayed women as silly, sentimental, ignorant, and vain to stories that dwelled on their physical and personality attributes, and from articles focusing on objections to suffrage to editorials that patronized women in general or opposed suffrage in particular.

A smaller number of newspapers came to support suffrage. Often edited by men active in or related to women active in the suffrage movement, these promoted woman's rights and suffrage in their editorials and news columns alike. These newspapers often established regular suffrage columns on their woman's pages, where suffrage organizations could publish news and arguments of the movement. They also supported the reform in editorials and editorial cartoons.

Newspapers occasionally presented both sides of the issue by publishing columns for or against woman suffrage on the woman's or church pages. These columns were submitted either by prominent individuals in the community or leaders of the various suffrage and antisuffrage organizations. They also published news articles covering speeches by suffragists or antis, reproducing verbatim the words of the speakers. During the period leading up to an election with suffrage on the ballot, some newspapers published "suffrage pages" in which they offered a variety of views from prominent members of the community and leaders of the opposing movements. Views for and against suffrage were also expressed through the many advertisements published by local suffrage and antisuffrage organizations immediately before elections in which suffrage proposals were on the ballot.

Because the campaign for woman suffrage in Wisconsin in 1911–1912 was so intense, all the readings in this chapter have been selected from Wisconsin newspapers. These readings are organized in two sections. The first section provides a variety of material in support of suffrage, including news stories, columns, advertisements, and editorials. Many of these provide the various arguments used at the time to convince male voters to support the reform. The second section provides a similar variety of published material opposing suffrage. Most of these selections seek to debunk the suffragists' arguments, with the two most common points being that women do not want the vote, and that their proper place is in the home with the family.

ARGUMENTS IN SUPPORT OF SUFFRAGE

By 1912 woman suffragists had argued their case for 64 years, but they still found the best way to convince male voters to vote in favor of the reform was to get the support of prominent men and have them argue their case for them. This is what they did for this article on the woman suffrage page (entitled "Vote For The Woman Suffrage Amendment Next Tuesday") of the Superior (Wisconsin) Telegram *shortly before the 1912 election. The article quotes more than 50 men of state and national prominence, including political, religious, educational, and labor leaders. Here is a sample of some of their statements, which cover most of the arguments for suffrage.*

Superior Telegram, 4 November 1912

MANY PROMINENT SUPERIOR PEOPLE INDORSE [sic] SUFFRAGE AMENDMENT

Emil Seidel, Ex-Mayor of Milwaukee: Women should have the right to vote, for the reason that there is "no reason on earth why they should not vote."

John Mitchell [labor leader]: I am in perfect harmony with the declaration of the American Federation of Labor, which has endorsed the demand that women be given the right to vote. I personally believe that it would be for the good of us all for women to be enfranchised.

Samuel Gompers [labor leader]: I am for unqualified woman suffrage as a matter of human justice. It is unfair that women should be governed by laws, in the making of which they have no voice. Men would feel that they were used badly if they did not have that right and women naturally feel the same.

Reverend Daniel Hudson, C.S.C.: The conviction grows stronger with me that when women have votes many evils, now regarded as irremediable, will be under easy control and much good accomplished. That woman suffrage is assured is a matter of rejoicing. Deo Gratias.

Horace A.J. Upham of Milwaukee: The evolution of our civilization has brought about the condition that men and women enter into the occupations of the business world and are competitors with each other. It is only a matter of justice to women that they be furnished with every means that the law can give, so that men who work side by side with them shall not have an undue advantage over them by possessing the vote.

Rev. L.K. Grimes: I am in favor of equal suffrage because it is a matter of right and justice to the women and because the average woman is better qualified, educationally and morally, than the average man. And another thing, because men have neglected their duties as citizens and are sending up a call for help to straighten out the muddle.

David Doble: Women should have the right of franchise because it is an inherent right of democracy.

Woman suffrage leaders were able to address readers directly if newspapers agreed to publish their columns, letters, or articles. In this article, Wisconsin suffragist and Milwaukee Journal *reporter Rosa M. Perdue counters the antisuffrage argument that women would abandon the home if allowed to participate in politics and worldly matters. Here, Perdue points out that women have already entered the working world and assures men that the franchise will only allow women to be better wives and mothers because it will give them a voice in civic reform. She also protests here the fact that male immigrants just made citizens have more rights than native-born women. This article appeared on the woman's page and was published as a column rather than as a news article. Perdue's name was used in her capacity as a suffragist rather than as a journalist, for the* Journal *rarely gave its reporters bylines at this time.*

Milwaukee Journal, 4 November 1912

Rosa M. Perdue: PLEA TO VOTERS TO GIVE WISCONSIN WOMEN THE BALLOT

Tide Which Has Swept Them Into Economic World Cannot Be Turned Back— Therefore They Should Have Ballot to Protect Themselves

The time approaches when the men of Wisconsin are to decide whether or not their mothers, wives and sisters may have a voice in government. I write to ask you on the behalf of our 50,000 working girls and wives and mothers to weigh the matter plainly and without prejudice. Thus far we have been disenfranchised in our own country, which we have loved and served all our lives, while many men who can barely qualify for their first papers are dictating through the ballot box who shall be our officers and what shall be the laws that govern us. Many such men as these, blinded by ignorance and prejudice, will vote at this election to keep us disenfranchised. Will not the true American citizen, the Scandinavian who knows his mother might vote in her native country, and every other foreigner who respects his wife and mother vote that she be made his political equal, as he knows she is in character and intelligence?

You need not fear that the simple fact of giving women a chance to be equal to express their opinions respecting aldermen, mayors, state and national officers is going to take women out of the home. Economic conditions beyond their control have already forced women into the industrial world, and they need the ballot to protect their interests there quite as much as men do. Nature has planted in the heart of most women that love of home which would keep her there, if a good home and the right kind of man is there for her. Voting against the amendment granting the franchise to women at this election will not restore woman to the home or restore to any man the coveted position which is now held by a woman.

In every city of this state there are clubs of women sincerely studying civic problems to better the conditions which surround their children and their homes. It is largely through the initiatives of good women that kindergartens and industrial training have been introduced in the schools. Playgrounds, parks, hospitals, infants' homes and hospitals detention homes, juvenile courts, trade schools, homes for the friendless, homes for working girls, social settlements and institutions for the cure of tuberculosis are among their various field of endeavor.

A Moral Force

They are earnestly in favor of city sanitation and a better moral environment in public places of amusement. They have long pleaded in vain for more women factory inspectors to protect the interests of working girls. The one woman factory inspector in the field is doing all she can, but it is a mere farce to expect one woman to even get a sight once a year at all the places in which women are employed. Women need the ballot to enforce their wise opinions concerning these matters of social welfare. The fact that there are women who do not vote [in places where their voting is permitted] is no reason for the continued disenfranchisement of the many who would feel it a privilege and a duty.

The fact that there are a few bad women and a few careless ones who might vote is no reason for depriving the majority of the privilege. I know no one will plead the majority of women are either willfully bad or careless.

Such arguments have not been held valid for the disenfranchisement of men. Why should they be urged against women?

Don't forget to vote on the separate ballot for the franchise of women.

Suffragists could also argue their case directly by placing political advertisements urging voters to support the suffrage amendment. With its reference to Abraham Lincoln and the enfranchisement of blacks following the Civil War in this advertisement, the suffrage committee compares women's current position to that of slaves before the civil war. This boxed advertisement (along with an antisuffrage advertisement) appeared in several Wisconsin papers in the week before the election.

La Crosse Tribune, 2 November 1912

Vote Yes On the Pink Ballot Nov. 5

<u>Abraham Lincoln Said:</u>
"No Class is Good Enough or Wise
Enough to Represent any
Other Class."

The woman who works with men, subject to the same laws as men, needs the ballot. The woman who maintains her home, who pays taxes, the woman head of the family whose future there is no husband to safeguard, needs the ballot. Women who do not work or pay taxes have as much moral right to the ballot as men who do not work or pay taxes.

We are asking for the right to vote. We have no voice in the matter. We put the question squarely up to you men's sense of fair play.

A million of your fathers fought to give the negro the right to vote.

If you think we women are as fit to vote as the negro, you can give us the Square Deal your fathers gave them, without going to war about it.

Do you want to sign our Emancipation Proclamation? Then put an X in the little square after the word YES on the Pink Ballot next Tuesday.

SUFFRAGE COMMITTEE.

Because women could neither vote nor hold office in most states, they could rarely be considered political figures. The wives of some politicians, however, were outspoken on political issues and were frequent speakers at public events and on occasion contributed columns to newspapers, particularly during political campaigns touching on issues regarding women. This was the case for Belle La Follette, the wife of U.S. Senator Robert M. La Follette. Both the senator and his wife were progressives and campaigned for suffrage. This column appeared on the woman suffrage page of the Milwaukee Free Press, *which itself was opposed to suffrage. The page—entitled "Should Women Have the Ballot?"—appeared periodically in the month before the November 1912 election and carried material from both the suffragists and the antis.*

Milwaukee Free Press, 6 October 1912

Belle C. La Follette: WISCONSIN WOMEN READY FOR BALLOT SAYS SENATOR'S WIFE

Only the expediency of woman suffrage is at issue today. The time is past when the abstract right must be contended for. And even the question of expediency is fast sinking into unimportance before the rising tide of examples of woman suffrage in successful operation.

The extension of suffrage to women is the great movement sweeping over the world. It surges from west to east and back again from east to west:—New Zealand, six of our own states, Finland, the great Australian commonwealth, Norway, China, all have in turn responded to the call toward broader democracy. Sweden is giving ear to the same call, and we are anxiously waiting to hear what response will be made in our own country where the question is now before the people in so many states that it is hard to keep count of them.

Neither individuals struggling singly nor organized groups can long stay the progress of such a movement. It comes with the steadiness and irresistibleness of a great elemental change. Even those who most dread its advent admit in their hearts that it is coming. It is an interesting sign of the times, as well as a renewed assurance of the sense of responsibility which women feel for the proper performance of duties entrusted in them that organized groups of anti-suffragists, in spite of their protest against the vote, are entering seriously upon the study of civic problems. Many of them will be well prepared to exercise the suffrage when the privilege is given them, and I think we may feel confident that the energy and earnestness now manifested in opposition will then be given in the service of the state....

Yes, suffrage is coming. We expect it to come in Wisconsin in November 1912, and the women of Wisconsin will be ready for it. They have shared the advantage of equal education in the public schools and the state university. They have taken their place in the industries of the state and in the professions. Singly and through their clubs, they have worked for better municipal, state, and national laws. They are mothers and teachers of the children of the state. They are as ready as the men of the state for the practical exercise of suffrage, except that they have not voted; and the only way to gain experience in voting is to vote. What is suffrage but an expression of patriotism—love for commonwealth, responsibility to our city, interest in our nation—and is that not common to all people?

Though male voters might not have been persuaded by Belle La Follette's arguments, they would be more likely to listen to her husband, a popular U.S. senator and former state governor. "Bob" La Follette had a loyal following among intellectuals and working men alike, and was one of the most prominent leaders of the progressive movement in the Midwest. A vigorous supporter of woman suffrage, he linked it to progressivism and enlightenment. For him, woman suffrage was a sign of the natural evolution of government toward complete democracy. This letter in the Chippewa (Wisconsin) Daily Independent, *which expressed these views, appeared in several other state newspapers.*

Chippewa (Wisconsin) Daily Independent, 5 November 1912

Robert M. La Follette: VOTES FOR WOMEN

Men would go out and be shot to pieces before they would surrender their ballot. It is their weapon, their shield, their only protection against tyranny and oppression in whatever form it may find expression in our modern life.

The ballot is an educator. The right to vote stimulates interest in public affairs and critical study of administrations and the records of public servants.

The State could not afford to disfranchise one-half of its men. No more can it afford to refuse to enfranchise its women.

What the ballot is to working men it will be to the seven or eight million working women in this country, of whom Wisconsin has its share.

Women are tax payers; they are in business; they are mothers and teachers; they have shared equality with men in education.

The women of Wisconsin are especially well-qualified to vote. They have long been interested in the struggle for a more truly representative government.

Equal suffrage is bound to come. It is part of the world's evolution in universal self-government.

Wisconsin as our foremost progressive state should stand for this Progressive movement which an enlightened legislature endorsed, when it submitted the amendment to the people, with only eighteen votes against it. The voters of Wisconsin should sustain the legislature on November 5th.

The Wisconsin State Journal, *published by prosuffrage Richard Lloyd Jones, was one of the few newspapers in the state to consistently support suffrage. In the months leading up to the 1912 election, the* State Journal *published dozens of stories reporting speeches and lectures given by prominent figures in support of the reform, including presidential candidate Theodore Roosevelt, Senator Robert M. La Follette, college professors, and religious leaders. In addition, the State Journal gave full coverage to the claims by suffragists that the liquor interests were working against them. These explanations were necessary for the public to be able to accurately assess the context of antisuffrage claims, but most newspapers ignored them or presented the suffragists' charges of corruption and collusion as hysterical and unfounded. In this news story, the* State Journal *uses a respected local church leader to denounce antisuffrage tactics. The general tone of the article is prosuffrage.*

Wisconsin State Journal, 4 November 1912

SCORES LEAGUE MAKING FIGHT ON SUFFRAGE
In Sermon Yesterday Rev. George E. Hunt Attacks Liquor Men's Political Dodger

AND BIG SUNDAY CROWD APPLAUDS
Madison Pastor Urges All Men To Support Equal Suffrage Amendment

The Christ Presbyterian Church was filled to its capacity last evening. Before this large audience the pastor, the Rev. George E. Hunt, held up for exhibit the dodger [flier] entitled "Danger," which has been issued at the eleventh hour by the retail liquor dealers of Wisconsin and circulated generously throughout the state.

Dr. Hunt asked the congregation to assume for the moment that they were not in a church but in a public hall and that he was speaking as a mere citizen of Madison rather than as a preacher. He then read the dodger, the text of which is printed in full in the editorial page of this issue.

This was the saloon keepers' appeal to the voters of Wisconsin to defeat woman's suffrage because it was dangerous for the saloon keepers to give the ballot to the women. The saloon keepers in this document frankly admitted that the women were not the best friends of the saloon. Mr. Hunt declared that this was the grossest insult that was ever offered the people of the state of Wisconsin; that it would act as a boomerang. He concluded his remarks by earnestly and eloquently urging his congregation in the interest of the home and in the name of Christian decency to vote "yes" for the "Votes for Women" amendment. His great congregation enthusiastically applauded during and at the conclusion of these remarks.

Sometimes the best arguments can be stated in just a few words. That's what the Wisconsin State Journal *did the day before the November election in this brief editorial statement.*

Wisconsin State Journal, 4 November 1912

VOTE FOR WOMEN

Vote for decency and progressive democracy. Vote "yes" for Votes for Women.

ARGUMENTS IN OPPOSITION TO WOMAN SUFFRAGE

A repeated argument of antisuffragists was that women did not want the responsibility of political participation and that where they had it they often did not use it or misused it. Underlying this argument was the idea that woman's real place was in the home under the protection of the men in her family and she should not be forced out into the world, which was corrupt, immoral, and dangerous. In the following editorial, written as the Wisconsin state legislature debated the bill that eventually resulted in the 1912 referendum, the antisuffrage Milwaukee Free Press *contemplates the results such an amendment might bring about and repeats the familiar argument that the majority of women do not want the vote.*

Milwaukee Free Press, 18 May 1911

WOMEN AND THE VOTE

The suffrage bill providing for a referendum on the question of "votes for women" has been passed by the assembly, as expected, and will undoubtedly be concurred in by the senate and signed by the governor.

The decision as to whether the franchise shall or shall not be extended to women in Wisconsin will, therefore, paradoxically enough, be rendered by the male voters at the November election of the next year.

It has long been regarded as a truism that whenever men become convinced that women really want to vote and will vote when the ballot is given them, they will not stand in the way of granting women the privilege.

The thing to be determined, therefore, during the next year and a half is whether a considerable majority of Wisconsin women is in favor of equal suffrage.

At present there is no reason to believe that it is. In this state as in other states, where there has been more or less successful suffrage agitation, a small and determined group of women, in no way representative of the interests, duties, employments and ideals of the great bulk of womankind, has raised sufficient dust to impress certain males of trip-hammer chivalry that the women of the community are pining away for want of the ballot.

The truth is that the women of Wisconsin make only the slightest use of such ballot privileges as they have, and that a like condition prevails in other states, where either whole or partial suffrage has been conceded after the novelty of the first ballot has passed.

Because the great rank and file of women do not actively oppose the suffrage seeking minority is no evidence of their passive acquiescence, but rather of their utter lack of interest. The average woman is too much occupied with affairs close to the true nature of her sex, to waste thought and time in public demonstration against the ballot.

However, whenever the question has come to an issue in cultural states of the union, the sex has become aroused and triumphantly repelled the attempt to burden it with a responsibility which it does not want. Thus, in Massachusetts, a referendum on the question of municipal suffrage for women, in which women were allowed to participate, resulted in but 22,204 favorable votes out of a total of 575,000 women of voting age.

The great national woman suffrage petition submitted to Congress in 1910, bore the names of but 163,438 women after the country had been scoured to obtain them....

The majority of women is instinctively opposed to its entrance into the field of politics and government, but there are vital reasons involving the inevitable changes which the grant of the ballot would bring about in woman's social and economic status, which if properly laid out before the sex, must add conviction to what as yet is an intuition.

It is an amiable delusion of the suffragist that she believes that "the revolution" she is furthering would end with the grant of the ballot, just as a Laura Jean Libby novel assumes that the wedding bell settles the happiness of two yearning lives. But just as in reality the true problem of future happiness but begins for the man and woman after they leave the altar, so will the real revolution implied in woman suffrage only begin with the grant of the ballot.

What that revolution must ultimately mean, not alone to the sex but to the race and its civilizations, the thoughtful opponents of suffrage will be under obligations to make known to Wisconsin in the coming months.

This message was reiterated succinctly in this political advertisement, which appeared in a number of Wisconsin newspapers during the week before the 1912 election. In the La Crosse Tribune, *this boxed advertisement was published directly above a prosuffrage advertisement on the same page.*

La Crosse Tribune, 2 November 1912

Woman Suffrage?
Vote NO!

On the Pink Ballot Nov. 5
The Madison Association Opposed to Woman Suffrage.
Mrs. Frank W. Hoyt, President

We believe the majority of the women in Wisconsin *do not* want to vote or assume the responsibility of government.

They believe their husbands and brothers are fully qualified to do the voting on public questions.

The women of Wisconsin are relying upon the men voters *not* to thrust suffrage upon them Nov. 5.

Vote NO!

On the Pink Ballot

Jokes, vignettes, and humorous cartoons were a common method for expressing hostility toward women and poking fun at suffragists. These were

*often supplied by plate services, which prepared editorial material to hun-
dreds of newspapers in quantity. The resulting boilerplate was usually
timeless and could be printed at any time. Much of this material was provided to the plate services by antisuffrage and liquor and brewing organizations, or organizations backed by them, though newspaper editors were
not always aware of this. This material was also frequently clipped from
other newspapers through mutual exchanges they agreed to, and therefore
appeared in multiple publications over time. This first vignette targets
male suffragists, whom antis frequently portrayed as henpecked and the
pawns of domineering women.*

La Crosse Tribune, 4 November 1912

Voting Under Compulsion

Wilbur F. Steele a Dakota legislator, took no stock in woman suffrage—
except when he was obliged to. Once a suffrage bill was before the house. A
call was made for a vote and the clerk proceeded to call the roll. When Mr.
Steele's name was reached he rose with the dignity of Demosthenes and
commenced: "Mr. Speaker, I am sorry that I can not support this bill, but—"
At this moment, a well-dressed lady was seen to bend over the gallery rail.
In a loud voice, she exclaimed: "W-i-l-b-u-r!" He glanced upward. It was
enough. He turned and said: "Mr. Speaker, I vote aye." The lady was Mrs.
Steele.

---

*This vignette uses humor to repeat the frequent charge that where they
could vote, women often didn't, for a variety of reasons. In this case, the suffragette (a term used to describe women campaigning for suffrage in England) is portrayed as a vain and flighty fool. If women think like this, the
reader concludes, why on earth should they be given the vote?*

Milwaukee Journal, 9 November 1912

WHY SHE DIDN'T VOTE

First Suffragette—Did you vote the Progressive Ticket?
Second Suffragette—I didn't vote at all.
First Suffragette—Why not? You registered, didn't you?
Second Suffragette—Yes, I registered, but I was afraid someone would
challenge my vote. You see, when they asked my age, I got so fluttered I gave
them my bust measure instead!

Like the suffragists, antis published letters and columns in newspapers to argue their position. Mary C. Hoyt was the president of the Madison Association Opposed to Woman Suffrage, hastily formed after the state legislature passed the suffrage amendment and put it on the November 1912 ballot. Suffragists claimed the organization was a front for brewing interests, which opposed woman suffrage. It never had more than a handful of members and disappeared from sight after the referendum was defeated. In this column listing some of the major arguments against suffrage, Hoyt ends with an appeal for funds to continue the antisuffrage campaign. The Oshkosh Northwestern, *in which this column appears, was published in a region of the state dominated by ethnic Germans and the brewing industry, both of which were opposed to suffrage.*

Oshkosh Northwestern, 30 October 1912

Mary C. Hoyt: WOMAN SUFFRAGE

AN APPEAL TO PUBLIC SENTIMENT, IRRESPECTIVE OF PARTY
(To the Voter)

Madison, Wis., Oct. 30—We earnestly urge you to vote NO on the question on woman suffrage on November 5th, for the following reasons:

1. Our country is now in a condition of ferment with its disrupting political factions. We already have a dangerously large electorate, therefore by adding a voting power which is untrained and undisciplined in matters governmental, we will but make more difficult an already distressing problem.
2. We claim that American women, judged as a whole, are suffering under no wrongs which need for their redress the violent overturning of the political machinery.
3. Burdened as we already are, first by nature, second by a highly developed civilization, why should we take upon our shoulders the additional weight of the world political?
4. Woman suffrage states have no remedial laws for woman or child that have not been duplicated in states where men only can vote. Colorado, where women have voted for nineteen years, has one of the most corrupt electorates in the United States.
5. An act conferring the franchise upon women is practically irrevocable. We cannot afford an experiment so dangerous to the welfare of the home, the woman or the child.
6. We ask you not to mistake the clamor of the suffragists for the expression of the majority of the women of your state.

We are in great need of funds to carry on the last two weeks of our campaign and any amount sent to us will be gratefully received by our organization.

> The Madison Association Opposed to Woman Suffrage
> By its President,
> (Mrs.) Mary C. Hoyt

The antis, like the suffragists, found community leaders to agree with them, and these individuals expressed their views in speeches and sermons that were then published in newspapers. The church pastor quoted in this story represents the majority of conservative religious leaders, especially those of the Roman Catholic Church, in his arguments against suffrage.

Oshkosh Northwestern, 4 November 1912

IS AGAINST SUFFRAGE

The Pastor of St. Josephat's Polish Church Gives His Reasons in a Sermon Sunday

That woman's sphere is in the home and not public life and that to give her the right of suffrage would take from her the great charm of womanhood were the contentions of Rev. Francis Laslow, pastor of St. Josephat's Polish Catholic church on Walnut street, in a sermon Sunday.

He came out strongly against giving women the ballot and stated his reasons for this view. He also read a number of extracts from an article in opposition to suffrage which was written by "Ouida," and printed in The North American Review. The pastor paid a compliment to woman by saying she was a queen who ruled over the kingdom of the home, but he said he thought she was going beyond her sphere when she went out trying to get into public life alongside the men. He held that there was much that she had not yet done to make the home the place it should be and she should set out to solve the home problems more fully before trying to take up the ones in other fields.

Woman suffragists were active at the polls on election day in an effort to gain support for the suffrage referendum. Their campaigning, however, may have had two paradoxical results. First, it may have alienated some of the men voters. Second, it may have caused some of the women in communities with school issues on the ballot to forget that they could vote on those questions (though this fact was reported early in the day and things might have changed as the day wore on). This article in the Milwaukee Journal, published in Milwaukee, where women could vote on a local question concerning school bonds, points out this failure in a long story reporting on the turnout in the city's different voting districts, first in a boxed text and then again in the story. These points seem to support antisuffrage arguments that most women were not interested in voting.

Milwaukee Journal, 5 November 1912

WOMEN FORGET TO VOTE

Mrs. Clara R. McLenegan was the only woman who had voted on the school bond question in the Sixteenth Ward up to noon. She voted at the third precinct and her vote was No. 162. About fifty women were registered in the precinct.

At 11 a.m. 160 had voted in Fourth precinct of the Fifteenth ward and 197 in the First of the Nineteenth. No woman had voted at either booth, but all the male voters voted the pink ballot on the suffrage question.

"Have any women voted here on the school bond issue?" asked a reporter of officials at the Second precinct, Ninth ward, where they vote in a schoolhouse.

"None," said an inspector.

"They raise families out here," volunteered the patrolman on duty.

Ald. Wittig visited a number of the voting booths to inspect the lighting facilities, which he declares very poor.

Women Forget School Bonds

Shortly after 9 a.m. Tuesday, 200 votes had been cast in the First precinct of the Ninth ward, and 25 or 30 men were in line waiting to vote. The woman suffrage question took the minds of many women voters entirely away from the fact that they had the privilege of voting on issuing school bonds. Very few women are voting on that question. In the First and Second ward not a single woman had voted up to 10 a. m. Of the 494 [men] registered in the Second precinct, seventy-three had voted at that hour....

In the Sixth ward voters appeared rapidly. Women are at work near all of the booths, distributing the pink ballot and urging support of the woman suffrage amendment....

In the First precinct 159 out of a registration of 253 had voted at 10:30 a. m. All are voting on the suffrage amendment. Women workers are stationed near all of the booths, urging support of the question.

An Irishman came into the First precinct booth, and when the inspector handed him a pink ballot, he asked, "What's this for?"

"That is to vote on the woman suffrage question," he was told.

"To the divil [*sic*] with woman suffrage," he cried. "Let the women stay at home behind the cookstove, with a cat," and thereupon he voted no before the very eyes of the inspector, and he did it with a vengeance.

When the suffrage amendment was lost in the 1912 election, antisuffragists interpreted this as a vindication of their beliefs, when, in fact, it simply meant that the majority of male voters did not support the reform. This view is expressed toward the beginning of this news story reporting the results of the election in Milwaukee.

Milwaukee Journal, 6 November 1912

REFUSE WOMEN POWER TO VOTE

SUFFRAGE CAUSE LOSES IN WISCONSIN BY VOTE OF MORE THAN TWO TO ONE

Milwaukee County Piles Up Plurality Against of 20,895— Madison "Antis" Greatly Elated

Voters registered an emphatic "no" to granting suffrage to women. The proposition lost in Milwaukee county by a vote of 39,533 to 18,643, a plurality of 20,895. Returns from other sections of the state indicate the defeat of the proposition by more than 2 to 1....

"The great majority of Wisconsin women will rejoice with us," said Mrs. Frank W. Hoyt, president Madison Association Opposed to Woman Suffrage, over the telephone from Madison. "We are grateful that the thoughtful and right-minded men of the state did not neglect to cast their ballots for the best interests of the home and womanhood. Our association is not militant and made no active campaign. It merely went on record in behalf of Wisconsin women who do not want suffrage thrust upon them."

Though suffragists had claimed that suffrage was inevitable and had acted as if they were confident of victory, when they were defeated in 1912, it was the antisuffragists who could say, "I told you so." The Oshkosh Daily Northwestern *maintains in this editorial that the referendum was defeated because not enough women wanted it, despite the fact that, paradoxically, it was men who voted on the issue.*

Oshkosh Daily Northwestern, 6 November 1912

Defeat of Woman Suffrage

The defeat of woman suffrage in the state election of yesterday will cause little surprise, even to those who were favorable to this plan. Regardless of whether the principle embodied in this question is right or wrong, there was no strong evidence that the women generally were inclined to insist on this concession. In fact, the evidence rather pointed to the fact that only a small portion of the women favored this plan. Perhaps the time may come when a readily apparent majority of the women will demand the "right," and if such time ever comes it is fair to believe their wishes will be respected by the male voters, who have it in their power to grant or refuse this extension of privilege. The campaign for "votes for women" will therefore very likely be continued by those who are personally interested in the question, with a chance that some future day may see a reversal of the verdict of this year.

QUESTIONS

1. In two separate lists, write down some of the principle arguments for and against suffrage. How did these arguments reflect conflicting contemporary views of woman and her place in society?
2. Why was it important for newspapers to provide the context of a story—by describing the background and interests of those supporting or opposing suffrage—to give the reader a complete idea of what was going on? Why might some newspapers have been reluctant to discuss or investigate the charges by suffragists that the liquor interests were plotting against them?
3. Jokes and humor are often based on stereotypes, yet they are supposed to be funny and the people making the jokes often say they mean no harm. How did jokes about women and suffragists serve as an insidious way of undermining them? Why would this be a particularly effective way for antisuffrage organizations to taint the press?
4. How does Senator Robert La Follette's endorsement of suffrage echo many of the themes of progressivism? How, according to this view, is suffrage inevitable?

NOTES

1. These organizations all had their own agenda to promote, but at some point came to include woman suffrage as a necessary reform. They all eventually

campaigned for suffrage and assisted the various suffrage organizations in their campaigns.

2. Elizabeth Burt, "An Arena for Debate: Woman Suffrage, the Brewing Industry and the Press, Wisconsin 1910–1919" (Ph.D. diss., University of Wisconsin, 1994), pp. 250–343.

3. Eleanor Flexner, *Century of Struggle: The Woman's Rights Movement in the United States,* rev. ed. (Cambridge: Belknap Press of Harvard University Press, 1975), pp. 304–19.

4. By the end of 1912, nine states had full suffrage. They were Arizona, California, Colorado, Idaho, Kansas, Oregon, Utah, Washington, and Wyoming.

5. Olympia Brown, "Bad Journalists," *Wisconsin Citizen,* May 1901, p. 1.

CHAPTER 16

Congress Adopts the Federal Income Tax, February 1913

T he adoption of the Sixteenth Amendment, which introduced the federal income tax, did not capture the public's interest with the same intensity as other issues of the Progressive Era, but it is the reform that eventually came to affect most directly the greatest number of Americans every day. The Sixteenth Amendment placed the responsibility for financing the federal government directly on the shoulders of the individual citizen. This was a radical departure from the system devised by the framers of the Constitution, who had instead required apportionment of taxes among the states based on population.

For most of the nation's history, the federal government's major source of income had been from custom duties, excise taxes placed on the sale of specific items, and, on occasion, death (or inheritance) taxes. An income tax was first introduced in the United States in 1862 in response to the financial emergency caused by the Civil War. That tax was collected on all wages, salaries, interest, and dividends, with a flat $600 exemption. It was modified in 1865, 1866, and again in 1870 by the introduction of the concept of a graduated tax determined by the individual's level of income. Although the income tax was successful in raising $376 million in 1866 alone, it was an unpopular measure among the general public. In 1872 Congress decided to let the statute die.

Some, however continued to support the idea of a federal income tax. Through the 1870s and 1880s, the Democratic Party supported it as a way of keeping tariff rates down and equalizing the distribution of wealth. In 1892 the Populists launched a campaign for the income tax and made it part of their platform. In 1894 Nebraska Democrat William Jennings Bryan led a movement in the House of Representatives to adopt an income tax and succeeded in attaching a tax provision to that year's tariff legislation. This, however, was struck down by the Supreme Court within the year. The Court held that a federal income tax was a violation of the Constitution's requirement that taxes be apportioned among the states on the basis of the population.

By this time, many members of the public had come to support the income tax as a way of leveling the widening chasm between the rich and the poor, the large corporation and the small business enterprise. That support was reflected by many in Congress, which began to consider amending the Constitution in order to authorize the tax. A constitutional amendment was also supported by Presidents Theodore Roosevelt and William Howard Taft as well New Jersey Governor Woodrow Wilson, who won the presidency in the election of 1912. It was opposed, however, by corporate and special interests that succeeded through lobbying, influence, and bribery in blocking a total of 33 proposals for an amendment made in Congress between 1895 and 1909.

The major arguments for an income tax (to be permitted by the constitutional amendment) were that it would provide additional revenue to the federal government in times of increased financial need (such as during war), permit lower tariffs, distribute the tax across all segments of society, and equalize the nation's distribution of wealth. There were many arguments against an income tax (and the constitutional amendment that would permit it). Those most concerned with the economic aspects of the tax claimed it would create double and even triple taxes on individuals who already paid state and municipal taxes and unfairly shift the nation's fiscal burden to the wealthy. As early as 1894, conservatives charged that it was socialistic in nature and hostile to the spirit of American institutions. Some believed it would usurp states' rights. Others claimed it was inquisitorial and would invade the individual's right to privacy.

By 1909 arguments in support of the income tax amendment in Congress outweighed those against it. In that year Rhode Island Republican Nelson W. Aldrich, the chairman of the Senate Committee on Finance, proposed an amendment to the Constitution. It stated: "The Congress shall have power to lay and collect taxes on incomes, from whatever sources derived, without apportionment among the several States, and without regard to any census or enumeration." Although Aldrich apparently introduced the amendment to distract support for a proposed income tax provision attached to the tariff bill currently under debate, the amendment quickly gained support. In less than two weeks, the Senate approved the amendment unanimously, and the House added its endorsement on July 12, 1909.

The Sixteenth Amendment received ratification from most of the 36 required states relatively quickly, with organized opposition coming only from those in the conservative and wealthy Northeast. The influence of the interests on Congress that had blocked the amendment's approval since 1894 had, perhaps, been momentarily weakened by the several Senate investigations into corruption that had been carried out in the previous three years. Eventually, the Sixteenth Amendment was ratified by the required 36th state on February 3, 1913 and went into effect February 25. It was the first Constitutional amendment to be passed in 43 years.[1]

Once the Sixteenth Amendment went into effect, Congress was able to write an income tax law, which it added to the Tariff Act of October 3, 1913.

THE HUNDRED-MILLION-DOLLAR BABY.

(Philadelphia Record.

"The Hundred-Million-Dollar Baby," *New Orleans Picayune*, 10 February 1913, p. 1. *Proponents of the Income Tax Amendment hoped it would raise as much as $100 million each year, decrease the need for high tariffs, and stimulate American trade and the economy. While Congress proposed the amendment, it could only go into effect if ratified by the state legislatures. This cartoon first appeared in the* Philadelphia Record *and was then reprinted in the* New Orleans Picayune.

The version that was finally adopted was a graduated tax that taxed individuals according to their income.[2] True to the predictions of its opponents, the Sixteenth Amendment opened the door to perennial taxation by the Congress. The federal income tax—originally proposed to be enacted only in time of national emergencies—eventually became a major source of revenue for the nation, totaling more than 50 percent of its budget receipts by the 1950s. The passage of the income tax amendment in 1913 inaugurated a new era in national politics whose effects on presidential and congressional elections were to be felt into the twenty-first century.

During the debates on the constitutional amendment, it was difficult for the newspapers of the period to present the issues of constitutional reform and tax law in both an informative and an interesting manner to a general reading public. When they did cover the issue, they typically focused on the colorful debates between opponents and supporters of the constitutional amendment or quoted known figures who spoke for or against it. Then, after July 1909, as the ratification process went forward, newspapers produced updates on the scorecard of states ratifying or rejecting the amendment. In the last few weeks before the amendment's ratification in early February 1913, they published frequent countdowns that listed the states that had already ratified, how many were still needed, and those that were expected to make a decision in the near future. On the editorial page, newspapers sometimes got into convoluted legalistic or statistical arguments, intended to support or oppose the amendment, that frequently overwhelmed the reader. Although this was a constitutional amendment that would eventually touch the life of practically every living American, most newspaper stories and editorials failed to drive this point home to the reader.

Once the tax amendment was ratified, newspapers continued to discuss it, especially on the editorial page. Some, particularly those that had supported it, predicted the tax would make citizens more aware of the government's expenditures and thus make government more accountable. Others, instead, warned that the tax could provide the government with a sense of unlimited resources and encourage it to spend money recklessly.

The readings in this chapter span the period between July 1909, when the amendment was debated in the House, to late February 1913, after it was ratified by the 36th state. The news articles and editorials in the first section illustrate some of the arguments against the income tax amendment, and include a few published after the amendment's ratification that predict dire consequences. Those in the second section represent some of the arguments made in support of the amendment and, once it was ratified, include some predictions of how the tax will alter citizen's behavior for the better.

OPPOSITION TO THE INCOME TAX AMENDMENT

The New York Times *represented the nation's conservative voice in its campaign against the constitutional amendment. Falling back on precedent and authority, it argued that Congress could easily apportion an income tax among the states according to their population, as the framers of the Constitution had designed. In this long editorial, the* Times *provides a historical and economic analysis of the results of the previous income taxes levied during the Civil War and attempted in 1894 that shows the wealthy Northeastern states will likely end up paying the bulk of the tax.*

New York Times, 8 July 1909

AN UNNECESSARY AMENDMENT

Why amend the Constitution? Congress might easily in a few words apportion an income tax among the several States "according to their respective numbers." The framers of the Constitution provided that taxes should so be apportioned. In the twenty years that preceded the Constitutional Convention a great deal had been said about taxation without representation. The members of the Convention were sensitive upon that subject. It was declared in the resolution introduced on July 16, 1787, that "representation ought to be according to direct taxation." The debates show that it was the sentiment of the Convention that "the apportionment of representation and taxation by the same scale is just." The danger was evident that, if this rule were omitted, a majority of the States might combine against a few others or against one State, and burden it with taxes far beyond its proportional representation in Congress. Accordingly, the Constitution, as adopted, declared that representatives and direct taxes should be apportioned among the several States according to their respective numbers.

The sound reasons that prompted the adoption of this principle still exist. So far from becoming obsolete, they have been strengthened and have taken on new validity with the lapse of the years. Democratic statesmen are continually prating about the wisdom of the Fathers. Republicans sometimes allude to it. Why should we depart now from the safe rule they laid down?...

In his argument before the Supreme Court against the income tax of 1894, which was declared unconstitutional because it was a direct tax and not apportioned, Mr. Joseph H. CHOATE referred to the working of the income tax imposed during the civil war, and pointed out to the court the very unequal distribution of the impost:

> "There was formerly an income tax law, and the last year it was in force was the year 1873. The exemption then was $2,000. In that year, the collections for that tax were such in the States of New York, Pennsylvania, Massachusetts, and New Jersey that even then, with that exemption, those four states paid four-fifths of the entire tax. What was their political representation in the lower house of Congress, which only can initiate and secure the passage of revenue bills? Eighty-three out of 356, or a little less than one-quarter. Anybody who knows anything about the operation of these income tax laws and as to the effect of changing the exemption from $2,000 to $4,000 knows that the inequality of the burden will, under the act of 1894, press upon those four states with vastly greater force. So that it is Massachusetts, New York, New Jersey, and Pennsylvania that, under this enactment, if it be allowed to stand, may pay not less than nine tenths of the entire tax, a tax imposed upon them by other States."

The corporation tax law passed the other day makes $5,000 the exemption figure—that is, corporations having a net income of not more than $5,000 will pay no tax. There is no reason whatever why there should be an exemption figure in a tax of this nature.... [I]t is safe to assume that the income tax which Congress would put upon us, should the amendment be adopted, will exempt incomes below $5,000. Exemptions for their states is exactly what the income tax advocates want, and the higher the exemption figure the smaller the sums collected in Texas, Iowa, the Mountain States and in other States where there is a ferocious desire that incomes shall be taxed. Having once removed the Constitutional safeguard of apportionment, there will be no check upon the power of the Populistic States to exempt themselves and make a few Eastern States pay all, or nearly all, the tax.

When the House approved the proposed amendment on July 12, 1909, the majority of representatives to vote against it were from the Northeast. This brief news story indicates their opposition.

New York Times, 13 July 1909

HOUSE FOR INCOME TAX PLAN

Votes 317 to 14 for Constitutional Amendment

Special to The New York Times

WASHINGTON, July 12—The House to-day, after strongly denouncing all forms of special taxation and the corporation tax in particular, through four hours of debate, passed the income tax constitutional amendment by far more than the required two-thirds vote. A roll call showed 317 Representatives for the proposed amendment and only 14 against it, one man answering present.

The fourteen opponents of the measure were all Republicans. They were Allen of Maine, Barchfeld, Dalzell, McCreary and Wheeler of Pennsylvania, Calderhead of Kansas, Fordney of Michigan, Gardner, McCall and Weeks of Massachusetts, Henry and Hill of Connecticut, and Olcott and Southwick of New York. Four of these are members to the conference committee on the Tariff bill that will have the corporation tax to consider—Calderhead, Dalzell, Fordney, and McCall. Another opponent of the tax and all similar levy was Hill, a member of the Ways and Means Committee.

The speeches and votes together both indicated a strong opposition, particularly in the East, to any of the special forms of taxation. Mr. Payne's speech was itself of that complexion, though he finally voted for the constitutional amendment on the ground that, while he hoped an income tax would never be levied in time of peace, he thought the Government should have the power in case of emergency.

The tax amendment was initially opposed by many New York state legislators as well as its governor, who argued that the individual states would be enslaved if they were to arm Congress with the income tax. Such arguments delayed the state's ratification for two years, but eventually individuals came to accept it. When the state legislature ratified the amendment in July 1911, the New York Times *denounced the Democratic legislators who had voted for the Republican measure, charging they had betrayed the interests of their state. It predicted that if the amendment resulted in an income tax law, New Yorkers would pay one-sixth of the revenues raised but reap none of the appropriations, which instead would go to the South and the West.*

New York Times, 14 July 1911

THE INCOME TAX VOTE

The confessions of faith made by those who have supported the Income Tax amendment are refreshingly frank. The best of all is that of the Arkansas advocate of the amendment, who declared that he was for it because for every dollar paid by Arkansas New York would pay a thousand dollars. This belief, or hope, is no doubt widely entertained in the States of the West and of the South....

A change of two votes in the Assembly from affirmative to negative would have defeated the amendment. It is amazing that this Republican income tax should have had even a majority in a Democratic legislative body. There is nothing Democratic about it. The amendment was of Republican origin, and it was brought forward not because the country stood in need of revenues but as a measure of political necessity. Mr. BRYAN is a great income taxer. It is understood that he had mixed in the contest at Albany, and his influence may have had something to do with the result. But Bryanism is not Democracy. The Democrats who voted for the resolution have betrayed the interest of their State, they have given aid to men who cherish designs not at all in the interests of this State. As Assemblyman MERRITT pointed out, New York will pay about one-sixth of the entire amount raised by an Income Tax law, and whatever that amount may be the South and West are ready to make use of it. The West wants $500,000,000 for deep-waterway improvement. Billions could be spent on irrigation projects without satisfying the demand for expenditures of that nature. But let New York or any Eastern State ask for an appropriation, opposition develops at once....

One innocent Assemblyman declared that we need fear no injustice at the hands of Congress under an Income Tax law. Some supporters of the tax have said that Congress would not impose any income tax unless in an extraordinary emergency, such as a foreign war. Having the power to lay the tax, we may be very sure that Congress will exercise it.

Resistance to the ratification of the amendment was not completely defeated in the New York State Assembly and an attempt was made to rescind that ratification when the assembly reconvened in the beginning of 1912. Here, the New York Times *explains the grounds for the resolution, which ultimately failed.*

New York Times, 2 February 1912

NEW YORK AND THE INCOME TAX

The sober judgment of the people of New York, we think, will approve the purpose of the concurrent resolution introduced by Assemblyman HAROLD J. HINMAN to rescind the resolution adopted at the last session of the Legislature approving the Federal income tax amendment to the Constitution of the United States....

Mr. HINMAN points out that there is no provision to secure uniformity throughout the Union in the incidence of the tax, and that is another departure from existing constitutional principle. The levying of the tax is not limited to war purposes, or to times of emergency. Certainly there is no present emergency demanding an increase of the Federal revenues from sources which State Governments need for their own existence. The need of additional revenue for the Government of the State of New York is somewhat urgent. We have recently been compelled to resort again to direct taxation. If the amendment should be ratified there can be no reasonable doubt that Congress would speedily avail itself of this new taxing power. By just that much the field open to State taxation would be diminished. We do not believe that the resolution ratifying the amendment, which was adopted last year by a vote of 35 to 16 in the Senate and of 91 to 42 in the Assembly, fairly represented the majority opinion of the people of the State. The adoption of Mr. HINMAN's resolution, we are confident, would meet with general approval.

New York's ratification of the amendment broke the resistance in the northeastern states, and in February 1913 the 36th state was added to those who had approved it, making the Sixteenth Amendment part of the Constitution. The Rocky Mountain News, *published in one of those Mountain States (Colorado) suspected by the* New York Times *of wanting to pick New Yorkers' pockets, feared Congress would exploit the new tax to raise new revenues.*

Rocky Mountain News, 6 February 1913

The Income Tax

Almost four years ago Congress submitted an Income Tax amendment to the states for their ratification. Thirty-eight states have ratified this amendment, two more than the necessary three-fourths majority.

There is, therefore, small doubt that the present session of Congress will witness the passage of an income tax measure. So long have the people waited for this reform—so intense is the public interest in it—that it is to be hoped that Congress will proceed wisely.

What is wanted by the people is a law that will make swollen fortunes bear a proportionate share of the public expense in order that the burdens of poverty may be lightened. If Congress, however, regards an Income Tax solely as a means of raising revenues for new expenses, the disappointment of the people will be bitter.

Another fear was that the partisan use of the income tax by the Democratic and Socialist parties would result in class discrimination and the exploitation of the wealthy.

New York Sun, 5 February 1913

Income Tax Now Possible

The adherence of Wyoming unexpectedly in advance of that of either New Jersey or New Mexico, makes the income tax amendment a part of the federal constitution. Congress at last has the power to lay a tax upon incomes, from whatever source derived, without apportionment among the states.

The exercise of this power is with congress, which submitted the resolution to the states on the general theory that it was a power to be used in an emergency in a last resort and not in the ordinary business of providing ways and means.

How far the new Democratic dispensation will depart from this original attitude toward the income tax idea, how strong will be the effort to make it the instrument of an odious class discrimination and inequality for Socialistic or near-Socialistic purposes wholly apart from the question of revenue, now remains to be seen.

The New Orleans Picayune *railed against the ratification of the tax amendment, arguing that it had been slipped through Congress while the public's attention had been distracted by the revolution in Mexico. The* Picayune *sees the tax as inherently unfair, and suggests that the amendment's approval is symptomatic of the growing tendency of people to profit at the cost of others.*

New Orleans Picayune, 20 February 1913

THE NEW CONSTITUTIONAL AMENDMENT

The Picayune did not support a movement to tax income earned by individual labor from industries. Incomes from property and investments are right enough, but taxes on incomes from personal earnings, from wages and salaries are taxes on labor. Moreover, people with incomes in order to escape the tax will cover up their affairs as much as possible and be loath to make public their revenue. Mr. Gladstone, the English statesman, in opposing an income tax in the United Kingdom, asked Parliament "If it was desired to make the country a nation of liars."

It is said that the income tax is collected in Germany more thoroughly than elsewhere, but it is largely through a strict inquisition and espionage which some persons believe would not be submitted to in the United States. But this assumption is not well-founded, for although the American people are showing every day their disregard for state and local laws, they display a wonderful willingness to put all public power in the hands of the National Government. Doubtless, the growing disposition of the people to look for generous appropriations and handouts from the National treasury is at the bottom of it.

As opponents predicted, Congress immediately moved to enact an income tax law and an inevitable outcry was raised in the business community. Here, in the words of E.H. Gary, chairman of the United States Steel Corporation—one of the nation's richest corporations—is a sample of what was to become the class war over taxes that began in 1913 and has continued into the twenty-first century. Gary predicts that businessmen may be reluctant to invest if their earnings are then taxed at a higher rate than the general population, an argument that has been repeated countless times by businessmen since.

Chicago Tribune, 24 May 1913

INCOME TAX LAW LABELED "WORST"

E.H. Gary Says Its Passage by Congress Calculates to Produce Classes

MONEY KINGS CAUTIOUS

New York, May 23—E.H. Gary, chairman of the United States Steel corporation, at the annual meeting today of the American Iron and Steel Institute, quoted President Wilson as saying that honesty had nothing to fear from the Democratic administration....

Tinker with Strange Subjects

Mr. Gary in his talk alluded to what he called "the disposition of legislative bodies to tinker with questions they are not well prepared to discuss or decide," mentioning particularly the passage of laws which he said were calculated to produce classes.

"I think, for instance," he continued, "the proposition to assess the income of men who have incomes of more than $4,000 and exempting the incomes of those who receive less than $4,000 a year is one of the worst things that has every happened in this country, because it immediately arrays 97 percent of the people against 3 percent of the people.

"I have no doubt that at the present time there is a disposition on the part of some of the leading financiers of the country, and perhaps those whose influence is needed to carry on the best interests of the country, to withdraw their financial support from extensions of various kinds, and that we are feeling the effect to some extent."

SUPPORT OF THE INCOME TAX AMENDMENT

The first breakthrough in the industrial states came in February 1910, when Illinois ratified the tax amendment. It was also the first northern state to do so. In the following editorial, the Chicago Tribune *debunks many of the arguments against the amendment offered by the more conservative states, particularly New York.*

Chicago Tribune, 11 February 1910

THE INCOME TAX AMENDMENT

The unanimous vote of the Illinois senate for the ratification of the income tax amendment shows that none of its members was affected by [New York] Gov. Hughes' argument against it. They did not share his fears that the federal government would destroy the credit and impair the power of the states and municipalities by taxing the income derived from their bonds.

Gov. Hughes has been effectively answered by Gov. Fort of New Jersey. He says:

"Suppose a 1 percentum of tax were to be levied upon income. Under such a tax, the holder of a $1,000 4 per cent state or municipal bond would pay an income tax on $40 a year, which would amount to 40 cents per annum. If the patriotism of our cities and the interest of our financial institutions who take and hold municipal securities are at so low an ebb as to cause such a tax to affect the value of the state or municipal securities, we are indeed in an unfortunate condition in the republic."

The general impression is that Massachusetts and New York will refuse to ratify the amendment. Perhaps the average citizen of those states is more affected by the possibility of the loss of 40 cents than is the average Illinoisian.

Gov. Fort's reply to the claim that congress might injure the states as such by taxing the income from their bonds is—

"First, the congress is representative of the states and elected by the citizenship thereof, and the remedy is in the hands of the people of the states by not returning such congressmen.

Second, the patriotism of our people is such that no congress could be elected that would lay any tax with a view of destroying the power or integrity of the states."

This is the sufficient answer to Gov. Hughes' assertion that the states would be enfeebled and enslaved if they were to arm congress with the income tax.

Illinois will be the first northern state to ratify the amendment. Its neighbors should not fear to follow where it leads. It has no apprehensions of the use to its injury by the congress of any power it may grant for the common defense and the promotion of the common welfare.

The New York governor's objection to the amendment played an important role in that state's deliberations on the amendment and dragged out debate for nearly two years. At the end of March 1911, as the state Senate hesitated over reaching a resolution, the New York World, *which had campaigned for the income tax since the 1880s, defined this as a critical moment for the entire country. In this editorial, the* World *urges the New York state legislators to fulfill their duty to their party—both the Democratic and Republican leadership had endorsed the amendment—and lead the nation.*

New York World, 30 March 1911

NEW YORK AND THE INCOME TAX

In deferring consideration of the Income-Tax resolution for another week, the New York Senate has neglected its plain and pledged duty. The Senate is expected to pass the resolution in the end, but this is a case where promptness is of value to the whole country.

Last year the differently organized Senate passed a resolution ratifying the Income-Tax amendment, but the Assembly twice voted it down. In six other States, New Hampshire, West Virginia, Virginia, Louisiana, Arkansas and Utah, one house has passed a ratifying resolution while the other has failed to do so. In three States both houses have rejected the amendment. In New Jersey the Senate only has voted in the negative. Nine States have not yet acted. In Maine the amendment will probably be defeated by a movement for a State income tax, although the Democratic State Convention specifically endorsed the Federal income-tax proposal. The Minnesota house has passed it unanimously. Twelve states failing in the end to ratify can defeat the amendment.

No Democratic legislator in Albany can consistently fail to vote for this resolution after accepting nomination and election upon State and National platforms, both of which expressly favor it. No Republican legislator need hesitate to further an amendment passed by a Republican Congress and strongly urged by the Republican President and the Republican Senator from New York.

*The New York governor's argument that with a federal income tax Con-
gress would, in essence, double tax those investing in state and municipal
bonds, was convincing to Connecticut legislators, who never did ratify the
amendment. In this editorial, the* Hartford Courant, *which supported the
income tax for emergency funding, uses exaggeration and ridicule to debunk the New York governor's arguments against it. In the process, the*
Courant *also debunks its rival, the* Hartford Times, *which had endorsed
Hughes's position.*

Hartford Courant, 15 July 1911

THE INCOME TAX

Our neighbors of the "Hartford Times," discussing the national income
tax, say that no answer has been made to the assertion by Governor Hughes
of New York to the effect that the national government might by this tax be
able to tax a state out of existence by levying against state and municipal
bonds. We had supposed this objection had gone under ground long ago.
"The Courant" is looking confidently forward to a time when bonds will not
be taxed at all by anybody, for they are nothing but evidences of debt and
have no value except as are based on some property somewhere which
itself is taxed. It is double taxation to tax a note and its security.

But coming to this precise statement of public peril, why isn't Hartford a
goner. The state of Connecticut taxes our municipal bonds. Are we doomed
to extinction? Why, indeed, isn't Connecticut herself a suicide? She taxes
her own bonds. Maybe she will some day get excited and tax herself right
out of existence. Where will we all be then?

In the opinion of "The Courant" an income tax is a fit and proper tax,
and that was the prevailing opinion through the United States until the
Supreme Court decided against the law that had passed. But it has been the
popular understanding all the time that such a tax in this country should, for
the present at least, be held back as an emergency resource. If the pending
constitutional amendment had contained the proviso that the proposed income tax should be levied only when the President of the United States
should declare that a great emergency existed, we believe it would have
gone through the states a-humming.

---

*At the very end, the last few states that were close to ratifying the amend-
ment raced each other to have the honor of being the 36th to do so. For days
in late January and early February, the press was practically breathless in
its speculation of which state would make it first. It might be Wyoming. No,*

wait. It might be New Jersey! But hold on. Maybe it would be Delaware! And Delaware it was. Once the 36th state had signed on, newspapers supporting the amendment greeted the news with triumph. The New York World, which had supported the reform since the 1880s, proclaimed the news with its typical hoopla. In its front-page story announcing the ratification, it even claims a role in the happy event.

New York World, 4 February 1913

INCOME TAX IS RATIFIED IN CLOSE RACE OF STATES

Long Fought For By The World, Measure Becomes Sixteenth Amendment To Federal Constitution When Delaware and Wyoming Adopt it in Almost Simultaneous Action

MAY RAISE AS MUCH AS $100,000,000 A YEAR

Final Action by Congress Putting Measure in Effect Will Be Taken at Extra Session—First Amendment in 43 Years

(Special to the World)

WASHINGTON, Feb. 3—There was great rejoicing in Congress this afternoon when announcement was made that the income tax amendment to the Constitution has been ratified by three-fourths of the States. It immediately became self-evident that enormous revenues, estimated all the way from $60,000,000 to $100,000,000 a year could now be obtained by levying a tax on incomes, thus offsetting to that extent reductions in duties covered by proposed tariff revision.

The honor of completing the ratification is practically conceded to Delaware, which put the amendment through barely ahead of Wyoming. Delaware's vote was said to have been completed at 10:55 A.M. Eastern time, and Wyoming's at 10:43 mountain time. New Mexico too indorsed the tax, but later in the day. New Jersey had been counted on to do so, but delayed.

Ratification follows a campaign vigorously waged by The World for thirty years, in which interest was aroused in all parts of the country, with the result that strong pressure was brought to bear on both Congress and the State Legislatures.

Sixteenth Amendment

In making the announcement in the Senate, Mr. Brown, author of the amendment, which now becomes operative, said:

"I am pleased to inform the Senate that advices from the States of Wyoming and Delaware to-day are to the effect that the income tax amendment has been ratified by both States. The joint resolution originated in the Senate and I congratulate the Senate on the part it played. The joint resolution having been favored by a special message by the President of the United States, I congratulate him, and I congratulate the American people on having ratified this sixteenth amendment to the Constitution."

It is not proposed to attempt income tax legislation this session of Congress. It will be brought forward in connection with downward revision of the Payne-Aldrich Tariff act.

Attention shifted immediately to the question of whether Congress would immediately levy an income tax and, if so, how it would affect individual Americans. While newspapers opposed to the amendment predicted a grim future, the Chicago Tribune, *which had supported the amendment, placed its faith in the wisdom of the nation's lawmakers.*

Chicago Tribune, 5 February 1913

THE SIXTEENTH AMENDMENT

The adoption of an amendment of the federal constitution authorizing congress to impose a direct tax upon incomes has been a foregone conclusion for some years. The trend of public opinion has been strongly in its favor, although naturally opposition has been concentrated and well directed. The equity which underlies the income tax plan in its theory seems very plain and incontestable to most voters, while whatever objections exist must prove themselves in the actual working of the law enacted. The objection which seemed so final to the masterful individualists of a previous generation of Americans, that this form of a tax is inquisitorial, carries less weight nowadays. The doctrine that "a man's business is his own affair," the doctrine of "the public be damned," are now admitted to have some sharp limitations.

The greatest obstacle that might have been predicted for a national income tax is the jealousy of the states, the objection that this type of taxation should be reserved by the states. But this objection did not prove formidable, evidently because the public felt that direct taxes might and would be imposed by both jurisdictions.

The sixteenth amendment is, of course, permissive merely, but its adoption will be promptly followed by a tax law. It is to be hoped this law will be drawn with wisdom and foresight, and that experience will prove we have in it a system more broadly just in its incidence than any other now existent in the United States.

One prediction for a positive outcome was that if people were paying for government expenses directly out of their own pockets, they would keep a closer eye on how the government spent that money. "Responsible citizens make for a responsible government," could have been the motto for this argument. This idea, put forward by Representative Hull of Tennessee, was seconded by the Atlanta Constitution. *In this editorial, the* Constitution *also praises the democratic nature of the income tax, which it believed would distribute wealth among the population more evenly.*

Atlanta Constitution, 5 February 1913

AN AWAKENING TAX

Representative Hull, of Tennessee, cited one of the first advantages of a federal income tax, now assured, when he declared it would provide an effectual check upon congressional extravagance. Where government is largely supported by money which comes directly from the taxpayer, as it will in this instance, people are apt to more intelligently scrutinize appropriations than under the present disguised and indirect system.

Most of us now contribute to the upkeep of the federal government and to its myriad improvement and reclamation projects, as well as to such fence-building grabs as dollar-a-day service pensions and the deepening and broadening of impossible creeks and imaginary harbors. But since we pay our share in the sugar-coated form of tariff revenues and internal revenue, the outgo is not so apparent and our incentive to keep a vigilant eye on the Washington spenders is not so keen.

When, however, a government official wearing the badge of the tax-gatherer waits upon the citizen once a year and takes an appreciable slice out of the latter's income, from that day forward said citizen is apt to scan the government budget and congressional expenditures with a jealous eye. The fact is brought home to him that it is his money being spent or misspent. Heretofore many of us have viewed federal appropriations as coming from some cryptic and mythical source concerning us personally in only a vague sort of way.

The income tax is going to jab the pocket-nerve. Therefore, the income tax is going to wake up a good many influential citizens in this country. It is true that the impost will be levied, probably, only on incomes of $5,000 a year and more. But there are enough people in America in this class to constitute a fair-sized and aggressive audience.

Other features of the tax, of course, are commendable in the extreme. The burden of government, with its yearly increasing expenses and facilities, is now likely to be apportioned more justly. The under dog will find his load less heavy. The enjoyer of a bloated income will be called upon to contribute according to his ability. Steps already being considered to lessen the inquisitorial feature of the tax are fortunately directed.

QUESTIONS

1. What was the legal point that prevented Congress from establishing an income tax before 1913? How would a constitutional amendment make the income tax possible?
2. What were some of the reasons given in support of a national income tax? What were some of the arguments against it? Why did states in the Northeast think they would be exploited by such a tax? How did the newspapers quoted here support or refute these arguments?
3. What were some of the characteristics of the *New York Times* that would make it oppose the constitutional amendment and the income tax? What were some of the characteristics of the *New York World* that would make it support the amendment and the tax? How would you describe the difference that separated these two newspapers on this issue? (Geographic? Economic? Class? Ethnic?)
4. Why would the *Chicago Tribune* be so proud of Illinois's "honor" in being the first northern state to ratify the amendment? (What was the historic role of Illinois in relation to some of the other northern states such as New York, Massachusetts, Vermont, New Hampshire, Maine, Pennsylvania, and Ohio?)
5. How did the *New York World* use its story about the amendment's ratification ("Income Tax Is Ratified in Close Race of States") to promote itself? In what way is this an example of sensationalism? How might this have appealed to the *World*'s readers?
6. How did the horse race type of reporting used in some stories (reporting which states had ratified, which had rejected, and which were still considering the amendment) add to the public's interest in the story? How much did it distract public attention from the more serious issues involved?

NOTES

1. The amendment had been ratified by 39 states by the time it went into effect. Five New England states were among those that either rejected it or took no action or only partial action on the amendment. The states that rejected it were Connecti-

cut, New Hampshire, Rhode Island, and Utah. The 5 states that took no action or only partial action were Florida, Massachusetts, Pennsylvania, Vermont, and Virginia.

2. The tax on individuals was set at 1 percent for single persons with annual incomes over $3,000 and for married persons with incomes over $4,000. A surtax, ranging from 1 to 6 percent, was imposed on incomes over $20,000. The tax on corporate income was fixed at 1 percent.

CHAPTER 17

The Prohibition Movement Gains in the States and Congress, 1900–1913

Carrie Nation was a woman with a mission. Tired of seeing the evil effects of alcohol and the failure of laws to regulate its sale, she loaded a pile of bricks and empty bottles into her buggy on the morning of June 6, 1900, and drove to nearby Kiowa, Kansas. Here, she drove up to three of the town's saloons and smashed their windows with her bricks and bottles while a crowd gathered. The saloons were operating against the state's prohibition laws, and someone should be punished, she announced from the back of her buggy. In the course of the next nine years, Nation expanded her territory to include places as far away as San Francisco and Coney Island, New York, and perfected her style. She would charge into saloons with a hatchet to chop up liquor crates and bricks to smash bottles of liquor, sometimes alone, sometimes with an entourage of reporters. She became known as the "Kansas saloon-smasher" and sold souvenir hatchets to encourage others to follow her example. A frequent speaker on the lecture circuit, she declared she was the right hand of God and had been commissioned to destroy the liquor traffic in the United States. During her brief but flamboyant career, Nation was imprisoned nearly two dozen times for disturbing the peace and destruction of property, was ridiculed, and was even declared insane before she retired to farming in Arkansas at the age of 62. After her death in 1911, some said her militant campaign had called public attention to the liquor traffic in the South and forced officials in those states to enforce the law.

Carrie Nation was probably the most colorful of the many reformers who took part in the one hundred years of the temperance and prohibition movements that culminated in 1919 with the ratification of the Eighteenth (Prohibition) Amendment to the U.S. Constitution. During their existence, these movements came to include middle-class housewives, society matrons, evangelical ministers, church leaders, scientists, medical doctors, college teachers, newspaper editors, factory owners, and mine operators. A few, like Nation, became public figures because of their extreme behavior in their campaign against Demon Rum. Most, however, waged a more moderate political and publicity campaign to educate the public and influence legislators to control, restrict, or prohibit the use of alcohol. What they all had in common was the belief that alcohol was responsible for many of society's problems, including poverty, unemployment, industrial accidents, vagrancy, crime, and spousal and child abuse.

The movement for the reform of alcohol began in the mid-1820s and continued until the enactment of the Prohibition Amendment in 1920. Some reformers worked on their own like Carrie Nation or through church and benevolence groups, but most became associated with more structured organizations devoted entirely to the remedy of the "liquor evil." Different organizations proposed different remedies. Some promoted behavioral change on the individual level, ranging from moderation to teetotal abstinence. Others campaigned for legal restrictions on the local, state, and national levels. These included local option, which allowed individual communities to choose or reject regulation, licensing, and outright prohibition.

Organizations sprang up across the country, but three grew to national prominence and persisted in their campaign against liquor until 1920 and after. The Prohibition Party was founded in 1869 to promote national reform through the election of prohibition candidates and the adoption of prohibition laws. The Women's Christian Temperance Union (WCTU), established in 1874, originally promoted moderation by securing temperance pledges from individuals and closing down neighborhood saloons. By 1910, however, the WCTU supported the complete prohibition of alcohol and had developed an extensive network with women's organizations to promote the reform through legislative petitioning, lobbying, and partisan politics. A third organization, the Anti-Saloon League (ASL), was established in 1894. A nonpartisan political pressure group, it initially focused on the abolition of the saloon then began to promote prohibition.

The prohibitionists ("drys") were relentless in their pressure not only on drinkers, saloons, and manufacturers but also on politicians and the general public. In the early years, WCTU women prayed in the streets outside saloons to convince men to take the temperance pledge. By the 1890s they had moved to lecture halls and national conventions. The ASL also appeared on the lecture circuit and conducted concentrated campaigns on local and state politicians. In 1909 it established a publicity bureau and poured out thousands of letters, fliers, pamphlets, and books designed to convince a variety of publics to support the reform.

The "Steady" Drinker

SCENE—Any Bar. TIME—Most Any Time.
BARTENDER—Where is your pal, Fred? I ain't seen him lately.
STEADY DRINKER—Oh, he couldn't handle the stuff and he had to go West for his health.

It's different with me. I drink right—just enough every day, so 's I can handle it.
   Of course the STEADY drinker will soon become an UNSTEADY drinker and go the same route as his friend. Not so fast, perhaps, but just as surely.

"The 'Steady' Drinker," *New York Evening Journal*, 24 April 1913, p. 1. *William Randolph Hearst's* New York Evening Journal *was one of the most outspoken newspapers to condemn alcohol, which it believed had ruinous effects on society. Some of the* Journal's *cartoons, like this one, poked fun at drunks. By the middle of the second decade of the century, many newspapers, including the Hearst papers, had "taken the pledge"— that is, they refused to accept liquor advertising.*

Both the ASL and WCTU began putting pressure on newspapers and magazines to refuse liquor ads, which represented a sizeable portion of their advertising revenue. By 1912 they claimed that at least 40 national magazines and a handful of major newspapers no longer accepted liquor advertisements, and this number grew steadily until prohibition went into

"Look for the Name," Old Saratoga Whiskey ad, *New Orleans Picayune,* **15 February 1913, p.** 4. *The antiliquor campaigns of prohibitionists and many newspapers were undermined by the liquor industry, which paid big money for advertising in newspapers and magazines. It was not uncommon to find an advertisement like this one on the same page as an article about saloons applying for a liquor license, prohibition meetings, and prohibition legislation. This Old Saratoga Whiskey ad was published right next to an article about liquor license hearings.*

effect.[1] To help with their crusade, both the WCTU and the ASL published newspapers with national and state editions. The WCTU established the *Union Signal* in 1883; the ASL began publishing the *American Issue* in 1903. They also inundated newspapers with press releases, publicity material to be published verbatim, and pleas for editorial support.

In the meantime, antiprohibitionists ("wets") also got organized. Opposition was spearheaded by a powerful coalition of individuals and groups with a vested interest in the brewing and distilling industries. The most prominent of these were the United States Brewers Association, founded in 1864, the National Retail Liquor Dealers Association (1893), the National Wholesale Liquor Dealers Association (1896), and the National Model License League, established in 1908 to represent distillers. Another group prominent in the opposition to prohibition was the National German-American Alliance, established in 1900. This group was opposed to prohibition for cultural as well as economic reasons, since many of its members were associated with the brewing industry. Another organization, the Personal Liberty League, promoted the idea that any laws dictating individuals' use of alcohol violated their personal freedoms.

Like the major organizations of the prohibition movement, the antiprohibitionists established publicity bureaus and published antiprohibition literature, letters to the editor, and guest editorials. They also used "plate services" to embed antiprohibition and proliquor articles, often in the guise of scientific or economic news and opinion, in "ready-prints"—whole pages of preprinted material about a variety of subjects that were then distributed to and published in hundreds of weekly papers. They also hired lobbyists to represent them on the local, state, and national levels and were known to resort to bribery in order to influence public officials.

In addition to those with vested economic interests, many people in society supported the antiprohibitionists. They did so on economic, cultural, constitutional, personal, moral, and practical grounds. Some argued that the liquor and beer industries were legitimate industries that employed millions directly or indirectly and raised significant taxes for local, state, and federal governments. Those who belonged to particular ethnic groups such as Italians, French, Germans, and Irish maintained that drinking beer, wine, or whiskey was an important cultural ritual around which many of their traditions were built. Constitutionalists opposed a national prohibition amendment on the grounds that it would violate state rights.

Still others claimed that prohibitionists were hypocrites who tippled themselves. Florida Governor Albert W. Gilchrist reflected this opinion in 1911, when he said, "My definition for a 'Prohabasse' is a man who while taking a drink himself, does not want to see any one else take anything else but stomach bitters or soft drinks."[2] One of the most persuasive arguments against prohibition was that where it had been enacted it failed to prohibit, and, in fact, encouraged illegal stills, "blind pigs" (places that sold intoxicants illegally), bootlegging, and graft. For those who argued this point, the key was not in prohibition but in the strict regulation of saloons through local option, liquor licenses, and police enforcement.

Despite increasingly organized resistance, prohibition began to prevail. By 1909 eight states and hundreds of towns, cities, and counties had passed laws that controlled alcohol through a variety of regulations.[3] State and local campaigns increased in frequency, making headway particularly at the local level through a variety of local option laws. These successes, however, increased the opposition, and in 1911 campaigns were particularly intense. In that year, various forms of liquor legislation were on the ballot in nine states—Utah, Texas, Kansas, Ohio, Kentucky, New Jersey, West Virginia, Oklahoma, and Maine.

In Texas, the referendum was a sensational one. The Methodist Church, which endorsed prohibition, threatened to excommunicate Governor Edgar Colquitt because of his antiprohibition stance. He also received death threats and was assigned a bodyguard to accompany him on his travels around the state.[4] Antiprohibitionists charged that prohibitionist "night raiders" had gone through the rural districts to intimidate blacks and warn them against going to the polls, fearing they would vote against prohibition.[5] The vote was a close one, with the wets defeating the prohibition amendment by just five thousand votes.

Once the Texas election was settled, attention quickly turned to the situation in Maine. Here the September election was particularly significant because that state had been the first to adopt statewide prohibition and had for years served as the example held up by the prohibitionists.[6] The vote was a close one, and for nearly two months the ballots were counted and recounted until November, when it was concluded that the drys had prevailed to retain the constitutional amendment by a margin of only 758 votes. Also in 1911, Congressman Richmond Pearson Hobson of Alabama proposed a federal prohibition amendment, which, though it failed, was an important breakthrough for the national reform movement.

In the next two years, more states and municipalities went dry and forbade the manufacture and sale of alcohol. However, liquor was still reaching dry communities through the mails and shipping by express companies, and violation of local laws was widespread. In early 1912 Congress took up a proposition that would ban liquor shipments into dry states and debated variations on the bill for 12 months in the House and Senate. The resulting Webb-Kenyon Interstate Liquor Bill moved forward quickly in January and February of 1913, with significant support in Congress, despite a concerted effort by the liquor interests to block its passage. Both houses of Congress approved the Webb-Kenyon Interstate Liquor Act. President William Taft, in the last days of his presidency, vetoed the bill on the grounds that it was unconstitutional, but his veto was overridden. The Webb-Kenyon Act, which went into effect March 2, 1913, was the first sign that a majority in Congress was amenable to federal regulation of alcohol.

The war in Europe in 1914 and the United States's entry into World War I in 1917 added impetus to the prohibition movement, which exploited the public paranoia about political corruption by the liquor interests and political influence and intrigues by the German-American-dominated brewing industry. The growing antiliquor sentiment culminated in Congress's passage of the Eighteenth Amendment in 1917 and its ratification by the states in January 1919. The Volstead Act, also passed in 1919, provided for enforcement of the amendment, and national prohibition went into effect in January 1920. It remained in effect until it was repealed by the Twenty-First Amendment in 1933.

Newspapers talked about the use of alcohol, its abuse, its regulation, and prohibition in their news stories, editorials, letters to the editor, and advertisements. They reported when new regulatory or prohibitory laws were proposed and then followed the debate on the proposals and their progress through the legislative system. They covered conventions of the Prohibition Party, WCTU, and ASL as well as those of the antiprohibition organizations such as the National Retail Liquor Dealers Association and the German-American Alliance. They provided space for arguments in support of prohibition as well as those opposed to it, and on the editorial page expressed their own opinions on the issue. Newspapers' advertising columns were often filled with advertisements proclaiming the nutritional value of beer, the purity of single-malt whiskey, and the healing powers of hot rum. Occasionally, however, a newspaper decided to refuse liquor advertising, and by 1912, the Anti-Saloon League reported that 250 daily newspapers no longer printed liquor ads. That number continued to grow until prohibition went into effect in 1920.

When prohibition was scheduled for a local or state election, prohibitionists and antiprohibitionists often took out advertisements to promote their position and attack their opponents. On occasion, a whole page in a Sunday newspaper would be devoted to the prohibition debate, with half the page devoted to the drys and half to the wets. And all the time, like an incessant background static, stories were published about drunks killing wives, killing each other, crashing cars, drowning, and getting into brawls. The seriousness of these stories was undercut, however, by the many would-be humorous stories, vignettes, cartoons, and jokes that showed the comic side of drunkenness.

The readings in this chapter are divided into three sections to reflect varying perspectives on prohibition reflected in the press. The first reading is a news article from the *New York Times* that does not take a position on the issue. Rather, it lays out the situation in nine states that were to vote on prohibition in the coming 1911 election, and gives the reader a good description of the many conflicting interests involved. The second set of readings generally support prohibition, or at least the control of alcohol. These include editorials and news items that, while they may not specifically argue for prohibition, describe the harm brought about by the abuse of alcohol, an argument that was often used by prohibitionists. In the third section, the readings oppose prohibition. Some oppose it because it infringes on the individual's liberty, others because they believe it is ineffective in prohibiting alcohol abuse. Some of these suggest that existing licensing regulations should be enforced rather than adding another law that will prove ineffective if not enforced.

DESCRIBING THE ISSUES INVOLVED

The year 1911 was a busy one for prohibitionists, who were challenged by the wets in nine state elections and dozens of city and county campaigns as well. While prohibition seemed to be moving forward in some states, it was under attack in others. The first election was scheduled in Texas, and all eyes were on it, for the outcome of this election could have an effect on all the others to follow. Shortly before that election was to take place, the New York Times *published a full-page story on the various campaigns in its Sunday magazine section. Here, the* Times *provides a good picture of the many interests in conflict whenever prohibition got on the political agenda.*

New York Times, 16 July 1911

PROHIBITION THE ISSUE OF 1911 IN MANY STATES

Maine, Texas, Kansas, Ohio and Kentucky Are Among the States Engaged This Year in a Struggle Over the Momentous Liquor Question

When Texas votes on the question of Constitutional prohibition at the special election to be held in the State next Saturday, the first gun will have been fired in a series of sensational liquor campaigns that are now upheaving several other States.

Maine is to follow in September with a crack at the prohibition clause that has been her primal law for more than a half century.

Ohio is torn by a "wet" and "dry" strife for the control of the coming Constitutional Convention.

Oklahoma sends out a wail against the "no license" features of her organic law.

Kansas liberals are preparing to fight a similar clause out of her Constitution.

West Virginia is getting ready to put one in hers.

Indiana is busy scattering municipal cases through the county Saharas of the State, and even conservative New Jersey—"The most liberal of the States," the liquor men's organ boasts—is thinking of taking Gov. Woodrow Wilson's tip that local option is quite a proper thing for her to enact into law.

Texas is not a stranger to liquor excitements. The temperance people have been restive there for a long time, and of recent years a rising tide of prohibition sentiment has threatened the State with the liquor row in which she is engaged to-day. A year or two ago this sentiment became strong enough to force the Legislature to action. The solons did not quite know at first what to do about it, but finally, they decided to ask the people whether they would like to have a prohibition constitutional amendment submitted to them for approval. In the State primaries last Fall the people said they would—by 100,000 majority. It was drawn and submitted, and they are to say next Saturday whether they really want it after all.

The incident that has thrown most ginger into the campaign over the pending amendment was the nomination, in the same primary, of Edgar Colquitt for the Governorship on the anti-prohibitionist platform.... Colquitt is as good a prohibitionist as any of the most ardent advocates of the pending amendment—and himself a total abstainer. But he does not think that State prohibition is the plan of procedure...and is an earnest advocate of county option.... [No sooner had he taken office] before he was on the stump arguing with all his fervor against the [amendment's] ratification at the polls....

While Texas is trying to get prohibition into her State Constitution, the State of Maine is trying to get it out of hers—where it has been for more than fifty years. Its presence there has long been an irritation to some elements in her population, and a growing sentiment has urged its elimination. The Democrats have made its submission to popular vote the pivotal issue in all their recent campaigns, and in each came closer and closer to winning the State on it. Two years ago they had reduced the fixed Republican majority of 30,000 to about 8,000 and last year they succeeded in planting the State in the Democratic column....

The date for submission has been fixed for Sept. 12, and the discussions it has aroused absorb people to the exclusion of all other topics. The Prohibitionists are struggling with the energy of fanatics to bring about a vote for retention. They have been so long "pointing with pride" to "the great prohibition State of Maine" as a beacon of light in the temperance cause that they cannot easily reconcile themselves to her loss. The license elements in the liquor ranks are, for just that reason, eager to take her from them. But it is said that some of the distilling and brewing interests are helping the Prohibitionists, on the theory that Maine absorbs more under the cover of her temperance constitution than she would care to guzzle in open licensed drinking places.

SUPPORTING PROHIBITION

Drunks were considered fair game for practical jokes and ribald humor, and newspapers often poked fun at them in news stories, jokes, cartoons, comics, and humorous vignettes. In 1900 Arthur Brisbane, the editorial writer for the antiliquor New York Evening Journal, *saw the tragedy behind the figure of the drunken clown and wrote the following editorial telling his readers that the consequences of drunkenness are no laughing matter. Brisbane may have meant only to scold the callous people who laughed at drunks, but this editorial could also be used as a poignant argument for prohibition.*

New York Evening Journal, 1900

Arthur Brisbane: Those Who Laugh at a Drunken Man

How often have you seen a drunken man stagger along the street!

His clothes are soiled from falling, his face is bruised, his eyes are dull. Sometimes he curses the boys that tease him. Sometimes he tries to smile, in a drunken effort to placate pitiless, childish cruelty.

His body, worn out, can stand no more, and he mumbles that he is going home.

The children persecute him, throw things at him, laugh at him, running ahead of him.

Grown men and women, too, often laugh with the children, nudge each other, and actually find humor in the sight of a human being sunk below the lowest animal.

The sight of a drunken man going home should make every other man and woman sad and sympathetic, and horrible as the sight is, it should be useful, by inspiring, in those who see it, a determination to avoid and to help others avoid that man's fate.

That reeling drunkard is going home.

He is going home to children who are afraid of him, to a wife whose life he has made miserable. He is going home, taking with him the worst curse in the world—to suffer bitter remorse himself after having inflicted suffering on those whom he should protect.

And as he goes home men and women, knowing what the home-coming means, laugh at him and enjoy the sight.

In the old days in the arena it occasionally happened that brothers were set to fight each other. When they refused to fight they were forced to it by red-hot irons applied to their backs. We have progressed beyond the moral condition of human beings guilty of such brutality as that. But we cannot call ourselves civilized while our imaginations and sympathies are so dull that the reeling drunkard is thought an amusing spectacle.

Many employers came to support prohibition because they saw how much damage a drunken employee could do to himself and others in an industrial or mining accident. Some employers even required that their workers take a temperance pledge and would fire them on the spot if they were caught drinking liquor on the job. A powerful argument for prohibition, then, was that it was already supported and enforced in the workplace. Here, Dr. Samuel Dickey, writing in the national publication of the Anti-Saloon League, uses government statistics to point out that what the saloon [bar] really does for its patrons is keep them from getting or keeping decent jobs. Better that prohibition shut down all saloons.

American Issue, January 1911

Dr. Samuel Dickey: What It Does

What does the saloon do for its patron in opening or closing doors of opportunity? The United States Department of Labor, using percentages based upon several thousand reports, found that 90 percent of railways, 79 percent of manufacturers, 88 percent of trades, and 72 percent of agriculturalists discriminate against employees addicted to the use of intoxicants as a beverage. The patron of a saloon may drive a garbage wagon or get a steady job as a doorkeeper of a dance hall, but he cannot drive a locomotive or secure employment as a paying teller in the bank. He may clean out cuspidors in a barroom and sweep up refuse on the street, but he cannot be trusted to run a stationary engine, drive a passenger omnibus, fire a boiler, amputate a leg, administer medicine, fill a prescription, keep a set of books, try an important case, manage a business corporation, or do any other work demanding a clear head and a steady hand. The saloon which takes its patron's money double-crosses him for disappointment and failure in the race of life.

When voters went to the polls in Maine in September 1911, the whole nation watched, for as the first state to have written prohibition into its constitution, Maine was the flagship of the prohibition movement. As votes were counted and recounted, Ohio newspapers watched with particular interest, for Ohio itself would shortly be facing its own constitutional revision at the polls. In the following editorial, the Cleveland Plain Dealer *points out that even if Maine's constitutional prohibition were defeated, a pre-existing state prohibition law would still be in force. The editorial comes down on the side of law and order and urges authorities to enforce the existing prohibitory laws.*

Cleveland Plain Dealer, 14 September 1911

The Result in Maine

By a margin so close as still to leave room for doubt Maine seems to have voted to retain prohibition in her constitution. The referendum campaign awakened intense interest in the state, and the vote was large and representative. The question to be settled was not the usual one of "wet" or "dry." It was far more significant. It was the question of whether state-wide prohibition that does not universally prohibit is better than local option and a regulated liquor traffic; whether illegal selling of liquor with the connivance of authorities is worse than a legalized traffic restricted to those communities that so signify in their preference.

It must not be considered that the large vote polled by the "wets" indicates that nearly a majority of the people of Maine are favorable to the general unrestricted dispensing of alcoholic drinks. It is a fact that many of the retail liquor dealers who have been carrying on an illegal trade in the cities were quietly supporting the "dry" side. And it is equally true that many of Maine's most respected citizens, including her governor, were strong in their opposition to constitutional prohibition.

Prohibition in Maine has become a tradition, and for the time being there will probably be no change. Maine has decided not to follow the example of the other New England States that tried state-wide prohibition, found it ineffective to attain the result desired, and replaced it with strict and enforceable laws....

Maine passed its first prohibitory law in 1846. This statute was repealed in 1856, but reenacted in 1858. It still stands on the statute books, so that a "wet" victory last Monday would not have made liquor selling legal. In 1884 the constitutional provision was voted in by a popular majority of nearly 3 to 1. The result at the resubmission is so close that it is likely there may be another referendum in the not distant future.

Meanwhile so much has been said both in and out of Maine regarding the weakness of the city enforcement of the prohibitory laws that temperance advocates of all classifications, including both prohibitionists and local optionists, should unite in an effort to make the existing laws effective. Authorities should be compelled to enforce the statutes and uphold the state constitution without hypocrisy, evasion, or the suspicion of "graft."

The joint resolution proposing a national prohibition amendment introduced by Alabama Congressman Richmond Hobson in December 1911 summarized in its first part many of the arguments for prohibition. It was published verbatim in a number of newspapers, including the Union Signal, *the publication of the Woman's Christian Temperance Organization, where it occupied the entire front page under a photograph of the congressman. Though Hobson's proposal eventually failed, the WCTU considered its introduction in Congress a great step forward in the campaign for prohibition.*

Union Signal, 7 December 1911

HON. RICHMOND PEARSON HOBSON INTRODUCES PROHIBITION AMENDMENT

On December 4, 1911, Congressman Hobson introduced in the House of Representatives the following resolution, which was referred to the Committee on Alcoholic Liquor Traffic and ordered to be printed:

Joint Resolution

Proposing an amendment to the Constitution prohibiting the sale, manufacture for sale, and importation for sale of beverages containing alcohol.

Whereas, Exact scientific Research has demonstrated that alcohol is a narcotic poison, destructive and degenerating to the human organism, and that its distribution as a beverage lays a staggering economic burden upon the shoulders of the people, lowers to an appalling degree their standard of character, thereby undermining the public morals and the foundation of free institutions, inflicts disease and untimely death upon hundreds of thousand of citizens, and blights with degeneracy their children unborn, threatening the future integrity and the very life of the nation: Therefore be it

Resolved by the Senate and House of Representative of the United States of America in Congress assembled, (two-thirds of each house concurring) that the following be proposed as an amendment to the Constitution which shall be valid to all intents and purposes as part of the Constitution when ratified by the Legislatures of three-fourths of the states: 1. The sale, manufacture for sale, and importation for sale of beverages containing alcohol, are forever prohibited in the United States and in all territories under their jurisdiction. 2. The Congress shall have the power to enforce, by appropriate legislation, the provisions of this article.

*A major argument against alcohol and for prohibition was that liquor ru-
ined lives and caused death. Shortly after the Webb-Kenyon Act became effective in February 1913, the* New York Evening Journal *published an
editorial proposing this idea. The editorial was placed in the top center half
of the page and was printed under a large two-column cartoon showing a
large bottle of whiskey standing at the head of a grave. The image in the
cartoon is powerful, as is the image painted by the words of the editorial.*

New York Evening Journal, 3 April 1913

The Most Expensive Tombstone in the World

Do you know any young man who is investing money in a tombstone like
this? If so, hand him this picture.

Here is the tombstone that stands at the head of tens of thousands of
graves. You cannot see it as you enter the graveyard, but the relations of the
man in the grave know that the tombstone is there.

This is the tombstone that costs more money than all kinds of tomb-
stones put together.

This is the tombstone that stands above ruined hopes, broken families,
disappointments, bitterness and all misery.

If you want to do something useful, without too much trouble, cut out
this picture and paste it up where it will be seen by those that need it.

The huge bottle and the small glass, the weak will, the blasted career—
and then the grave with the tombstone—that is the story.

OPPOSED TO PROHIBITION

*Many opposed prohibition on the grounds that it did not prohibit, but, par-
adoxically, favored drunkenness, illegal activity, and public corruption.
Some who truly did want to control and regulate the liquor trade favored
local option and license regulation, which they believed could realistically
be enforced at the municipal level. Many of these arguments were used by
antiprohibitionists in their attempt to remove the prohibition amendment
from the Maine Constitution. In this editorial just five days before the
Maine election, the antiprohibition* New York Times *reviews many of
these arguments. Its tone is sardonic as it suggests that prohibition con-
tributes to the liquor trade, the extermination of drunkards and the preser-
vation of the middle class.*

New York Times, 7 September 1911

MAINE'S PROHIBITION FIGHT

Article V. of Maine's Constitution, which contains the prohibition clauses, is defended during the campaign which is to end next Tuesday by a curious alignment of forces. Not only the temperance people of Maine wish to keep the article intact, but the very worst and most pernicious of the liquor interests. There are thousands of retail liquor dealers within the State doing an illicit but "protected" business. There are the express companies, which, since 1884 have thriven on the transportation of spirits into the State from neighboring borders. There are many wholesale liquor dealers in Boston, especially, who would lose a chief part of their trade if a license law were substituted for the prohibitory amendment. And throughout the State of Maine the peddlers of poisonous "splits" and the keepers of the "kitchen bars," from which spirits of the worst character are purveyed, are secretly working in aid of the consecrated efforts of the devout men and women who comprise the Anti-Saloon League, the Christian Civic League, the Women's Christian Temperance Union, the Maine Sunday School Association, and the boys and girls enlisted with the Young Campaigners for Prohibition. The meetings and the marchings under the "Vote No" banners win both a frank and a sinister approval.

But while the local liquor interests are opposed to any disturbances of their business in Maine, the National organizations of the brewers and distillers seek to overthrow prohibition there as a matter of principle. If extended to all the States, prohibition would outlaw and destroy their manufactories of liquor. Whenever a State is gained, while its inhabitants may become no more abstinent than they were and the sales of liquors in original packages or under corrupt protection may bulk as large, the property in the breweries and distilleries within its confines is destroyed. Therefore, the great liquor interests are allied with bodies of respectable citizens who believe that, since prohibition fails to prohibit, the liquor traffic should be legalized in Maine under a heavily taxed system of licensing. It is a nonpartisan campaign, since Republicans and Democrats favor one side or the other according to their personal convictions.

The plea that prohibition fails to prohibit would be quite valid if it could be shown that any license system succeeds better in regulating the liquor traffic. Police administrations fall down in the attempt to restrict illicit selling of liquors in any community where the traffic is licensed. Prohibition does throw the business into disrepute. It clears the main thoroughfares of the saloons, and removes them from the sight of the young, who are taught that the business is outlawed and disreputable. The drunkards for which it is incidentally responsible, die off rapidly, for they are tempted to drink the worst and most powerful decoctions. Prohibition may kill the poor and miserable tipplers, but it tends to preserve the middle classes. Perhaps the interests of the middle classes will prevail in the coming election.

The most naked reason for opposing prohibition was self-interest. The brewing, liquor, and saloon industries were against it simply because it would destroy their livelihood. In their publications, correspondence, and promotional literature, they exhorted their members to do all in their power to influence public officials and the voting public to defeat prohibition. Prohibition publications often reprinted these statements as evidence of the industries' desperation as well as of illegal activity such as bribery and vote-buying. The WCTU's Union Signal *seized on this paragraph published in a leading national publication of the liquor industry to exhort its own members to increase their zeal in the campaign for the earlier version of the Webb Bill being debated in Congress.*

Bonfort's Wine and Spirit Circular, December 1912

"This Bill Must Be Killed" (?)

This bill is the most dangerous measure ever aimed at the liquor traffic. What have you done to defeat it? This bill must be killed. If you fail to do your part, don't complain if the bill is passed and your business is ruined.

Many antiprohibitionists argued for education and temperance rather than prohibition and restrictive laws, though temperance organizations had been preaching this to no avail since the early 1800s. When it appeared that Congress would approve the Webb-Kenyon Bill, the New Orleans Picayune *reflected on the unintended results of attempting to prohibit undesirable behavior. Prohibitory laws, it charges, actually encourage exactly what they attempt to restrain and drive that behavior underground. This argument has surfaced repeatedly over the years, particularly in regard to laws against teenage drinking, smoking, and drug use.*

New Orleans Picayune, 11 February 1913

DISCIPLINE BUT DO NOT DESTROY

Human nature is born in our race. There is much that is evil in the natural man and much that is good, but the natural capacities for good must be developed by discipline, education and encouragement, while the evil is the most natural, the most spontaneous and, in the beginning, most ready to assert itself.

Wisdom, based on experience, tells us that the evil in human nature cannot be extinguished, but it can be put under restraint, and even directed into channels where it is less injurious. Wise men have used restraint and training to modify and moderate much that would otherwise be extremely pernicious to individuals, and pernicious to society. While well-meaning, but thoughtless and shortsighted, individuals have undertaken to change and revolutionize natural laws as manifested in human passions without realizing how entirely it is an impossibility.

Thus we enact prohibition laws, and in closing the saloons fill the homes with drunkards. We forbid racetrack gambling, and fill the city with innumerable private gambling clubs.... But while we know that the evils it is sought to extinguish are just as prevalent and powerful as ever, we are gratified at the fact that they are not in such plain view as they were, and that is all we have accomplished. We have not made men and women better. On the contrary, we have made many more than there were bad, because they can now do in secret what they would not have dared to do in the open light of publicity.

The thing that wisdom counsels is not to attempt to change human nature, not to seek to extinguish human passions and lusts, but to restrain them, to discipline them, and even to lead the natural force and energy behind them into harmless and even useful directions....

Human desires and passions are not inherently evil. They are energies of the soul, neither good nor bad in themselves, but, like dynamite, they are capable of varied uses, some frightfully destructive, and others eminently useful, heroic and noble. These energies can drive men to extremes of crime or of virtue, to savagery or civilization, to art, vice, insanity, love, lust or religion, according as they are directed. Therefore, wisdom counsels us not to attempt to suppress and extinguish human nature, but to discipline, to educate, to regulate and guide it in the right channels to right uses.

Some antiprohibitionists claimed that drinking was actually increased by prohibition. In this editorial, published shortly after Congress approved the Webb-Kenyon Bill, the New Orleans Picayune *uses Internal Revenue statistics to prove it.*

New Orleans Picayune, 28 February 1913

INCREASED CONSUMPTION OF STIMULANTS

Never in the history of this republic was the movement against intoxicating liquors and drugs so strongly backed and so generally supported as now. Many of the states have made prohibition laws against the sale of liquors. Prohibition is urged and argued in newspapers maintained for the purpose; it is preached in pulpits and on public platforms; it is the fundamental doctrine of a political national party that puts up presidential candidates in rivalry with the others, and never has the cause had such backing and support. Congress has just enacted a law forbidding the shipment of liquors into states where prohibition state laws are in force.

Nevertheless, the reports made by United States Commissioner of Internal Revenue Roy E. Cabell, at Washington, show that the people of the United States are drinking more whiskey, smoking more cigars and cigarettes, and chewing more tobacco than ever before in history.

From July to February the nation has consumed 94,000,000 gallons of whiskey, an increase of 5,000,000 over the corresponding period the previous year.... [F]or the first seven months of the current fiscal year, the people of the United States have drunk 38,364,000 barrels [of beer], an increase of 1,850,000 over the last year....

There is no doubt that the consumption of liquors is increased by the prohibitory laws. The very fact of this prohibition excites thirst and arouses a determination in people to have the stuff, despite the laws, and, of course, there are means of getting it.

There was an additional objection to the Webb-Kenyon Bill—and any federal prohibitory law. This was that it was unconstitutional, and that it would violate states' rights. In its attempt to regulate interstate commerce, detractors contended, the federal government would violate individual states' rights. President William Taft, who was serving the last days of his presidency, opposed the bill on these grounds, and vetoed it. In the following editorial, the New York World *applauds his action and chastises Congress for attempting to impose the legislation on the entire country to please a handful of prohibition states.*

New York World, 1 March 1913

A RIGHTEOUS VETO

The Liquor bill which President Taft vetoed yesterday was a weak and cowardly measure. It was passed by Congress in response to a demand that the nation come to the assistance of the States which have adopted prohibition. It was weak and cowardly because practically every man who voted for it knew it was of dubious constitutionality, and because, even if it were constitutional, it used the Federal power to bolster up State laws which most of those who passed them did not expect to obey.

Like the bill abolishing the army canteen, it was supported by members of Congress who did not have the courage to stand for the right. In this case Congress dodged the issue openly, in the belief that the President would meet a situation which it lacked the courage to face.

The boldness with which Mr. Taft killed this humbug shows that this confidence was not misplaced, but no credit attaches to anybody else.

QUESTIONS

1. How might a newspaper's editorial position on prohibition be contradicted by other material published in the newspaper?
2. What were some of the economic pressures on newspapers to oppose prohibition?
3. Do you think it was a contradiction for a newspaper to accept liquor and beer advertising but then support prohibition on the editorial page?
4. In "Those Who Laugh at a Drunken Man," why does Arthur Brisbane accuse his readers of being uncivilized as long as they find "the reeling drunkard" an "amusing spectacle"?
5. Locate the section in the editorial "Maine's Prohibition Fight" in which the *New York Times* reveals its major argument against prohibition. How does it support this argument?
6. In "The Result in Maine," what does the *Cleveland Plain Dealer* suggest as the solution to the "Maine problem"?

NOTES

1. The magazines to refuse liquor advertising included a number of women's magazines like *Ladies Home Journal,* but also general interest magazines such as *McClure's Magazine* and *Collier's.* Two newspapers to drop liquor advertising were the *Detroit Times* and the *Chicago American.* By early 1915, the Anti-Saloon League claimed 520 daily newspapers no longer accepted liquor or beer advertising. This number continued to grow in the next five years.

2. "Opinions on the Results," *New York Times,* 12 September 1911, p. 2.

3. The states that had prohibition by 1909 were Maine (1846), Kansas (1880), North Dakota (1889), Oklahoma (1907), Georgia (1908), Mississippi (1908), North Carolina (1908), and Tennessee (1909).

4. "Bodyguard for Colquitt," *New York Times,* 4 June 1911, p. 1.

5. "Wets Probably Win in Texas Election," *New York Times,* 23 July 1911, p. 1.

6. Maine enacted prohibition as a state law in 1846 and wrote it into its constitution in 1884.

CHAPTER 18

Women March for Suffrage in Washington, March 1913

I n 1913 two radical suffragists, Lucy Burns and Alice Paul, grew tired of the ladylike strategies used by the majority of the mostly middle-class suffragists. Burns and Paul had worked with the militant suffragettes in England, whose campaigning had escalated to include acts of destruction such as breaking windows and setting fires in public buildings and the homes of government officials. While rejecting such violence, Burns and Paul adopted the suffragettes' boldly defiant style of campaigning that featured more action and less talking. This included aggressive lobbying, street-corner demonstrations, and parades that would make their cause highly visible to the general public and apply constant pressure on political figures with the power to make legal change. They were appointed by the board of the National American Woman Suffrage Association (NAWSA) to spearhead the campaign for a federal amendment.

Women, who were denied the vote in the U.S. Constitution, had first organized for suffrage in 1848. In the next 65 years they built a national movement in the face of indifference, ignorance, and outright opposition from a range of groups including Catholics, antifeminists, social and political conservatives, and members of the beer and liquor industries. They gradually won support from prohibitionists, Socialists, feminists, and progressive reformers of many brands. By 1913 women had won full suffrage (the right to vote in all elections) in only nine states and territories—Arizona, California, Colorado, Idaho, Kansas, Utah, Oregon, Washington, and Wyoming. All attempts to pass suffrage in states east of the Mississippi had failed, as had numerous attempts to pass a constitutional amendment. (See Chapter 15.)

In 1913, NAWSA decided to put more energy into the drive for a federal amendment and turned the task of promoting it over to Burns and Paul. The two women decided to take advantage of the crowds that would flock to

Washington, D.C., for the March 4 inauguration of President Woodrow Wilson. For the day before the inauguration, they organized a suffrage parade of some 10,000 women who would march down Pennsylvania Avenue with banners and flags.[1] Most would be on foot, but some would defy propriety by riding astride on horseback. In addition, the parade was to include silent tableaus to be set on floats that would demonstrate various historical moments in women's history and progress.

At a time when woman's prescribed place was still in the home and she was expected to behave docilely and stay out of the public eye, Paul and Burns fully expected to attract the curiosity and attention of the half-million spectators flooding to the capital for the inaugural celebrations. Above all, they hoped to impress the incoming president with their determination and the worthiness of their cause.

For weeks, women prepared for the parade. One group, which planned to march all the way from New York City to Washington, D.C., practiced in New York City's Central Park. Other groups from Chicago, Denver, and California chartered train carriages to carry them to the capital. Some prepared elaborate costumes and banners, and suffrage organizations across the country deluged the public and the press with suffrage literature.

The parade certainly attracted attention, but it quickly deteriorated into a near riot as drunken men and boys blocked the avenue, harassed the marchers, and mobbed the tableaus. Women were pushed and shoved, knocked over, and injured while the outnumbered Washington police stood by passively. The following day, outraged public leaders called for an investigation into the police's failure to control the mob. A Senate investigation was called immediately and the hearings that followed provided the suffragists, though bruised and battered, an excellent forum to air their arguments for suffrage and women's rights. The inquiry ultimately led to the dismissal of the Washington chief of police, and the suffragists were regarded as heroes when they returned home.

Perhaps as a result of this fiasco, the campaign for the constitutional amendment picked up new momentum and spurred a national petition drive that culminated in an automobile procession to the Capitol on July 31 to present a group of senators with petitions carrying more than 200,000 signatures. Suffrage agitation, including more suffrage parades, continued unabated for the next seven years. More states were added painstakingly to the suffrage column and finally, in June 1919 Congress passed a federal suffrage amendment. The Nineteenth Amendment was ratified by the required 36 states in August 1920, and women were allowed to vote in national elections in every state of the union for the first time in November 1920.

Alice Paul and Lucy Burns had organized what we would today call a "media event." They were wildly successful in attracting newspaper coverage to all phases of the parade, including plans for it beforehand, the adventures of various women's groups making their way toward Washington to participate in it, the parade itself, the riot during the parade, the outcry following the riot, and, finally, the inquiry into the failure of the Washington police to maintain order. Though initial stories of plans for the parade tended to treat the women as curiosities and the parade as a gimmick, the

WHAT IF THE COLLEGE BOYS DO INTEND TO LOOSE MICE ON THE SUFFRAGETTE PARADE

"What if the College Boys Do Intend to Loose Mice on the Suffragette Parade," *Rocky Mountain News,* **8 February 1913, p. 6.** *Newspapers frequently ridiculed women in general and woman suffragists in particular. Here, the cartoonist uses a female stereotype—women (perhaps spinsters) with cats—in his vision of the suffrage parade to be held in Washington, D.C., the following month. Most people would say this cartoon was only in fun and didn't hurt anyone, but even this kind of humor discouraged people from taking women and their demands for the vote seriously. In fact, the march in Washington didn't turn out nearly as well as the one illustrated in this cartoon, for a crowd of bullies harassed the women and turned the parade into a rout.*

ensuing coverage during the Senate investigation elevated woman suffrage to an issue of national attention.

An examination of these stories reveals many of the prevailing notions about women and gender in 1913, and the suffragists in these stories are typically described according to female stereotypes of the time. In the stories leading up to the actual event, they are frequently described as pretty, inexperienced, and either naive or a bit silly. Much attention is devoted to their appearance—their hair, their figure, and their manner of dress. A lot is said about their "pluck" and "determination," since these were not attitudes expected of women during this period. Only a few news stories focus on the professionals, businesswomen, and women church and social leaders participating in the event.

Many initial stories covering plans by individual groups of women to march in the parade are reminiscent of the newspaper stories about the early stages of Coxey's march on Washington in 1894. (See Chapter 6.) Little is said about their actual arguments for suffrage, but much fun is poked at their efforts to mobilize. Just as newspapers had covered the difficulties encountered by Coxey's army, newspapers followed New York's "Gen. Jones" and her suffrage "army" on its "hike" to Washington as they were caught in a snowstorm, got lost, suffered casualties to blistered feet and the flu, and marched through towns and cities to the cheers and jeers of crowds gathered to witness their passage. More sober women, like Mrs. Knute Nelson, the wife of a Minnesota senator, who planned to march in Norwegian costume, as well as the seasoned officers of suffrage associations, were described in more respectful terms.

When the marchers were mobbed by the crowds and lost control of the parade, this, too, fit the prevailing notion of women as weak and unable to control the circumstances around them. Even the descriptions of the shaken and sobbing suffragists during and after the riot fell back on stereotypes of women as fragile creatures in need of men's protection. No men stood up to protect them, except an unexpected troop of cavalry from a nearby fort, a few military men in the crowd and some Boy Scouts, who were hailed as valiant knights coming to their rescue. The suffragists' inability to deal with the unruly crowd clearly indicated that this was neither an appropriate place or proper activity for a woman. Only a few newspapers described the parade as a legitimate attempt to promote and publicize a needed reform.

Woman suffrage remained in the news for the next weeks, as outrage focused first on the mob, then on the Washington police who had failed to maintain order. Most newspapers, whether in support of suffrage or not, denounced the mob's actions. How could they possibly be in support of a mob of hoodlums roughing up a bunch of middle-class ladies bent on a respectable (if misguided) cause? However, even here, some embedded in their denunciations a number of messages reflective of the writers' own perspectives on woman's role.

The readings in this chapter all reveal prevailing notions of woman and her role in American society. Few of these discuss the merits of suffrage, but in some, the newspaper's position on the reform is revealed through its tone or choice of words in discussing the parade and the women participating in it. These readings have been organized in four sections. The first group of readings can be said to be positive toward the suffrage parade and the women in it. The news stories and editorials in the second section ridicule the suffragists, either by making fun of their enterprise or by using a patronizing tone. In the third section, the readings express the writers' criticism of the parade as either illogical or ill planned, and in so doing, reveal their opposition to suffrage reform. In the fourth section, the selections denounce the behavior of the men in the mob as well as the failure of the Washington police to control the situation. These tend to fall back on gender stereotypes of women as fragile creatures who should be protected by men, and, conversely, of men as powerful, decisive actors whose proper role is to defend women against harm.

POSITIVE TOWARD THE SUFFRAGE PARADE AND SUFFRAGISTS

Though the goal of the parade was to promote woman suffrage, few, if any, newspaper stories explained suffragists' arguments as to why women should have the vote. Few even provided an explanation of what this parade was to accomplish. This reporter for the Rocky Mountain News *(published in Denver, Colorado, where women had had the vote since 1893) asked for an explanation and got a clear and succinct answer.*

Rocky Mountain News, 22 February 1913

WOMEN OF COLORADO TO "HIKE" IN PARADE

Mary Bradford, Mrs. Shafroth and Mrs. Taylor Consider Joining in Great Demonstration

Several of Colorado's most representative women will "hike" in the suffrage parade at Washington the day before inaugural day, which promises to mark the most spectacular suffrage demonstration ever seen in America.

Mrs. Mary C.C. Bradford will carry the Colorado Suffrage association banner in the parade.

Mrs. John Shafroth and Mrs. E.T. Taylor, both members of the Colorado association, have been invited to take part in the great suffrage demonstration.

Mrs. Bradford will be in Philadelphia a week preceding the parade, attending the national meeting of state school superintendents and will go on to the capital for the demonstration. Mrs. Minnie Reynolds Salabrino and Congressman Addison W. Rucker will also represent Colorado in the parade.

The suffrage leaders of Colorado are strongly in favor of this method of advertising the power of the woman's movement to obtain the ballot for women. "The men at Washington say they will give women the franchise when they want it," says Mrs. Dora Phelps Buel. "This demonstration will show that we want it."

Mrs. Harriet G.R. Wright, president of the Colorado Equal Suffrage association, believes that by following the modern idea of representing suffrage in a spectacular way, the women of America will draw the attention of the world to a great cause.

Though an estimated 10,000 women were expected to participate in the parade, it was the participation by male political leaders that set the tone for this story. By describing first the senators and congressmen planning to march in the parade, and then their wives, the various suffrage leaders, and the business, professional, and working women, this Chicago Tribune *story lends the parade an air of weight and legitimacy. The* Tribune's *correspondent lists the participants in that order, reflecting a kind of "who's who" in the social hierarchy in the process.*

Chicago Tribune, 2 March 1913

SENATORS TO JOIN WOMEN'S PARADE

Eight Members of Lower House Also Will March in Capital Streets

MANY OFFICIALS AID

Wives and Daughters of Nation's Leaders Will Have Large Part in Move

(BY A STAFF CORRESPONDENT)

Washington, D.C., March 1—[Special]—Official Washington will be represented Monday in the first woman suffrage parade and pageant ever held in Washington.

In response to the invitation extended to members of both houses of congress, Senators La Follette, Chamberlain, Dixon, Smoot, Poindexter, Gronna and Sutherland and Representatives Kent, Knowlands and Baker of Colorado, Lafferty, Mondell, French, and Murdock have pledged themselves to march in the men's section, led by Representative Hobson of Alabama.

Mrs. John W. Keen, wife of the Indiana senator; Mrs. Miles Poindexter, wife of the Washington senator; Mrs. La Follette and her daughter, Miss Fola La Follette, who will lead the actresses; Mrs. William Kent, Mrs. Claude U. Stone, wife of Representative Stone of Illinois, and the two daughters of Representative and Mrs. Prouty of Iowa are among those who will march with their State delegations.

Miss Julia Lathrop of Chicago, chief of the children's bureau, will march with the government department clerks.

Makeup of Big Parade

The parade will start from the Peace monument at the foot of the capitol; Mrs. Richard Coke Burleson, wife of Lieut. Burleson, U.S.A., and Miss Inez Milholland of New York will ride at the head of the procession as grand marshal and herald, followed by the officers of the National American Woman Suffrage Association.

The parade will consist of seven sections, portraying the history of the woman suffrage movement. In the first section, led by Mrs. Carrie Chapman Catt, president of the International Suffrage Alliance, the first division will be made up of floats representing the countries where women have full suffrage.

Another name to catch attention was that of Nellie Bly (Elizabeth Cochran), the daredevil stunt reporter of the 1880s and 1890s who had traveled around the world in just 72 days for Pulitzer's New York World. Bly had disappeared from newspaper work to marry and then, upon becoming a widow, to embark on a brief and disastrous career as a businesswoman. She returned to news reporting as a correspondent for the New York Evening Journal in 1913. Though her name no longer had the same cachet it had enjoyed in the 1890s, it was still popular enough for the sensational Journal to use in its headlines. Bly was given this assignment perhaps because she was to ride on horseback in the parade as a herald. This is a typical Nellie Bly story, full of gushing, wide-eyed, and enthusiastic first-person descriptions. What is remarkable about this story is that it is entirely positive toward the parade and the women in it and only briefly toward the end mentions the chaos that overcame the marchers.

New York Evening Journal, **4 March 1913**

"MARCHING WOMEN HAVE MADE HISTORY,"
DECLARES NELLIE BLY

Washington, March 4—Can you imagine it? Ten thousand women in line? They say that was the number by actual count. I believe there were more.

Picture if you can an endless chain of butterflies, divided into sections according to color. Image ten thousand of these beautiful dreams of color fluttering along and it will give a little impression of the exquisite parade which made history.

Add to this the knowledge that women of ability and fame in all lines of art, literature, medicine schools—why waste space repeating all the fields occupied by women today?—was represented and still add to this the knowledge that women in that parade came from every state in the Union with a few from foreign countries, and some slight conception of the appearance and quality of the paraders may be conceived.

The march was to start at 2:30 p.m. At 8 a. m. the pavements were packed and the streets along the route became rapidly impassable. Balconies, grandstands and windows were filled with sightseers.

Women Eclipsed All

I did not hear anyone speak about the new President, who was doubtless on his way toward the mecca of his dreams at that hour. His train was due about 3. No one, excepting his reception committee, seemed to care. This was not his day with the public. It was out to see the women, and it meant to see them. Everything was yellow. [Yellow ribbons represented woman suffrage.] Public and private conveyances were trimmed in yellow. Vendors sold yellow flags and balloons. Mothers were trudged after by their children—boys, as well as girls—adorned in yellow. Florists filled their windows with yellow flowers and the stores put all their yellow goods on view.

I believe every suffragette ate her luncheon calmly and then proceeded orderly to her designated starting point. The management and the obedience to orders was unexcelled.

On the minute those 10,000 splendid women, wonderfully skillful, without long organization or training, started on the walk that will resound around this mysterious globe upon which we are glued.

Men parade. They like it, you know. And don't they look like funeral directors or freaks when they do? They will never want to parade again, these men who witnessed the beauty of the day's memorable affair.

When men parade—if it is a big affair, certain public appropriations are always made for them, and certainly the line of travel is held sacred for them.

They Must Pay for All

Not so with the women. They have to pay for everything out of their own limited funds. And even Congress refused to set aside the line of travel for their sole use during the parade.

I am sure more public men will either declare themselves in favor of suffrage or be less violently disposed against after this.

It was a large, visible, radiating soul-compelling sign which they read—a sign of what is coming. I saw serious thoughtful expressions on the faces of many prominent men after the parade.

You will see all the pictures and read descriptions of the floats and I won't attempt to tell you about that. I find you can't be in a parade and tell everything about it except your own little space. So I must leave this to the reporter who observed us from a stand. The crowd was unmanageable and much will be written of the hoodlumism of the spectators. The police powerless. The same thing occurred in New York in the first parade. A complaint to the authorities brought better treatment the second time.

The parade ended at the Continental Hall and as usual when men had the management of the affair, this was badly managed. There are three large doors leading to the vestibule. By some strange occurrence only one could be forced open, and the great mass of women had to pass almost single file to get into the building at all.

Where's the Man to Match?

It is worth while inside, however. Inside it is beautiful. Dr. Anna Howard Shaw presided at the meeting, and Mrs. Catt and Mary Johnson, the writer, spoke.

Where is the man who can match Mrs. Judith Smith of Boston? Mrs. Smith came to Washington to be in the parade. She made a brief speech in which she said she had worked in the cause for sixty years. Mrs. Smith is not afraid to tell her age. A woman, too. She said the way to keep young was to engage in an interesting and absorbing fight. Mrs. Smith is ninety-two years old. Now, Mr. Man Voter, bring on your active, fighting ninety-two-year-old fighter....

I never was so proud of women; I never was so impressed with their ability; I never so realized their determination and sincerity. I am glad I am one.

RIDICULING THE SUFFRAGE PARADE AND THE WOMEN IN IT

Miss Rosalie Jones of New York got a lot of attention when she announced her plans to march a contingent of suffragists from New York City to

*Washington, D.C., to participate in the parade. When she and her com-
rades got together in Central Park to practice their marching skills, they
quickly caught press attention. This story in the working-class* New York
World *describes the women in amused, somewhat patronizing tones. The
story, which was accompanied by a collage of photos of the women practic-
ing their march, includes a number of descriptions that accentuate their
feminine characteristics. Readers must have asked themselves, "This is all
very amusing, but can these women be serious?" Ironically, in its attempt to
humorously dramatize the situation, this story foreshadows the violence the
women would actually encounter on March 4.*

New York World, 30 January 1913

SUFFRAGETTE PILGRIMS PRACTISE FOR THE BIG HIKE TO WASHINGTON

Moving Picture Men on Their Trail in Central Park Almost Routed by Police

The suffragette pilgrims hiked to Central Park yesterday to break their
feet in for the hike to Washington and had an encounter with the movies.
The stunts of the hikers were so realistic—such visions of ankles, such wind-
blown cloaks and waving staves, such determined stands and sudden
rushes to cover—that a blood-curdling whistle was presently heard and a
group of mounted police came dashing from every direction to save the pilgrims from threatened danger.

The police were about to charge upon the picture men, amid the shrieks
of the suffragettes, when they discovered their error. After the excitement
was over Gen. Rosalie Jones explained the situation, introduced the hikers
to the mounted men and offered to convert the force.

It was 10 A.M. when the brown-cloaked and hooded figures dropped off
cars and emerged from autos at the Seventy-second street entrance on Central Park West. Everybody was sporting new shoes, which were carefully inspected for their swelling capacity and rubber heels. The General, by virtue
of her standing, had assumed a very large soft felt hat, which she wore
under her cowl, only its daring front elevation betraying its military preten-
sions.

Col. Ida C. Craft had beneath her cloak a mackinaw coat so prolific of
pockets that she constantly made exploring expeditions through them to assure herself that they had all remained stationary. Elizabeth Freeman was
garbed in red and yellow as a gypsy. She will drive the yellow cart which figured in the Ohio campaign. Her dress follows tradition by associating all
travelers with the pilgrims on sacred missions for the protection of their

companions on the high roads till in the end the occasional travelers caught the infection and became nomads themselves.

Corpl. Martha Klatchen was in charge of the recruits, Mrs. Mary Baird, Mrs. Hettie Graham, and Mrs. John Boldt, whose pilgrim cloaks and scrips were new. The veterans proudly displayed the Albany notch on their staves [from a previous march on the New York state capital]. Mrs. Richard Schultz, the scout who will dash ahead and line the way to Washington with posters, was there with her auto.

When the pilgrims had marched and counter-marched on the brow of a neighboring hillock, and then like the king's men, marched down again, they were piled into the auto. Then the highly decorated votes-for-women crew, through the snow and sleet, were raced about in mad circles and semi-circles with the movies in full chase.

While the auto was in full flight a little boy walking with his mother came into view and cried at the top of his voice: "I want a ride!" He got it. He was tossed from one suffragette to another till he found himself on the knee of somebody next to the driver, and then they were off. The mascot, as he was promptly named, was small Joseph Spingarn.

Rosalie Jones's band of suffragists continued to attract attention, especially as they started their march and began to run into problems. Though these were surely the difficulties anyone would encounter in a two-hundred-mile trek (especially wearing the kind of footgear women wore in 1913 and traveling the mostly unpaved roads that existed at that time), they seemed all that more comical because they were happening to these foolish women.

Rocky Mountain News, 22 February 1913

BLISTERED FEET STOP HER HIKE

"Colonel" Ida Craft, Suffragist "Army," Drops Out in Mud on Way to Capital

HAVRE DE GRACE, Md., Feb 21—With slightly depleted ranks, "General" Rosalie Jones' little band of suffrage pilgrims struggle into Havre De Grace just as dusk this evening after a march over the worst and muddiest road the "army" has encountered since it started last week on the march to Washington.

Three of the hikers were missing when the main body reached here, but they marched into town. One of the trio, "Colonel" Ida Craft, was suffering intensely with blistered feet. The other two remained behind to assist her. So bad was the walking in stretches that when the "troops" reached northeast for luncheon, the marchers looked more like mud images than women.

To add to their troubles, the commissary automobile suddenly took fire on the road, but it was quickly extinguished with but slight damage to either the car or its contents.

The "army" expects to leave here in the morning, stopping at Belair, Md., tomorrow night.

Criticizing the Suffrage Parade and the Women in It

Many supporters and opponents compared the American suffragists' tactics to those of the more militant English suffragettes. Though this editorial in the San Francisco Chronicle *uses the comparison to praise the American suffragists for their restraint, it includes an implied warning that to date they have been tolerated only because they have not been militant. The writer also notes that the parade, while of publicity value, does little to appeal to logic and reason. This is followed by a brief editorial paragraph expressing the same sentiment, published by the* Chronicle *the same day.*

San Francisco Chronicle, 21 February 1913

SUFFRAGE PUBLICITY

Difference Between the English and the American Methods

Two very different ways of advertising the woman suffrage cause are being demonstrated by the on-to-Washington "hikers" in this country and the militant women in England, who on Wednesday caused the destruction of the country home of Chancellor of the Exchequer Lloyd-George and then said the act was "fine."

In its beginning the suffrage movement in England had very much the same object as the similar movement in the United States, namely to attract attention. But the object is no longer to make the male voter take notice, but to cause him alarm. In other words, by resorting to bomb throwing and other acts of violence, the English suffragettes have substituted for their campaign of publicity a campaign of coercion.

Of course nobody will pretend that walking from one city to another distant one is a form of logic calculated to appeal very strongly to the reason. But as a publicity measure—a means of keeping alive the cause of woman suffrage—it certainly is successful.

In this country the attitude of the male public toward the suffragists is generally good-natured. This is because their efforts to obtain publicity have not become an annoyance or a menace.

This difference between publicity and violence is one which the suffragists of the Pankhurst type[2] have lost sight of. And in losing the distinction they are quickly losing the sympathy and exhausting the patience of the English people.

* * *

The ability of a woman to walk a long distance hardly established her fitness to vote, but certainly blowing up buildings doesn't either.

Some opponents insisted on linking the American suffrage movement to the more violent movement in England as a way of signaling how much danger the movement posed to social stability. One way of doing this was by constantly mentioning the violence in the English movement when discussing the American movement. Another was to refer to the American suffragists as "suffragettes," a word used specifically for the English movement. The San Francisco Chronicle *still had not gotten over the fact that California had adopted woman suffrage following a narrow popular vote in 1911. Here, the writer warns that the passage of a federal amendment— the goal of the parade—would infringe on states' rights and increase the federal government's centralization.*

San Francisco Chronicle, 3 March 1913

DEMANDS OF THE SUFFRAGETTES

They Ask for Votes Through an Amendment of the National Constitution

Smashing windows, ruining mail matter and committing arson is not convincing evidence of fitness to vote, nor is the hiking of a lot of tired women to Albany or Washington. It is no evidence either way of the desirability of woman suffrage, but it is very good evidence of the unfitness for the suffrage of the particular women who engage in such folly or such crime, yet it would be evidence of the same kind against men.

But the march on Washington seems to be connected with the now formulated demand of the suffragettes that they should be given the right of suffrage in all states through the means of an amendment to the Federal Constitution.

There they are treading on sacred ground. From the birth of the Republic it has been left to the states to determine for themselves who should vote and who should not, and as opinion has greatly varied, qualifications of electors have varied more or less among the states.

In so large a country and so unequally settled the desires and the needs of the people have varied to some extent and consequently the laws. In no country, we believe, but our own does universal suffrage exist, or universal masculine suffrage, in regard to local affairs nor are we sure that it exists in all the states. It might be that the time would come when some State would desire a restricted suffrage for certain purposes.

At all events, the qualifications of electors are now determined solely by the states with the single exception that no State may deny or abridge the right of any citizen to vote by reason of race, color or previous condition of servitude.

It is now generally confessed that this Fifteenth Amendment, passed at a very emotional period [shortly after the Civil War], has not worked well at all and has probably rather injured than benefited those whom it was intended to help. No one will pretend that it has secured a better government for all the people in any State. And it may yet make us much more trouble. It is making us trouble.

An amendment to the Federal Constitution forbidding any State to deny or abridge the right of any citizen to vote by reason of sex would doubtless be valid. The sovereign people of the United States can do anything.

But if that should happen to give women the right to vote in communities where sentiment was strongly against it, it would not help but injure the women in those communities, and if the women, then everyone else.

The best way for the women to get the ballot if they want it is that adopted by the women of California—reason the thing out.

But whether that is best or not, the proposal that the people of the Nation shall in their highest sovereign capacity bestow the right to vote upon women in states which are opposed to it raises a question much greater than that of woman's suffrage, and is sure to receive vigorous opposition from motives not connected with woman's suffrage. It will be opposed by all who see danger to the Republic in increasing centralization.

When the suffrage parade was mobbed, everyone, even suffrage opponents, uttered public condemnations of the mob's actions and the police force's inaction. Nevertheless, they also realized that this could be used by the suffragists and would harm the supposed moral position of the antisuffragists. In reflecting on this, this writer for the antisuffrage New York Times *cannot resist commenting that the mistreatment of the women in the parade is one of the suffragists' few legitimate complaints. The message here is that since*

*American women have no real complaints about the way they are gener-
ally treated (although this assumption was by no means accurate), why do
they need suffrage?*

New York Times, 5 March 1913

Anti-Suffragism Gets a Hard Blow

Opponents of woman suffrage ought to be prompt, and will be, in common fairness as well as from intelligent policy, in denouncing the failure of
the police of the District of Columbia to protect from assault, insult, and interference the participants in Monday's parade.

Whatever one may think of the object for which the women were marching, what they did was in the exercise of a right the legality and legitimacy of
which, as an expression of sentiment and desire, are beyond question. Like
other American citizens similarly employed, they were entitled to protection. They did not get it, partly because policemen on duty were in number
pitifully inadequate for the handling of a crowd which their superiors knew
beforehand would be of enormous size and therefore hard to control, and
partly because this inadequate force, according to the testimony of many
witnesses, was in sympathy with the rioters rather than with the paraders,
and did not do what it could to keep clear the line of march and to preserve
order and decency.

Herein lies full justification for demanding a rigid inquiry to fix responsibility where it belongs, and then for action severe enough to cause any
repetition, in Washington or elsewhere, of these outrageous negligences
and proceedings. Major SILVESTER [*sic*] [commander of the District police]
enters a plea…saying that the force at his command was inadequate for the
task imposed on it. The defense is worthless. It should have been made before the parade, not after it, and the Major should have used this argument,
not in palliation of disgraceful failure, but as a reason for supplementing be-
times his inadequate force with others that good-will and appreciation of
the needs of the case could easily have secured.

The suffragist women do well to exploit their grievance since it is a real
one, and of real grievances they have had few in this country, but after their
natural anger has subsided, they will see that "the cause" can hardly fail to
profit from what happened to themselves. The opposing cause will suffer to
precisely the same extent, and that is why the decent and intelligent antagonists of woman suffrage have a special reason, apart from the general and
common reason, for lamenting and denouncing the abominable treatment
of the paraders.

DENOUNCING THE BEHAVIOR OF THE SPECTATORS AND POLICE

Most newspapers expressed shock at the treatment the woman suffragists received at the hands of the mob. Whether or not they supported the parade or woman suffrage, they were outraged that American women should be treated this way. Furthermore, they were outraged that the police, whose job it was to maintain order, had failed to protect the marching women. Several newspapers picked up on the irony of the cavalry coming to the rescue. The New York World *even featured this in its headline on its front-page story, creating a story of mythic proportions, with a battle between good and evil, and the rescue of defenseless maidens by knights in shining armor.*

New York World, 4 March 1913

CAVALRY SAVES SUFFRAGE PARADE FROM HOODLUMS

[Special to The World]

WASHINGTON, March 3—Five thousand women, marching in the woman suffrage parade today, practically fought their way foot by foot up Pennsylvania avenue through a surging mob that completely defied the Washington police, swamped the marchers and broke their procession into little companies.

The women, trudging stoutly along under great difficulties, were able to complete their march only when troops of United States Cavalry from Fort Myer were rushed into Washington to take charge of Pennsylvania avenue.

Later in Continental Hall, the women turned what was to have been a suffrage demonstration into an indignation meeting, in which the Washington police were roundly denounced for their inactivity and resolutions were passed calling upon President-elect Wilson and the incoming Congress to make an investigation....

The marchers had to fight their way from the start and took more than one hour in making the first ten blocks. Many of the women were in tears under the jeers and insults that lined the route.

It was a hostile crowd through which the women marched. Miss Inez Milholland, herald of the procession, mounted on a white horse, distinguished herself by aiding in riding down a mob that blocked the way and threatened to disrupt the parade.

Another woman member of the petticoat cavalry struck a hoodlum a stinging blow across the face in reply to a scurrilous remark as she was passing....

Cavalry Drive Mob Back

Around the Treasury the crowds were massed so tightly that repeated charges by the police were seemingly ineffective. When the cavalry suddenly appeared there was a wild outburst of applause in the reviewing stand. The men in brown virtually brushed aside the mounted and foot police and took charge.

In two lines the troops charged the crowds. Evidently realizing they would be ridden down, the mobs fought their way back.

The parade in itself was a great success. The greatest ovation probably was given to Gen. Rosalie Jones, who led her little band of "hikers" from New York over rough roads and through snow and rain to march for the "cause."...

More than 300,000 people saw the "Votes for Women" parade. The marchers represented every civilized nation on earth and wore every color of the rainbow....

Drunken Men Tried to Climb on Their Floats, Women Say

This statement was issued from Woman Suffrage Headquarters to-night:

"While police by the score stood by and laughed, hoodlums, drunken men and toughs this afternoon did all but break up the great suffrage procession in which more than 10,000 women participated.

"Only the timely arrival of a squad of the Fifteenth United States Cavalry, who rode to the rescue on the gallop, the manliness of several score United States soldiers and marines recruited from the streets and a band of Boy Scouts kept the great suffragist army from being routed."

In a sense, the mob played right into the suffragists' hands. One of the arguments for woman suffrage was that if immigrant, ignorant, and uneducated men could have the franchise, nice, well-behaved, middle-class, educated women (how suffragists pictured themselves) certainly should also. That contrast between the uncouth masses of men and the genteel suffrage women is captured in this clever editorial, which notes the irony of considering male drunkenness superior to female hysteria.

Chicago Tribune, **5 March 1913**

HOODLUMS VS. GENTLEWOMEN

Maj. Sylvester, superintendent of the Washington police, and the Washington authorities appear to be stout advocates of the fine old doctrine that if there is a contest between gentlewomen and hoodlums for possession and use of the streets the privileges are inherently and inalienably with the hoodlums.

This superiority of the hoodlum over the gentlewoman is one of the grounds upon which the suffragists ask for consideration and relief, but they would have been willing to avoid being knocked over the head by the argument during the parade.

The suffragists will be puzzled to discover wherein they offended the law or why they found themselves outside the protection of ordinary courtesy and ordinary police efficiency. They had obtained a license to parade in the streets, reluctantly granted, it is true, but granted. It is recalled that Maj. Sylvester protested he would be unable to protect the marchers from insult, and this at the time seemed strange, as it put Washington in contrast with New York, where the suffragists paraded and heard nothing but cheers. The strangeness of the contrast is the more remarkable now.

Probably the suffragists will count the experience a profit in that it called attention to a considerable lack of essentials in government, and called attention in such a way that indifferent men will take notice.

It is reported that as a result to the parade, a number of cases of hysteria were entered in the hospitals, which may be regarded as a feminine expression of astonishment that gentlewomen in considerable numbers could not walk in the street of the national capital without being insulted.

It is further reported that a much larger number of cases of inebriety were treated, which may be regarded as a masculine expression of superiority, intellectuality, and strength of character.

It was ironic that, prior to the parade, many had been critical of the violent actions of the British suffragettes, fearing that this might become the style adopted by their American sisters. Now, however, the tables had turned. It was the American public that had become violent. This was shocking to many, especially since the violence had occurred in the nation's capital.

Atlanta Constitution, 5 March 1913

RUFFIANS

The conduct of the Washington mob that jostled and insulted the parade of suffragettes on Pennsylvania avenue is a blot upon the inauguration ceremonials, and a stinging reflection upon the ability of the Washington police.

We have heretofore prided ourselves that the movement for woman suffrage in this country was not attended by any of the violent and disgraceful scenes by which it has been accompanied in Great Britain. But the heckling, the torment and the deliberate, reckless affronts meted out to these women in the nation's capital is hardly less than reprehensible in spirit if not in kind than the anarchy visible in England.

The spectacle is a reflection upon that prevailing American courtesy and chivalry we have so long boasted as differentiating us from other nations. The mob that so glibly exhibited its gutter instincts may well have disagreed with the creed of these women without resorting to the tactics of the bar-room and the dark alley.

There is consolation at least in the fact that the conduct thus insolently staged is wholly unrepresentative and un-American. Incidentally, it should be the business of congress to mercilessly investigate to the end of disclosing the cause for the singular apathy and inefficiency of the local Washington authorities.

The mob was faceless, and individual men could not be singled out for recrimination or punishment. The Washington police, on the other hand were an official organization with a superintendent who could be held accountable. Here, the New York World, *which prided itself in its record on investigating municipal and congressional corruption and ineptitude, blames the Washington police for the riot and demands that Congress take action.*

New York World, 5 March 1913

WASHINGTON'S SUFFRAGE-PARADE SCANDAL

During the suffrage parade in Washington the police proved their utter inefficiency. When the hoodlum element became unruly the police force not only did nothing to restore order or protect the marchers, but some of its members are charged with addressing insulting remarks to women in line. What is needed evidently is a drastic overhauling of the department from Chief Sylvester down.

Arrangements for the suffrage parade were made long in advance with the permission of the local authorities. If the Washington police have not learned of the policeman's business to handle a crowd and deal with disorderly characters it would have been a simple matter to call in the help of the military for a few hours. No great foresight was needed to guard against such scenes as disgraced the nation's capital. No great courage was called for to disperse the rowdies who broke into the parade. A little energy at the start would have ended the disturbance. A few arrests would have put a stop to the hoodlumism along Pennsylvania avenue.

The trouble is the Washington police did not try. They made a shameful exhibition of themselves, and if Congress does what it should it will speedily provide for a better police force in Washington.

QUESTIONS

1. Compare the suffrage march of 1913 to the march of Coxey's army on Washington in 1894. In what ways were both of these organized as political actions? As publicity actions? What were some of the similarities in their strategy for winning public support and newspaper coverage of the march? What are some of the similarities in the way newspapers treated them?

2. Social movements frequently organize colorful events and spectacles to catch public and media attention. How does this attention serve the movement? How does it harm the movement?

3. Few of the news stories and editorials discussed in this chapter (and published during the period) dealt with the political ideas of the suffrage movement. Do you think the public actually knew what woman suffrage was all about? If people did not learn about it in newspapers, where else might they learn about it?

4. The *New York World*'s article about Gen. Jones's hike in Central Park describes the suffragists in terms often used by newspapers to describe women of the period. What are some of the words, phrases, and themes (about women) used in the article? How would these descriptions of the suffragists actually undermine the suffrage movement?

5. The parade would probably be considered a failure by most organizers, but suffragists were able to turn it into a success that animated the campaign for a federal suffrage amendment. What role did the press play in turning this defeat to victory?

6. Many of the newspapers covering the parade, such as the *New York Times* and the *San Francisco Chronicle*, were opposed to the federal suffrage amendment. They frequently expressed their position outright in editorials and indirectly in their choice of stories, headlines, photographs and language. Do you think this influenced their readers' opinions on suffrage? Do you think any single newspaper can sway public opinion one way or another?

NOTES

1. This was not the first suffrage parade, for two had already been held in New York City in campaigns for suffrage in that state. This was, however, the first to be brought to the nation's capital.

2. Emmeline Goulden Pankhurst was the leader of the English militants.

CHAPTER 19

The Seventeenth Amendment Reforms the Senate, May 1913

The U.S. Senate came to be known as the "Millionaires' Club" during the Progressive Era because of the way in which vested interests were often entrenched in that body of the government. According to the rules laid out in the Constitution, the members of the Senate were chosen by the state legislatures, not by popular vote. State legislatures used this power to reward prominent politicians who would advocate their state's interests or to punish those who betrayed the interests of their constituents. In selecting U.S. senators, state legislators were often influenced by pressures from their most powerful constituents—those who controlled local and regional business and industry. In the most egregious cases, wealthy and powerful men were able to buy Senate seats for themselves or their friends.

As a result, corruption, inefficiency, disorder, and even paralysis existed at the level of both the state legislatures and the U.S. Senate. The business of state legislatures was repeatedly held up by warring factions trying to elect or defeat nominees to the Senate. Between 1901 and 1903, for example, Delaware was not represented in the Senate at all because of its legislature's failure to elect senators. In 1905 it took the Missouri legislature months to settle on its selection of a senator, and its final session on the issue deteriorated into a brawl in which several members were injured. Between 1912 and 1913, it took the Illinois legislature more than nine months to select a replacement for U.S. Senator William Lorimer, who had been unseated following charges of bribery and corruption. In cases like these, the wrangling over whom to appoint to the position kept the state legislatures from their other business, while their failure to take action prevented the U.S. Senate from operating with a full complement of officers. Those who suffered the most were the constituents, whose interests were not being represented either at the state or the federal level.

Reformers maintained that a constitutional amendment allowing the direct election of senators by the voting public was the best way to prevent corruption in the Senate. The suggestion was first made in 1826 and again in the 1850s and 1860s by Andrew Johnson in his successive roles as state representative, U.S. senator, and president. But Johnson's resolutions faced entrenched opposition from the Senate, which, according to the Constitution, must approve any amendment by a two-thirds vote. In the 1880s and 1890s, the movement for reform resurfaced. It became a plank in the Populist program at every election after 1892 and was in the Democratic Party platform in every presidential election year between 1900 and 1912. It gained enough support in the House of Representatives so that between 1893 and 1902, the House adopted a constitutional amendment calling for the direct election of senators five different times. In each case, however, the amendment died in the Senate, where few members were willing to abolish the system to which they owed their seats.

At the same time, the move for the popular election of senators moved slowly forward on the state level through a variety of methods. The first of these, the statewide preference primary, was enacted in Oregon in 1901 and became referred to as the "Oregon System." With this method, voters could indicate their preference for the state's U.S. senators, and the state legislature would then officially elect the winner. The second method, adopted by Wisconsin in 1904, allowed for direct primaries in which members (rather than the leadership) of each party selected the party's nominees for public office, including its candidate for the Senate. By 1912, 29 of the 48 states elected their senators through either preference or direct primaries, but the *direct* election of senators by voters still did not exist.

Those who supported a constitutional amendment to allow voters to vote directly for their senators argued that this would elevate the Senate's tone and membership, increase its responsibility to the people, and decrease the opportunity for corruption. They also maintained this would allow greater citizen participation, though few noted that few women (women did not have full suffrage in all 48 states until 1920) or blacks in the South (where many voting requirements made them ineligible) would be able to vote in these elections. Those who opposed a constitutional amendment argued it would be an invasion of states' rights or that it would turn Senate elections into popularity contests. Others doubted it would increase voter participation or make voters more responsible than legislatures. Some southern states (some of which already had primary elections) feared the amendment would give the federal government control over elections and put an end to the practice in the South of barring blacks from the polls on the basis of residency, property, tax, or literacy requirements.

The debate became more salient on those occasions when a particular scandal or investigation reached public attention, often through the press. In 1906, for example, muckraking journalist David Graham Phillips exposed the workings of the Senate in an investigative series for *Cosmopolitan*. In "The Treason of the Senate," Phillips charged the Senate was ignorant and corrupt and provided specific examples and documentation exposing individual senators. The first article in the series was introduced by publisher William Randolph Hearst as a "terrible arraignment of those who, sitting in the seats of the mighty in Washington, have betrayed the public to that cruel and vicious Spirit of Mammon which has come to dominate the nation."[1] Hearst was perhaps exaggerating the situation for the purpose of boosting his magazine's circulation, but this indictment rang true enough for the general public. The series was a hit, and *Cosmopolitan*'s circulation and advertising increased significantly in the year during which the series was published.

The scandal that finally brought public opinion to a pitch and increased pressure on the Senate to amend the Constitution was launched by a story in the *Chicago Tribune* in April 1910. In that story, the *Tribune* reported the statement of Illinois Representative Charles A. White, who said he had received bribes from the Democratic leader of the lower house as well as another Democratic legislator in 1909 to vote for U.S. Senate candidate William Lorimer. According to White, the money had been part of the "jackpot," a general corruption fund distributed after every legislative session. The *Tribune* story was picked up by newspapers across the country, and investigations were immediately launched by the Illinois state attorney, the Illinois General Assembly, and the U.S. Senate itself.[2] The investigations continued through the next two years, during which other lawmakers came forward with stories of bribery, and the election of at least one other senator, Isaac Stephenson of Wisconsin, was investigated. The continuous press coverage of the charges and investigations, which Lorimer claimed were instigated by the "newspaper trust," eventually led to his expulsion from the Senate in July 1912.[3]

As the Lorimer case dragged on through the summer and fall of 1910, the House launched another direct-election amendment. Although by this time more than half the states had their own direct primary laws, the proposal met stiff opposition from some southern and mid-Atlantic states that argued it infringed on states' rights. An attempt to meet this objection was made by revising the amendment to include wording that would give states rather than the federal government control over the election process. This revision, which became known as the "race rider," only prolonged the hag-gling, for some northern states argued it would remove federal power to bar racial discrimination at the polls.

Eventually, the House resubmitted its original proposal; the Senate rati-fied it in June 1911, and the House concurred in the final version on May 13, 1912. The joint resolution went immediately to President William Taft for his signature and was then submitted to the states. The required 36 states ratified the Seventeenth Amendment by May 1913. As approved, its first paragraph stated: "The Senate of the United States shall be composed of two Senators from each State, elected by the people thereof, for six years; and each Senator shall have one vote. The electors in each State shall have the qualifications requisite for electors of the most numerous branch of the State Legislatures."[4]

The new amendment was welcomed by the recently inaugurated Presi-dent Woodrow Wilson and formally proclaimed by his secretary of state, William Jennings Bryan, on May 31, 1913. It went into effect immediately so that the senators in office on that day were to be the last to hold their seats at the behest of their respective legislatures. Neither corruption in the Sen-ate nor probes of that corruption ended with the change of the election law, however. Just a month earlier, Wilson had launched an attack on the power-ful lobby of business interests that was attempting to defeat his low-tariff bill. On June 2, one day after the Seventeenth Amendment went into affect, the Senate launched an investigation of its members' ties to business inter-ests. The investigations were to reveal more sordid details of gifts, favors, bribery, and outright corruption that sullied more than one reputation and once again undermined public confidence in elected officials. The investi-gation eventually led to laws requiring people operating in the legislative lobby to register, as well as laws requiring senators and congressmen to de-clare their financial interests.

The readings for this chapter include news articles and editorials pub-lished during various phases of the movement for Senate election reform, from the proposal of a constitutional amendment in 1896 to the adoption of the Seventeenth Amendment in 1913. These have been organized in two sections. In the first, the stories and editorials support Senate election re-form, either through a constitutional amendment or primaries. These main-tain that the reform will clean up the Senate, reduce corporate influence, make citizens more involved in government, and generally enhance democ-racy. In the second section, the readings are opposed to the reform on a va-riety of grounds, including arguments that it will infringe on states' rights, counteract the intentions of the framers of the Constitution, fail to make voters more involved and responsible, favor wealthy candidates, and turn Senate elections into popularity contests.

SUPPORT OF SENATE ELECTION REFORM

In 1896 the time seemed ripe to introduce a constitutional amendment for Senate reform. The Kentucky and Delaware legislatures were deadlocked in attempts to fill vacant Senate seats, which added ammunition to the arguments for the reform. The proposal, which would have established the Sixteenth Amendment, died in the Senate. This news article provides the various arguments for the amendment but none of those against it.

Chicago Tribune, 22 May 1896

PEOPLE MAY VOTE FOR THE SENATORS

Mitchell Will Bring Up His Proposition for the Sixteenth Amendment Tomorrow—House Would Pass It.

Washington, D.C., May 21–[Special]–According to a notice given by Mitchell of Oregon the Senate will be called upon on Saturday to consider the proposed amendment to the Constitution providing for the election of Senators by the people. This amendment makes but little change in the Constitution of the Senate itself, requiring that each State shall be represented by two Senators, but providing that they shall be chosen by a plurality vote of the people in the State, the voters to have the same qualifications as are requisite for electors of the more numerous branch of the State Legislature. When vacancies occur in the Senate they are to be filled by the Governor of the State until the next general election for Representatives in Congress. The amendment was reported favorably from the Committee on Elections two months ago, and Senator Mitchell, Chairman of the committee, purposes to do all in his power to press it to a vote. The committee urged that the amendment proposes a change in the mode of election only and does not alter at all the position of United States Senators as representatives of the States in their sovereign or political capacity. The friends of the proposed constitutional amendment urge that the present system is a reflection on the honesty and capacity or both, of the voting classes of the several states.

It is shown in the report that the material interests of the State suffer by reason of protracted Senatorial contests in the Legislature, which are frequent occurrences. Often these contests are carried on not only for weeks but sometimes for months, and in many cases, besides the ill-feeling and actual strife, there has been complete failure to elect, and the State has been deprived of its representation. The situation in Kentucky and Delaware today is cited by the committee as an argument in favor of election of Senators by the people, and that, too, by a plurality vote.

There is but little doubt of the fact that if the Senate could be brought to pass the resolution, the House would adopt it with a hurrah, and the amendment to the Constitution would therefore be submitted for ratification by three-fourths of the Legislatures, and if adopted it would become the sixteenth amendment.

While proposals for a constitutional amendment like the one put forward by Senator Mitchell floundered in Congress, progress was made in individual states. In 1904 Wisconsin was the first to adopt the direct primary, and it was soon followed by others. In this editorial, the Milwaukee Journal *expresses its faith in the ultimate success of the progressive reform. At the same time, it gets in some digs at politicians known to be allied with the moneyed interests, specifically, millionaire lumberman, banker, and newspaper owner Isaac Stephenson. The 79-year-old Stephenson had already served two terms in the state assembly and three terms in the U.S. Congress. In May 1907 he had been elected to the U.S. Senate to fill the seat of Senator John C. Spooner, who had resigned.[5] Here, the* Journal *suggests that that he will be a real opponent to any constitutional amendment for reform that might make its way to the Senate.*

Milwaukee Journal, 24 August 1908

WHAT? NOT SENATE REFORM! WELL, THAT'S A SURPRISE!

More rapidly than many people realize, the United States senate is being reformed. It is being converted from a corporation to a popular body.

One force at work for the accomplishment of this end appears to be the popular primary law as applied to the nomination of United States senators. During the last two years the passage of primary laws has resulted in the adoption of this method of choosing nominees in no less than twenty-seven states. This is more than half of the republic.

And the first tests of these laws are showing that it is not easy for the corporation man to stand against the popular primary. In Oregon, Fulton went down. In Kansas, Long gave way to Bristow. In South Dakota, Kittredge was defeated. In North Dakota, Hansbrough has the same kind of trouble to go against....

With all this evidence of what her sister states are doing, are the people to permit Isaac Stephenson, who represents the power of Money in Politics, to be Progressive Wisconsin's contribution to Senate Reform?

Even if Wisconsin stumbles over the Bar'l, the movement will succeed, for it is in the right direction. Cheer up. The rule of Aldrich, Elkins, Scott, Hale & Co. is drawing to a close.

Slowly but surely, states that had opposed direct election began to consider change. In 1910 the Massachusetts Assembly adopted a resolution favoring direct elections. Though the resolution by no means guaranteed success, the Chicago Tribune *hailed it as a step forward for progress, especially since it had occurred in a conservative New England state. In the following editorial, the* Tribune *does not name specific moneyed interests, but nonetheless implies that "unwholesome influences" have corrupted the system.*

Chicago Tribune, 12 May 1910

DIRECT ELECTION OF SENATORS

The lower house of the Massachusetts legislature has actually adopted a resolution favoring the direct election of senators by the people. This is indeed progress. Conservative New England is beginning to lend its support to a popular movement which has made so much headway in the south and west.

It is not because of a suspicion that money has been used to secure senatorial seats that New Englanders are gradually coming to distrust the supreme wisdom of their legislatures. But they are alive to the fact that through the control of party machinery and the judicious use of patronage legislatures are sometimes induced to put into the senate or keep there men whom the people would not have favored if they had been consulted. The voters are beginning to think that they have as much political wisdom when it comes to electing a senator as their respective legislatures have.

It is needless to say that the action of the lower house of the Massachusetts legislature does not have the approval of Senator Lodge or, for that matter, of any New England senator. It is not in their power to kill off the new idea which is taking root in New England. Through a constitutional amendment, or in some roundabout way, the voters of New England states will in time select their senators at first hand instead of leaving it entirely to state legislators, who are too often controlled by unwholesome influences which could not affect the many of the electorate.

In 1911 the New York legislature became bogged down for more than two months in an attempt to select a U.S. senator, with the result that many of the original individuals interested in the position dropped out in disgust or discouragement. According to some, the stalemate was due to a power play by the Democratic Party boss, Charles F. Murphy. The New York World, *which often railed against the Senate for corruption—and had even taken to referring to the influence of business interests on the Senate by speaking*

of "Senator Sugar," "Senator Wool," "Senator Lumber," and so on—took
this as a perfect example to support its campaign for Senate election reform.

New York World, 29 March 1911

Must the Legislature Be an Ass?

How much longer will the New York Legislature make an ass of itself for the edification of [Democratic Party leader] Charles F. Murphy?

Sixty ballots have been taken in a futile attempt to select a United States Senator. The contest has already extended over seventy-two days of the legislative session. It has cost the taxpayers tens of thousands of dollars. It has discredited not only the [Governor] Dix administration and the Democratic party but the State of New York itself. During all this time the one obstacle to the election of a Senator has been the boss of [Democratic machine] Tammany Hall.

All the original candidates for the office are out of the contest. Mr. Depew, the Republican caucus nominee, has withdrawn. Mr. Sheehan, the Democratic caucus nominee, has released his supporters. Mr. Shepard, who was Mr. Sheehan's chief opponent, retired long ago. Depew, Sheehan and Shepard are out, but Murphy is still in, and day after day the Legislature allows the Tammany Boss to make it an object of national ridicule. Its constitutional powers, its statutory powers, its intelligence, its independence, its self-respect—all are sacrificed to Murphy and to Wall Street interests that are behind him. All of Murphy's voting-trust caucuses have a single object, which is to prevent the election of a Senator unless the Legislature allows him to name the candidate.

This has been the most disgraceful spectacle of subservience to boss rule that New York has known in a generation. It is the more disgraceful because the Legislature's servitude is voluntary, self-inflicted. Not only can it elect a Senator any day it chooses, without regard to Murphy and the corporations behind him, but it can enact direct-primary laws that will utterly destroy Murphy's power as a Boss and strip him of all his inflated authority. It can drive Murphy out of business, yet it permits him to usurp its own constitutional powers. Men who have taken a solemn oath of office make themselves puppets of the Tammany Boss and jump whenever he pulls the strings. Instead of electing an honest, capable, worthy United States Senator who would represent the State and the public welfare, the Legislature waits on the word of Murphy and allows him to nullify the will of the majority while he seeks by trickery to bring about the choice of a Senator who will be the tool of Wall Street and Fourteenth Street.

Must the Legislature be an ass?

Congress finally approved a constitutional amendment in May 1912, and 36 states (including New York) had ratified it by May 1913. Georgia was one of the states that did not ratify it, although it already had adopted senatorial primaries within the state. Like other southern states, Georgia feared that federal control over state elections would force it to end its practice of barring blacks from the polls through a variety of legal requirements. The Atlanta Constitution, *the voice of the New South, differed with its legislature on this point. This editorial dismisses the fear that Congress would foist any such "force bills" (federal laws imposed on states that challenged states' rights) on the South and hails the amendment's ratification as a reform long overdue.*

Atlanta Constitution, 11 April 1913

SENATORS FROM THE PEOPLE

With the ratification of the seventeenth constitutional amendment providing for direct election of United States senators—a reform for which the nation has long clamored, and for which Georgia's senatorial primary blazed the way—reaches fruition. Henceforth the men who sit in the upper branches will come straight from the people. Henceforth if one wants to discuss "tainted senators" it will be necessary to indict the people of an entire commonwealth instead of a powerful and possibly corrupt coterie of politicians.

The change, so far as average wisdom can now see, is a salutary one. Like all other political alterations of a fundamental nature the test of time must be required to prove it. The innovation is notable in that it is wholly in line with the prevalent effort to get the government closer to the people, to approximate as nearly as possible under the constitution a pure democracy. The drift is a wholesome one, but it carries its responsibilities. The greater the power of the man with the ballot, the more circumspectly must he exercise that power both as to men and measures.

The [Atlanta] Constitution does not now and never has taken stock in the bogie that under the terms of the new amendment congress might foist "force bills" on the south. Conceding, even that the amendment gives it that authority, there is no disposition to exercise it. The nation is too near one in understanding, too mutually comprehensive of the Negro problem, to fear that it would indorse any reversion of this nature.

Some interpreted the passage of the Seventeenth Amendment as a sure sign of the inevitable march of progress—the inevitable overthrow of the old by

*the new, of the inefficient by the efficient, and of corrupt government by
clean government. This editorial predicts somewhat naively that the direct
election of senators will "end for all time" corruption in the Senate.*

Rocky Mountain News, 10 April 1913

THE NEW ORDER

The world is not alone moving, but it is surely moving along right lines.
Old systems and methods, which had come to be regarded as fixtures, are
being forced into the zone of desuetude. The political schemes and conspiracies which had shamed states and communities are well-nigh things of
the past. In infrequent cases and places only do they remain, and, even
there, the march of progress and the determination of the people for better
things and better government have them on the run. The organized corrup-
tions and briberies of the past have gone in large part never to return.

This week the people finally placed their seal of approval on the constitutional provision for the election of United States senators by direct vote.
The adoption of the amendment to the national constitution marks an
epoch in this government. It ends for all time the scandals, the crimes
against the people and the assaults on the very foundations of democratic
government, which were, in too many instances, associated with the election
of senators by the legislatures of the states. It effectually places a quietus on
the crooks and grafters who were wont to haunt the legislative halls and
place in pawn the souls and honor of men as the price of their illy-concealed
briberies. But, above all, it is the splendid culmination of many years of
struggle to give to the people their undoubted right to elect any and all of
their servants by their own direct action.

The historians of future senatorial conflicts will not have to chronicle the
degradations and debasements of Montana, or Delaware, or Illinois. The citizenship dowered with the new right will not have to blush for the exhibitions
of open-handed corruption that befouled the convention system of nomina-
tions. No more will there be barter in the market place of iniquity for the control of the individual or delegated influence. And the politician who has any
wisdom left will keep his ear close to the ground, not for the voice of a boss or
the rumblings of a packed and purchased convention, but for the current of
sentiment that tells unmistakably of the coming will of the whole people.

OPPOSITION TO SENATE ELECTION REFORM

*Not everyone was convinced that election reform would make the situation
better. Direct or preferential primaries had been adopted by 29 states by*

1912, but one of their frequent failures was a poor voter turnout. Some, like the writer of this editorial, wondered if direct elections would be any more representative of the will of the people than the system they were replacing, and might, instead, favor the wealthy who could afford to run in two elections—one for the nomination and another for the election. They also wondered if direct elections would turn elections into nothing more than popularity contests. These, of course, became major concerns for all elections as voter turnout declined and the cost and superficiality of campaigns increased steadily through the twentieth century.

Boston Herald, 10 May 1912

First Fruits of "Progress"

The disgraceful and country-wide turmoil over the choice of Chicago convention delegates, unprecedented in our political history, shows that we have as a people bitten off quite enough in the way of progressive ideas.

The really small representation in popular primaries of any sort makes it gravely open to question whether they are any more representative of the "will of the people" than the system which they have supplanted.

In the states, North and South, which are picking out their senators in this way, the quality of the output has distinctly deteriorated. The expense under preference primaries of two campaigns, one for the nomination and another for the election—shown in the case of Isaac Stephenson of Wisconsin—gives the rich man an undeserved power in politics.

The frequency with which the public is summoned to the polling-booth lessens popular respect for the ballot as an institution, and so cheapens the operations of government all along the line.

Any contest between party candidates at the polls is usually one of principles. Between aspirants for a nomination it inevitably degenerates into personalities.

Despite such arguments, the U.S. House of Representatives and Senate finally passed a constitutional amendment and turned it over to the states for ratification in May 1912. The amendment's success was by no means guaranteed, and by December 1912, only two state legislatures— Massachusetts and Minnesota, the only two in session after the joint resolution was passed—had acted to ratify it. Thirty-six state legislatures were to convene in January 1913, among them the New York State legislature. When newly elected New York Governor William Sulzer made his inaugural address in the beginning of January, he charged the state legislature to ratify the amendment. The New York Times, *which opposed the amendment, dismissed Sulzer's arguments as "claptrap."*

New York Times, 2 January 1913

GOV. SULZER'S TASK

The Governor earnestly recommends the ratification of the amendment to the Federal Constitution providing for the election of Senators by the people, instead of by the Legislature. He says the people have demonstrated their ability for self-government, and that "if the people cannot be trusted, then our government is a failure and the free institutions of the fathers doomed." These are the familiar arguments of those who advocate the direct election of Senators. The words sound well, very well, so well that it would be easy to assume that they express a well reasoned political idea. In truth, they are claptrap, by which we mean no reflection upon Mr. SULZER—he talks merely as the others have talked. Of course, the people are capable of governing themselves. They have proved it by a century and a quarter of the experience of this Republic. But a Government whose laws are enacted by a Congress of which one branch is made up of men chosen by the Legislatures of the States is as truly self-government as one where both branches of Congress are elected by direct vote.

The attack is not on the Senate, not on elections by Legislatures, but on the representative principle. The people can govern themselves, can make their own laws, but we know very well that they would make an awful mess of it if they tried to make laws by their own direct action. On the average, as a general principle based on experience, the people would make a choice of Senators less wise that that made for them by their chosen representatives. Popular election of Senators is a short way of lowering the standard of ability and dignity and authority of the United States Senate. Mr. SULZER says that "forty-eight Senators can prevent the enactment of a good law or the repeal of a bad law," and this, he thinks, "is too much power for forty-eight men to have in a free government of 100,000,000 of people." We should say a government is pretty safe in which the co-operation of as many as forty-eight men would be required for the defeat of good laws or for the defeat of bills repealing bad laws. At any rate, it is a condition quite as likely to arise under the policy of direct election of Senators as under our present practice.

New York became the 3rd state to approve the Seventeenth Amendment on January 15 and it was quickly followed by 33 others, so that by April 9, 1913, it appeared that the required 36 states had ratified the amendment. (Wisconsin signed the wrong form of the amendment and had to approve it a second time, so by a technicality, the amendment was not officially ratified until May 13.) Those who still opposed the amendment now predicted that this would mean a shift of political power from the state in general to their urban centers where most voters reside.

New York Times, 10 April 1913

SENATORS BY POPULAR ELECTION

Connecticut, the thirty-sixth State to ratify the amendment passed on May 13, 1912, providing for the popular election of United States Senators, has effectually evinced the prevailing lack of faith in Legislatures properly to represent their States. Heretofore, the Federal Senate shall consist of two Senators from each State elected by its people for six years. When vacancies occur the Governor of the States shall issue writs for a special election, but it is provided that the Legislature may empower the Executive to make a temporary appointment until the vacancy shall be filled by election as directed by the Legislature. The incumbency and term of service of no Senator now elected will be affected by the amendment.

By their own vote a blow has been struck at the dignity and good name of the several States composing the Union. They have decided that they cannot elect Legislatures fit to choose their representatives, as States, in the Federal Congress. What assurance is there, then, that the people can choose fit Senatorial representatives themselves? The amendment violates the principle of the short ballot, adding another to the long roll of elective offices: moreover, as Senator HOAR expressed it, the new method "transfers the seat of political power in great States, now distributed evenly over their territory, to the great cities and masses of population. The people now elect but two Federal officers, the President and the Congressmen. Now they can elect three.

The first blow having been struck, the second impends. While the States voted as Sovereigns by means of their Legislatures, the fact that one State was rich and populous and another small, poor, and newly settled, made no difference—the majesty of each was represented by its two Senators at the Federal capital. Now that their election is reduced to the terms of the popular vote, the people of the States must stand up and be counted. By what right should the 20,000 voters of Nevada have an equal voice in the deliberations of the Nation's upper house with New York's 1,560,000 voters? Such questions will be raised and with the coming years more insistently.

Connecticut was the 36th state to ratify the amendment, which assured its adoption. While much of the nation applauded this action, the Hartford Courant *was dubious that direct election would make any real difference in the quality of the Senate or its members. In this editorial it criticizes as*

*naive those who think ordinary citizens will now take more responsibility
or act more intelligently in elections.*

Hartford Courant, 1 May 1913

THE REAL NEED

This week the "Outlook" rejoices and is glad over the Seventeenth Amendment. "The people," it exultantly says, "have taken from the Legislatures and into their own hands the right to name senators of the United States." It says farther—

"There are only two ways of securing improvement in public business. One is by improving the breed of professional politicians—that is the method of benevolent despotism. The other is by simplifying the process of selecting representatives through direct elections, direct primaries and the short ballot, so that the ordinary citizens can take their part—that is the method of free government."

The ordinary citizens were just as able to "take their part"—if they cared to—before the Seventeenth Amendment was born or thought of as they ever will be under the new dispensation. There hasn't been a time within living memory when they—those to whom nature gave white skins, at any rate— were not perfectly free to vote, and to make their ballots tell for the kind of representation and government they wanted. They are the sovereign source of power in this country. They have always had the electing of delegates, legislators and congressmen in their own hands. In the case of great multitudes of them, the threshold difficulty has not been to induce them to vote carefully and discriminatingly, with intelligence and good judgment, but— as all campaign managers know—to get them to vote at all. What solid grounds are there for a belief that they are going to be so vastly more alert and critical in the choice of their United States senators than they have been in the choice of their Legislators? If any, what? The "Outlook" will have our best wishes in any well-directed efforts it may make to improve the politicians, but the vitally important thing is to improve the citizens.

The terms of thirty-two senators of the United States run out in 1915; the terms of as many more run out in 1917. For these senators it is a case of re-election (by direct popular vote) or retirement. The new plan may have its compensating advantages—more than compensating; we won't stop now to consider them. It has the obvious drawback that every one of the senators who desire to stay on at Washington is now under a new temptation to think of his popularity when he should be thinking only of the country's interests and his senatorial duty.

Questions

1. What were the major arguments for and against changing the way in which U.S. senators were elected? How might these arguments be affected by an individual's (or newspaper's) political affiliation or geographic area? Which method of electing senators (by the legislature, by preference primaries, by direct primaries, or by popular vote) do you think has the best results?

2. Some opponents of the constitutional amendment argued that it was a force bill, that is, a federal law imposed on states that challenged states' rights. This was an argument used especially by southern states and is referred to in the editorial quoted from the *Atlanta Constitution*. Why were southern states like Georgia particularly sensitive to the loss of states' rights?

3. Newspapers' descriptions of the debate over Senate reform often lined up the opposing sides by using terms that connoted good and evil. Make a list of those nouns, adjectives, and verbs that were associated with each side in the debate. Note which newspapers used these terms.

4. Newspapers in favor of election reform used a number of terms to describe the groups that attempted to influence officeholders. What are some of these terms? How are they used in such a way as to connote negative meanings? Note that as these terms were used in specific contexts they came to mean much more than their dictionary definition. Discuss how the use of a word or term in a specific context can become packed with meaning.

5. Note the optimistic tone of the *Rocky Mountain News* editorial "The New Order." Why is this editorial such a good example of Progressive Era ideology? Pick out the phrases that represent the ideals of the period.

Notes

1. "The Treason of the Senate: An Editorial Forward," *Cosmopolitan*, February 1906, p. 478.

2. "Tells of Bribes to Elect Lorimer," *New York Times*, 1 May 1910, p. 1.

3. The Senate first voted in March 1911 to allow Lorimer to keep his seat. Then, in May of that year, with a brace of newly elected members, it reopened its investigation, and, in July 1912, voted 55 to 28 to oust him on the grounds that his election had been procured by bribery and corruption. Instead, Stephenson was exonerated by the Senate in March 1912. Ironically, one of the senators to vote for his exoneration was Illinois Senator William Lorimer, who at that time still held his seat.

4. The amendment also provided for the filling of vacancies in the Senate and would not affect the election or term of senators already chosen before it was to go into effect.

5. Stephenson was reelected in March 1909. Charges were made that he had bought his election by bribing voters and he became the subject of investigations in both the Wisconsin legislature and the U.S. Senate. In 1912 he was exonerated of all corruption charges, and he held his Senate seat until March 1915.

CHAPTER 20

The Ludlow Mine Massacre, April 1914

As tensions built in Europe and revolution broke out in Mexico during the spring of 1914, a more local war raged in the foothills of the Colorado Rockies between striking coal miners and mine owners. One of the bloodiest incidents in American labor history occurred on April 20, 1914, when state and private militia fired on the tent encampment of striking miners and their families in Ludlow, Colorado, with machine guns and cannons. In the course of the 14-hour battle, militiamen torched the tents where women and children had hidden to escape the bullets. As the panic-stricken victims huddled in smoke-filled pits beneath the tents, the militia opened fire on the fleeing survivors. Forty-five people—including 13 women and children—died in the incident and scores were injured.[1]

The incident at Ludlow was the most shocking of many incidents that occurred in the 15-month-long battle between labor and mining interests. The strike had begun in September 1913, after the Rockefeller-controlled Colorado Fuel and Iron Company refused to honor several state employment laws and rejected the miners' demands for union recognition and the abolition of the camp guard system. Once the walkout began, the miners were evicted from their company-owned shacks on company-owned land. Some 13,000 men, women, and children set up tents supplied by the United Mine Workers on the prairie and in the nearby hills near the mouths of canyons and along the railroad lines leading to the mines. The miners refused to work and attempted to keep out nonunion strikebreakers.

The mine owners at first attempted to control the situation with private security forces made up of a combination of camp guards, hired guns deputized by the local sheriff, and detectives supplied by the Baldwin-Felts Agency (a Virginia agency similar to the infamous Pinkerton Agency). (See Chapter 4.) When these proved insufficient, the mine operators put pressure on Governor Elias Ammons to supply troops from the Colorado National Guard, which he did in late October. Violent acts by the miners decreased under the state of martial law declared by the militia commander, but the striking miners were held under a state of virtual tyranny. Union leaders and speakers, including the octogenarian Mother (Marry Harris) Jones, were harassed, arrested, and deported from the state. The miners' weapons were confiscated, and they were forbidden from congregating or speaking publicly in support of the union.

In the meantime, attempts by union, state, and federal officials to bring the owners to the negotiating table failed. The mine operators represented the most powerful industrial lobby in Colorado and were backed up on the national level by the powerful Rockefeller family, which owned a controlling interest in the Colorado Fuel and Iron Company. Their combined influence was powerful enough to effectively block state and federal intervention on the miners' behalf, and in late November the mine owners succeeded in convincing the governor to allow them to bring in strikebreakers.

The strike dragged on through the winter, as a federal grand jury indicted 25 members of the United Mine Workers for "maintaining a monopoly of labor" and "conspiring in the restraint of trade." At the same time, the House Subcommittee on Mines and Mining began hearings on the situation. In late February Governor Ammons became impatient with the skyrocketing cost of maintaining the Colorado National Guard and began to withdraw it from the strike zone. By April 17, a single troop of only 34 men remained. Mine owners quickly organized a second troop ("Troop A") of 130 men made up of mine guards, pit foremen, sheriff's deputies, and vigilantes. These were the men who fired on the Ludlow camp and set it ablaze on April 20.

The Ludlow incident galvanized the strikers. Miners from nearby union camps joined them to swell their ranks to more than two thousand. The state Federation of Labor issued a call for all crafts to organize their men, arm them, and send them to help the striking miners. The governor attempted to match their strength by calling out the entire state militia. In response, the hitherto uninvolved Typographical Union adopted a resolution calling for Ammons's impeachment or recall and appropriated funds to buy arms and ammunition for the strikers.

At the same time, Italian, Greek, and Austrian miners among the strikers appealed to their consular representatives for protection, and the president of the local union called for aid from the Red Cross. More than two hundred women and children—referred to as "refugees"—escaped to nearby Trinidad, seeking temporary housing and aid. In the four days following the Ludlow incident, the fighting spread to nearby mining communities in

Trinidad, Lynn, and Aguilar; eventually six mines owned by other companies were engulfed in the action.

When a truce was called on April 24, 60 lives had been lost in the preceding four days, and destruction of property totaled more than one million dollars. President Woodrow Wilson finally decided the situation could not be contained by the Colorado National Guard. He acceded to requests for federal troops, and in the beginning of May, by which time nearly one hundred lives had been lost, sent more than 1,600 U.S. Army troops to keep the peace.

NOT IN MEXICO, BUT IN COLORADO!!

"Not in Mexico, but in Colorado!" *New York World,* 28 April 1914, p. 10. *The* World *regularly took up the cause of the workers, and it did so with a vengeance when state militia and a private army hired by mine owners slaughtered women and children along with striking miners in Ludlow, Colorado. The incident took place just as the United States was preparing to intervene in a revolution in Mexico to uphold law and order and protect Americans living there. Critics could not help but note the irony of the situation.*

The stalemate between strikers and mine owners continued through the summer and fall. Rockefeller turned down a request from Wilson to intervene, the mine owners refused to submit to arbitration or consider negotiation, and the miners refused to return to work. Meanwhile, in June Rockefeller hired publicist Ivy Lee to craft a comprehensive national public relations campaign through which he not only absolved himself of any wrongdoing but also succeeded in disqualifying the union's demands and the strikers' actions.

Backed by Rockefeller's millions, the Colorado mine owners were able to hold out for the duration of the strike. The United Mine Workers ultimately ran out of funds and was forced to end the strike in December 1914. The union won no concessions from the mine owners, and hundreds of out-of-work miners were left without strike benefits. Many left the region rather than return to work on the operators' terms. In 1915 the United Mine Workers raised a monument to the Ludlow dead on the site of the massacre.

Newspaper coverage of the Colorado mine strike and even the Ludlow Massacre was surprisingly minimal in national papers. The *New York Times,* for example, ran several stories during the week April 21–29, but none of these were written by its own reporters and accounts instead relied on other newspapers on the scene such as the *Rocky Mountain News* (which *did* give the events significant coverage). The *Times* stories were all positioned well inside the paper, anywhere from pages 7 to 22, while stories on the situation in Mexico covered the front several pages each day. The *Chicago Tribune,* which published only one story and one editorial on the Colorado mine war that week, also failed to note the situation until April 24. The usually anti-Rockefeller *New York Journal* didn't publish anything at all until April 24, and that story appeared on page 6. Then, on April 29, its front-page banner headline declared, "Three Wars Now in Progress." The three wars were those in Mexico, Ulster (Northern Ireland) and Colorado. Even the *New York World,* which gave the Ludlow Massacre the most coverage in both its news and editorial sections, gave it only a fraction of the space devoted to the deteriorating situation in Mexico and the deployment there of American troops.

Several speculations can be made as to why there was so little coverage and editorial comment in the national news. First of all, the Colorado mine strike was just one of a number of labor strikes that troubled the nation in 1913–1914. Second, at a time when the military coup in Mexico and the United States's subsequent intervention were jostling for space in crowded newspapers, the Colorado strike was just one of many other events deemed newsworthy. Third, many of the newspapers published in Colorado and the region were owned, controlled, or influenced by mine owners and tended to downplay the situation. Because these newspapers fed stories to other parts of the country through the wire services, national coverage was limited. The exception to this was the independent *Rocky Mountain News,* and its vivid stories describing the violence against the miners served as the source for many of the wire stories published in other newspapers. Fourth, on the national level, Rockefeller was able to control public policy and public opinion through financial and political influence as well as a comprehensive public relations campaign. Rockefeller-generated publicity created an effective blackout in some instances and tended to influence news coverage and editorial comment when these did occur.[2]

The readings in this chapter all deplore the violence in the Ludlow incident and the subsequent battles between the strikers and the forces representing the mine operators. Likewise, most of these point to the need for a return to law and order. Beyond this, however, these selections present a number of perspectives as to who was responsible for the violence or what should be done. These readings are organized in four sections to reflect these different perspectives. In the first section, the news stories and editorials are critical of the mine operators or Rockefeller and sympathetic toward the strikers—either explicitly or in the way in which they describe the events. The first two stories, for example, describe the desperation and panic among the strikers and the brute force employed by the militia against them. The editorials condemning the mine operators or Rockefeller refer to "corporate greed" and the oppression of labor as being motivating factors for the stalemate and resulting violence. The readings in the second section instead place the blame for the violence on the strikers. Several editorials in this section point to the union's demand for a "closed shop" at the mine or the unwillingness of the strikers to compromise as being responsible for the violence. Readings in the third section blame the state of Colorado or Governor Ammons for failing to maintain law and order and prevent violence. Here the different writers blame this on the state's inefficiency, corruption, or vested interest in collusion with the mine owners. The final section provides several selections in which the writers call for federal intervention or hail the decision by President Wilson to replace the "disorderly" state militia with federal troops in order to restore order. These reflect the Progressive Era ideal that the federal government is fair, enlightened, and the embodiment of the progressive spirit.

CRITICAL OF THE MINE OWNERS AND SYMPATHETIC TO THE STRIKERS

One newspaper to give the strike and the massacre thorough coverage was the 16,000-circulation Rocky Mountain News. *This Denver newspaper exhibited a strong sense of independence, perhaps because it had only re-cently been purchased by Chicago publisher John Shaffer. When congres-sional hearings that winter began to reveal the conditions in the coalfields, Shaffer assigned reporter Harvey Deuell to cover the strike and brought in editorial writer William Chenery. Their resulting coverage was harshly critical of the mine owners and sympathetic toward the miners. The* Rocky Mountain News*'s first story on the Ludlow Massacre paints a picture of desperation and panic among the miners and their families, who, despite their defiance, are clearly outgunned by the militia.*

Rocky Mountain News, 21 April 1914

ARMED MINERS RUSHING IN TO EXTERMINATE GUARDSMEN

Fighting Rages 14 Hours and Small Force of Militia Sweeps Hills With Machine Guns to Hold Back Determined Band of Union Workers

Thirteen dead, scores injured, the Ludlow strikers' tent colony burned and hundreds of women and children homeless was the result up to mid-night of one of the bloodiest battles in labor warfare ever waged in the West. Four hundred striking miners were intrenched in the hills back of Ludlow this morning awaiting daylight to wipe out 177 members of the state na-tional guard, with whom they fought for fourteen hours yesterday. The known dead are [identifies two dead and one injured].

Eleven unknown strikers are declared to have been killed, and one non-combatant. The injured among the strikers are said to number twenty. Fif-teen hundred armed strikers from the southern camps were reported to be rushing toward Ludlow at an early hour this morning.

HILLS ARE SWEPT BY MACHINE GUNS

For three hours late last night strike leaders say the militia swept the hills where the union men were intrenched with six machine guns.

Throughout the day a blasting fire swept Ludlow. Bullets rained on the railroad station. Shortly after 6 o'clock last night flames swept through the tent colony and women and children ran screaming to the station, where they crouched on the floor.

Two women and a child, say union men, were killed in the dash from the tent colony by the soldiers' bullets. This has not been confirmed.

From Trinidad and Walsenburg and Lamar all the available troops are being rushed to Ludlow for the battle which will break with daybreak.

Renewed fighting surpassing that of yesterday is expected. Residents of all the nearby towns and camps are panic-stricken.

Battle Rages Throughout Whole Day

Efforts of sheriffs and deputies to get to the scene were unavailing. No one could venture near Ludlow by automobile or any other conveyance.

At Trinidad, 15 miles away, citizens barricaded themselves in their homes. The streets were deserted.

According to reports the battle began yesterday morning at 7:30. Firing above Cedar Hill attracted the soldiers, and Lieutenant Linderfelt of Cripple Creek with a detachment of sixteen of the men stationed at Ludlow, was sent out to investigate.

He was cut off by the blaze of the strikers, and with his men took up a position on Water Tank hill and began returning the fire.

Throughout the day the fighting raged over an area of three square miles, a district bounded on the west by Berwind and Hastings, Barnes Station on the east, the Ludlow colony on the north, and Raneyville on the south.

Strikers Entrenched for Battle

The strikers entrenched themselves behind the embankment of the Colorado and Southeastern and stubbornly held their post. They cut telephone and telegraph lines and so badly crippled all means of communication that it was hours before news of the battle could be sent to Trinidad.

Fifty members of the newly organized Troop A were called out and sent aboard a special. Trainmen, when they heard of the battle, refused to pull the train. An hour's delay followed....

The reinforcements detrained below the Colorado and Southeastern crossing and in the face of a fierce fire from the strikers in the hills and below the railroad embankment, rushed for a string of steel freight cars.

PUMP HOUSE RIDDLED BY BULLETS

There they began firing on a body of strikers barricaded in a pump house. This building was riddled by the fire from the Springfield rifles. It was here that the strikers suffered their heaviest loss of the day.

As dusk settled down the strikers retreated up a gully back of the blazing tent colony, the soldiers followed slowly, sweeping the valley with their machine guns. At 9 o'clock firing ceased and the hills which had echoed to the crash of rifle fire throughout the entire day were silent save for the echo of an occasional shot.

From the entire district, strikers began slipping through the hills toward the main camp. They came armed and ready to join in the battle this morning.

When day breaks there will be 600 to 700 strikers waiting to crush the soldiers.

By the next day the death count had increased. Some of the grisly details of the battle began to appear in newspaper reports, and their headlines captured the horror of the situation. "Mothers and Babies Slain in Safety Pits/ Tents are Fired and Victims Perish From Smoke While Men, Trying to Rescue Their Families, Are Killed by Machine Guns and Rifles; Renewed Battle Expected." the Rocky Mountain News *reported. "Women and Babes Killed by the Colorado Militia/ Alleged That the Soldiers Used Machine Guns on the Tent Colony of Strikers. Women and Children Had No Chance of Escape," reported the* Atlanta Constitution. *The story did not make page one in the* New York Times, *but did get three columns on page seven. The Times story identifies many of the victims and uses vivid eyewitness accounts to describe their deaths. Much of this story is taken verbatim from a story by Harvey Deuell published that same day in the* Rocky Mountain News.

New York Times, 22 April 1914

45 DEAD, 20 HURT, SCORE MISSING IN STRIKE WAR

Women and Children Roasted In Pits of Tent Colony as Flames Destroy It

HID FROM HAIL OF BULLETS

Miners' Store of Ammunition and Dynamite Exploded, Scattering Death and Ruin

TO RESUME BATTLE TO-DAY

Men From Other Union Camps Join Fighters In Hills to Avenge Their Slain

MILITIA TROOPS HEMMED IN

Decisive Engagement Planned by the Soldiers, Who Are Preparing a Machine Gun Sortie

Special to The New York Times

TRINIDAD, Col., April 21–Forty-five dead, more than two-thirds of them women and children, a score missing, and more than a score wounded is the result known to-night of the fourteen-hour battle which raged with uninterrupted fury yesterday between State troops and striking coal miners in the Ludlow district on the property of the Colorado Fuel and Iron Company, the Rockefeller holdings.

The Ludlow camp is a mass of charred debris, and buried beneath it is a story of horror unparalleled in the history of industrial warfare. In the holes which had been dug for their protection against the rifles' fire the women and children died like trapped rats when the flames swept over them. One pit, uncovered this afternoon, disclosed the bodies of ten children and two women....

To Resume Battle at Dawn

With arms ready, both sides after a day of ominous quiet, now await the coming of dawn, when, it is predicted, the battle will be resumed with greater bloodshed that that which had occurred. The militia, which yesterday drove the strikers from their tent colony, and, it is charged, fired it, involving thereby the greatest loss of lives, are preparing for a machine gun sortie at daybreak from their position along the Colorado and Southern Railroad tracks at each side of the Ludlow station.

On the surrounding hills, sheltered by rocks and boulders, 400 strikers await their coming, while their ranks are being swelled by grim faced men who tramped overland in the dark, carrying guns and ammunition from the neighboring union camps....

On the outcome of the engagement tomorrow may depend the fate of the strike. Both sides face it as a battle to the death with no thought of quarter asked or received. At a late hour it was said here that the battle could only be averted with the arrival of overwhelming reinforcement for the troops of Denver....

Battle Over Three-mile Area

Throughout the day yesterday and intermittently during the night the fighting raged over an area of approximately three miles square....

Within the doomed camp last night explosions of cartridges which had been stored there by the miners added to the horror of the flames which swept over it amid a hail of lead with which the soldiers raked the tents.

An unidentified man driving a horse attached to a light buggy dashed from the tents waving a white flag just after the fire started. When ordered to halt he opened fire with a revolver and was killed by a return volley from the militia.

Terrified by the bullets which whistled through the blazing canvas above their heads, the women and children apparently more afraid of the lead than the flames, remained huddled in their pits until the smoke and heat carried death to them.

Some, braver than the rest, ran into the open and dashed aimlessly among the two hundred tents, which by that time had become so many torches which swirled their fire and sparks and lighted the scene with a ghastly brilliancy. Two women dashed toward the militia position.

"Dynamite," they screamed.

An instant later the ammunition remaining in the camp exploded, sending a shower of lead in all directions.

A seven-year-old girl dashed from under a blazing tent and heard the scream of bullets around her ears. Insane from fright, she ran into a tent again and fell into the hole with the remainder of her family to die with them. The child is said to have been of Charles Costa, a union leader at Aguilar, who perished with his wife and another child.

Instances of individual heroism were numerous. James Fyler, financial secretary of the Trinidad local union and a witness in the recent Congressional investigation, died with a bullet in his forehead as he was attempting to rescue his wife from the flames....

Lewis Tikas, leader of the Greek colony and one of the most prominent organizers in the district, was shot as he attempted to lead a group of women away from the camp in the direction of an arroya [*sic*] which offered shelter. According to witnesses of his death, Tikas threw up his arms to show that he carried no weapons. The troopers yelled at him to run, and shot him as he fled.

In an effort to rescue his sister from danger, Frank Snyder, 10 years old, son of William Snyder, a striker, met death in the colony later in the afternoon. The girl ventured from the pit where the family had taken refuge. The boy jumped out to draw her back and a bullet struck him in the back of the head, killing him instantly.

When it appeared no more men remained in the colony the militia ceased firing and went to the work of rescue. Women ran from the burning tents, some with their clothing afire, carrying their babies in their arms. Many, in order to save the babies at their breasts, were forced to abandon their older children to their fate. Among these was Mrs. Marcelina Pedragon. With her light skirt ablaze in several places she carried her youngest child to the open, but left two others behind. Hope for them has been abandoned.

Trembling, hysterical, some apparently dazed, the women were escorted by the troops to the Ludlow [station], where they were held until this morning, when a Colorado and Southern train brought them into Trinidad. In the haste of departure families became separated. Efforts to unite them by the United Mine Workers in many instances proved in vain.

The camp was abandoned to its fate following the departure of the women, and for hours the light of the fire lit the sky a bright red. By its light the strikers retreated to the arroyas [*sic*] back of the colony and to the surrounding hills. The camp fell at 8:30, just fourteen hours after the fight commenced.

Even as fighting continued in the Colorado hills, newspapers quickly condemned the violence, particularly the militia's actions, as well as the state's inability to maintain order. In the following editorial, The Rocky Mountain News *condemned the actions of the militia and compared them to the Indian slaughter of frontier families and Poncho Villa's barbarities in Mexico. The writer traces the responsibility for the violence to the mine owners and, ultimately, John D. Rockefeller, Jr., described here as "the richest man in the world."*

Rocky Mountain News, 22 April 1914

The Massacre of the Innocents

The horror of the shambles at Ludlow is overwhelming. Not since the days when the pitiless red men wreaked vengeance upon intruding frontiersmen and upon their women and children has this Western country been stained with so foul a deed.

The details of the massacre are horrible. Mexico offers no barbarity so cruel as that of the murder of defenseless women and children by the mine guards in soldier's clothing. Like whitened sepulchers we boast of American civilization with this infamous thing at our very doors. Huerta murdered Madero, but even Huerta did not shoot an innocent little boy seeking water for his mother who lay ill. Villa is a barbarian, but in his maddest excess Villa has not turned his machine guns on imprisoned women and children. Where is the outlaw so far beyond the pale of human kind as to burn the tent over the heads of nursing mothers and helpless little babes?

Out of this infamy one fact stands clear. Machine guns did the murder. The machine guns were in the hands of mine guards, most of whom were also members of the state militia. It was private war, with the wealth of the richest man in the world behind the mine guards.

Once and for all time the right to employ armed guards must be taken away from private individuals and corporations. To the state, and to the state alone, belongs the right to maintain peace. Anything else is anarchy.

Who are these mine guards to whom is entrusted the sovereign right to massacre? Four of the fraternity were electrocuted recently in New York. They are the gunmen of the great cities, the offscourings of humanity, whom a bitter heritage has made the wastrels of the world. Warped by the wrongs of their own upbringing, they know no justice and they care not for mercy. They are hardly human in intelligence, and not as high in the scale of human kindness as domestic animals.

Yet they are not the guilty ones. The blood of the innocent women and children rests on the hands of those who for the greed of dollars employed such men and bought such machines of murder. The world has not been hard upon these; theirs has been a gentle upbringing. Yet they reck not of human life when pecuniary interests are involved.

The blood of the women and children, burned and shot like rats, cries aloud from the ground. The great state of Colorado has failed them. Her militia, which should have been the impartial protectors of the peace, have acted as murderous gunmen....

In the name of humanity, in the name of civilization, we have appealed to President Wilson. His ear heard the wail of the innocent, outraged and dying in Mexico. Cannot the president give heed to the sufferings of his own people?

Think, Mr. President, of the captain of the strikers, Louis Tikas, whose truce with the gunmen was ended with his murder. Think of the fifty-one shots which were passed through the strike leader. Think of his body, which has lain exposed since his infamous killing. Then, with the vast power which has been committed to you as the executive of a great nation, attend to the misery wrought by an anarchistic lust for dollars. Without your speedy aid the poor and the needy, betrayed by the state, may be slaughtered to the last smiling babe.

John D. Rockefeller made a public-relations mistake when he snubbed President Wilson's attempts to introduce a mediator in the situation earlier that year and again after the Ludlow Massacre—a misjudgment that opened him up to criticisms such as those leveled in this editorial. The New York World, *which blasted "monied interests" and the "Wall Street gang" on a regular basis, was quick to point the finger of blame at Rockefeller as the representative of "organized capital" in this bloody war. Here, it describes the millionaire as a self-proclaimed dictator who has usurped the powers of the state.*

New York World, 24 April 1914

THE COLORADO INFAMY

The disorders in Colorado grow out of conditions like those which we are seeking to improve in Mexico. In the territory controlled by Mr. Rockefeller's Fuel and Iron Company constitutional government has ceased. There is no security for life and property. Industry has come to an end. Civil war exists.

One of the greatest beneficiaries of organized capital, Mr. Rockefeller has taken the ground that labor should not organize. To enforce his views in this respect he has exercised sovereign powers. He has exiled a whole community. He has employed armed forces. For his benefit the civil law has been suspended. As an auxiliary to his own troops, the State militia has been employed as in actual war.

This is the way some of our Latin-American neighbors carry on what they call government. It is in situations like this that their revolutions are fomented. When governments take sides, promoting strife instead of preventing it; when they permit one interest to exceed its rights and deny in another interest even a hearing; when in controversies that ought to be settled with reason they use cartridges instead of courts, what do they expect?

Republican government has ceased in the whole region of Colorado dominated by Mr. Rockefeller's agents. It has been succeeded by Rockefeller government, which is as tragic as any that we have seen south of the Rio Grande.

The State of Colorado has gone out of business. Its paramount duty is to rehabilitate itself; to assert its supremacy over riotous Rockefellers as well as riotous miners; to restore peace and order, and above all, to reopen its courts and restore law and justice.

CRITICAL OF THE STRIKERS AND THE UNION

Predictably, some criticized the strikers for bringing the violence down on themselves, even as they condemned the actions of the state militia and the governor's failure to take control of the situation. The New York Times, *which in most labor disputes supported negotiation and condemned any action by the workers, attributed a good part of the responsibility for the slaughter to the strike organizers and the United Mine Workers. The* Times's *interpretation of the situation (in this editorial it describes the mine workers as "contented") was likely influenced by publicity and information provided by the mine owners during the long months preceding the Ludlow Massacre.*

New York Times, 23 April 1914

THE LUDLOW CAMP HORROR

Somebody blundered. Worse than the order that sent the Light Brigade into the jaws of death, worse in its effect than the Black Hole of Calcutta, was the order that trained the machine guns of the State Militia of Colorado upon the strikers' camp of Ludlow, burned its tents, and suffocated to death the scores of women and children who had taken refuge in the rifle-pits and trenches.

Law and order in Colorado must be preserved. The strike organizers who invaded the camps of the Colorado Fuel and Iron Company with threats and arms, to force nine-tenths of its contented workers to unionize, may not escape their full measure of blame for the labor war that is now on. But no situation can justify the acts of a militia that compels women and babes to lie in ditches and cellars twenty-four hours without food or water, exposes them to cannon and rifle fire, and lets them die like trapped animals in the flames of their camp.

The State of Colorado has been worse than weak in its attempts to re-store order in the mines. In the recent and continuing labor conflicts in England, Germany, France, and South Africa, the Government authorities have worked with strength and firmness to quell disturbances. From the first acts of the authorities of Colorado have served only to make confusion worse confounded. Mr. JOHN D. ROCKEFELLER, Jr., in his statement before the House Committee in Washington, that "a strike has been imposed upon the country from outside" to intimidate an army of peaceful miners, declared that the "local authorities in Colorado have not been able to provide ade-quate protection for the employees of the Colorado Fuel and Iron Com-pany." Therefore it became the first duty of the company to provide such protection. But it was not the disciplined forces of a private company, it was the crazily officered troops of the State that made the Ludlow camp horror possible.

This terrible blunder has precipitated a situation more grave than that which exists between this country and Mexico. Here is an intestine war that has arisen in other States as well as in Colorado, now breaking out with the ut-most virulence because of a grievous wrong committed. GOV. AMMON [*sic*] has been asked to convene the Colorado Legislature in special session to shape the policy of the State. Hitherto the labor interests have not been ashamed nor afraid to introduce laws preventing railways from transporting "strike-breakers." They were solicitous, often bold in their demands. Solicitude and boldness will now change to defiance and insistence. Pointing to Ludlow, they will justify the legalizing of any act of usurpation. Their doctrine is to deny the right of any man to work for whom he pleases, and they have sought to undermine the law that protects every citizen in rights equal for all. They are now nerved to take this citadel by storm. The right to work becomes in their eyes the right to prevent others from working. In defense of that right they have used bombs, firearms, even artillery, and against sleeping enemies of any sex or age. But when a sovereign State employs such horrible means, what may not be expected from the anarchy that ensues?

The Boston Evening Transcript *was a conservative paper that often rep-resented middle-class, "Yankee," and business interests. In a series of edito-rials on the "Colorado situation" during the week April 22–29, it invariably blamed the strikers for starting the war and causing the escalation of violence. At the same time, some of these editorials compared the anarchy to the situation in Mexico, some—like this one—scolded the state and the militia for losing control of the situation, and some called for federal intervention. Here, the writer unfairly blames the strikers for putting their families at risk by keeping them "within the range of hostilities." Unfortunately for the destitute strikers—who had been evicted from their company-owned homes by the mine operator—there was nowhere else to keep their families. The "range of hostilities" was where they lived, in their makeshift tent city.*

Boston Evening Transcript, 23 April 1914

Colorado's Horrors

Worse and worse grows the situation with each day's development in the Colorado mining camps. It seems to be a battle to the death between the strikers and the militia. The right of men who were willing to work was violently challenged by those who were not, and it was the duty of the State to assert its supremacy and power to protect those engaged in peaceful industry. But evidently authority has been recklessly if not barbarously exercised. It is a shocking record that has been made by the battles of the week. Forty-five dead, more than two-thirds of them women and children, is a grewsome [*sic*] tale of tragedies that can hardly fail to appall the public mind no matter what the provocation, and no matter if the miners themselves kept their families within the range of hostilities with the expectation that their own helplessness would provide their own protection.

The strike organizers went to the camps of the Colorado Fuel and Iron Co. with arms in their hands and forced or tried to force workers who were satisfied with their conditions to organize. In other words, they started the war, because they were guilty of violent compulsion that no State would permit to continue. But the remedy seems worse than the disease. The State troops have shown neither discipline nor discrimination. They have not observed even the ordinary rules of warfare. They have killed more women and children than men. They have evidently expended their ammunition along lines of least resistance. They have adopted the execrable tactics of the men whom they were sent to restrain or punish, and a condition little short of anarchy has ensued.

It is humiliating that we should have a Mexicanizing process in one of our own States. Machine guns have been trained upon the strikers' camps, fires have resulted and women and children have been burned or suffocated. It is as though in attempting to take a hostile city the guns were turned upon its residential sections where its homes were located. The troops were not sent to make reprisals in kind, but to do the work of soldiers and not engage in a slaughter of the innocents. Of the original cause of the quarrel the public knows little, but certainly it was not sufficient to give warrant for all that followed. This situation is cruel and disgraceful.

CRITICAL OF THE STATE

Perhaps the most egregious aspect of the Colorado mine wars was the inability of the state to impose law and order and in so doing protect both the lives of the strikers and the property of the mine owners. Here, the New York World *accuses the state of abdicating its powers to the mine operators, thus losing any authority to control the situation and protect its citizens.*

New York World, 23 April 1914

THE COLORADO MASSACRE

If such an atrocity as that reported in Colorado had been chargeable to Villa or Huerta in Mexico the whole country would have been aflame at the horror of it. Whole families have been wiped out as a result of a strike war between mine guards and militiamen on one side and miners on the other. Of the dead and wounded the majority are women and children.

There could be no such massacre as this if the State of Colorado had not surrendered its government to the Rockefeller Fuel and Iron Company. It has done even worse than that. Having permitted the inhabitants of a large section of its territory to carry on hostilities for months, it has openly taken sides. Instead of using its great authority to compel peace and establish justice, it has assailed the weaker of the antagonists with all the fury of the savages who once roamed its valleys.

Whatever the rights and the wrongs of the quarrel between Mr. Rockefeller and his employees may be, it is the duty of the State of Colorado to enforce its laws without fear or favor. This it has not been done. It has hidden in a cowardly way behind a pretense of martial law. Its own armed agents have been more intent upon serving Rockefeller than upon serving the State.

Mr. Rockefeller's son recently testified that he was willing to sink his entire investment in Colorado rather than yield to the demand of his employees that they be permitted to organize. He has not sunk and he does not intend to sink his entire investment, but he has debauched an American commonwealth, and the blood of women and children is on the hands of his barbarous agents, private and public.

Some compared the situation in Colorado to a civil war. In this editorial, the writer vents frustration at the pro-industry bias that had crippled the congressional investigation and attacks Colorado's record of corrupt and inefficient government.

Chicago Tribune, 24 April 1914

ORDER FIRST

The civil war in Colorado—because it can be called no less—breaks out at an ill timed moment.

That state has furnished the worst example of popular government afforded in this country, and even before this last outbreak it showed no signs of improvement.

The public at large has been unable to get at the truth of its labor disputes. And the evident bias of the congressional investigating committee has made confusion worse confounded. The affairs of Colorado must be cleaned up. Justice and honest dealing must be compelled.

The essential first step at this, however, is the restoration of the authority of the government. Anarchy can bring nothing but misery and murder.

This editorial writer goes a step further by accusing the Colorado authorities of intentionally enlisting on the side of the mine owners and waging war on the strikers.

New York Tribune, 23 April 1914

War in Colorado

It is grave news that comes from the Trinidad mining district in Colorado—so grave that not even the big events below the Rio Grande can blot it out. Meagre [*sic*] reports are as yet available. But clearly the charge of grave crimes lies at the door of the State of Colorado which explanations can but little palliate.

The fundamental quarrel between the mine owners and the strikers has been much expounded. In that quarrel sides can be taken as one's convictions run. But we can conceive of no convictions and no facts which will justify the wholesale shooting of women and children with machine guns. Unless disproof comes quickly, the belief will grow stronger and stronger that here, as in the State of West Virginia, the authorities have far exceeded their constitutional duty to maintain order and are entering upon a campaign of war and destruction in behalf of the mine owners of the state.

As workers from nearby minefields went out on sympathy strikes and swarmed to join the embattled strikers at Ludlow and Trinidad, the governor gave up any pretense of controlling the situation and called for federal assistance. At a time when the U.S. military was recruiting men to take part in the Mexico intervention, this would place an undue burden on the already undermanned U.S. Army. This editorial criticizes Colorado for not being able to solve its own problems. It also notes the hypocrisy of America's intervention in the Mexican crisis to bring that country American ideals while it is unable to uphold those ideals within its own borders.

Boston Herald, 28 April 1914

TROOPS FOR COLORADO

It is a curious circumstance that just when thousands of our fellow-citizens are eager to rush into Mexico to elevate her ideals, Gov. Ammons of Colorado should ask for federal troops to suppress anarchy at home. But for the crisis in Mexico the civil strife in Colorado would have held foremost place in the news. Violent as have been our industrial struggles in the past, none has surpassed in barbarity the conflict between the mine owners and militia and the striking miners. It little behooves us to point the finger of scorn at Mexican atrocities when women and children in Colorado have been mowed down by machine guns. Nor is this item a fabrication of the sensational press, any more than the reprisal of the strikers in imprisoning a score of men and women in a burning mine.

Gov. Ammons's request is virtually an admission that he is unable to cope with the situation. At a time of stress and trial for the national administration he asks that its troops, preparing for emergencies in Mexico, be sent to settle an industrial dispute. That this is the character of the struggle is revealed by the President's appeal to John D. Rockefeller "to bring about a settlement."

Colorado should settle her own difficulties. The time for the President to turn toward that state will be when Mexican troubles are over, and then, not with troops, but with plans for remedying the conditions that underlie its industrial ulcer. The questions involved are more important to the welfare of this country than the attempted applications of our ideals of government to thirteen million neighbors of mixed Aztec, Spanish, Indian and Negro blood.

The ministers who had so much to say on Sunday of the need of carrying American ideals into Mexico should recall that we have not completed the job in a part of our country taken from Mexico in 1848.

PROMOTING FEDERAL INTERVENTION AND MEDIATION

Even as they deplored the violence in the Colorado minefields, some worried about the effect such upheavals might have on national business interests. It was commonly believed that labor unrest in one part of the country could easily lead to sympathy strikes and labor disputes in other regions. Although the United Mine Workers had sought futilely for months to negotiate concessions with the mine operators, to the outside world it seemed time to bring in external mediators. This editorial writer takes this a step further and promotes the concept of compulsory mediation and arbitration. The logical party to enforce this would be the federal government.

Atlanta Constitution, 24 April 1914

UNHAPPY COLORADO

Within the past few days the labor disturbances in southern Colorado have occasioned about as many deaths and disabilities as our taking of Vera Cruz, reckoning with American losses only.

The entire national guard of Colorado is to be called into action. A virtual state of anarchy prevails. The mandate of the state seems to go for nothing, either as between the striking miners or the operators.

It ought to be impossible for such a situation to exist in a civilized country. There might be slight palliation if the disturbances had merely begun, and the disorder could be attributed to the natural friction engendered by the early bitterness of partisans.

But for several months violence and upheaval have been the program in the mining districts of Colorado. Time and time again state troops and disaffected miners have clashed, blood has been shed and bad feeling created. There was the unfortunate incident of "Mother" Jones, which at one time threatened farspread and disastrous circumstances.

In some respects, the situation in Colorado, West Virginia, and Michigan shows parallel lines.

In each instance there is organized obstinacy from both disputants and their partisans.

Efforts to bring about compromises are met with indifference or with a spirit of unreasonableness.

Neither side seems disposed to admit that concessions should be made mutually, and both sides exhibit a continuous contempt of the rights of that great third party, the public.

The question as to whether the strikers or the operators in these three states have merit on their side is not the cardinal issue.

The point that matters is that lawlessness has supplanted law, and that business interests near and remote from the immediate industries are badly affected. And the longer strife continues, the deeper and more costly will be the scars left upon the entire industrial fabric.

The more one contemplates conditions of this nature the greater becomes the conviction of the necessity for compulsory arbitration, compulsory mediation or compulsory publicity.

When President Wilson agreed to send federal troops into Colorado, most observers believed order would be restored and the dominance of the mine owners would be eliminated. This was certainly representative of the Progressive Era belief that wise, informed, qualified, and impartial government would bring about fairness, justice, and democratic aims. By predicting that the entrance of the federal government into the controversy would ensure a "square deal" for both sides, however, this writer was being naive. Although the federal troops did, indeed, put an end to the violence, by the end of the Colorado strike in December 1914, the strikers were clearly the losers. Most lost their jobs, some were imprisoned, and the owners won their fight to keep the union out.

New York Tribune, 29 April 1914

Ending the Colorado Scandal

The sending of the United States cavalrymen to the scene of the Colorado mining troubles should put an end to the wholesale murder of women and children there. The state of private warfare will end. The United States will be in charge and it will be competent to keep order and do justice as between the two parties of the controversy. The first step will doubtless be to disarm the strikers and the mine guards. The federal troops will be able to protect the property involved and there will be no occasion for the mine owners maintaining their private soldiery. It was a disgrace for the State of Colorado to turn over this function to private organizations.

Where the armed guard in labor disputes appears there bloodshed is most likely to take place. It is impossible to apportion the blame, but the state which abdicated in favor of the private armed guard invites trouble. It was so at the Carnegie strike [in Homestead, Pennsylvania] years ago. It was so in the disgraceful affair in West Virginia, which terminated a year or so ago, only when the protests of the entire country made that state's acquiescence in the scandal no longer possible.

The entrance of the United States into the Colorado controversy means a square deal for both sides. The truth will soon be known, for the Colorado strike has now become a national matter. And when public opinion has had an opportunity to assert itself the strike will end with the doing of substantial justice on whichever side it may fall.

Even in 1914, the presence of American soldiers inspired a sense of confidence that freedom, justice, and democracy would prevail. This was more an ideal than a reality, for since the Civil War the major role of the American soldier had been in the Indian wars and in suppressing or supporting various insurrections in South and Central America—and the losing side in those encounters would hardly argue that justice had prevailed. This writer clearly upholds the ideal.

Cleveland Plain Dealer, 30 April 1914

Regulars in Colorado

The sending of federal troops into a state to restore order has been very seldom resorted to; fortunately it has very seldom appeared necessary or wise. When conditions demand such action, however, it would be the height of folly to refuse it.

There will be general agreement that the president was justified in dispatching troops to Colorado. An intolerable situation had developed. The state authority had failed in the task of re-establishing peace. Conditions were getting worse, instead of better, with the passage of days.

Every effort was made by the administration to avoid the necessity of interposing the national authority in arms. Mr. Wilson even went the length of sending a personal representative, a member of the house of representatives, to interview John D. Rockefeller and urge him to submit the Colorado issue to a peaceful settlement. The refusal of the younger Rockefeller to accede to the wish of the executive apparently left the president no alternative but to use the soldiers of the United States for the restoration of order in the mountain state.

Fortunately, the regular army enjoys the confidence and respect of all classes. All parties to the controversy in Colorado agree that the sending of troops was wise under existing circumstances.

And the government of the United States, represented in the bloody fields at Trinidad by the regulars, will take no sides between disputants nor endeavor to determine on which side the right lies. The army is there to re-store order—to keep the peace until the passions of men cool sufficiently to permit a settlement in justice.

The spectacle of a nation's soldiery keeping domestic peace by force of arms is not pleasant. It is pleasanter, however, than the spectacle of riot and bloodshed which Colorado has been showing the world for some weeks past.

QUESTIONS

1. How was the public's right to know undermined by financial interests in the case of the Colorado mine strike? What, if any, safeguards existed in 1914 to protect this right to know? Would the fact that many competing newspapers existed in 1914 increase the probability of the public's get-ting the whole story?

2. The newspaper stories quoted here refer to the Ludlow incident as if it were a military battle. Note how they refer to the two sides in the battle and the military terms they use to describe them. How does the use of these terms prescribe legitimacy to one side or the other?

3. A Marxist interpretation of the Ludlow incident would argue that it was a class battle between capitalists and workers. Further interpretation would argue that the capitalist press continued the class war by the way in which it reported the Ludlow incident. What terms and phrases are used in these stories and editorials to support this interpretation?

4. How do the editorials "The Massacre of the Innocents" and "The Lud-low Camp Horror" reveal the opposing perspectives of the *Rocky Moun-tain News* and the *New York Times*? Which of these two editorials best reflects the beliefs and values of the Progressive Era? Explain.

5. Consider the sources of information available to the public in 1914. Based on the information provided in this chapter and the articles and editorials cited, do you think an individual in 1914 would have had the ability to determine the truth of the Ludlow incident? Would that indi-vidual be able to rely on either of the editorials ("The Massacre of the Innocents" and "The Ludlow Camp Horror") to reach an opinion on who was responsible or what should be done?

NOTES

1. For an excellent detailed analysis of the Colorado mine strike and its national ramifications, see George S. McGovern and Leonard F. Guttridge, *The Great Coalfield War* (Boston: Houghton Mifflin Co., 1972).

2. In contrast to the meager coverage provided by newspapers, a number of national magazines of the moderate-to-left spectrum covered the Colorado struggle intensively. These included socialist publications like *The Masses* and *Appeal to Reason* as well as general circulation publications like *Harper's Weekly, Collier's Weekly, Nation,* and *Everybody's.*

Appendix: Newspapers Cited—
Publication Information, Circulation
Figures and Political Affiliations

Note: The information provided below was obtained from the N.W. Ayers Annual Newspaper Directory and Annual series published between the years 1889 and 1915. Information was provided to the directories by publishers and is incomplete in some cases; circulation figures may not be accurate. In cases where a newspaper is cited only from a single year, information is provided for only that year.

CALIFORNIA

San Francisco Chronicle

> M.H. DeYoung, editor and publisher (1889–1913), editor (1915); Chronicle Publishing Company (1913–1915)
> Independent
> Morning circ.: 48,397 (1899); 61,156 (1895); 75,000 (1900); 80,626 (1904); 50,000 (1910); 60,000 (1913).
> Sunday circ.: 52,619 (1899); 68,434 (1895); 90,000 (1900); 93,569 (1904); 70,000 (1910); 70,000 (1913); 92,090 (1915).

COLORADO

Rocky Mountain News

> Thomas M. Patterson (1889–95, 1904); T.M. Patterson, editor, News-Times Publishing Co. (1910–1913); John C. Shaffer, editor; Denver Publishing Co. (1913, 1915)
> Democratic (1889); Populist (1895); Independent (1900, 1904, 1910, 1913)

Morning circ.: 12,856 (1889); 23,940 (1895); 25,752 (1900); 33,681
(1904); 31,512 (1910); 26,182 (1913); 39,376 (1915)

Wednesday circ.: 4,800 (1889); 5,500 (1895); Thurs.: 5,116 (1900);
2,914 (1913); 7,400 (1915)

Sunday circ.: 30,588 (1895); 33,699 (1900); 66,200 (1904); 57,902
(1910); 51,644 (1913); 64,337 (1915)

CONNECTICUT

Hartford Courant/Connecticut Courant

Hawley, Goodrich, & Co., editor and publisher (1889); Hartford
Courant Co., publisher (1895–1915); Charles H. Clark, editor
(1910–1915)

Republican

Morning circ.: 6,700 (1889); 8,200 (1895); 9,800 (1900); 10,350
(1904); 13,500 (1910); 15,000 (1913); 15,000 (1915)

Thursday circ.: 6,400 (1889); 8,000 (1895); 8,900 (1900); 9,800
(1904); 9,800 (1910); 9,000 (1913); 9,000 (1915)

GEORGIA

Atlanta Constitution

Constitution Publishing Company (1889–1915); Clark Howell, editor (1900–1915)

Democratic

Morning circ.: 10,751 (1889); 20,000 (1895); 18,330 (1900); 18,330
(1904); 35,454 (1910); 41,405 (1913); 47,323 (1915)

Sunday circ.: 20,750 (1889); 30,000 (1895); 24,500 (1900); 24,500
(1904); 46,630 (1910); 44,102 (1913); 49,341 (1915)

Tuesday circ.: 116,807 (1889); Monday: 174,870 (1895); 89,798
(1900); 89,798 (1904); Monday-Wednesday-Friday: 108,990
(1910); 101,474 (1913); Tuesday-Thursday-Saturday: 104,435

ILLINOIS

Chicago Tribune

Tribune Company, editor and publisher (1889–1904); R.W. Patterson, editor; Tribune Co., publisher (1904–1913); James Kelley,

editor (1913); Robert R. McCormick and Joseph M. Patterson, editors and publishers (1915)

Republican (1889–1904); Independent Republican (1910–1915)

Morning circ.: 48,087 (1889); 75,000 (1895); 75,000 (1900); 75,000 (1904); 150,000 (1910); 220,000 (1913); 303,316 (1915)

Sunday circ.: 63,613 (1889); 128,500 (1895); 125,000 (1900); 175,000 (1904); 300,000 (1910); 300,000 (1913); 459,728 (1915)

LOUISIANA

New Orleans Picayune

Nicholson & Co. (1889–95); Estate of Mrs. E.J. Nicholson (1900–1904); Nicholson Publishing Co. (1910–1913)

Democratic

Morning circ.: 16,143 (1889); 20,000 (1895); 21,000 (1900); 21,000 (1904); 20,000 (1910); 19,000 (1913)

Sunday circ.: 24,960 (1889); 30,000 (1895); 32,000 (1900); 32,000 (1904); 30,000 (1910); 32,500 (1913)

Thursday circ.: 15,798 (1889); 19,000 (1895); Monday and Thursday: 19,000 (1900); 19,000 (1904); 10,000 (1910); 5,500 (1913)

New Orleans Times-Democrat

Times-Dem Publishing Co. (1889–1913); Page M. Baker, editor (1895–1910); Ashton Phelps, editor (1913)

Independent Democratic

Morning circ.: 17,500 (1889); 25,000 (1895); 22,500 (1900); 22,500 (1904); 20,000 (1910); 20,129 (1913)

Sunday circ.: 24,000 (1889); 40,000 (1895); 37,500 (1900); 37,500 (1904); 30,000 (1910); 34,252 (1913)

Saturday circ.: 16,000 (1889); Friday: 15,000 (1895); Tuesday and Friday: 12,500 (1900); 12,500 (1904); 10,000 (1910); Thursday: 6,000 (1913)

New Orleans Times-Picayune

Times-Picayune Pub. Co. (1915)

Independent Democratic

Morning circ: 54,081 (1915)

Sunday circ: 70,000 (1915)

Thursday circ.: 6,576 (1915)

MASSACHUSETTS

Boston Herald

> Boston Herald Co. (1901)
> Independent
> Daily circ.: 138,072 (1891); morning and evening: 150,000 (1901);
>   morning: 75,000 (1910)
> Sunday circ.: 111,619 (1891); 100,000 (1901); 90,000 (1910)

Boston Pilot

> James Jeffrey Roche, editor, Pilot Publishing Co. (1901)
> Catholic
> Weekly circ.: 72,000 (1891); 75,000 (1901); 75,000 (1910)

Boston Transcript

> Boston Transcript Co. (1901, 1910)
> Independent Republican
> Evening circ.: 15,000 (1891); 23,745 (1901); 30,083 (1910)
> Saturday circ.: 31,000 (1901); 42,500 (1910)

Boston Traveller (Founded 1824, changed spelling to *Boston Traveler,*
1898)

> Boston Traveler Co. (1898–1910); John H. Fahey, editor (1910)
> Republican (1891); Independent Republican (1898–1901); Inde-
>   pendent (1910)
> Evening circ.: 16,000 (1891); 65,000 (1898); 71,235 (1901); 88,378
>   (1910)

NEW YORK

New York Evening Journal

> W. R. Hearst, publisher (1900–1904); New York Evening Journal
>   Pub. Co. (1910–15); Arthur Brisbane, editor (1913–1915)
> Democratic
> Evening circ.: 700,000 (1904); 600,000 (1910); 800,000 (1913);
>   797,477 (1915)

New York Evening World

> Joseph Pulitzer, editor and proprietor (1889); Press Publishing Co.
>   (1895–1910)

Democratic (1889); Independent (1895–1915)

Evening circ.: 90,000 (1889); morning and evening: 484,075 (1895); evening: 350,000 (1904); 401,259 (1910); 404,855 (1913); 386,505 (1915)

New York Herald

James Gordon Bennett, publisher (1889–1910); New York Herald Co., publisher (1910–1913); E. S. Drone, editor (1900–1904); James Gordon Bennett, editor (1915)

Independent

Morning circ.: 100,000 (1889); 80,000 (1895); 120,000 (1900); 130,000 (1904); 100,000 (1910); 100,000 (1913); 109,192 (1913)

Sunday circ.: 110,000 (1889); 100,000 (1895); 245,000 (1900); 245,000 (1904); 200,000 (1910); 220,000 (1913); 220,000 (1915)

Wednesday circ.: 20,000 (1889); 18,000 (1895)

New York Sun

W. M. Laffan Publishing (1889–1904); Chas. A. Dana, editor (1889, 1895); Paul Dana, editor (1900); Wm. Laffan, editor (1904); Edward P. Mitchell, editor (1915); Sun Printing & Pub. Assn. (1910–15)

Independent

Morning circ.: 80,000 (1889); 120,000 (1895); 120,000 (1900); 120,000 (1904); 90,000 (1910); 90,000 (1913); 67,071 (1915)

Evening circ.: 100,000 (1913); 122,763 (1915)

Sunday circ.: 120,000 (1889); 150,000 (1895); 150,000 (1900); 150,000 (1904); 100,000 (1910); 100,000 (1913); 90,283 (1915)

Wednesday circ.: 65,000 (1889); 55,000 (1895)

New York Times

New York Times Publishing Co.

Republican (1889); Democratic (1895, 1900, 1904); Independent Democratic (1910, 1913, 1915)

Morning circ.: 40,000 (1889); 75,000 (1895); 40,000 (1900); 100,000 (1904); 175,000 (1910); 200,000 (1913); 259,673 (1915)

Tuesday and Friday circ.: 5,000 (1889)

Wednesday circ.: 40,000 (1889); 50,000 (1895)

Sunday circ.: 80,000 (1895); 50,000 (1900); 175,000 (1910); 150,000 (1913)

New York World

Joseph Pulitzer, editor and proprietor (1889); Press Publishing Co. (1895–1915)

Democratic (1889–1915)

Morning circ.: 180,000 (1889); 484,075 (1895); 250,000 (1904); 361,412 (1910); 383,955 (1913); 380,056 (1915)

Sunday circ.: 260,263 (1889); 324,904 (1895); 450,000 (1904); 459,663 (1910); 486,364 (1913); 463,280 (1915)

Wednesday circ.: 100,000 (1889); Tuesday and Friday: 110,000 (1895); Monday-Wednesday-Friday: 135,000 (1904); 84,735 (1910); 82,296 (1913); 73,992 (1915)

Monthly circ.: 125,000 (1900)

OHIO

Cleveland Plain Dealer

Plain Dealer Publishing Co.

Democratic (1889–1900); Independent Democratic (1904–15)

Morning and evening circ.: 21,500 (1889); morning: 37,500 (1895); morning and evening: 30,000 (1900); 65,280 (1904); morning: 79,601 (1910); 105,703 (1913); 112,132 (1915)

Sunday circ.: 21,300 (1889); 27,000 (1895); 25,000 (1900); 59,275 (1904); 102,725 (1910); 132,192 (1913); 153,048 (1915)

Friday circ.: 26,600 (1889); 28,000 (1895); 25,000 (1900)

PENNSYLVANIA

Pittsburgh Press

Press Publishing Co. (1892)

Independent (1892)

Evening circ.: 38,790 (1892)

Sunday circ.: 20,000 (1892)

TENNESSEE

Memphis Daily Commercial

Commercial Publishing Co. (1892)

Democratic (1892)

Morning circ.: 7,560 (1892)
Sunday circ.: 10,000 (1892)

Memphis Free Speech

Free Speech Co., publisher; Ida B. Wells, editor (1892)
Republican (1892)
Saturday circ.: 1,850 (1892)

WISCONSIN

Chippewa Daily Independent

T. J. Cunningham, editor, Chippewa Valley Publishing Co. (1912)
Democratic
Morning circ.: 700 (1912)

Milwaukee Free Press

Milwaukee Free Press Co.
Independent Republican
Morning circ.: 34,392 (1912)
Sunday circ.: 31,110 (1912)

Milwaukee Journal

L. W. Nieman, editor (1910–1912); Journal Co. (1910); L. T. Boyd,
    publisher (1912)
Independent (1890); Democratic (1897); Independent (1910,
    1912)
Daily circ.: 8,500 (1890); 18,000 (1897)
Evening circ.: 15,750 (1897); 58,787 (1910); 64,627 (1912)

Oshkosh Northwestern

Hicks Printing Co., Publishers (1912)
Republican
Evening circ.: 10,348 (1912)

Wisconsin State Journal

Richard Lloyd Jones, editor; State Journal and Printing Co. (1912)
Republican
Evening circ.: 6,149 (1912)

Bibliography

Books and Articles

Amott, Teresa L., and Julie A. Matthaei. *Race, Gender and Work: A Multicultural Economic History of Women in the United States.* Boston: South End Press, 1991.

Barkan, Elliott R. "Race, Religion, and Nationality in American Society: A Model of Ethnicity—From Contact to Assimilation." *Journal of American Ethnic History* 14:2 (Winter 1995): 38–75.

Bernstein, Richard B., with Jerome Agel. *Amending America.* New York: Times Books, 1993.

Bordin, Ruth. *Women and Temperance: The Quest for Power and Liberty.* Philadelphia: Temple University Press, 1981.

Boyer, Paul, et al., eds. *The Enduring Vision.* Lexington, Mass.: D. C. Heath, 1990.

Brands, H. W. *The Reckless Decade: America in the 1890s.* New York: St. Martin's Press, 1995.

Buenker, John D., John C. Burnham, and Robert M. Crunden. *Progressivism.* Cambridge, Mass: Schenkman Publishing Co., 1980.

Burt, Elizabeth V. "An Arena for Debate: Woman Suffrage, the Brewing Industry, and the Press, Wisconsin, 1910–1911." Ph.D. diss., University of Wisconsin, 1994.

Campbell, W. Joseph. *Yellow Journalism: Puncturing the Myths, Defining the Legacies.* Westport, Conn: Praeger, 2001.

Clements, James, ed. *Encyclopedia of American Immigration.* Vols. 1–4. Armonk, N.Y.: Sharpe Reference, 2001.

Conzen, Kathleen Neils, et al. "The Invention of Ethnicity: A Perspective from the U.S.A." *Journal of American Ethnic History* 12:1 (Fall 1992): 3–41.

Crunden, Robert M. *Ministers of Reform: The Progressive Achievement in American Civilization, 1889–1920.* New York: Basic Books, 1982.

Dulles, Foster Rhea, and Melvin Dubofsky. *Labor in America: A History.* 5th ed. Arlington Heights, Ill.: Harlan Davidson, 1993.

Flexner, Eleanor. *Century of Struggle: The Woman's Rights Movement in the United States*. Rev. ed. Cambridge: Belknap Press of Harvard University Press, 1975.

Gould, Lewis L. *America in the Progressive Era, 1890–1914*. Harlow, England: Pearson Education, 2001.

Heyer, Paul. *Titanic Legacy: Disaster as Media Event and Myth*. Westport, Conn.: Praeger, 1995.

Hofstadter, Richard. *The Age of Reform: From Bryan to F.D.R.* New York: Knopf, 1956.

———. *The Progressive Movement, 1900–1915*. Englewood Cliffs, N.J.: Prentice Hall, 1960.

Irwin, Will. *The American Newspaper: A Series Appearing in Collier's Magazine, January–July 1911*. Edited by Clifford F. Weigle and David C. Clark. Ames: Iowa State University, 1969.

Kent, Noel Jacob. *America in 1900*. Armonk, N.Y.: M. E. Sharpe, 2000.

Link, Arthur S., and Richard L. McCormick. *Progressivism*. Arlington Heights, Ill.: Harlan Davidson, 1983.

Marzolf, Marion Tuttle. *Civilizing Voices: American Press Criticism, 1880–1950*. New York: Hastings House, 1991.

McGovern, George S., and Leonard F. Guttridge. *The Great Coalfield War*. Boston: Houghton Mifflin Co., 1972.

Nesbit, Robert C. *Wisconsin: A History*. Special edition edited by William F. Thompson. Madison: University of Wisconsin Press, 1989.

Neuzil, Mark. "Hearst, Roosevelt, and the Muckrake Speech of 1906: A New Perspective." *Journalism and Mass Communication Quarterly* 73:1 (Spring 1996): 29–39.

Riis, Jacob. *How the Other Half Lives*. Rev. ed., with a preface by Charles A. Madison. New York: Dover Publications, 1971.

Royster, Jacqueline Jones, ed. *Southern Horrors and Other Writings: The Anti-Lynching Campaign of Ida B. Wells, 1892–1900*. New York: Bedford Books, 1997.

Schiller, Dan. "An Historical Approach to Objectivity and Professionalism in American News Reporting." *Journal of Communication* 29 (Autumn 1979): 46–57.

Smythe, Ted Curtis. "The Reporter, 1880–1900: Working Conditions and Their Influence on News." *Journalism History* 7 (1980): 1–10.

Solomon, Barbara Miller. "The Intellectual Background of the Immigrations Restriction Movement in New England." *New England Quarterly* 25:1 (March 1952): 47–59.

Sundquist, James L. *Constitutional Reform and Effective Government*. Washington, D.C.: Brookings Institute, 1986.

Sweeney, Michael S. "'The Desire for the Sensational': Coxey's Army and the Argus-Eyed Demons of Hell." *Journalism History* 23:3 (Autumn 1997), 114–125.

Tax, Meredith. *The Rising of the Women*. New York: Monthly Review Press, 1980.

Von Drehle, David. *Triangle: The Fire That Changed America*. New York: Atlantic Monthly Press, 2003.

Wertheimer, Barbara Mayer. *We Were There: The Story of Working Women in America*. New York: Pantheon Books, 1977.

Wiebe, Robert H. *Search for Order, 1877–1920*. New York: Hill and Wang, 1967.

Wilkerson, Marcus M. *Public Opinion and the Spanish-American War*. Baton Rouge: Louisiana State University Press, 1932.

Some Useful Web Sites Organized by Subject

The Masses. A collection of political cartoons and covers published by *The Masses* can be found at http://marxists.anu.edu.au/subject/art/visual_arts. For cartoons by artist John Sloan published in *The Masses*, articles by Max Eastman and more, see links provided at http://www.spartacus.schoolnet.co.uk/ARTsloan.htm.

Riis, Jacob. *How the Other Half Lives*. First published in 1901. Hypertext edition. http://tenant.net/Community/Riis.

Temperance and Prohibition History. Provides information about prohibition, Frances Willard, the Anti-Saloon League, cartoon from the Prohibition Party, speeches by prohibitionist legislators. http://prohibition.history.ohio-state.edu.

Index

About the Author

ELIZABETH V. BURT is Associate Professor at the School of Communication, University of Hartford. She is the author of *Women's Press Organizations, 1881-1999* (Greenwood Press, 2000), and has published many
articles and book chapters on issues of the Progressive Era, social movements, and the woman suffrage movement.